Books by Keith O'Brien

Paradise Falls: A Deadly Secret, a Cover-Up, and the Women Who Forged the Modern Environmental Movement

Fly Girls: How Five Daring Women Defied All Odds and Made Aviation History

Outside Shot: Big Dreams, Hard Times, and One County's Quest for Basketball Greatness

CHARLIE HUSTLE

CHARLIE HUSTLE

The Rise and Fall of Pete Rose, and the Last Glory Days of Baseball

Keith O'Brien

Pantheon Books
New York

Grateful acknowledgment is made to the following for permission to
reprint the following images: page 9: Courtesy of Janice Wiethorn;
pages 35, 115, 175, and 307: Courtesy of Getty Images

Library of Congress Cataloging-in-Publication Data
Names: O'Brien, Keith, [date] author.
Title: Charlie Hustle: the rise and fall of Pete Rose, and
the last glory days of baseball / Keith O'Brien.
Description: First edition. New York: Pantheon Books, 2024.
Includes bibliographical references and index.
Identifiers: LCCN 2023020621 (print). LCCN 2023020622 (ebook).
ISBN 9780593317372 (hardcover). ISBN 9780593317389 (ebook).
Subjects: LCSH: Rose, Pete, 1941—Cincinnati Reds (Baseball team)—History.
Baseball players—United States—Biography. Sports betting—United States.
Classification: LCC GV865.R65 C53 2024 (print) | LCC GV865.
R65 (ebook) | DDC 796.357092 [B]—dc23/eng/20230515
LC record available at https://lccn.loc.gov/2023020621
LC ebook record available at https://lccn.loc.gov/2023020622

www.pantheonbooks.com

Jacket photograph: Cincinnati Reds' Pete Rose in action vs. Pittsburgh Pirates,
1972 NL Playoffs, by Heinz Kluetmeier / *Sports Illustrated* / Getty Images
Jacket design by Eli Mock

Printed in the United States of America

First Edition

9 8 7 6 5 4

For the People
in the Bleachers
on a Warm Summer Day

Anyone who would appraise Pete Rose would be wrong to do so by the numbers. For he is not so much a ballplayer as he is an emotion, an attitude, a symbol.

"Pete Rose," Commissioner Peter Ueberroth said, "is baseball."

He is, at least, what baseball ought to be.

—*The Cincinnati Enquirer,* September 12, 1985

He can't run. He can't throw and he doesn't have a good pair of hands. All he does is bust his tail and beat you.

—Dick Williams, manager of the Oakland Athletics

But this is a Pete Rose story . . . and Pete Rose had a gambling addiction. . . . Pete's addiction got out of control.

—Tommy Gioiosa, friend and associate of Pete Rose

CONTENTS

AUTHOR'S NOTE

I grew up in Cincinnati when Pete Rose was at the peak of his fame, and I was there when he self-destructed, when he lost everything.

I know the part of town where he grew up—the West Side—because, briefly, as a child, I lived there, too. I went to school with guys like him. And like every Cincinnatian—and every baseball fan who was alive during that time—I have felt just about every emotion about Pete Rose: pride, disgust, frustration, pity, and confusion. Only one thing hasn't changed over the years: my fascination with his story. He was Icarus in red stirrup socks and cleats. He was the American dream sliding headfirst into third. He was both a miracle and a disaster, and he still is today.

This story is a work of nonfiction, built with the help of thousands of pages of previously unutilized federal court documents, newly released FBI files that I requested and obtained, raw television footage, decades of newspaper articles, Major League Baseball's voluminous 1989 investigation into his misdeeds, and more than 150 hours of interviews with Pete Rose's friends; enemies; former teammates; family members; two former commissioners of baseball; three people who placed his bets on the game; four different investigators who dug up his secrets; the special counsel who led that charge, John Dowd; and Pete Rose himself. Rose met with me in person and spoke to me on the record for twenty-seven hours in 2021, before he stopped calling back, before he shut down.

The narrative takes no license with facts, characters, scenes, or chronologies. If something appears in quotation marks here, it means it is verified—taken directly from a legal deposition, courtroom testimony, a memoir, a recorded interview, or a press account—or, in rare instances, confirmed by reliable sources who were there. Every effort has been made to portray the events as they occurred, to depict emotions as they were felt at the time, and to document them as accurately as possible for history.

CHARLIE HUSTLE

INTRODUCTION

September 1985

THE STANDING OVATION lasted for seven minutes, long enough that the umpires stopped the game and the pitcher sat down on the mound. Seemingly bored, and with nothing to do, the sad hurler for the visiting San Diego Padres crossed his arms and rested them on his knees, while the subject of the endless applause, the Cincinnati Reds player standing on first base, finally broke down. He finally cracked.

Pete Rose began to cry.

For more than two decades, baseball fans had come to expect raw emotion from Pete. It was part of both his public persona and his internal character. He sprinted out walks, slid headfirst into bases, shouted at pitchers to intimidate them, knocked over catchers at home plate, and once broke a man's shoulder in a meaningless game as he tried to score the winning run. But this—crying—was new for fans. And so, when the crowd at Riverfront Stadium in Cincinnati saw him bow his head, hide his eyes beneath his shiny red batting helmet, and wipe away his tears with his new white batting gloves, the people cheered even louder. They loved Pete even more on this warm night in September 1985 because he had done it. He was now the hit king.

With his latest single—a clean, low-looping line drive to left-center field off that pitcher for the Padres—Pete had compiled more hits than any other player in baseball history: 4,192. More than Cobb and Musial, more than Aaron and Mays. Seven hundred more hits than Yaz. Twelve hundred more hits than the Babe. Fifteen hundred more than Teddy Ballgame. Nearly double the total of Joltin' Joe, the Yankee Clipper, and as many as Bench and Berra combined. Pete had joined the list of the Immortals, players known far and wide by a single name. Indeed, he had surpassed them, all of them, and he would never look back, in part because Pete isn't built for self-reflection and in part because he would never have to reexamine this part of his story.

Decades later, his hit record still stands. In a country where twenty-five million children might swing a bat every spring—and some sixteen thousand men have done it at the highest level, coming to the plate in a major-league ballgame with the dream of slapping a double down the line—no one has ever come close to matching Pete Rose's hit record, and they probably never will. It stands there like a monument to the man himself.

Yet on this night in 1985, the fans in Cincinnati loved him for a different reason. For the reason they had always loved him and for what they knew to be true. Pete Rose wasn't special. He was almost ordinary. Arguably, the most ordinary extraordinary athlete in the history of American sports. Hardscrabble and gritty. Less talented than tough. A Rust Belt hero for a Rust Belt town. He was just like the fans, the people cheering him now on this night in September. He was white, working-class, and midwestern.

"And again the flashbulbs go off all over the ballpark," the city's radio play-by-play man cried from the press box over home plate. "Hit number 4,192."

"It's a slider inside," the television color man added in the next booth over, as the network replayed the record-breaking hit in slow motion. "And Pete hits the ball probably like he's done four thousand times—a line drive over shortstop. And right there he knows it's a base hit. He knows that's it. And he rounds the bag the way he always does: all out."

"This is his game. It is his town and it is his moment," still another broadcaster added. Then, in a preplanned advertising stunt that's impossible to imagine today, the broadcaster stood up in the booth, turned toward the camera, hoisted a can of Budweiser, and toasted Pete on national television.

"This Bud's for Pete Rose—and baseball," the announcer said. "Just breathe it in."

—

On first base, in that moment, Pete exhaled and shook his head, acknowledged the crowd, looked up, and then looked down, and as his gaze settled on his customary black cleats, he would have seen them squarely planted on the infield dirt. Pete was safe at first, as usual.

But the world had changed in the twenty-five years that he had been playing professional baseball, and it was changing still, even as Pete stood there at Riverfront Stadium that night, awash in the praise and the flashbulbs. The game that Pete had loved as a boy was no longer an unpolished American pastime, populated by men who had learned to play by hitting bottle caps in the streets and who worked off-season jobs in the winter to survive. It had become a big business where even the worst players made three times more than the average American, the biggest stars earned ten times more than the president of the United States, and owners operated like modern-day railroad tycoons. In 1985, baseball was on the cusp of its first billion-dollar television deal with CBS, and viewers tuning in to watch this modern game saw a product that looked different in ways that thrilled some people and rattled others.

Baseball—a sport that had been almost exclusively white in the 1950s—was now much more diverse. Thirty percent of the league was now Latino or Black, and by 1985 the biggest stars were players of color: Darryl Strawberry, Doc Gooden, Ozzie Smith, Fernando Valenzuela, Rickey Henderson, Kirby Puckett, Dave Winfield, Tony Gwynn, and both Rookies of the Year in 1985—Vince Coleman and Ozzie Guillen. No big-city columnist was going to publicly celebrate a star player for being white, as they had once celebrated Pete and others of his generation, and no reporter was going to protect Pete either, because the chummy beat writer was gone now, too.

These writers—always men and often friendly enough with the players to go out carousing with the team on the road—had been replaced by a new generation of sports reporters, raised on Woodward and Bernstein. And these scribes weren't beholden to the athletes in any way. What they wanted was a story, and they had competition to get it. New networks like CNN and ESPN were going to be happy to document a star player's missteps, foibles, flaws, and errors, because scandal was good for ratings, and no scandal was going to be more captivating in the 1980s than Pete Rose's.

It was almost as if he were standing in quicksand that night at Riverfront Stadium—only he was unaware of the world beyond him. Pete didn't know it, but he was sinking.

In the next few years—a shorter time frame than anyone ever could have imagined—the cheering stopped and the toasts did, too, as baseball officials and reporters did something they had declined to do in the past. They pulled back the curtain, stripped away the myth, dismantled Pete Rose the icon, sold off the pieces, and revealed the man, naked and broken, for who he was, for who he had always been, though no one had ever dared to say it out loud for fear of tarnishing America's pastime. Pete wasn't working-class. He was maybe low class. He was uneducated and unpolished beneath his New Money shine. He was consorting with a screwball collection of bookies, railbirds, lackeys, dope dealers, and wannabe mobsters, and he had surrounded himself with a small group of young admirers who were thrilled to be his friends and were willing to do anything to protect him. They would satisfy Pete's addictions and keep his many secrets. They wouldn't tell anyone that he was sleeping with young women, that he was betting on baseball, and that he was lying about all of it.

These revelations, still to come, would forever alter the game, ruin Pete Rose, change life in the proud baseball town of Cincinnati, spark endless debates about fame and forgiveness that still linger decades later, and mark the end of the age of innocence in sports. By the time it was over, Pete was no longer just a man; he was a fault line, separating the past from the present, the time of heroes from the time of cheaters. Nothing in American sports would ever be the same again. We wouldn't even think about gambling the same way.

Sports wagering is now legal in almost every state. In some cities, baseball fans can place bets on the game at kiosks at the stadium. In most states, people can wager with the flick of their fingers on their phones while they cheer from the cheap seats or from just behind the dugout, and baseball, once opposed to gambling in all its formats, isn't frowning on the new craze. It's actively promoting sports gambling with corporate partnerships and in-game graphics broadcast on national television, giving viewers live betting odds of the current batter's chances of hitting a home run in that very moment.

There's simply too much money in play not to be involved. In 2023, fans in America wagered more than one hundred billion dollars on sports, enough money that they could have pooled their cash to buy the Cincinnati Reds a hundred times over or purchase every single Major League Baseball team—and still have billions of dollars left in their pockets.

These are changes that no one saw coming—least of all Pete Rose, the baseball executives who put their careers on the line to investigate him, or Pete's friends who were forced to make difficult choices in the white-hot klieg lights of a prying national media. As the FBI began to close in on Pete's associates in the late 1980s, and baseball executives started asking questions of Pete himself—questions that they had ignored for years—everyone around Pete had to make a decision: Were they going to tell the truth and expose him for his gambling? Or were they going to lie and potentially go down with the man? What price were they willing to pay? What story were they going to tell? Which side were they on?

The answers to these questions changed people's lives forever—including Pete's. And more than three decades later, these decisions still reverberate like shock waves through a universe that Pete created with his own hand. In this mythical place, Pete Rose is the sun, burning brightly in the center, and the people in his life, everyone else, are planets in orbit, trapped by shared history, Pete's charisma, and above all his gravitational pull. Each was drawn to him for different reasons, and some in this universe are no longer in need of his light, of Pete's warmth and attention. They orbit in distant rings, cold and dark. Still, they cannot escape, and certain disturbances—like phone calls, say, from a writer, or fresh allegations, new stories—set off a chain reaction. Those closest to Pete will still do what he says, while others on the outside—the dark planets gone cold—will crack up if they spend too much time remembering what it was like to live in the warm light of Pete's sun. Put simply: people cry, break down, get angry, or go off when they talk about Pete Rose. They love him or hate him so much that he has destroyed them.

But all that comes later, in the wreckage of this story, in the aftermath of one of America's great tragedies. In the moment—Pete

Rose's greatest moment, on that night in September 1985—everyone was happy, Pete most of all. He was a player at his peak standing on first base with the flashbulbs firing, and the people cheering, and the television broadcasters raising their beer cans in the booth behind home plate.

Somewhere in the stands, Pete's mother hugged friends and family. In the seats around her, strangers embraced, too, and at some point Pete couldn't take it anymore. He looked up at the sky and then buried his face into the shoulder of his first-base coach, his longtime friend and former teammate Tommy Helms.

"I don't know what to do," Pete told Helms, as the ovation continued at Riverfront Stadium unabated.

"That's okay, boss," Helms replied.

Pete didn't have to do anything anymore.

"You're number one," Helms assured him. "You deserve it all."

ACT I
RISE

1

BEFORE THE BRIDGES went up, the interstates went in, and the circle freeway carved a path through the valley, there was only one way to cross the Ohio River on the West Side of Cincinnati. It was the little side-wheel ferry down the hill in front of Pete Rose's house.

Pete was about twelve years old when he got hired to work on the boat. The ferry operator, Mr. Kottmyer, paid Pete a menial wage to dart amid the cars and collect the crossing fares—thirty-five cents for automobiles, five cents for passengers. Mr. Kottmyer knew what he was doing; his family had run the ferry since the Civil War, purchasing the business from a string of other ferry captains, including George Anderson—the man who had given the entire neighborhood its name: Anderson Ferry. But Mr. Kottmyer had misjudged his new hire, Pete Rose. The little kid, two sizes too small for his age, wearing dirty dungarees and old leather shoes, probably would have done the job for nothing. Pete liked riding across the river, back and forth between Ohio and Kentucky, with people pressing silver coins into his hand. It was like traveling, only they were never far from home. Wherever they were on the water, wherever Mr. Kottmyer steered the ferry, swinging the bow into the current, Pete could see his house on the Ohio side rising above the riverbank on Braddock Street.

The two-story clapboard house in which Pete was born had been built into the hill in the 1880s, and it was showing its age. The house felt as if it were teetering there, held together by cinder blocks and mortar, and inside the house there wasn't much room for the Rose family. Pete shared a bedroom with his younger brother, Dave. His older sisters doubled up as well, and all of them took turns using a single bathroom, lining up outside the door during the busiest times of the day. But the house was also a survivor. From its perch on the hill, it had dodged catastrophic floods over the years that had washed other homes away. And perhaps most important to Pete, his home on Braddock Street was at the center of everything that mattered in the neighborhood. Schulte's Gardens and the Trolley Tavern—Anderson Ferry's two local drinking establishments—were both right there on the two-lane highway that hugged the water's edge, U.S. 50, River Road. Pete could be at either of them in a minute just by running down the hill, with the coins he earned from Mr. Kottmyer jangling in his pants pockets.

Sometimes, outside Schulte's, Pete gambled with these coins or whatever other money he had made by collecting discarded beer bottles and redeeming them for cash. The game was called lagging pennies. From a short distance away from Schulte's brick exterior wall, two boys pitched pennies at the building. Closest penny to the wall won the round, and the winner grew richer by the moment. He stuffed the other boy's penny, the loser coin, into his pants pocket and gathered himself to throw again.

Pete was good at the game. He could lay his penny right up against the wall. But more often, Pete used the wall outside Schulte's for a different activity. He threw a rubber ball against it and then fielded the bounce off the wall—again and again and again—with a singular intensity that people noticed at the time and then forgot. They had no reason to remember, because most people who visited Anderson Ferry were just passing through. They were on a barge pushing south to New Orleans, on Mr. Kottmyer's little boat crossing over into Kentucky, or in a car on River Road rambling east toward downtown Cincinnati.

There, at the city center, the landscape looked decidedly different than it did in Pete's neighborhood. A rail yard bustled at the edge of town. The Cincinnati Reds' ballpark, Crosley Field, stood just beyond the tracks. A cluster of newly built high-rise buildings reached toward the sky along the waterfront, and people scurried between the buildings on weekdays, perhaps one building most of all: the world headquarters for the Procter & Gamble Co. at Sixth and Main. P&G's roots in the city dated back to the 1800s, and its flagship product, Ivory Soap, seemed to capture the essence of Cincinnati more than anything else. The soap was said to be pure—"99 and 44/100 percent pure"—and P&G produced it by the truckload. During the day, workers churned out soap at a factory north of town, and in the evening the P&G executives retired to private clubs to dine with their wives, throw dinner dances for their daughters, or discuss Republican Party politics.

It was a world that existed just seven miles from Pete's house on Braddock Street, but it felt unattainable to him and to other children growing up on the West Side, especially Anderson Ferry. In this neighborhood of machinists, meat cutters, truck drivers, pipe fitters, and clerks, no one ever escaped, and Pete Rose wasn't getting out, either.

Everyone knew that he wasn't even going to do as well as his father.

2

The man's full name was Harry Francis Rose, but everyone on the West Side knew him as Big Pete. According to the story, it had something to do with a horse of the same name that Harry Rose had loved when he was a boy. But the nickname was more likely rooted in a practicality that few in the Rose family liked to discuss. Big Pete's parents had divorced when he was just a baby, and his mother had remarried Harry Sams, a railroad worker on the West Side.

The nickname, Pete, made it easier to distinguish the stepfather from the boy, and in time no one—not even his own mother—called him Harry anymore. He was just Pete, growing up behind the rail yard a couple miles upriver from Braddock Street and making a name for himself as a scrappy fighter with fists the size of coffee canisters and a face like chiseled rock. At age fifteen, competing under the name Pete Sams, Pete Rose's father first thrilled sports fans in Cincinnati when he defeated a flurry of young boxers at the Franklin Avenue Armory over the course of two days to claim a district championship. He continued to fight. Then, around his eighteenth birthday, the young man quit boxing and trained his sights on other sports.

In winter, Pete Rose's father played basketball for Christ Church in the Ohio Valley League. In spring and summer, he played third base for the Tresler Comets, batting .300, and every fall Big Pete dominated the semipro Feldhaus football league, a rugged collection of workaday men willing to sacrifice their bodies for a game that was meaningless in every way except two. The players often placed side bets on the outcomes of the games, and they knew a good player could get noticed. He could receive an invite to try out for a pro club in Green Bay, Chicago, or Cleveland.

A flashy halfback and a punishing defender, Big Pete had as good a chance as anyone of getting such a call. He was always scampering into the end zone, throwing for touchdowns, cutting down opponents at the knees, and intercepting the ball. In his first nineteen seasons, Big Pete won the Feldhaus league title an unprecedented twelve times, making himself a West Side star. The newspapers wrote feature stories about him, and at least one local television station invited him to come in, wearing his football uniform, to demonstrate his gridiron prowess on TV.

"Let's show them what you do on the field," the television host said.

Pete Rose's father ducked and moved that day, bobbing his head, shaking his hips, and hitting the hole at speed. He sliced between barriers set up inside the television studio with a football tucked under his arm. The host told viewers to prepare for an exciting finale. He set up a desk chair at the far end of the studio and asked Rose to display his raw power—the same way he speared opposing runners during games on Sundays. Only to make it fair, and cushion the blow, the host asked a stagehand to drape the chair with a blanket.

Big Pete nodded. He was happy to do it. He had just one request.

"Take the blanket off," he said through clenched teeth. "You think I'm a sissy?"

—

That day, inside the television studio, Big Pete broke the desk chair. He slammed into it with such fury that he knocked off one of the chair's arms, dented the seat back, and left it splintered, good furniture smashed to pieces on the floor. The host had hoped to have Rose hit it a couple of times to end the program, but that was impossible now, and the station didn't want to sacrifice another perfectly fine chair for the show. So the host faded out, thanking Big Pete for coming. "Pete Rose," the host said, "the most famous semipro athlete in the history of greater Cincinnati."

It was high praise for Rose's father, and also, as it turned out, it marked the pinnacle of his career. He would never be more than a semipro ballplayer. He was good enough for the Feldhaus football league maybe, or the Tresler Comets, or a small-time television program in Cincinnati, but not much else. The Green Bay Packers weren't calling. The Cleveland Browns weren't, either. And even if they did—even if, by some miracle, a pro scout discovered Big Pete playing halfback on the West Side on a crisp Sunday afternoon—he wouldn't have been able to leave home. The man had obligations.

Late one winter, between basketball and baseball seasons, he had married a young German girl with big eyes and a fondness for Tareyton cigarettes—Laverne Bloebaum. The new couple settled into Laverne's house on Braddock Street in Anderson Ferry, with a whole mess of Bloebaums, including at times the young bride's father, her younger brother, her older sister, and her sister's husband. To contribute, Big Pete needed to get a job, and he found one at a local bank. Monday through Friday, he commuted to Fourth and Walnut downtown and sat at a desk, punching and cranking an old adding machine. He was a bookkeeper.

The work helped scrape and claw the Roses to the edge of the middle class. By 1940, Big Pete was making $1,400 a year—the equivalent of about $40,000 today. But it was tedious work, and not at all what Big Pete wanted to be doing with his life. Reading the balance sheets gave him terrible headaches and forced him to wear eyeglasses—another thing that sissies did. Perhaps worst of all, the pay he took home never seemed to be enough for the growing family. Sometimes, to supplement the family income, Laverne had to take work waiting tables or serving drinks at the Trolley Tavern down the hill. They had two girls to support—Caryl and Jacqueline, born in quick succession in the 1930s—and then in the spring of 1941, their third child, a boy, Little Pete.

Big Pete was obsessed with his son's greatness from the start. He forced him to swing a baseball bat and throw a ball left-handed, even though Little Pete's dominant hand was obviously his right, to make him a more valuable asset to Little Pete's youth baseball teams. He once used the family allowance to buy boxing gloves for Little Pete instead of shoes for the older girls. With those gloves, Pete sparred with his father in the tiny yard on Braddock Street, and with whatever time they had left before sundown, they played baseball at a ragged diamond not far from the house called Bold Face Park. Big Pete always had an eye on the future and remained laser-focused, it seemed, on his oldest son, even after Laverne gave birth to another boy, Dave, in the late 1940s. Once, when Little Pete broke a window at the house, shattering the glass with a well-hit ball, Big Pete refused to fix it. The broken window, he told Laverne, was proof of the boy's first hit. It had to remain shattered—for history—just in case Little Pete ever became a great ballplayer. Big Pete believed it was possible. The kid just needed to work. "Hustle, Pete," the father said. "Keep up the hustle." He thought that with hard work Little Pete could overcome anything—his lack of money, his lack of talent, and even his lack of size.

Little Pete was always one of the smallest kids out on the field at Bold Face Park. By middle school, other boys towered over him; Little Pete, Puny Pete, "Pee-Wee" Pete, they called him. He couldn't keep up. Still, his father kept pushing. Most dads on the West Side weren't able to watch their sons' games—work at the factory or the rail yard kept them away—but Big Pete found a way to be there. Pete's teammates remembered seeing him at the field more than their own fathers, cheering in foul territory or meeting with the coaches to demand that they let Pete be a switch-hitter, batting from both the left side and the right. Big Pete was hustling, as he wanted his boy to do. His only break was the occasional weekend afternoon, when he drove his kids fifteen miles across town to the far reaches of the East Side, down by the river near the county line, to spend the day at the city racetrack, River Downs.

Pete loved baseball, but these afternoons at the track were some of the happiest moments of his childhood. At River Downs, he didn't have to play or perform. He didn't have to hustle or keep up with anyone. He could just stand along the homestretch and cheer. Among men clutching racing forms, dollar bills, betting slips, and dreams, Little Pete could be a boy, screaming like crazy for his daddy's horse to win.

3

Catholic high schools ruled Cincinnati in the 1950s. Everyone who mattered—the Procter & Gamble executives, the Eisenhower Republicans, the Stevenson Democrats, the families with money, and the working-class Catholics concerned for the everlasting souls of their children—did whatever they could to send their boys to learn from the grim-faced priests at high schools named Elder, Roger Bacon, Archbishop Moeller, and St. Xavier. But the Roses on Braddock Street were neither religious nor wealthy. Big Pete didn't like that they were always asking for money at church, and he and Laverne made a different plan for their firstborn son. In the fall of 1955, they enrolled Little Pete at a public school, Western Hills High.

West High, as the locals called it, was a sprawling campus about four miles north of Pete's home, straight up the hill. The campus included both a middle school and a high school—six grades in all, with almost three thousand students, all West Siders, and many of them quintessentially so. The kids descended from Uchtmans and Wollenhaupts, Scheidenbergers and Schindlers, Zieglers and Otts, Kisers and Kohls. Almost everyone in the school was white, and from the start they were thrilled to be at West High. The school had an orchestra, a choir, a business club, an archery team, a cheer squad—

the Sparkettes!—a state-of-the-art library with built-in bookshelves, a swimming pool with a synchronized-swimming coach, and, most important to the young Pete Rose, a thriving tradition of male sporting dominance that began every fall with football season.

The school's football games could draw more than ten thousand people at a time. But no game mattered more than West High's annual Thanksgiving Day showdown against rival Elder High School. Elder was a West Side school, too. But it was private and Catholic and only for boys. A party was thrown every year. The West High faithful called it the "Pow Wow." Every Thanksgiving eve, a police escort and the school marching band would lead a parade away from West High, until there were West Siders a mile long heading up Glenway Avenue to Oskamp Playfield, where there would be a massive bonfire, celebratory speeches, and rousing applause for each senior on the team. Then the West High dads, sufficiently lathered up and ready to see their boys thrash Elder the next day, gathered to drink beer late into the night at Lutz's Gardens.

Pete Rose wanted in on this tradition. As a freshman, he went out for the reserve football team, and saw time at tailback, punt returner, and placekicker—a toe-ball kicker running at it head-on. But his performance on the field for the Mustangs—both as a football player and as a freshman baseball player in the spring of 1956—was entirely forgettable, to the point that later classmates asked themselves, "Was Pete Rose even there?" In a large school with hundreds of young male athletes, many of them already growing beards and sprouting chest hair, Little Pete did what kids sometimes do: he vanished into the crowd.

Part of the problem was that Pete didn't look like an athlete at all. He was still small, all sinew and bone, with gaps in his teeth, a goofy smile, and a lumpy buzz cut. While other boys crafted their hair every morning before school with gels and oils in front of their mirrors—sculpting perfect flat tops, crew cuts, or ducktails—Pete's hair stuck up in all the wrong places. Popular upperclassman athletes didn't even want to be seen with him in the halls between classes. They wanted to walk with their girlfriends, not chat with Pete Rose. Pete also failed to distinguish himself in the classroom. He enjoyed geography and learning to read maps, but hardly anything else. He had no interest in studying. And even when it came to his favorite subject, Pete refused to apply himself for reasons he could easily explain to anyone who asked. Did he need to know the capital of Greece or the largest river in France to be a good athlete? "I don't think so," he said.

At the end of his freshman year, in the spring of 1956, Pete found proof that he was taking the right approach. A regional manager for a coupon company, S&H Green Stamps, was putting together a team of teenagers to compete in Class A of Cincinnati's prestigious Knothole baseball league. The man traveled the country for work, he told parents. He always made it a point to watch youth baseball games when he was on the road. He believed that Cincinnati boys played the game as well as anyone, and he began assembling a roster to reflect that local talent, starting with his own son, Jerry Paner.

Paner—one of Pete's classmates at West High, bound for a baseball scholarship at Bowling Green State University—would play shortstop. Jim "Ost" Oster—another West High kid and a future electrician—would handle the catching duties. Art Luebbe—a giant left-hander, already at least six feet tall, with blond hair, blue eyes, and honor-roll grades at St. Xavier High—would pitch. The Witsken twins—Carl and Howard, the sons of West Side dairy farmers, who had learned to play baseball on the back side of their father's farm—would do damage at the plate, and the Green Stamps would hope to get timely hitting from a scrappy second baseman from Anderson Ferry: Pete Rose.

Pete looked as if he could have been Art Luebbe's little brother. Standing in his baggy white uniform pants with his ball cap on, he didn't even reach Luebbe's shoulders. He lacked size and power, and could be, some thought, a bit of a distraction. Pete sometimes couldn't stop himself from horsing around. But at the plate and in the field, he channeled this energy into a hot coal of confidence. He had quick hands and good vision. He could manufacture runs by bunting and stealing—even when he wore his dungarees to practice—and that's all the Green Stamps needed from their undersized second baseman. As it turned out, the Stamps were a juggernaut.

Behind Art Luebbe's powerful left arm, they rolled all the way to the city championship game that summer, faced Solomon's Grocery in the finals, and beat them 2–0. Luebbe was nearly perfect that day. He struck out thirteen and never allowed a hit. But Luebbe himself made it clear just how important Pete was to the squad. When the Stamps won a national Knothole tournament one week later—beating teams from Ohio, Kentucky, and Tennessee at the end of August 1956—the Stamps' star pitcher let Pete hoist the trophy.

The piece of hardware was enormous. Pete needed two hands to hold it, and he laughed at the absurdity of its size, smiling his big, goofy grin as he stood next to Luebbe on the field. But it seemed like a fitting way to end the season—and the summer.

Harry Rose's kid was clearly no Art Luebbe, no Witsken twin, no Jim Oster, and no Jerry Paner. All those boys were bigger than Pete and better. Yet Pete had something. It was intangible perhaps, but it was something, and on this team it came with an official title. The Green Stamps named Pete their captain.

About six weeks later, the Stamps gathered one last time as a team at a downtown hotel for the city's annual baseball awards banquet. Everyone dressed for the occasion, even Pete. He wore a white shirt, a dark tie, the best shoes he owned, and argyle socks. The group posed for a team picture, and at some point in the evening Pete stood for one more photo at the request of *The Cincinnati Post.* The newspaper wanted a shot featuring the team captains from each of the championship squads in the city: Don McClure from Grote Post; Bob Roncker from St. William; Sam Hollingsworth from Myers Dairy, and Pete Rose from the S&H Green Stamps.

The photograph ran in the *Post* the next day, and it should have been a moment of celebration for the Roses. Big Pete's dreams were coming true, and Little Pete's were, too. The boy was in the newspaper; he was becoming *someone.* But inside the house on Braddock Street, it didn't feel that way, for reasons that didn't make it into the newspaper and for reasons that neither the father nor the son wished to discuss, especially, it seemed, with each other. In the greatest hour of his childhood, in the afterglow of the Knothole championship, Pete Rose felt like a failure.

He had been cut from the football team at West High.

4

THE BAD NEWS about the football team came down sometime that August in the way bad news often does: it was delivered quietly, through the back door. Pete Rose wasn't cut from the football team at West High so much as he wasn't invited to play. Other sophomore boys got the call to come out for varsity. Pete did not. He was out.

Both the father and the son struggled to process this news, but perhaps the father most of all. Had there been some kind of mistake? He was Harry Francis Rose, Big Pete—one of the greatest semipro football players in the city, the man on local television, showing off his moves, tackling chairs, and breaking them, never a sissy, and this was his son. Clearly, the school had made an error. The coach must have cut the wrong kid.

There was no mistake. Little Pete, with legs like staircase spindles, would not play football in the fall of 1956. He'd miss one of the greatest seasons in recent West High history, watching from the stands while his classmates Harry Panaro and Wayne Streibig played tailback and became local stars. On just the second play of the season, Panaro ripped off a forty-seven-yard touchdown run. Minutes later, he scored again, almost single-handedly beating West High's first opponent of the year, and the Mustangs were off and running. They outscored their first four opponents 107–14, didn't lose until almost the end of October, won the city's public high school league, and entered the all-important Thanksgiving Day game against Elder that November with a record of 8-1 and everything on the line. Elder had won the city's Greater Catholic League that fall, meaning the Thanksgiving game would serve as a de facto city championship. The undisputed top private school was playing the best public school. "The winner of the Western Hills–Elder classic," one newspaper wrote that week, "can lay claim to the mythical city crown."

The halls at West High felt almost electric in the days leading up to the game. For the first time in years, the kids believed they could beat Elder. The student council made plans for a Victory Dance, and the pregame "Pow Wow" that Thanksgiving eve featured all the usual pomp and circumstance. Just after nightfall, the West High marching band led the students up Glenway Avenue to Oskamp Playfield, where the bonfire was roaring and the school's cheerleading squad, the Sparkettes, were cheering. *"This is my school!"* Afterward, the West High dads retired to Lutz's Gardens, as usual, and the next morning, with a thin layer of fresh snow on the ground at Elder Stadium and some eleven thousand people shivering in the stands, West High took it to Elder. The Mustangs won 20–13.

In the celebration afterward, jubilant football players mobbed West High's head coach and carried him off the field. But the closest Pete got to the action was the ride home. Harry Panaro smuggled him onto the team bus because, Pete informed him, he had no way to get back to campus and wished to avoid making the two-mile walk in the cold, if possible. The whole way home, Pete hid in Harry's seat at the back of the bus—*with* the football team, but not *on* it, an insult that felt to the boy like a screwdriver in his heart. It turned and turned like the wheels of the bus as it lurched out of the parking lot at Elder and drove the kids home to West High.

"Fuck school," Pete thought.

If he couldn't have football—if he couldn't be a part of this—he didn't care anymore. What was the point?

"Fuck school."

It was just a notion in his mind at first—one of a million stupid teenage notions, flittering through the frontal lobe of his brain, here and gone—and then it crystallized into something resembling a plan. Without football, Pete decided he would quit going to class. He'd get on the bus in the morning at his usual stop on River Road in Anderson Ferry and ride it to West High, but never enter the building. Or he'd intentionally miss the bus and head downtown instead. He'd walk around all day, pretend to be someone else. And on the rare days when he did attend class, he wasn't really there. Pete fired rubber bands at the other kids in class, got in fights, or stared out the window of the classroom, brokenhearted and lost.

Harry Panaro was among the first to notice. Pete seemed to be falling in with the wrong crowd, Harry thought. He ran with the motorheads and the losers now. Like one of the ferries along the river, Pete had lost his moorings and was drifting away, caught in a current of his own making and wrestling with a new feeling: loneliness. It was only a matter of time before teachers and administrators noticed, too, and placed a call to Big Pete and Laverne on Braddock Street to talk about their wayward son.

At best, administrators informed his parents, the boy would have to repeat his sophomore year. At worst, he'd never come back. Folks on the West Side believed Pete might just drop out—a thought that infuriated his father. More than once that year, Big Pete came to the school for meetings with teachers, and at home he scolded the boy to the point that Little Pete stopped listening to his father, maybe for the first time in his life.

It was a tenuous moment that required intervention, a parent's love, a careful approach, and perhaps some well-intentioned consequences. In many houses, both then and now, it likely would have meant no more sports, no more activities. A child failing out of school should not play ball, should not play anything. But the Rose house was different because Big Pete was different. Amid his son's troubled sophomore year, the father opted to enroll his son in athletics outside of school. He decided it was time for Little Pete to get into a boxing ring and fight, and he sent him to train with a rugged West Side character named Jimmy Schlank.

Schlank—a Syrian American with dark hair, thick eyebrows, long arms, and an easy smile—was a former amateur boxing champion in Cincinnati. He had won the lightweight crown in 1936 when he was nineteen years old and earned the right to compete in the national championship in Chicago. He had made it all the way to the semifinals there, knocking out opponents in front of twelve thousand raucous fans. The key was his mentality. Schlank would get knocked down and bounce back up again. He feuded with fighters he didn't like outside the ring and approached bouts with a fury that at times felt personal. As boxing beat writers noted, Schlank was known to "lose his head."

Now forty years old, he owned a bar on the West Side called the

Fishing Club, about a mile from Pete's house, on the ridge overlooking the river. Yet it was fighting that Schlank really loved, and he did everything he could to stay in the game, training young boys in an empty lot behind the bar. It wasn't a real gym; he didn't even have a real boxing ring. Schlank's students trained in the belly of an old, abandoned swimming pool, and sometime during his sophomore year of high school Little Pete Rose became one of them—if, perhaps, a little reluctantly.

He didn't care much for boxing. There was too much practice, and not enough actual competition for his taste. Training inside Schlank's swimming pool felt absurd. "A swimming pool," Pete groused. "A swimming pool, with no fucking water in it." And Schlank was hard on him to the point that Pete thought his trainer a little crazy, and maybe a little mean. If given the choice, Pete would have rather played football or baseball. But with the walls of the pool acting as the ropes of the ring, Pete listened to Schlank. He learned how to stick and move, how to work the jab, how to protect himself, and how to pursue his opponent. He learned how to be mean, too, or at least how to survive, and he took from Schlank an ethos—something bigger than boxing. It was important, Schlank said, to "fight your fight." It was important to fight and keep fighting.

Soon, a date was set for a proper match. In April 1957, three days before his sixteenth birthday near the end of his lost sophomore year, Pete Rose stepped into a real ring for his first fight. The location was the Findlay Neighborhood House—a brick building on the edge of downtown, a short walk from the Reds' stadium, Crosley Field—and the opponent was, for Pete anyway, a total unknown: a sixteen-year-old fighter named Virgil Cole.

For Big Pete in the crowd that day, it must have felt as if his life had come full circle. The father had entered the ring as an amateur at age fifteen, winning the district title in 1929 to the thrill of the crowd. His son Little Pete could certainly do the same, and on the boxing card this flyweight matchup—Rose versus Cole—seemed like a fair one. Both boys were the same age and the same size. Each weighed in at 112 pounds. If anything, Virgil was smaller.

But if Pete thought he had it tough growing up on Braddock Street in Anderson Ferry, young Virgil could have easily disabused him of that notion. He was the third of nine children, born into a segregated public housing development, capable of housing a thousand families on the edge of downtown, all of them Black. By the time Virgil was sixteen and stepping into the ring at the Neighborhood House, his father was gone, and his mother was dead. He was living with an aunt, and he entered the ring with more experience than Pete. He'd fought before and was on his way to winning a local crown—just as Schlank himself had once done. Virgil was afraid of no one, least of all this West Side novice standing before him, Pete Rose, with his lumpy buzz cut and his trainer, sparring with kids inside an empty swimming pool.

On the night of the fight—April 11, 1957—the beating commenced with the sound of the first bell. Virgil pounded Pete about the head and body, so hard and so often that Pete could do nothing to stop it or even fight back. He flopped around in the ring like a hooked fish on a dock while his oldest sister, now twenty-one, watched in horror amid the crowd, crying out for her father to stop the madness. Stop the fight.

"They're killing him," she said.

At first, Big Pete refused to acknowledge it. He couldn't admit what he was seeing with his own eyes.

"He's not getting hurt," he told Pete's sister, to assuage her fears.

By the end of the fight, however, everyone knew that was a lie, including most notably the fighters themselves. Virgil won by decision and won easily, and then the storytelling began, though how each boy would tell this story was different with time.

In the decades to come, Virgil Cole would go on to be a factory worker and a janitor for the Cincinnati public schools, speaking little, if at all, about the time he trounced Pete Rose. For most of his life, Virgil held the memory close, like a secret. Still, the achievement gave the man a measure of local fame that he could not escape. And as the legend of Pete Rose grew over the years, so too did the unlikely tale of Virgil Cole. For years on the West Side, his photo hung on the wall of a popular pizzeria. At his death in 2003, at the age of sixty-two, Virgil earned lead obituary status in *The Cincinnati Enquirer*—with a photo and a big headline: "He Once Bested Pete Rose"—and his wife buried him in Cincinnati beneath a tombstone etched with boxing gloves and a single word: "Champ." Though he rarely talked about his fight with Rose, Virgil Cole believed it to be important. He believed he had changed the course of history by pushing the young Pete Rose out of the boxing ring and into baseball.

Meanwhile, Pete told the story differently. Never keen on discussing his losses or appearing to be weak, he used what happened that night in April 1957 to gild the edges of his own mythology. Yes, he had lost to Virgil Cole, and, yes, he had lost badly. But inside the ring that night at the Findlay Neighborhood House, getting pummeled in front of the crowd, he didn't quit. He hadn't even gone down, and that was a lesson that Pete liked.

"He couldn't knock me out," Pete told his mother afterward.

5

THAT FALL—THE FALL of 1957—Pete Rose began mounting the first comeback of his life.

He reported to Western Hills High School, committed to repeating his sophomore year. Despite the shame of failing a grade and falling behind his fellow classmates, he dedicated himself to his studies, and this new and improved Little Pete impressed his teachers and coaches. By the spring of 1958—what should have been his junior year, but instead was his second sophomore campaign—Pete was batting leadoff for the West High baseball team. He was getting on base any way he could, setting the table for Jerry Paner, his former Green Stamps teammate, and the center fielder Ron Flender, who would soon be signed by the Cincinnati Reds. Little Pete also wasn't so little anymore; he was seventeen and getting stronger by the day. In a legion ball game around the Fourth of July that year, Pete hit two home runs, staking his new summer squad, Postal Employees Post, to a 25–0 win.

The varsity football coaches at West High couldn't ignore him any longer. In August 1958, they finally asked Pete Rose to suit up for the Mustangs. He was on the team—wearing No. 55—set to play halfback and kicker, and he was ready for the opportunity. Pete scored touchdowns against Central, Woodward, Hamilton, and Hughes. He broke free against Walnut Hills for a fifty-seven-yard score. He helped lead the team to a public school championship that November and prepared to play Elder at the end of the month. Then, on Thanksgiving morning, Pete and his teammates served up a beatdown. They buried Elder, 31–14, with Pete scoring one of the team's touchdowns and kicking the lone field goal. He helped beat Elder—the one thing every West High boy wanted in life—which almost made the baseball season that year an afterthought. In the spring of 1959, in Pete's last year of athletic eligibility in high school, he was the starting second baseman for the Mustang nine.

The on-field heroics earned him a few mentions that year in the school newspaper, *The Western Breeze.* "Pete Rose is providing thrills galore," the paper wrote. "The junior scatback has not failed to bring the fans to their feet." But just like his days with the S&H Green Stamps, no one thought that Pete was the best player at West High. Quarterback Ralph "Golden Boy" Griesser got the credit for the Thanksgiving Day victory over Elder. Fullback Charlie Schott was voted the "All-Around Boy" at the annual West High sports banquet that year, and on the baseball squad someone was always better than Pete—whether it was Jerry Paner, Ron Flender, or the newest West High prospect, Eddie Brinkman. The Washington Senators would soon sign Brinkman to a reported $75,000 contract—a stunning amount of money that most major leaguers at the time never received, not even the stars. In the early 1960s, Mickey Mantle was making between $60,000 and $70,000 per year. But the Senators were an expansion team. They needed young talent, and Brinkman's numbers suggested that he was going to be an all-time great. One summer on the West Side, Brinkman batted .560.

"Watch," said the Senators' manager, Gil Hodges, shortly after Brinkman joined the big club in the 1960s. "Watch Brinkman go to his right, deep in the hole, turn, and throw to first. This boy will be around for a dozen or more years. He has the attitude, range, and arm. Makes all the plays and will hit more than enough."

Hodges looked at Brinkman and saw the future.

"I'll tell you one thing: he makes this Washington picture a lot brighter."

The suggestion to Pete Rose was clear. He was no Flender. He was no Brinkman. He was no prospect worth $75,000. Even his own high school baseball coach didn't think so. Pete was a good bunter, the coach told scouts who inquired. He ran hard. But scouts didn't need to look at him. "Too small," the coach said. At best, Pete was bound for a life in the shadows, playing semipro ball like his father and finding a way to eke out a living doing something else, perhaps in the rail yards or, if he was lucky, on one of the river barges.

In the fall of his senior year, with no eligibility left at West High—due to the fact that Pete had repeated a grade—he couldn't play sports with his classmates and instead joined a team in his father's Feldhaus league. He suited up for the Groesbeck Green Devils on Sundays and squared off against such teams as the Eastern Merchants and Mousie's Café. Then, unable to play high school baseball in the spring of 1960 for the same eligibility reasons, Pete turned to a family connection for help, the only relative he knew who had ever truly escaped Anderson Ferry, the West Side, and seen the world on the other side of the wall.

Pete called his mother's oldest brother—his uncle Buddy Bloebaum.

6

Buddy was a full decade older than Laverne, and among the Roses anyway he was royalty. Like most in Pete's family, Uncle Buddy quit school after eighth grade, and as a result he had been forced to take a series of working-class jobs. He was a machinist in his teens, a pool-hall manager in his twenties, and these days he was lucky to have a position at a factory in Dayton, sixty miles north of Cincinnati: the National Cash Register company.

But as a young man in the 1920s and 1930s, Uncle Buddy had been a local athletic standout. He starred on a semipro baseball team called the Duckworth Democrats, batting leadoff, playing shortstop, and, according to the local papers, "making plays of the sensational variety." At a minimum, he was a far better baseball player than Pete Rose's father had ever been, and in 1932, Uncle Buddy briefly tasted the sweet elixir of baseball glory. The Cincinnati Reds signed him to a Class D minor-league contract and sent him to Iowa to play for the Cedar Rapids Bunnies in the Mississippi Valley League.

It was the lowest rung of professional baseball, and the Bunnies struggled to compete against the likes of Davenport, Rock Island, and Keokuk in 1932. Fans rarely turned out to Bunny Park to watch. Uncle Buddy played most of his games in an empty stadium, and he lived that entire summer under a cloud of doubt. The owners in Cedar Rapids, deep in debt, threatened to shut down the Bunnies before the Fourth of July, and then, the following spring, they made good on that promise. In April 1933, Cedar Rapids folded and sold its players off to other teams. Uncle Buddy was now the starting shortstop for the Peoria Tractors, though not for long. In the second game of the 1933 season, he collided with his own left fielder while trying to make a diving catch behind third base and injured his leg.

It was, for Uncle Buddy, a stroke of Roy Hobbsian bad luck. Even before the injury, he was thirty, too old for Class D baseball. Now he was old, and injured, and done. At the end of May 1933, Uncle Buddy informed Tractors ownership in Peoria that he was going home. He was limping back to Cincinnati. The next time he played baseball, it would be for the Solway's Furniture team and Schulte's Gardens on the West Side.

But Buddy Bloebaum's brief moment of baseball success wasn't entirely wasted. At Bunny Park in Cedar Rapids, he got the chance to play night games under newfangled floodlights—a celestial experience, reporters gushed, "seventy-five times as brilliant as the brightest moonlight," and a sensation that major leaguers wouldn't experience for three more years. He batted .285—proof that he had belonged—and he made connections that would help him, and his family, for decades to come. In Cedar Rapids and Peoria, he befriended the young man playing next to him on the infield: Phil Seghi, a light-hitting third baseman from Illinois. Seghi had a narrow face, a long nose, a pipe-smoking habit, and a batting average thirty points lower than Bloebaum in Cedar Rapids. Not a star. But unlike Pete's uncle,

Seghi was in his early twenties at the time. He avoided serious injury, and he stayed in the minors for the next twenty years, logging stops as a player and manager in Winnipeg, Sioux City, Tallahassee, Green Bay, and Fargo—until somehow Seghi and Bloebaum ended up in the same place again. In the 1950s, the Cincinnati Reds hired both men as scouts.

The job of scouting was a primitive shadow of the science it would later become. There were no analytics, no spreadsheets, and often no real plan. To find young talent, Seghi and Bloebaum would typically hold open tryouts on dusty diamonds across the Midwest, looking to find the next great Cincinnati Red amid soybean fields. They promoted the events by placing advertisements in local papers, and hopefuls were reminded that they had to supply their own cleats, gloves, and uniforms for the tryouts.

For Bloebaum, it was part-time work, and strictly local. After finishing his shift at the cash register factory in Dayton, he hit the fields in rural southwestern Ohio and informed the front office in Cincinnati if he found any prospects of note. But before long, he was reporting directly to his former teammate Phil Seghi, who from the start of their scouting days had moved up on a different track. While Bloebaum focused on Dayton, Seghi traveled the country, covering ground from Texas to Wisconsin, Nebraska to Ohio. His job with the Reds was full-time and all-consuming, and getting bigger by the day. In 1958, the Reds appointed Seghi as interim farm director, and the following year they made the position permanent. Seghi was now overseeing the club's entire minor-league operation—roughly two hundred players across eight different teams. It was Seghi who decided which prospects to sign and which ones to promote, and Buddy Bloebaum had a direct line to the man, making him a valuable resource to the young Pete Rose, the greatest uncle he could ever have.

In the spring of 1960, during his final weeks at West High, Pete huddled with Uncle Buddy to discuss his playing options. He was desperate to play ball somewhere. He couldn't live without it, and Uncle Buddy directed him to a small amateur league in Dayton in the heart of his scouting territory, not far from his factory job. Pete earned a roster spot with the Lebanon club there, and he proceeded to have the greatest spring of his life. Playing against the K. C. Bailey Realtors and the Dorothy Lane Markets, the nineteen-year-old son of Harry Francis Rose batted .500 in May and June.

Maybe it was just a hot streak; the sample size was small. But Pete didn't think so. He was starting to develop a philosophy around hitting. He liked to get into a deep crouch at the plate so that his head was almost level with the top of the strike zone. He wanted his eyes on the ball from the moment it left the pitcher's hand, and he wanted his bat moving through the top of the zone. This way, everything he hit would be down. He'd eliminate easy pop flies and maximize his chances of getting on base with line drives, choppers, seeing-eye ground balls that got through the hole, and weak dribblers that died in the grass. That's how you hit .500, he figured, and that's how you get noticed. Keep it simple.

"See the ball," he said, "and hit the ball—hard."

Whatever it was, it worked, and at some point that spring Uncle Buddy did what good uncles do. He put in a word for his nephew with the Cincinnati Reds.

Phil Seghi wasn't thrilled with the idea of signing Pete Rose. Privately, Seghi said, the club didn't need another "Punch-and-Judy hitter," a raw, undeveloped, soft-swinging second baseman who struggled to hit the ball over the fence. The Reds, like almost every team in 1960, were looking for power—both at the plate and on the mound. They wanted the next Ernie Banks, one of a few National League players capable of hitting forty home runs a year, or the next Don Drysdale, the league's strikeout leader in 1959. In recent months, Seghi had signed a towering six-foot-five, 220-pound first baseman from Alabama. He had inked a six-foot-two pitcher-shortstop for a reported $100,000—a massive deal in 1960—and he was proud to say that he already had under contract two of the country's best young infielders: the second baseman Bobby Klaus from the University of Illinois and the shortstop Tommy Helms from North Carolina.

The fact was, the Reds didn't need another middle infielder or any other player from West High. Seghi had already signed Pete's former teammate Ron Flender to a reported $15,000 contract and then gone out of his way to make sure everyone knew it. Seghi invited newspapers to take his picture with Flender as he and the phenomenon from the West Side smiled, holding his freshly printed Reds contract. No doubt, Flender was going to be a great one. As the baseball beat writers noted, Flender showed exceptional promise and had all the tools to succeed: "Ron has the equipment to move up."

Pete Rose, by comparison, did not. The promise was harder to see and the tools less obvious. But it was hard to ignore his .500 batting average in the Dayton league. By June, Pete was batting twenty-nine points higher than the next-best hitter. He was perfect at the plate on many days, hitting triples, doubles, singles, never getting out. He was willing to play any position—shortstop, second base, outfield, even catcher—and Seghi trusted Bloebaum. If he was willing to vouch for his nephew, Seghi would at least listen.

On June 16, 1960, a Thursday, Pete led his Lebanon squad to a 20–8 victory over Wright-Patterson in the Dayton league, starting the game at catcher—anything to help the team. The next day, Uncle Buddy shirked his scouting duties at a tryout camp in Piqua and showed up at the Roses' house on Braddock Street. He wanted to talk business with Pete and his father, and on Saturday the three men from the West Side—Uncle Buddy, Pete, and his dad—reported to the Reds' stadium, Crosley Field, to sit down with Phil Seghi and a couple other scouts to discuss a possible contract with the Reds' minor-league affiliate in Geneva, New York. Pete was clearly no Flender, no Klaus, no Helms, and no Brinkman. Seghi wasn't going to cough up Eddie Brinkman kind of money—$75,000—for Pete Rose, even if he did know his uncle. This was a different sort of conversation. Geneva was A-ball, Class D—the ranks where Seghi and Bloebaum had once toiled in obscurity thirty years earlier and a level of baseball so low that it doesn't even exist anymore. Seghi was just looking for a fresh body to put on the infield there, and for that, Pete would do just fine—especially if he was willing to accept a financial offer that was less than one-tenth of what Brinkman got and half of what Flender was set to earn. Seghi was willing to pay Pete $7,000.

Little Pete could barely contain his excitement. The money felt to him like a fortune—*riches.* He would have gone to Geneva for the bus fare, he would have gone for free, and now Seghi was trying to pay him to do it. Little Pete wanted a pen and he wanted to sign, right away. But his father saw the contract for what it really was—

a lowball offer, in the lowest rung of baseball, a gift, a favor, almost nothing—and he began to negotiate with Seghi.

At the very least, Big Pete wanted to wait and see if another team might make his son a better offer. Several scouts were attending games in Dayton, and there was a rumor that the Baltimore Orioles were also interested in Pete. Maybe the Roses needed to wait for the Orioles, Pete's father said.

At this point, Little Pete began to panic. "Goodbye, seven thousand dollars," he thought. "Goodbye, Cincinnati Reds." His father was frittering it away, talking about what-ifs and maybes. Little Pete couldn't believe it, and he finally spoke up. He spoke up in his own defense.

"I'd like to sign," he told Seghi.

For $7,000, he'd go to Geneva—or anywhere else.

"I want to go right now."

Seghi and the other men laughed. At the very least, Seghi told Pete, he had to wait for the plane. It wouldn't be leaving for a few days.

Back home on Braddock Street, Pete Rose bounced from room to room, unable to sit still or hold a thought in his head, except this one: He was out. He was leaving. Despite all the odds stacked against him—his lack of size, his limited talents, his working-class West Side roots, and his inability to do almost anything right in the classroom—he had the chance to do the thing his father had never done. He was going to play real ball, be a professional, and he was determined not to squander the opportunity. To prove he was serious—and fill the horrible void of dead time between that weekend and his plane trip to Geneva—he even considered playing another game in the Dayton league. Then Pete thought better of it and chose a more prudent course. He packed a suitcase, said his goodbyes, officially signed his contract with the Reds the following Thursday, and headed to the airport to catch his plane.

On the flight to New York, the first flight of his life, Pete looked out the window of the twin-engine propeller plane as it took off from the airport in northern Kentucky, excited and a little afraid. He was pretty sure that he was going to die. He couldn't understand how the propellers and wings were keeping him aloft. But as the plane leveled out over the river valley west of Cincinnati, banking to the north and to the east, a calmness washed over him.

Out the window down below, Pete thought he could see his house, his neighborhood, the ball fields of his youth, Bold Face Park, the ferry landing, River Road, Crosley Field, and the bank where his father worked downtown—everything he had ever known.

It was all there and then it was gone, disappearing out of view.

ACT II
SHINE

7

Geneva, New York, wasn't the worst place to play baseball, but it came close.

The city itself was a summertime destination for New Yorkers drawn to its location on the northern shores of Seneca Lake. But it was small, with a population of only seventeen thousand. It was an hour's bus ride from the nearest commercial airport. It was cold and wet well into May. It was in a state that was shedding minor-league teams at an alarming clip. New York had lost almost two-thirds of its franchises since 1949. It was in a division that was hardly doing any better. The New York–Penn League, a loose collection of small-town teams, had been shrinking for years, and the Geneva Redlegs couldn't do much to save the league from financial doom. The Redlegs didn't even have a real stadium.

Their field, Shuron Park, sat on the edge of town next to the eyeglass factory, Shur-on Standard Optical, for which it was named. Around first and third base, there were hazardous slopes and dips, worn in by years of high school games. In left field, there was a bald patch where the grass was slow to grow. Players fought to shower first after games, due to a limited supply of hot water, and they approached the outfield wall with caution. It was a metal structure—some kind of aluminum or tin—and players, leaping at the wall to chase down a home run or a double in the gap, had been known to slice open their wrists on the top lip of the fence.

"We want baseball in Geneva to succeed," Phil Seghi told locals. But the 1959 season had ended with a fire ripping through the concession stand and the team teetering on the edge of bankruptcy. The 1960 campaign was troubled from the start. On the forty-hour caravan trip north from spring training, a car broke down, leaving the team manager and two players stranded somewhere between North Carolina and New York. The marooned Redlegs had to place an emergency call to Geneva and ask the team chairman, Lefty Venuti, a beefy man who owned a local tavern, to wire $30 to cover the cost of the repairs just to get back on the road. It was money that Venuti didn't have. But there was no rush, really. As it turned out, Shuron Park wasn't anywhere near ready to open for the season.

On the cusp of opening day, the Redlegs had no field and, also, no ball caps. The order hadn't come in. To take batting practice, they needed to use a college diamond nearby, swinging hatless in the cold. Meanwhile, jerseys were missing, too, and supporters were just about nonexistent. Advertisements in *The Geneva Times* declared, "It's Fun to Be a Fan!" But ticket sales were sluggish. Paid attendance on opening day that April was 715 people, and Venuti knew that was a generous figure. The actual number was roughly half that.

A spate of rainouts followed—in Geneva and across the New York–Penn League. Within the first three weeks, nearly half of all games were canceled due to foul weather. In the press box, sportswriters joked that the persistent rain might do what even a world war could not—kill the league. Geneva was especially in danger of folding. The Redlegs were nearly $10,000 in debt, taking out loans just to make payroll in May and playing in an empty ballpark on the nights when they did manage to take the field. The average home attendance that spring was 387 people, a dreadful figure that put Venuti in a dark mood. After the Redlegs' seventh home rainout that spring, he announced that the team might have to disband. "The next thirty days," he said, "could see the end of baseball in Geneva." Who wanted to watch the dismal Redlegs in a soaking rain? Or at all?

Players booted routine grounders, chucked the ball around like a circus squad, and lost pop flies in the lights, making ridiculous errors—even for A-ball, Class D. In one game that June, the Corning Sox beat the Redlegs 10–4, and all ten of Corning's runs were unearned. This loss came amid a five-game losing streak in which the Redlegs committed a total of twenty-eight fielding errors, and that embarrassing statistic almost made the team's sixth consecutive loss, the next night, feel like a moral victory. Yes, the Redlegs lost again—this time 16–1—but at least they had committed only one error, and at least they found out that help was on the way. In June, Seghi promised that the big club, the Cincinnati Reds, would float the Geneva Redlegs financially at least until the end of the year. He sent a check for $1,200, and he promised to send some new players, too. A shortstop, some pitching help, a left-hander plucked out of retirement, and an unheralded second baseman from West High in Cincinnati, Pete Rose. "We are doing all we can," Seghi informed Geneva.

But Seghi had run the math, and he knew the reality. Of the 200 players in the entire Reds minor-league farm system, only about 140 of them were real prospects. Only about 25 of those were considered "top-notch." Less than half of these so-called topnotchers would ever sniff the major leagues. If they ever did, Seghi thought, it would take five to seven years, and more than likely not a single one of them was playing in Geneva that June, because that would have been a waste of young talent. Between the errors and the losses, the lack of ball caps and the lack of fans, the Redlegs were doomed to have one of those seasons. A season of darkness. In the lowest rung of baseball, they were flirting with last place.

8

PETE ROSE DIDN'T know the first thing about the Redlegs, their history, their financial troubles, or their record. All he cared about was the future. On the flight to New York in late June 1960, it felt as if the world had cracked wide open for Pete, as if anything were possible, including perhaps the stewardess on the plane. Even years later, Pete would remember what she looked like—her blond hair and her green eyes—and he would recall that he wanted to speak with her. He wanted to tell her who he was: *Pete Rose of the Cincinnati Reds.* Or, at least, Pete Rose of the Geneva Redlegs.

The plane landed in Rochester before he got his chance. No team officials waited outside Shuron Park when Pete's bus pulled up outside. It was a Friday, and the Redlegs were set to play the Elmira Pioneers, the Class D affiliate for the Philadelphia Phillies. The lights in the outfield were buzzing to life. About three hundred people were trickling in through the gates, and Ace Brooks, Geneva's public address announcer, almost mistook Pete Rose for another fan walking into the ballpark that evening. The young player stood out to Brooks only because he was carrying a suitcase, with a few baseball bats strung up on top. And inside the stadium, he announced himself with a certain cocksure authority that Brooks, a much older man, found notable, even strange.

"I'm your new second baseman," Pete said.

Brooks directed Pete to the clubhouse, where again the new recruit explained who he was and why he was there. He specifically said that Phil Seghi had sent him to Geneva and that he was supposed to be playing second base. But Lefty Venuti had other plans for Pete. He parked him in a chair in his office, directed him to fill out some paperwork, and then dispatched him to a hotel for the night. The Redlegs had lots of reinforcements coming in that week, including three new players that day alone. They didn't need Pete in the lineup against Elmira, and they possibly didn't need him at second base at all. Geneva already had its second baseman. His name was Atanasio Pérez—*Tony* Pérez—a player who would mean more to Pete and the Reds than anyone suspected in the moment, perhaps because Pérez couldn't give interviews in the mostly white locker rooms of the New York–Penn League or walk up to Ace Brooks to say anything.

Pérez didn't speak English. He was from a town called Violeta in rural Cuba. The fifth child of a sugarcane farmer raised in a three-room house, Pérez attended school until sixth grade and then went off to harvest sugar himself. There was no other option for a boy like him in Violeta. Except, for Pérez, there would be. On weekends, he played for the sugar company baseball team, Central Violeta. Local men noticed him there—tall and skinny, but with surprising power. Pérez moved to a better team and then finally to Havana, where a Cincinnati Reds scout, and a Cuban native, made Pérez the offer of a lifetime. For $2.50—the price of a visa to the United States—the scout would send Pérez to the Reds' spring training in Florida in February 1960.

People in Violeta were excited for the Pérez kid—*Tahnny,* they called him. In Florida, though, life was hard for the seventeen-year-old. His uniform was two sizes too big for his six-foot-one, 147-pound body. The Reds jersey hung off his wispy frame like a poncho and made him an easy target for ridicule. His Latino teammates nicknamed him Flaco—*Skinny*—and everyone else kept calling him Tony, which wasn't his name. Yet there was no point in objecting. Pérez was pretty sure he was going to get cut and shipped back to Violeta. Phil Seghi didn't like the looks of him and intended to let him go.

But the scout who had discovered Pérez fought Seghi to keep his prospect in Florida, and by the end of spring training Pérez had earned a spot on the roster in Class D Geneva. It was a spot that Pérez intended to keep. He started the season with a triple, batted .421 through the first week, vied for the best batting average in the league into early June, nearly won a wristwatch when he narrowly missed hitting the scoreboard at Shuron Park with an early-season home run, and led the Redlegs in hits. Of everyone on the team, Pérez seemed least likely to lose his job to the new guy from Cincinnati with his suitcase, his buzz cut, and his over-the-top enthusiasm about playing second base.

But in the days before Pete Rose walked into Shuron Park, Tony Pérez fell into a slump that he couldn't shake. His batting average dipped below .300 for the first time all year. Instead of hitting three doubles in a game, he went hitless—0 for 2, then 0 for 5, then 0 for 3. He went 2 for 17 for the week, and it wasn't as if Pérez were making up for his offensive woes with flashy plays in the field. On the night Pete arrived in town, Pérez dropped a routine pop fly behind first base with two outs and two runners on in the top of the ninth and the Redlegs clinging to a 2–0 lead—an error that nearly cost the Redlegs the game. The ball was in Pérez's glove, and then inexplicably it was out, bouncing around on the ground.

It was time to make a change.

—

On Saturday morning, less than twenty-four hours after Pete Rose had shown up in Geneva, the manager placed Pérez on the disabled list and inserted Pete into the lineup against Elmira. He was playing second base and batting third—Tony Pérez's usual spots—and he made an impression immediately.

At the plate that Saturday night, Pete went 2 for 4 with a run batted in. The next day, he remained in the lineup for a doubleheader against the Erie Senators. And though it wasn't his best day—Pete was just 1 for 9, and the Redlegs dropped both games to Erie—Pete returned to the ballpark on Monday to find himself penciled into the lineup yet again. He was back at second base, and that's where he stayed for most of the summer. When Pérez returned from the disabled list in early July, he was moved to third.

It wasn't as if Pete were setting the league on fire; he wasn't. After three weeks in Geneva, he was batting just .234. He managed to strike out almost as many times as he got a hit. He committed errors in the field—a Redleg specialty—and got picked off trying to steal second base. These failures weighed on Pete as he watched other guys on the team—sometimes with better statistics and more experience—get cut to make room for someone else. He knew the reality. When someone faltered in Geneva, that was often the end of the line for him. He might never play baseball again, and it worried Pete's parents enough that at one point that month Big Pete and Laverne got into the family Ford and drove 350 miles to see a Redlegs game on the road in Erie, Pennsylvania.

That night, in the stands, Big Pete watched, swelling with both pride—and fear. His son, he thought, was improving. A few weeks in the minor leagues had already made him a better player, yet Big Pete had underestimated just how good the competition would be. Even here—in A-ball, Class D—players were bigger, stronger, faster than anything he had ever seen on the West Side of Cincinnati. And talking to the Redlegs' manager after the game filled Big Pete with dread. He got the sense that the manager had no idea who his kid was and no idea what he could do. In a conversation that lasted just a few minutes, the manager must have rattled off a thousand things wrong with his son.

For once, Big Pete was stunned into an uneasy silence, a feeling he tried to hide when his boy emerged from the showers, excited to see his parents. Maybe this wouldn't last long. The drive home to Cincinnati that night was surely a quiet one for Big Pete and Laverne. But there was something about Pete that made his teammates believe it might end differently for him. In Geneva, Pete rented a room inside a house on Copeland Avenue that belonged to a local clerk in his early sixties, Sherman McGuire. The house was about half a mile from the ballpark, close enough, players joked, that on a clear night you could hear Pérez and the other Cubans on the team yelling at each other in Spanish. Mr. McGuire's other boarders were also ballplayers, and everyone in the neighborhood got to know Pete Rose that summer. He'd visit with folks on their porches on his way to the stadium, hitch rides into town, talk with strangers. He'd tell them that one day he was going to be famous. They'd read about him in the newspaper, he said.

At least one neighbor cracked that Pete would be lucky just to escape Geneva. But Pete didn't let the naysayers discourage him. On long rides on the team bus that summer, he continued to predict his future greatness, telling teammates in the seat next to him to watch. "Just watch," he said. He was going to make the majors. He had it all planned out, and while some of his teammates thought his confidence was misplaced, they learned not to doubt Pete because, as folks liked to say in Geneva, he was a "pepper pot." He was loud and brash.

Norm Jallow, the Redlegs beat writer for *The Geneva Times*, noticed it from the moment that Pete stepped on the field at Shuron Park in that first game against Elmira in late June. "Rose is an aggressive and eager ballplayer at second," Jallow wrote in his column after Pete's debut, "and gives promise that he could be a good hitter." Pete ran out walks in Geneva as if he'd gotten a hit, because, Pete said, the sooner he got to first base, the faster he'd get to second. He slid headfirst into bases—something that almost no one else did. He cheered for his teammates, he shouted a lot, and he cursed with such ferocity that the words echoed for all to hear in the tiny ballpark—a habit that Jallow tried to summarize for his readers in a euphemistic fashion. "He adds life," Jallow said, "to the infield."

What Pete didn't add were wins. One month after his arrival in Geneva, the Redlegs weren't just flirting with last place anymore; they owned it. The club was twenty-three and a half games out of first. On some nights, fewer than two hundred people came out to watch, and Lefty Venuti was reduced to begging. If the people wanted baseball in Geneva, he said, they needed to start showing up. "Otherwise," Venuti explained, "we'll die by the wayside." Phil Seghi had to see this mess for himself.

In late July, Seghi traveled all the way from Topeka, Kansas—where he had been scouting another Reds minor-league team—to visit Geneva, survey the empty stands, meet with Venuti, and watch the underperforming Redlegs in action. The visit was well timed. On the night Seghi arrived, the Redlegs lost two games by football scores—21–17 and 13–3—and Seghi made sure everyone knew that he was disappointed. He publicly called out a few of the players by name, including a highly touted pitcher who had lost his control and Pete's old high-school teammate Ron Flender, who had been assigned to Geneva, like Pete, and should have been doing better. The West High star—once coveted by Seghi—was batting just .207 for the Redlegs that summer, which made no sense to the Reds' front office.

"It's hard to believe," Seghi said. "We sent ballplayers in here we felt sure would help."

About a month later, Seghi picked up the phone in Cincinnati, called the manager of the Redlegs in Geneva, and asked him to resign, a conversation that didn't go well. The manager refused to cooperate. He didn't like Seghi. So Seghi fired him instead. Then Seghi hung up the phone and announced his decision to the press. The Reds were starting over in Geneva, he said, and the 1960 season soon sputtered to its inevitable conclusion: a last-place finish.

At least Pete Rose had dodged Phil Seghi's wrath. In the Reds' estimation, Pete lacked polish, talent, power, and ability. He struggled to make double plays, had a weak arm, couldn't hit left-handed, probably shouldn't be a switch-hitter, and couldn't run. But the numbers suggested that Pete had improved as a hitter over the course of the summer. In the last six weeks of the season, he nearly batted .290, and with improved contact at the plate Pete managed to bring his season average up to .277, a respectable finish that tied Pete with Pérez for the second-highest batting average on the team.

Perhaps just as important, Pete had endeared himself to the fans in Geneva. They liked that he was fiery. He was known as "a fiery youngster . . . a holler-guy." People appreciated his style more than his stats, and in an ugly season, with so little to cheer, they remembered one play in particular. It came against the Wellsville Braves on the last day of July, with the score tied 4–4 in the bottom of the seventh.

Pete led off the inning with a walk. The next batter then slapped a slow roller to shortstop, which seemed to set up an easy double play for the Braves. But Pete was barreling into second base, intent on taking out the Braves' infielder Lou Haas by any means. He slid hard, almost tackling Haas at the knees—a rolling block, not a slide exactly. Both men went down, their bodies tangled up together, and then they popped up, throwing wild punches at each other.

In the ensuing melee, both benches cleared and Pete Rose found himself transported back in time. He wasn't on the field at Shuron Park in Geneva. He was in Jimmy Schlank's empty swimming pool on the West Side of Cincinnati, pursuing his opponent, fighting his fight, and proving a point. He was going to do whatever it took to win—even now, against Wellsville, in a meaningless game, in front of a tiny crowd, with the season unraveling. He was never going to quit.

In the bleachers at Shuron Park, the crowd roared. The people loved it, and Pete's teammates responded, too. In the aftermath of Pete's fight with Lou Haas, Geneva put up six runs, won the game 10–4, and then beat Wellsville in the nightcap, too—the Redlegs' first sweep of a doubleheader in almost two months and a moment that fans in Geneva would not forget.

At the end of the season, they voted Pete Rose the most popular player on the team, an award that came with a prize—a brand-new suitcase.

Pete was going home in style.

9

The Redlegs players scattered that fall, leaving Geneva for their hometowns and their winter jobs. Tony Pérez and the other Cuban players on the team went back home or to Puerto Rico to play baseball until spring training. Several players reenrolled in college, hoping to resume their studies. One was going to work for his uncle, a fruit wholesaler. Another hoped to get rehired in his old job at a gas and electric company, and Pete Rose thought it would be fun to spend the winter in Cincinnati selling sporting goods—gloves and balls and bats. He told everyone in Geneva that this was what he planned to do.

It was not meant to be. Instead, when he returned home to Braddock Street, he got a blue-collar job like almost everyone else in his neighborhood. He got hired to work in the rail yards just west of Crosley Field. Pete pulled the overnight shift there, midnight to eight o'clock in the morning, loading and unloading freight cars for a company called Railway Express, manual labor. It didn't pay much—$2.83 an hour—and it was difficult work, even dangerous. When trains and loaders moved about the yard, the workmen needed to be careful not to be crushed between cars or flattened by falling equipment—accidents that happened in the yard with alarming regularity. When the temperatures dipped below freezing, Pete was cold. Whatever the elements were, he was out in them, working. And when the boxes were heavy—as they often were—he strained to move them on or off the conveyor belt, into or out of the railcar. Selling sporting goods, it was not.

Still, Pete didn't mind the work. From the rail yard, he had a clear view of the white facade of Crosley Field, the place where he longed to be. In winter, the outfield grass at the stadium was frozen, the concourses quiet, and the grandstand empty. But Pete liked to imagine himself playing there, all the same. He could cast a glance over his shoulder and picture what the future could be. And there was at least one other perk of the job. In the rail yard that winter, Pete got stronger. Day after day, box after box, railcar after railcar, Pete was effectively working out, building his core, strengthening his legs, and pumping his arms. Almost by accident—with no offseason regimen and no trainer whatsoever—he was getting bigger. Then, back in the old house on Braddock Street, he worked out by doing one rudimentary exercise by choice.

Every day, Pete swung a training bat that his uncle Buddy had given him. The bat was much heavier than the one Pete used in games, and for Pete, swinging it became a sort of religion. He'd take fifty swings from the left-hand side and fifty swings from the right. He'd reach down for imaginary balls on the outside corner and climb the ladder for high fastballs down the middle. He'd swing in front of a mirror upstairs in his childhood bedroom almost every night before going to work. He'd swing it, and he'd swing it, and he'd swing it.

Some nights, his younger brother, Dave, would lie in bed watching Pete in the gauzy darkness of the little room. Fifty swings, down and away. Fifty swings, high and tight. Fifty swings, fifty swings, fifty swings. And sometimes, if it was really late and he was tired, Dave, who was still just twelve years old, would remind Pete that he had to get up for school in the morning. Maybe it was time to put the bat away and let him go to bed.

But Pete just shook him off.

"I'm swinging," he told his brother.

The following spring, the Reds assigned Pete to the Tampa Tarpons in the Florida State League. Like the Redlegs in Geneva, the Tarpons were A-ball, Class D. They had played poorly in 1960 and were struggling financially. For a time that spring, the Reds weren't even sure if they should assign players to Tampa, because it wasn't clear that the Tarpons would be around for much longer. In almost every other way, Pete thought that Tampa was better than Geneva. He enjoyed the warmer weather. He liked walking around the docks in the harbor or slurping down black bean soup, cooked up by Cubans in Ybor City. He could go to three different places to gamble in his free time—a horse track, a dog track, and late-night jai alai games—

and he had a manager who was a star or at least a curiosity: Johnny Vander Meer.

Vander Meer was the only pitcher in major-league history to ever throw back-to-back no-hitters. He did it for the Reds in 1938, then never came close to achieving that level of sustained dominance again. He suffered from arm and back pain, finished with a lifetime record of 119-121, and spent the last few years of his career back in the minors, trying to find it again and failing, until there was no point in trying anymore. Vander Meer drifted away into a string of small-time minor-league managerial jobs. He ran a hardware store in the winter in Tampa. He worked for the Dixie Division of the Schlitz Brewing Company and did advertisements for Camel cigarettes. "They're mild," Vander Meer said, "and sure taste great!" He was now forty-six and a full decade removed from playing a meaningful major-league game.

Still, he was Johnny Vander Meer—Double No-Hit Johnny, the Dutch Master, Vandy Vander Meer, one of the all-time greats. People knew his name. Baseball men respected his opinion, and Vander Meer was about to form some strong opinions about the player who reported to Tampa that spring with a brand-new suitcase in tow: Pete Rose.

Ron Flender barely recognized Pete when he first walked in the door at Al Lopez Field in Tampa. Flender figured his old West High teammate had put on twenty pounds over the winter. Pete was now listed at five feet eleven, 170 pounds, and that extra weight appeared to be all muscle. Flender took one look at Pete and thought, "What the heck has he been doing?"

Vander Meer was less enthused. Phil Seghi had thrown together the Tampa roster at the last moment because of the team's financial difficulties. Just days before the season started, Vander Meer had no idea who was going to be on his team, and the players who had been confirmed on his roster were hardly impressive. Only about half of them had ever played professional baseball before and none of them seemed to have any sort of power. At best, Vander Meer figured, it was an adequate team with serviceable players, many of whom were unknown. In preseason interviews with local sportswriters, Vander Meer didn't mention Flender at all, and what he said about Pete Rose didn't sound encouraging. According to Vander Meer, Pete was just another "infield candidate" who was obscure enough that the press bungled his name: *Peter* Rose, one reporter called him.

But Vander Meer understood how to work with adequate players. In many ways, he had been one himself, and he liked a few things about this Tarpon squad. "Sure, I could use a couple of power hitters," Vander Meer said before opening day. But he never did measure a player's worth based on how many home runs he could hit, and Vander Meer knew such a thing was especially meaningless at Al Lopez Field, a cavernous ballpark bigger than some major-league stadiums. Vander Meer needed guys who could hit the gaps. Find the holes in the defense, and then run, stretching singles into doubles and doubles into triples.

"We will be hustling," Vander Meer said, "all the time out there."

Pete wasn't sure how to feel about Vander Meer's comments or the fact that some people in the press didn't even know his name. And briefly that March, before the season started, he felt lonely, lost. Even with the extra muscle he had gained in the rail yard over the winter, he was still smaller than most of his teammates. What if he batted .277 again? "Keep hustling," his father told him, trying to lift his son's spirits, during a visit to Tampa that spring. It was what Vander Meer wanted; it was also the only thing Pete could control.

He'd have to make up for his lack of size by working harder, by running harder, and on opening night for the Tarpons, he did not disappoint. He knocked in the first run of the season with a triple. Then, with the game tied and the bases loaded in the sixth, Pete slashed yet another triple into the outfield and broke the game wide open. For the night, he finished 3 for 5 with four RBIs. The Tarpons won easily, and for the first time in months Pete felt great.

It wasn't just his stat line for the night that pleased him. With each plate appearance, he was gathering data about what pitchers threw and when. He was logging their tendencies away, and he was honing his eyes to identify their pitches immediately. He wanted to know by the way the ball was spinning if it was a screwball or a knuckler, a slider or a curve. And since he was crouched over the strike zone—his body coiled like a spring—he snapped to the ball, making it hard for any pitcher to throw something by him. Especially here, in A-ball, Class D.

In the first two weeks in Tampa, Pete hit eleven triples. That was three triples shy of what that year's major-league leader would collect over the course of the *entire season.* He led the team in RBIs, from the leadoff position. He nearly hit .500, and he impressed fans in Tampa the same way he had in Geneva: by sliding headfirst and sprinting down to first base on a walk, behavior that most people had never witnessed before. The *Tampa Times* dubbed Pete "the Toast of the Tarpons" before the spring was over. Sportswriters learned his name, and then they changed it to fit. The press started calling him "Scooter Rose," and the tone inside the Tarpons' front office changed as well. He was no longer considered an "infield candidate." Pete was labeled the "finest prospect to come out of Tampa—perhaps ever."

The label was maybe premature. This was a player who had batted .277 the previous summer and was now only sixty-three at bats into a new season. He couldn't continue at this pace. And yet he did. The 1961 version of Pete Rose offered the clearest glimpse of his future self. For the year, Pete batted .331, led the team in runs scored, hit thirty triples—a new Florida State League record, two triples shy of the all-time minor-league record, and his own hustle probably ruined his chance at that record. He legged two would-be triples into inside-the-park home runs, sliding into home plate, dripping in sweat and covered with dirt.

There was no stopping the Tarpons. They made it all the way to the league championship series against the Sarasota Sun Sox that September, won the Florida State pennant, and put fans in the seats at Al Lopez Field for the first time in years. Some nights, during the title run, the Tarpons had crowds exceeding 1,500 people. The team owner broke even that year, and he decided to award each player with a special gift for their hard work. At the end of the season, he handed out championship-engraved Zippo lighters.

Pete thought the gift was both ironic and stupid. He didn't drink alcohol, he didn't smoke cigarettes, and he couldn't understand why the owner of a baseball team, or Johnny Vander Meer for that matter, would encourage his players to light up. Pete was all about baseball in a way that could make him irritating, even to other ballplayers. They thought him a "hot dog" for running down to first on walks and sliding headfirst into bases, an approach that one teammate called a joke. They thought he was showing off, or showing them up, or both. They teased him because he couldn't sit still and was always swinging a bat, real or imaginary. Teammates assigned to board with Pete on the road would wake up in the morning to find him swinging in his underwear in the soft light of a little motel room. They wanted to sleep and he wanted to work—obsessive-compulsive about his performance or just obsessed. And players disliked him for one other reason: during his year in Tampa, Pete was always telling them how good he was—as though they hadn't seen that morning's box score or didn't know his batting average. They didn't understand why Pete couldn't just play, hit his triples, and shut up.

But Johnny Vander Meer loved it. In the offseason that fall, Vander Meer couldn't say enough about his second baseman. He called Pete a "can't-miss prospect." He praised his desire, his ability, and his habits. "Excellent habits," Vander Meer said. He liked that Pete was the first one on the field and the last one to leave the batting cage, that he was always on time, that he was ready to play, and that he was versatile. In Vander Meer's assessment, Pete could play second, third, shortstop, and outfield. "And he runs like a scalded dog." In the face of any pitcher or any moment, he wouldn't back down.

"He's got more stomach," Vander Meer said, "than a parachute jumper."

10

THE BIG CLUB in Cincinnati was starting to take an interest. That fall and winter, Pete wasn't going home to Braddock Street to work in the rail yard. The Reds assigned him to stay in Tampa and play in the Instructional League where the best young players could get more experience, more at bats—and more looks from scouts.

Pete soon settled into a comfortable routine befitting a twenty-year-old player with a small measure of local fame. He played baseball during the day; frequented a tavern at night a few miles from Al Lopez Field with a history of murder, narcotics, and underaged drinking; sipped soda or juice at the bar while his teammates played pool and drank beer; picked up a bartender, who, Pete boasted later, was an acrobat in the circus and could move her body in "unbelievable" ways; and then woke up the next day to do it all over again. Meanwhile, on the field, Pete played good baseball that winter. Scouts noticed and pointed him out to reporters. The press started writing stories about him, and rumors swirled that the Reds could cash in the lottery ticket that had become Pete Rose. They could trade their minor-league infielder for a chunk of money and get as much as $150,000 for him—a nice return on Phil Seghi's $7,000 investment.

Instead, in 1962, the club assigned Pete to the Macon Peaches in the Class A Sally League in Macon, Georgia—a few steps above both Geneva and Tampa, but hardly a glamorous post. Macon was a racially segregated paper mill town, and the Peaches' ballpark, named after a white banker who had risen to prominence in the city during Reconstruction, was located close enough to the mill that teams were often forced to play in a cloud of odors and a haze of exhaust. Everyone complained about the smell, and outfielders dreaded the haze. Some nights, it was thick enough that they could lose fly balls in the lights. Pete checked in at the ballpark that spring, secured a room at the local YMCA—his lodging for the summer—and then began getting ready for the season with a player he'd first met over the winter in the Instructional League: his toughest competition for ever making it to the big leagues, Tommy Helms.

The son of a cotton mill worker from rural North Carolina, Helms had yellow hair, a narrow face, ears as big as soup ladles, and a problem with management. He didn't want to be a Macon Peach and play near the paper mill. In the spring of 1962, Helms thought he was good enough to be with the Reds' Triple-A affiliate in San Diego, and he knew he was a better infielder than Pete Rose—an opinion that the Peaches' manager, Dave Bristol, happened to share. Bristol planned to play Helms at shortstop that season and Pete at second—assuming Pete even made the team. "I don't know about that Rose kid," Bristol said just before the season started. Sometimes, in the dugout, Bristol would just sit there staring at Pete and spit his tobacco juice.

But Bristol had more in common with Pete than he wanted to reveal. Like Pete, he approached each game as if it were a barroom brawl. Even a handshake was an opportunity for competition. He'd squeeze another man's hand as if he were trying to induce pain, and he had a plan for Pete Rose. Not long after Pete arrived in Macon—faster and stronger, with another fifteen pounds of muscle on his body after his winter in the Instructional League—Bristol got out a stopwatch and clocked him. He timed Pete running from home plate to first base in 3.8 seconds after a swing, and 3.6 seconds after a bunt. That was good enough for Bristol and good enough for Pete to bat leadoff—right in front of Tommy Helms.

The lineup clicked almost immediately. In one early season game, Macon thumped the Greenville Dodgers, 32–5, as both Pete and Helms fed off each other. Pete collected six hits that night, Helms got four, and it was a sign of what was to come. For the year, Helms batted .340, ten points higher than Pete. Yet Pete had more triples, more home runs, and more RBIs, and he provided more excitement for the locals. Fans enjoyed Pete's headfirst slides. They appreciated the way he sprinted to first base on a walk, like the umpire might change his mind, and by midsummer local sportswriters were penning entire columns about Pete, not Tommy Helms.

That alone could have been enough to pit a couple of young players against each other. In a remote baseball outpost like Macon, everyone wanted to be noticed. But Helms couldn't help himself. He liked Pete—his swagger, his confidence, the way he lived to play baseball, and how nothing seemed to stop him or even slow him down. Not the naysayers. Not his size. Not the next day's pitcher. Not even little Macon. In the one season they spent there, Pete joked that they were "Makin' Out."

The Peaches traveled in a convoy of Corvair Greenbrier Sportswagons, eight guys to a vehicle, and once to break the monotony of a long drive to Asheville or Savannah, Pete sneaked out the back window while the Sportswagon was moving and climbed up onto the roof. He broke curfew at the YMCA to stay out late or date pretty women—"the prettiest girls in town," he bragged. He persuaded a teammate to flirt with a local switchboard operator with bad teeth, just so he and the other players could make long-distance phone calls for free, and in one of those phone calls Pete arranged to meet his mother and brother in Knoxville to pick up the first big purchase of his professional baseball career: a new Corvette, paid for with the earnings he'd been saving for two years. The color was mint green, and his drive back to Macon surprised almost no one who had been paying attention that summer.

Somewhere in rural Georgia, with Helms in the passenger seat of his new Corvette and Rose shifting into gear, they got pulled over for speeding.

The officer that day shook down Rose and Helms for all the cash they had in their wallets, but it didn't matter. Neither man figured he was returning to Macon in 1963—a guess that proved true, though not in the way they imagined at the time.

The following spring, Helms held out for more money. He had spent four years in the minors at that point, had logged five hundred more at bats than Pete Rose, and believed he was worth more than the Reds were paying him. He went home to North Carolina and stayed there working at a grocery store for most of March to prove a point, while Pete reported to spring training in Tampa to compete for a job with the top second basemen in the Reds organization: Bobby Klaus, who had played at Triple-A San Diego the previous summer, and the Reds' starter in 1962, Don Blasingame.

"The Blazer," as the guys in the clubhouse called Don, was a ten-year veteran, with a pregnant wife at home in Cincinnati and allies in every stadium. When he was traded away from the St. Louis Cardinals a few years earlier, his teammates threw him a going-away banquet and named him the most valuable player of the "Friendship League." At the very least, in Cincinnati, the Blazer was a known commodity. The Reds knew what they were going to get out of him—a reliable glove and okay bat. But by 1963, they also knew what they *weren't* going to get. The Blazer was almost thirty-one years old. He couldn't run anymore, and, apparently, he couldn't hit, either. In two of the past three seasons, Blasingame hadn't even managed to bat .240, and with that sort of average it didn't matter how many friends he had in the National League. The Blazer was in trouble with the Reds' manager, Fred Hutchinson.

Beat writers loved Hutchinson because he made companions of them on the road. He would let them into his hotel room at night and talk baseball until the wee hours in an ever-thickening cloud of cigarette smoke. Then he'd sneak in a round of golf just after dawn the next day and come traipsing into the hotel lobby with his clubs slung over his shoulder and a fresh cigarette in his mouth, when everyone else was just getting up, ready to head to the stadium and do it all over again. What wasn't there to love about Hutch?

The players found it harder. They called him "Old Stoneface," because they never knew how he felt, except when he was yelling, which he seemed to do a lot. The joke among the writers was that Hutch didn't throw tantrums, "he threw rooms." When the Reds lost, he was known to toss stools across the clubhouse, turn over tables, dump the postgame meal on the floor, tear off his jerseys, rip them to shreds, or worse. At least once, he broke every light in the tunnel outside the dugout. He simply couldn't tolerate mediocrity, and that was bad news for the Blazer.

Hutch wasn't going to stand by Blasingame if the veteran second baseman couldn't turn things around. But Hutch also wasn't inclined to follow the established line of succession at the position. He didn't seem likely to give the job to Tommy Helms, who wasn't in camp, or Bobby Klaus, who was. Quietly, Hutch was leaning toward a different player, a minor leaguer who was just twenty-one years old. He was thinking about Pete Rose.

"If I had any guts," Hutch grumbled that winter, "I'd put Rose on second base and forget about him."

11

In the first game at spring training that March—with all the returning major leaguers in camp and all the top prospects joining them there—Hutch hesitated to find his courage. He started the Blazer at second, as usual. Then, when he had a chance to make a substitution, he brought in Klaus. The two infielders went 0 for 5 in the game. Cincinnati lost to the Chicago White Sox 1–0, and the next day Hutch's squad struggled against the Sox again. Heading into the ninth inning, it was 0–0 and beginning to look as if the Reds might never score. In the first seventeen innings of spring training, they had yet to cross home plate once.

On the bench, Pete was pretty sure he wasn't getting in the game. At first, he hadn't even been there. He had been on a nearby diamond taking batting practice with a lesser squad. Klaus had gotten the start at second base that day, and Klaus seemed to be doing well. He had two hits, all of which made it clear to Pete that this wasn't going to be his day. He got up to leave the bench and go for a run. One of the assistant coaches stopped him and told him to stick around—just in case—and when left fielder Wally Post doubled for the Reds in the bottom of the ninth, Hutch had his opportunity to put Pete in the game.

Post had been in the majors for a decade and was going to be an opening day starter, but he wasn't as fast as he could have been, and he had struggled in recent seasons with his weight. Pete went in as a pinch runner and then stayed in the game as it crept into extra innings, still tied. In the bottom of the eleventh, Pete got his first chance at the plate and, for once, he was nervous. He had been auditioning for years to play with the Reds, but never quite like this: on a field with big leaguers and Hutch watching. He swung at the first pitch, just so he wouldn't have to think about it, and connected. The hit—a long drive into the gap in left-center—was good for a double.

Then he hit another one in the fourteenth, and this time he scored, sliding into home—safe. The Reds had beaten the White Sox 1–0.

"How 'bout that?" Pete said, celebrating after the game.

In the next morning's papers, the local beat writers revived his old nickname from his days with the Tarpons. They started calling him "Scooter Rose" again. Hutch put him in the starting lineup that afternoon, and Pete kept hitting. Amid a windstorm against the St. Louis Cardinals in St. Petersburg that felt almost hazardous at times, he walked, singled, and would have had two other hits, had he not been robbed by strong defensive plays. In the press box, Earl Lawson sat up over his typewriter and started to pay closer attention.

Lawson was forty years old and had spent more than half his life working for Cincinnati newspapers. He started as a copyboy at the *Times-Star* when he was seventeen, moved up to city desk reporter, kept his job when the *Times-Star* merged with *The Cincinnati Post* in the 1950s, and had spent the last dozen years covering the Reds for both the *Post* and *The Sporting News*—"The Baseball Paper of the World." His body carried the mileage of press-box living. He was soft in places where he should have been hard, gray around his temples, and at least twenty pounds overweight, depending on the length of the most recent road trip.

But Lawson was also more cosmopolitan than many baseball writers. He had fought in the Pacific during World War II, survived Leyte and Okinawa, been cited for his courage there, and revolutionized baseball writing back home. Lawson didn't want to regurgitate box scores for readers. He wanted to tell stories, and to get them, he became one of the first reporters to venture into the clubhouse before and after games. He hung out there, gathering scenes, and when he wrote, he tried to introduce his readers to the players—a sanitized version of the players, at least. Because he was always around, Lawson became a member of the Cincinnati Reds family. The players gave him a nickname; they called him Scoops. And since he was family, since they considered him one of them, sometimes they fought with him, too. On two occasions in prior years, players assaulted Scoops, angry over what he had written about them.

The latest assault, from a year before in 1962, had been over the word "hustle." Scoops didn't think some players were *hustling* enough, and outfielder Vada Pinson took offense at the criticism, punching Scoops in the face one afternoon in Pittsburgh—a choice that led to a scuffle, a scandal, and briefly a court case. "I'm sick and tired," Scoops said, "of being punched by ballplayers." But nothing changed. Scoops was back the next day and Pinson was, too. There was no investigation. No suspension. The *Post* didn't even remove Scoops from his beat during his court battle with Pinson. He finished the 1962 season with the team. He was back in 1963, and on the ground at spring training that year Scoops began preaching the gospel of Pete Rose as soon as he saw the gap-toothed twenty-one-year-old player running around the field with his crew-cut hair. "Hustle is young Pete's middle name," Scoops wrote in mid-March, in one of the first stories to mention "hustle" in connection to the player. Yes, he wrote again and again in his pieces, "the kid is a real hustler."

Scoops knew Hutch had to agree, and after Pete's first two games against the White Sox and the Cardinals, the Reds' beat writer pressed Hutch to announce that he was considering Pete for the big club. Scoops knew what Hutch liked, and Pete had it all. He was brash and young, Scoops said, with ready wit and ability. Why not just say it? They both knew that Pete was working harder at spring training than anyone else. Finally, Hutch relented. Fine, he said. He was officially considering Pete Rose for a roster spot.

"I'm going to take a real good look at him," Hutch told Scoops.

Then the New York Yankees came to town.

The Yankees were not only the best team in baseball at the time; they were the most noble and prestigious franchise in American sports. They had reached the World Series in thirteen of the previous sixteen seasons. They had won it a staggering ten times during that span. They were the two-time, back-to-back defending world champions coming into the season in 1963, and they had some of the biggest names in baseball on their roster: catcher Yogi Berra, the team's beloved elder statesman, entering the last season of his eighteen-year career; slugger Roger Maris, who was two seasons removed from breaking Babe Ruth's single-year home-run record; pitcher Whitey Ford, a Cy Young Award winner and World Series hero in the prime of his career; and one of the most feared power hitters in baseball history, with 404 home runs to his name, Mickey Mantle.

With this cast of legends, fans flocked to see the Yankees wherever they went, and spring training was no different. For the Reds' exhibition game against them at Al Lopez Field on the third Sunday of March 1963, fans began buying tickets at nine o'clock in the morning, four and a half hours before the 1:30 game. Eight thousand people soon filled the stands—a record turnout that included Pete's father, who wouldn't miss the chance to see his son play against a legendary baseball team. While Big Pete settled into a seat behind home plate, others scaled light posts in the outfield and perched themselves there to get a better view. Television stations in Ohio and New York broadcast the game live. The scoreboard lit up. The organist began to play, and Pete Rose bounced out of the home dugout to take his spot in the field. He was starting at second base against the mighty Yankees.

Pete wasted no time in making his presence known. In his first at bat in the bottom of the first, he punched a single into center field, took second and third on balks, and then scored the first run of the game, hustling home moments later on a liner to left. It was classic Scooter Rose. He was manufacturing runs out of the infield dust, and the Reds were up 1–0, just not for long. In the fourth, Mickey Mantle hit a towering home run that flew out of the park like one of the rockets NASA was launching that summer at Cape Canaveral. The Reds' pitcher had Mantle down in the count, no balls and two strikes, and then Mantle made him pay, trotting around the bases while the ball took its time falling back to earth.

Fans were thrilled; this was what they had come to see: the Yankees putting on a show. But New York subbed Mantle out after the big hit. The $100,000 slugger had been nursing a groin injury that spring. Management didn't want him to push it in the preseason, and the Reds jumped all over the Yankees the rest of the way, compiling twelve hits to win 6–3. The Reds' first baseman Gordy Coleman and outfielder Wally Post both hit home runs to put Cincinnati out in front for good, but Pete stood out, too. He bunted to start a two-run rally in the fifth inning. He sprinted down to first base, beating the throw. He then barreled into second base to break up a double play and finally, in the ninth, he turned a double play of his own to close out the Yankees and end the game.

It would be two more weeks before Hutch made his final decision on whether to roster Pete that spring, but in some ways he made the call that day in the dugout watching Pete play against the Yankees. The Blazer was about to lose his job. Klaus was about to return to Triple-A San Diego, and Tommy Helms would be joining him there, if he ever left the grocery store in North Carolina, signed his contract, and reported to camp. There was simply no way Hutch would cut Pete—a reality that even some of the Reds' veteran players were beginning to recognize. In the clubhouse after the Yankees game, the Reds' outfielder Frank Robinson, a future Hall of Famer and the 1961 National League MVP, put it this way. "Rose," Robinson said, "is the type of player who can force you to keep him around—even though you might not think he's ready."

But no one would ever call Pete Scooter again. That changed during the Yankees game, too. In the fifth inning, when Pete bunted and beat the throw to first, Mantle found the play both audacious and ridiculous, almost entertaining. Bunting for a hit? In spring training? Really? Mantle would have sooner worn a sundress to the plate than play the game like that, and with his teammate Whitey Ford he coined a new nickname for Pete in the visitors' dugout that day. Pete was Henry Hustle, they said. No, the Charlie Hustler. He was, everyone finally agreed, Charlie Hustle.

Mantle and Ford—baseball's golden boys, imbued with talent from birth, and seemingly touched by the hand of God—intended the name to be an insult. They were laughing at Pete. They thought he was working too hard. But Pete refused to see it that way. He knew that hustling was the secret to his success, the key to every room he would ever enter. He happily wore the name. "The Mick gave it to me," Pete bragged that summer. "He and Ford," he crowed. "Mantle said to me, 'Hey, Charlie Hustle.'"

Pete told the press it was a compliment.

12

OPENING DAY WAS like a holiday in Cincinnati. Shops closed after lunch. Executives cut out of the office early to meet their wives and children at the midafternoon game. A local fixture, "Peanut Jim" Shelton, greeted the crowd outside the stadium selling roasted nuts from a two-wheeled cart, and for three decades a massive parade snaked past Peanut Jim, down the streets, through throngs of people on either side, and up to the gates of Crosley Field. On opening day 1963, this parade included a color guard, brass bands, cheer squads, Boy Scout troops, and the governor of Ohio himself. He was going to throw out the first pitch at the game in front of a sold-out stadium. Attendance: standing room only.

This was a celebration unlike any other in the country, because Cincinnati had a history unlike any other. It was a baseball town through and through. Cincinnati was home to the first professional baseball franchise. The Red Stockings, formed in 1869, predated the Yankees, the Red Sox, the Dodgers, the Giants, and every other team, and they were a shining example of pure baseball dominance from the start. The Red Stockings went 57-0 in their first season, beating everyone they faced in front of large crowds, and usually by enormous scores. They defeated the New Orleans Southerners 35–3; the St. Louis Unions 70–9; the Milwaukee Cream City Club 85–7; and the Cincinnati Buckeyes 103–8. It would be more than a year, in fact, before the Stockings lost a game—to the Brooklyn Atlantics in extra innings.

The team president at the time didn't linger on the loss. He said he'd rather run the Red Stockings in Cincinnati than be President Ulysses S. Grant in Washington, and though this team soon disbanded and one of the star players brought the Red Stockings name to Boston, city leaders in southwest Ohio established a new ball club under the same flag. In time, this version of the Red Stockings became known as simply the Reds, and over the decades, through a sea of changes, the franchise made Cincinnatians proud. The Reds were the first team to play at night, the first to travel by air, and the champion of two World Series—though the team's first title, in 1919, over the Chicago White Sox felt cheap, maybe even stolen. Mobsters and gamblers had gotten to the heavily favored White Sox that fall and persuaded a handful of players to throw the World Series, to let the Reds win, to lose on purpose—for money.

Pete left Tampa on an overnight train on the first Wednesday of April. He wasn't officially rostered yet, but he hadn't been cut, either. With just six days to go before opening day, he was heading north with the Reds and the White Sox for a barnstorming tour through Macon, Lynchburg, Charleston, and Indianapolis en route to Cincinnati.

It was after nine o'clock when the train finally inched out of the station in Tampa, and no one seemed likely to get much sleep before the afternoon game the next day in Macon. The train cars were bursting with baseball players, laughter, card games, revelry, and the fresh promise of a new season. Everyone on board could convince themselves that this was going to be their year as the train rolled north in the night, and no one was doing more convincing than Pete.

"I deserve this chance," he told a reporter after the train arrived in Macon in the morning.

Hutch still wasn't sure. He was worried that Pete might struggle against big-league pitching, and he was concerned that he'd be putting too much pressure on him by bringing him up so fast. Players didn't jump from the Class A Sally League to the majors. Pete probably needed to go to San Diego with Klaus and Helms and avoid the circus that would come with a roster spot in Cincinnati, a circus that was already starting. Before the train even arrived in Macon, reporters were knocking on the door at 4404 Braddock Street, asking questions of Big Pete and Laverne, and Hutch knew this was only the beginning. If he added Pete to the roster, it would be a public relations bonanza. A West High boy was coming home.

But Hutch couldn't shake his instincts. That Saturday night, after the barnstorming stops in Macon and Lynchburg and the game in Charleston, West Virginia, Hutch gave Pete the news he had been waiting to hear his whole life: Pete was on the team. He was about to celebrate his twenty-second birthday, and he was going to play for the Cincinnati Reds. There was just one catch. After arriving back home in Cincinnati on Sunday, Hutch told Pete to check in at the Netherland Hilton Hotel downtown. He was not to spend the night with his mother and father, Big Pete and Laverne, jumping with excitement on Braddock Street.

"Go home and see your folks, kid," Hutch told him. "Then come back to the hotel."

He needed him to get some rest and stay focused.

"You're starting against Pittsburgh tomorrow."

13

FOR WEEKS, DON Blasingame had seen it coming, and he didn't flinch when he got the news. Even though his wife was eight months pregnant, and Hutch's decision would have significant financial ramifications for his family, the Blazer refused to blame Pete for his demotion to the backup second baseman. Instead, in Indianapolis, the day before the opener, he wished the rookie good luck and offered him a bit of advice. "You've got a chance to make a lot of money in this game," the Blazer told Pete. "Don't do anything foolish."

Other players on the team were less gracious. They had quietly disliked Pete for the hotdogging, for sprinting to first base on walks, for his oversized ego, which didn't seem to fit under his ball cap, and for the whole aggressive Charlie Hustle vibe to which Mickey Mantle had given a name. Now they disliked him because he had jumped the line. He hadn't waited his turn. He had taken the Blazer's job. In the clubhouse that April, Pete would find himself relegated to hanging out with the team's two outspoken Black stars, Frank Robinson, the 1961 league MVP, and Vada Pinson, the outfielder who had punched Scoops Lawson in the face the previous summer.

In the years to come, Pete would reframe this moment to make it seem like this was no big deal, and in some ways, that was probably true. Ever since he reported to Geneva in June 1960 and joined Tony Pérez in the locker room there, Pete had been living and playing next to Black and Latino players. A baseball locker room—though still mostly white, and by no means progressive—was more integrated than most of America, and as a result, a young white ballplayer like Pete was exposed to different cultures in a way an average person was not.

Still, it had to be jarring for him to be exiled to an island with Robinson and Pinson. In the 1960s and even into the 1970s, players often self-segregated along racial lines, and Pete seemed like a prime candidate to fall in with the white crowd, with his Joe Friday crew cut, his white working-class roots on Braddock Street, and his education at West High, where, in the 1950s, school plays were sometimes performed in blackface. He didn't see the world like Robinson and Pinson. He didn't talk like them, he didn't command a vocabulary that grasped the complex racial politics of the moment, and he couldn't appreciate the depths of the slights that Robinson and Pinson faced, even after hanging out with them on the road, even after they became friends.

That summer, a prominent and conservative white sports columnist for the New York *Daily News* wrote that Robinson and Pinson had formed a "Negro clique" in Cincinnati—an angry one—that was dividing the Reds' clubhouse. "The Negro players think they are being picked on," the columnist wrote, "and the white players think the Negro players are getting away with murder, and that is the climate of our time."

Robinson was furious about the comment—so furious that he would dedicate an entire chapter to the topic in his memoir twelve years later. He couldn't understand why the columnist had singled him and Pinson out or why he wrote about their alleged clique at all, when there were cliques in every clubhouse for all kinds of reasons: racial, religious, who drank and who didn't. "The clique thing," Robinson said, "was just nonsense." But if reporters didn't criticize him for that, he figured, they would have attacked him for something else. "I suppose if Vada and I weren't so close," he said, "they might have started calling me a 'loner,' and blaming *that* on the decline of the ball club. Either way, I probably would have gotten it." Pete, on the other hand, could just play baseball, talk about baseball, focus on baseball.

Yet the kindness that Robinson and Pinson showed him that season did change Pete in subtle ways. In the years to come, young Black players spoke warmly about how Pete welcomed them into the clubhouse in Cincinnati. He didn't really understand them, and his comments, at times, made that clear. He was known to make inappropriate and stereotypical "Black" jokes where watermelons and short ribs figured in the punchline. Still, they liked him—because Pete was different than many other white players. He knew what it was like to feel unwanted, too.

On the morning of opening day 1963, Pete would awake inside the Netherland Hilton cognizant of a few things: his teammates hated him, he didn't have many friends, and this was his chance—maybe his best and only chance to make it in the big leagues.

The day dawned cool and cloudy on Braddock Street, with a dark gray sky stretching over Anderson Ferry and a weather forecast for the afternoon that left the Roses with little to cheer. There was a threat of rain.

But Big Pete and Laverne didn't linger on the thought for long. For them, it was like Christmas morning, VE Day, and the Fourth of July wrapped into one. They were pulling Pete's little brother, Dave, now fourteen, out of school for the game, and they were getting dressed in their Sunday best before they headed down River Road to Crosley Field in the family car.

Laverne made sure her eyebrows were plucked, lined, and perfect. She wore a light-colored frock, buttoned to the neck, as if she had been invited to the Queen City Club for lunch with the fashionable wives of the P&G executives. Dave pulled a sport coat over a white collared shirt, and Big Pete donned a dark suit for the occasion, complete with a pocket square and a skinny tie. At the time, Dave was just excited to be skipping school, riding downtown with his parents, and walking into the stadium with a near-sellout crowd of twenty-nine thousand other fans, including the mayor of Cincinnati and the governor of Ohio. But later Dave would weep for the memory of this moment: his mother so proud; his father so happy; and his big brother, Pete, about to change everything for all of them. In a family photo that day, staged by the Reds to mark the occasion just before the first pitch, Big Pete almost smiled.

Up until that moment, Little Pete hadn't felt a single twinge of anxiety. He wasn't nervous when he reported to the park. He wasn't worried when he sat in front of his new locker in the Reds' cramped clubhouse in the bowels of the stadium, and he didn't feel anything approaching fear when he tried on his new uniform for the first time, white with red pinstripes and stitched with his new number—fourteen—which had been randomly assigned.

Seeing his family changed that. Suddenly, it hit him.

"I'm starting," Pete thought. "I'm starting for the Reds on opening day."

It was the one thing he had wanted in life. "My whole fucking life." And now it was upon him. It was happening.

"I'm starting."

At 2:27, the lights clicked on at Crosley Field to cut through a gray mist, and then Pete Rose bounded out of the Reds' dugout with the rest of Cincinnati's starters to take his position at second base. The crowd roared. Fans had high expectations for the team—and for Pete. *The Cincinnati Enquirer* called it "Pete Rose Day" in the city and predicted he would win the Rookie of the Year award. The results that day were less inspiring.

Pete walked to start the game, hustled down to first to the delight of local fans, scored moments later when Robinson hit a home run, helped turn three double plays in the game, and the Reds beat the Pirates that afternoon, 5–2. But Pete also booted a ball for an error, overthrew the pitcher at one point getting the ball into the infield, went hitless, and struck out looking in the seventh inning—on a pitch right down the middle that Pete couldn't stop replaying in his mind after the game was over.

"I saw the pitch the whole way," he said, trying to make sense of it. He couldn't understand why he had just stood there when what he wanted to do was swing, and soon Pete would have a lot of time to think about his mistakes. After just one week in the big leagues, he was 2 for 23 at the plate, batting .130, and bound for the bench. Hutch replaced him with the Blazer just before a nine-game road trip, and reporters speculated that the team would dump Pete in San Diego when the Reds hit the West Coast the following week. Pete would fly out with the team, they said, and not come back. He'd probably get assigned to Cincinnati's Triple-A club there and reunite with Tommy Helms.

But as the starting second baseman, the Blazer did no better than Pete. The Reds lost five of their first seven on the road. The Dodgers outscored them 14–1 in two games in Los Angeles. Cincinnati fell to second-to-last place in the National League, and Hutch didn't feel like leaving Pete in San Diego so much as he felt like throwing things in the clubhouse—stools, a table, something. After the cellar-dwelling Colt .45s held the Reds to one hit the next night in Houston, Hutch could barely contain his anger in front of the press. His team was perfect, he declared. Perfect for making mediocre pitchers look like Hall of Famers. "Trot 'em on out," Hutch said, seething with sarcasm, "and we'll get 'em started. We'll make 'em look good." Then, almost impulsively, the ornery manager announced a change for the next night's lineup.

"Rose will replace Blasingame at second base," he said.

This time, Pete was intent not to squander the opportunity. On the bench, he hadn't sulked, but studied, often sitting right next to Hutch. He wanted to know what pitchers were throwing—and when. He absorbed everything that Hutch said, and he paid careful attention to how Frank Robinson ran the bases—because Hutch instructed him to do so. Now, back in the lineup, Pete hoped to show everyone he could run like Robinson, too. He just needed to get on base more, and this time he did.

Crouched over the plate with his eyes on the ball and his bat moving through the top of the zone, Pete batted .338 over the next three weeks. Then .403 over a fifteen-game stretch in June. Anytime he saw a pitcher twice, he was better than he had been the time before. He remembered what they threw and how they threw it. He was waiting for it now, and he didn't try to kill it when he saw the pitch coming. He'd bunt for a single. Or if the infield was expecting a bunt, he'd hit it just over their heads. He'd find the soft grass in front of the outfielders or he'd walk, sprinting down to first base while the pitcher shook his head, quietly cursing Pete Rose.

"The kid," Hutch said, "looks like money in the bank."

He was good enough, anyway, that at the end of June the Reds sold Don Blasingame to the Washington Senators for a small, undisclosed amount of money. The Blazer and his .161 batting average were gone. He'd be out of the majors in three years and banished to the outer reaches of the baseball universe, managing the Nankai Hawks in Japan.

Meanwhile, Pete was just getting started. He wanted to be named Rookie of the Year, like *The Cincinnati Enquirer* had predicted. He wanted a new car, something better than his mint-green Corvette. And after considering a Jaguar E-Type coupe—a sporty model that had been showcased in James Bond movies—Pete settled on a vehicle that seemed to fit him a bit better: a chocolate-brown Pontiac Grand Prix convertible. It was a car he could afford on his league-minimum, $7,500 salary, and it looked good on the streets of the city, rolling up to Crosley Field or to River Downs, the racetrack on the East Side of town that he had frequented as a boy with his father and started to frequent again now.

Sometimes that summer, on off days or before games, Pete would go and bet on the horses. It was just something to do before baseball, though it wasn't always about the horses. One day that July, while peering through his binoculars, he spotted something else that interested him. It was a young woman with auburn hair, hazel eyes, and sculpted cheekbones. She was standing near the finish line in high heels and a short powder-blue sundress that was cinched around the waist, and Pete knew what had to happen next.

He needed to meet her.

14

KAROLYN ANN ENGELHARDT didn't know the first thing about baseball, the Reds, horse racing, or silence. She was a talker, up close and personal, and loud. People heard Karolyn before they saw her, but Karolyn made sure they saw her, too. She smoked Salem cigarettes because she thought they made her look sexy. She wore four-inch heels to appear taller. She refused to skimp on makeup, lip gloss, or eye shadow. Of the latter, she would come to prefer a particular shade of powder blue—roughly the same color as her dress that day at River Downs. And though she was barely five feet tall, Karolyn usually managed to make herself the center of attention with her looks, her laughter, her smile, her big mouth filled with curse words, and her general ferocity for life. Even on a quiet, cloudless afternoon, Karolyn was a hurricane, spinning unfettered through the world.

It was the last thing anyone would have ever expected from an Engelhardt. Her father, Fritz, was German-born and German-raised, an immigrant and a carpenter from a place called Gelsenkirchen. He had come to America with $25 in his pocket, settled in Cincinnati, and made sensible decisions there because he knew what it was like to have nothing. He changed his name to Fred and then worked his way up by building staircases in department stores and other commercial buildings in the city. It was his one great talent, and in time Fred Engelhardt's carpentry skills gave him everything: his wife, their family, and their home, a small two-bedroom apartment on Central Parkway in the city's most German neighborhood—Over-the-Rhine.

Karolyn, his first child and only daughter, was expected to be sensible, too. A German-Catholic girl in Over-the-Rhine couldn't choose a different path. But the nuns at Our Lady of Angels High School in Cincinnati—an all-girls school devoted to the teachings of the Virgin Mary—couldn't beat the spunk out of her. At graduation in 1960, Karolyn's classmates voted her Miss Extrovert. It wasn't as great as being named Miss All-American or Miss Cutie Pie, yet it was decidedly better than being called Miss Arrogant or Miss German—unfortunate names bestowed on other girls. Karolyn was somewhere in the middle, and she hoped that this station in life might be good enough to land her one of her three dream jobs. She wanted to be either a Roller Derby queen, a go-go dancer, or a stewardess.

A series of disappointments followed. The airlines refused to hire Karolyn; she was too petite to reach the overhead compartment. And the other jobs simply didn't exist in Cincinnati. With nowhere to go, Karolyn ended up getting hired out of high school as a bookkeeper. She ran numbers at a textbook company downtown, and she was afraid to admit that her numbers rarely added up. Worst of all, time was slipping away. While some of her classmates from Our Lady of Angels were getting married and settling down, Karolyn was still living at home with her parents and her little brother three years after graduation. A catch for some man perhaps, but not for everyone due to her oversized personality, and one quality that her German father and the Catholic nuns at Our Lady of Angels would have appreciated. Karolyn wasn't going to have sex with any man until she was married.

It was something Pete Rose could not have known as he spied her through the binoculars at the racetrack in Cincinnati in the summer of 1963. All he knew was that she was beautiful, and he made his approach, introducing himself. He was Pete Rose, he said, the second baseman for the Cincinnati Reds. Karolyn had never heard of him.

Their courtship that year was swift and explosive. At one point late in the season, Karolyn called Pete in his hotel room on the road—only Pete wasn't there. He was in the lobby flirting with another woman, an indiscretion that he openly admitted to Karolyn when he called her back. He wasn't big on apologies, and sometimes they argued. One night after a fight, Pete rode off in his Grand Prix convertible, and even decades later Karolyn remembered what he said as he left. He told her that he was finished with her forever because of how far she would or would not go with him. "I'm through with you, Blessed Virgin Mary," he said.

But Pete came back that night, and Karolyn was happier with him around. She didn't care that the Reds were mediocre that year, finishing in fifth place in the National League, twenty-three games behind the Dodgers. She didn't worry about her boyfriend's .273 batting average, and she didn't think about awards like Rookie of the Year. None of that mattered to her. She just liked Pete. If he said he was going to pick her up at seven o'clock for dinner, he arrived ten minutes early, always punctual. When he met her parents, he charmed them with his smile and his entertaining stories until Karolyn's mother doted on him like a second son. Her mother was soon calling Pete whenever the Reds were on the road to make sure he didn't oversleep. And though Pete tried to act cool—with his fast car and his fast life—Karolyn knew the secret: he wasn't. Once, on a date at a Cincinnati restaurant that specialized in fried shrimp and butter-broiled steaks, Pete tried to smoke one of Karolyn's cigarettes after dinner as she often did and ended up doubled over at the table, coughing. She was sure he was the one.

That fall, after the season ended, Pete enlisted in the U.S. Army reserves—a move that had less to do with patriotism than self-protection. By volunteering as a prominent athlete, he could earn privileged status and avoid getting drafted in the war in Vietnam that many worried might be coming. Still, Pete had to report to basic training at Fort Knox in Kentucky. He trimmed his crew cut even shorter than usual. He had to awake before dawn and live in a barracks, two hours from Karolyn, for much of the fall. And it was here, after Thanksgiving, that Pete's life changed in two important ways. He learned that the baseball writers had voted him Rookie of the Year, and he announced that he'd be marrying Karolyn. A date was set for late January.

Some teammates were shocked; Pete was just twenty-two, and given his eye for acrobatic bartenders and other attractive women on the road, he didn't seem like the settling-down type. His teammate, starting pitcher Jim O'Toole, didn't understand what Pete was doing. But Karolyn's mother was thrilled. As she saw it, Pete and Karolyn were perfect for each other. "Because nobody else," Karolyn's mother said, "could put up with either one of you." The only problem, for her, was the wedding date.

"You're supposed to be at the baseball writers' dinner that night at the Netherland Hilton," Scoops Lawson informed Pete around Christmastime that year. The writers were going to be honoring Pete. He was even supposed to give a speech. It was the sort of event that a young player might schedule around or skip in favor of his bride. One's own wedding was about the best excuse one could have to miss a dinner, another dinner, on baseball's endless winter banquet circuit, but Pete figured he could do both and told Scoops not to worry.

On the big day, he met Karolyn at St. William church on the West Side and married her in a Catholic ceremony, per her wishes, that in Pete's estimation lasted way too long. "Are we married yet?" he kept asking Karolyn. About a thousand guests were watching and waiting, a crowd that included former athletes from West High, all the good girls from Our Lady of Angels, Pete's teammates with the Reds, guys he had met in the minor leagues, men who liked to gamble at the racetrack, hundreds of German-Catholics from Over-the-Rhine, everyone who mattered in Anderson Ferry, and a cross section of white, working-class Cincinnati—the Zimmers, the Beebes, the Bloebaums, and the Engelhardts. Then, when it was over and everyone drove deeper into the West Side to attend the reception inside an old gym, Pete drove alone in the other direction. He went downtown to accept his award and give his speech at the baseball banquet, ready with a joke as usual. He would be going for more doubles in 1964, Pete told the crowd at the Netherland Hilton that day, because, as he noted with comedic timing, "I'm not a singles man anymore."

It was a good line. It made the papers, and at some point later that night Pete did manage to make it back to attend his own wedding reception, where there were drums of punch, cases of champagne, and roughly five hundred wheels of pizza to feed the crowd. But what everyone remembered from the evening was that Pete was gone for most of the night. At his own wedding reception, he was thinking about baseball and about himself, not Karolyn. He was spending time with reporters, not with her. She had to entertain alone, floating in a sea of admirers and trying to make the best of it.

It was a role she would have to learn to play well.

15

PETE AND KAROLYN put off their honeymoon until March, working around Pete's army obligations, and even then it was a squeeze. The young newlyweds had to celebrate their love for each other at spring training, and in order to afford the trip, Karolyn had to return many of their wedding gifts. The dinner plates, the electric can openers, the silverware—it was all going back. She didn't mind. Karolyn couldn't wait to get to Florida.

For ballplayers, spring training was the greatest time of year. In Tampa, there was sunshine, warmth, the sounds of baseball at the park, and the scent of attractive women at the bar. In prior years, Cincinnati players had stayed at the Causeway Inn and had frequented a tavern there called the Dugout Lounge, where the waitresses dressed as major-league "bat girls" in tight-fitting, high-cut, one-piece dresses made to look like Reds uniforms. This year, they were moving up to the International—a sprawling eight-acre resort near the beach with a twenty-four-hour coffee shop, a hopping dining room scene beneath a three-story glass rotunda, a late-night lounge open until three o'clock in the morning, and a roster of beautiful hostesses dressed to reflect the hotel's global theme. There was a Dutch Girl, a Swiss Girl, a French Mademoiselle, and a Spanish Señorita—and no one seemed to care that the Señorita's real name was Darlene. Pete was glad to be back in Florida.

But a real honeymoon, it wasn't. Since Pete wasn't especially popular with the other players, Karolyn wasn't popular with their wives. She sat by herself at the pool, languishing on the fringes. And when the players and their wives did gather together, the mood was off, everyone whispering about bad news. Just weeks before spring training, Hutch had found a lump in his chest—lung cancer. No one knew how long he would last. Hutch couldn't even get through practice some days without sitting in a special lifeguard's chair set up behind home plate so that he could survey the field.

Pete convinced himself that Hutch would make it—a coping mechanism, perhaps. He already had enough on his mind. He had earned a small raise for the 1964 season, but not before Phil Seghi lowballed him for most of the winter and even tried to slip a clause into his new contract forcing Pete to take a pay cut if he got demoted to Triple-A. Pete found the whole thing insulting.

He wasn't going back to the minors. He wasn't satisfied being Rookie of the Year. He didn't think that his .273 batting average in 1963 was even close to his maximum potential, and he wouldn't entertain any talk that he might struggle in his second season due to bad luck, due to the dreaded sophomore jinx. Instead, going into the new season, Pete was consumed with three obsessions: He wanted to be a great hitter, a .300 hitter. He wanted to make money—"good money," Pete called it—and he wanted to prove the press wrong. As far as he was concerned, there was no such thing as a sophomore jinx.

Pete proceeded to have a terrible April. He batted .174, and he struggled at times in the field. In one game alone that month, he dropped two pop flies at second base and let a third fall for a hit. Reporters labeled him a happy bridegroom but an unhappy hitter, and in May, Hutch finally had no choice. He benched Pete in favor of his old rival Bobby Klaus.

Like Blasingame the year before, Klaus had a chance to keep Pete on the bench for good. It was the greatest opportunity of Klaus's life. But like Blasingame, he failed. He batted .183 in place of Pete, and by late July, Cincinnati placed Klaus on waivers. He was bound for the worst team in baseball: the New York Mets. Still, Pete wasn't safe. His troubles only mounted. Hutch was in pain all summer, his cancer spreading. He took a medical leave for a while, and when he did, the interim manager, Dick Sisler, seemed to lose control. Coaches fought—throwing punches at each other during rain delays at least once—and Pete continued to falter at the plate. At one point that summer, he worked himself into a 2-for-28 tailspin.

But despite everything, the Reds found themselves only five and a half games out of first place on Labor Day. Pete rediscovered his swing, and his confidence, batting .313 in the final month of the season, and somehow Cincinnati had a shot at the National League pennant with two games left to play. All the Reds needed to do to secure first—and at least a tie for the league crown—was hold on to a 3–0 lead against the Philadelphia Phillies, at home at Crosley Field, in the eighth inning, on the second-to-last day of the season. They needed six outs.

The Reds' pitcher Jim O'Toole, who had allowed only three hits all night, retired the first batter to start the frame. Five outs to go. Then the next man hit a soft blooper between Pete at second base and shortstop Leo "Chico" Cárdenas, an athletic, young Cuban player who had made his first All-Star team that year. It looked like an easy out. But inexplicably, neither Pete nor Cárdenas broke hard on the ball. It fell for a hit, and from there it all unraveled. The Phillies scored four in the inning. The Reds lost the game by a run, and the pennant slipped away.

Afterward, in the clubhouse, O'Toole could have been angry with Cárdenas or Pete—or both. One of them should have caught the ball, and both of them had just stood there, waiting for the other one to do something. Frank Robinson, one of Pete's only friends on the team, thought both Cárdenas and Pete were responsible, and at least two beat writers seemed to think Pete was the one at fault. The ball, they wrote, was closer to second base.

Cárdenas, however, was an easier target. His lack of English often made him the subject of cruel jokes around the clubhouse or in the press box. In a television broadcast earlier that year, the Reds announcer cracked that the biggest improvement on the team was that "Cárdenas learned fifty more words of English." And the Reds players that night were already angry at their shortstop. In the inning prior, Cárdenas had charged the mound after getting hit with a pitch, momentarily waving his bat around like a weapon. The benches cleared and the melee seemed to awaken the Phillies, meaning Cárdenas had not only let the ball hit the grass; he had sparked the rally in general. O'Toole made up his mind. He came at Cárdenas, venting his frustration, and the shortstop, feeling cornered and angry, grabbed the first thing he saw to defend himself: an ice pick. "You say I miss the ball," Cárdenas said. "I get you."

The brawl inside the clubhouse sounded worse than it was. With Robinson and others holding O'Toole and Cárdenas apart, neither man came within a dozen feet of the other. But everyone heard it. Reporters cupped their ears to the clubhouse door while the players raged inside—a fitting end to a lost season. The Reds had turned on themselves.

Hutch was dead before Thanksgiving, and Pete was shipped off to play winter ball in Venezuela, where young players were sent when they weren't meeting expectations. Lots of guys would be there: Pete's former teammate in Macon Tommy Helms; Pete's former teammate in Geneva Tony Pérez; the future Hall of Famer Luis Aparicio; the future leader of the World Series champion Mets, Davey Johnson; and a thirty-year-old failed player who had never made it in the big leagues but was working his way up as a manager with the Navegantes del Magallanes, the Magellan Navigators, George "Sparky" Anderson.

They'd play a hundred games over the winter and make more than four thousand bolivares a month, roughly $1,000—"good money," as Pete liked to say. But Pete, who was assigned to the Caracas Lions, knew he couldn't stay the entire winter. He'd need to take a leave of absence in December. Karolyn was pregnant with their first child, and she was due any day.

The baby, a girl, was born in Cincinnati four days after Christmas 1964. Pete and Karolyn named her Fawn, and they brought her home to the West Side.

Karolyn's parents had bought a small house there next to Elder High School, Pete's old rival from his West High days, and Pete and Karolyn lived in an attic space on the third floor, rent-free. They had a separate entrance and a full bathroom, but only one bedroom, and many nights in the months ahead Karolyn slept there alone with baby Fawn, a young mother tending to her crying newborn in the dark. Pete had already returned to Venezuela.

But Karolyn understood the deal. She knew why Pete couldn't stay. There was a season to play and money to make, and given his lackluster performance in 1964, there was also, Karolyn knew, a lot on the line for her husband. Pete was potentially one bad April or one more slump away from returning to the minors or losing his job to someone better than Don Blasingame or Bobby Klaus, and Pete's first few weeks in Venezuela proved just how tenuous things were for him. Early in the season, on the road in Valencia, Caracas fans turned on Pete after he committed three errors in a single game. The crowd booed him, and Pete responded by allegedly spitting at some fans—a decision that reporters said cost him about 10 percent of his monthly paycheck.

The incident received almost no media attention back home. Unlike Chico Cárdenas, who was labeled a hothead, volatile and childish, for his behavior against the Phillies the previous fall, Pete dodged any criticism whatsoever for the alleged spitting affair in South America. He earned a pass—and even got a chance to explain it away. His pal at *The Cincinnati Post,* Scoops Lawson, wrote an entire column that winter where Pete denied spitting on anyone. He got fined, he told Scoops, for refusing to take the field after the fans started whistling at him. "Those people down in Venezuela are nuts," Pete said. "I really mean it."

By the following spring, when beat writers did ask him about the incident in Venezuela, they didn't even mention the spitting or his refusal to take the field. They focused instead on the positive. They wrote that Pete had responded to the angry fans by practicing more, working harder, and compiling hits. He ended up batting .351 that winter, the sixth-highest batting average on the Venezuelan circuit, and he showed up at the International in Tampa in the spring of 1965 brimming with confidence.

"I know I'm a better ballplayer right now than I was last year," he said. Pete was right. That year, for the first time in his career, he batted over .300, and then he replicated the feat in 1966. He made the All-Star team for the first time and became a leadoff man whom opposing pitchers didn't want to face. All he needed to really compete was a better team around him—a common complaint for many athletes, but one that many had in Cincinnati at the time. Before the 1966 season, the Reds traded away their best player, Frank Robinson, possibly for all the wrong reasons.

Robinson had rankled the Reds' front office since 1961, when he was arrested for carrying a concealed handgun after a verbal dispute in a late-night burger joint. According to Robinson, the police officers kept calling him "boy." Robinson knew he shouldn't have had the gun in his pocket that night. But in Cincinnati, after dark, he felt that he needed the protection, and the reaction to his arrest in the Reds' front office told Robinson everything he needed to know about where he stood with the team. The Reds' owner, Bill DeWitt—a longtime baseball executive with a round face and a thick neck—was so upset that he declined to send someone down to the city lockup to bail Robinson out. The job would fall to Scoops Lawson instead. Scoops interviewed him, then helped him secure bail.

Now, after a season in which he had hit thirty-three home runs, Robinson was gone, traded for nothing, and Pete was befuddled. "That's an awfully big bat to take out of the lineup," he complained the night of the trade. But changes were coming that would remake the Reds and forever shape Pete's life both on and off the field. Six months before trading Robinson, the Reds drafted a seventeen-year-old catcher, Johnny Bench, out of Binger, Oklahoma, who was handsome, well spoken, part Choctaw, and already hitting twenty-three home runs a year in the minors. Everyone loved him—scouts called Bench the best prospect they had seen in years—and the young catcher made it onto the Reds' roster within months. By the time he arrived, both Tony Pérez and Tommy Helms were established there, too, and they were playing for the tobacco-chewing manager whom Pete had learned to love in Macon: Dave Bristol. The Reds finally had a nucleus of young talent. Then, in early December 1966, Bill DeWitt announced he was selling the team to a group of investors, the largest of which was the publisher of *The Cincinnati Enquirer.* The purchase price was $7 million, nearly twice what DeWitt had paid to buy the Reds four years earlier, and the new owners made it clear on day one that they intended to win with this team and modernize baseball for Cincinnatians in every possible way.

They were committed, they said, to moving out of the antiquated facilities at Crosley Field. They were determined to develop a new and better stadium closer to the river. They were pushing out Phil Seghi—within a year, the old front-office man would be gone—and they were bringing in a new baseball executive who had won a World Series in St. Louis and had a clear vision for the Reds in Cincinnati.

His name was Bob Howsam, and he planned to build around the team's 1966 player of the year, the player with hustle and local connections. Howsam loved Pete Rose.

16

HOWSAM LOOKED MORE like a middle-aged math teacher than a baseball power broker. He was big and burly, with horn-rimmed glasses and a fondness for short-sleeve button-down shirts. He wore them almost every day during baseball season, pairing the shirts with forgettable ties, the more conservative the better, and he spoke with a voice that sounded too soft for his large body. It was probably the farmer in him; the Howsams raised bees and produced honey in the San Luis Valley of Colorado, not far from the New Mexico border. But they had first moved there in the 1890s to pan for gold, and the prospector blood ran strong with the Reds' new general manager. His whole life Bob Howsam had been chasing a fortune in sports.

In his twenties, he ran the Western League, a collection of six baseball teams in Colorado, Nebraska, and Iowa. In his thirties, he and his father bought one of those teams, the Denver Bears, and built a new ballpark for the club on land that had previously been used as a dump. The Howsams called the park Mile High Stadium when it opened in 1948, and it was soon packed with people. The Bears drew almost half a million fans at their peak, more than some major-league franchises. Howsam then founded a professional football team, the Denver Broncos, and sold everything. He considered himself a businessman, and he felt ill-equipped to compete with the oil tycoons buying other teams. But Howsam remained interested in sports. So when the beer magnate August Busch offered him the job as general manager of the St. Louis Cardinals in the summer of 1964, Howsam accepted. That fall, the Cardinals won their first World Series in almost twenty years, and over the next two seasons,

Howsam made bold hires and trades that set up St. Louis for future pennants. The key, he believed, was finding value where others didn't and promoting the team as a reflection of the community. That's how you won games, Howsam believed, and that's how you won fans.

Howsam was now intent on doing it in Cincinnati, but it had to be his way, by his rules. On Howsam's teams, there could be no beards, sideburns, mustaches, or long hair, and everyone had to dress the same way on the field. Players were required to wear black cleats with no logos, and they were barred from wearing high socks. At a time when many young Americans were starting to let their hair go, putting on bell-bottom jeans, flashing peace signs, and driving Volkswagen buses to the coast, Howsam wanted the Reds to project wholesomeness—"the wholesome theatrical aspect of baseball."

It was perfect for Cincinnati. In the presidential election the following year in 1968, people here would vote Republican, as they almost always did. Cincinnati was Richard Nixon country. But Howsam probably would have enforced the same rules if he was running a team in New York or San Francisco, and he definitely wasn't going to overpay for any player, even the player he planned to build his team around, Pete Rose.

In 1967, under new management with Howsam, the Reds agreed to pay Pete $46,000, twice as much as the average player and about five times the average American, but still less than many doctors and lawyers earned and only a third of what Willie Mays was getting paid in San Francisco. Not enough, Pete believed. At least not enough to keep Pete from working a second job after the season was over. In the winter of 1967—after batting .300 yet again—he bundled up against the cold, stuffed his hands into his pockets, and walked a car lot on the West Side two blocks from Karolyn's parents' house, moving inventory at Glenway Chevy. "Attention Baseball Fans and New Car Buyers!" advertisements read in Cincinnati. "Pete cordially invites you and your family to come out and see the all-new line of . . . *Chevrolets.*"

Like many jobs, it was boring; no one cheered for Pete on the car lot. But he got a Corvette out of the deal. He drove it around town as an advertisement for Glenway Chevy, and there was one night late that year that Pete would never be able to shake from his mind. It was a Monday, cold and dark. He was working late. It was snowing outside, and a twin-engine TWA jetliner en route from Los Angeles to Cincinnati came in flying low over the West Side. Too low. As it crossed the river to land in northern Kentucky, it crashed into the hillside, tumbled through an apple orchard, and exploded into a ball of fire about a mile and a half short of the runway.

Across the city that night, people could see the ferocious orange glow of the doomed plane in the distance. It flickered and pulsed on the horizon, and thoughts immediately turned to the passengers on board, eighty-two of them, according to the live reports on the radio. Pete had to get closer. Instead of going home after work, he drove down the hill, five miles to the river, easing his Corvette to a stop near Mr. Kottmyer's ferry landing and his childhood home on Braddock Street. Then he sat there in the cold, watching the snow fall and the plane burn across the water. Only twelve passengers would survive.

It was something that Cincinnatians who were alive at the time always remembered. They knew where they were on the night that Flight 128 went down in the apple orchard. But the crash seemed to occupy an outsized space in Pete's memory, perhaps because it was so close to his old neighborhood. He could imagine the plane flying in low over the rooftops, he could imagine the families and business travelers coming home, and he knew exactly what the wreckage looked like because he had seen it up close. "I could see it on the other side of the hill in Kentucky," he'd remember decades later. "I could see it burning."

Taken together, it felt like a close call, like a near miss, as if it could have been Pete on that plane, as if it could have been him on that hillside, and it seemed to fill him with a sense of urgency both on and off the field going into the 1968 season.

For starters, he and Karolyn moved out of her parents' house and into their own place—a two-bedroom apartment in a cozy complex of squat buildings a few miles away on the West Side. The complex was called Hilltop Garden, and the Roses' unit in Building E was barely big enough to hold Pete's Rookie of the Year trophy. It stood like a towering lamp on an end table in the main living area, which also doubled as the kitchen. Still, it was better than the attic space in Karolyn's parents' house. There might have been just four rooms in the new apartment, including the bathroom, but there was a small balcony off the back. There was a swimming pool down the hill for Karolyn and Fawn to enjoy. It was an easy commute to Crosley Field for Pete, and there were lots of friends nearby. Enough young Reds players lived at Hilltop Garden that they could carpool to Crosley Field together, rambling down the hill in a single vehicle and listening to Pete talk about baseball—and his salary, what he should be making.

"Get me straight," Pete told reporters in early 1968. "I don't play for money." But his paycheck did matter. "I like to get what I'm worth," he said. And he had a figure in mind. It was Willie Mays money, Mickey Mantle money—a $100,000 deal. He hoped to be the first $100,000 singles hitter in baseball, and unlike other players he didn't mind speaking openly about his financial ambitions, because he figured he was worth it, and he knew he was an important attraction. He was, Pete declared in 1968, one of the two most exciting *white* players in baseball.

Pete denied making the comment when the quotation first appeared in *The Cincinnati Enquirer.* But one of the Reds' beat writers remarked that it sure sounded like Pete, and it didn't surprise anyone that he might have said something that was both controversial and honest about the changing face of the sport. Baseball had evolved to a point where a star player's whiteness *was* notable—at least for those people holding on to the past.

A decade earlier in 1957, the National League had fielded a starting lineup at the All-Star Game that had featured three Black stars: Hank Aaron, Willie Mays, and the Reds' Frank Robinson. But the American League had trotted out a lineup that was exclusively white. The AL's two Black players that day barely made it onto the field—one of them didn't see action at all—and neither team had a single pitcher who was Black.

At the most recent All-Star Game in 1967, the American League continued to lag behind anything reflecting the diversity of the country; only six players on the roster were Black or Latino. But this time, two starters—Rod Carew and Tony Oliva—were players of color, and the National League fielded a team that was nothing short of historic for any fan paying attention. Half the team was Black or Latino, and it was these stars who carried the National League that night. The first five men to bat were Lou Brock, Roberto Clemente, Hank Aaron, Orlando Cepeda, and Dick Allen—all Black or Latino. The NL's starter was Juan Marichal, an imposing fastball pitcher nicknamed the Dominican Dandy. The next two NL pitchers were Ferguson Jenkins and Bob Gibson, both Black. A white man didn't even toe the rubber for the National League until the ninth inning. And Pete Rose's teammate Tony Pérez was the biggest star of the night. Pérez hit a home run in extra innings to win the game for the National League.

In other ways, the game looked exactly the way it did two decades earlier when Jackie Robinson became the first Black player in the majors, and one of the places that was slowest to change was the press box. In the late 1960s, it remained all male—women weren't permitted in the clubhouse—and almost all white, especially in the places where it mattered most. Every major sports column in every major American newspaper was written by a white man. And while many of these reporters wrote flattering feature stories about the game's Black and Latino stars, they gravitated to Pete Rose. He looked like them, he spoke like them, he was working class like them, and he was willing to give interviews all day, filling their columns with colorful quotations and stories. In their minds, he didn't need to run from his comment about being exciting and white. Pete was just stating the facts of the matter.

"He *is* the most exciting white ballplayer in baseball," columnists wrote in 1968. "The most electrifying player in the game today—purple, orange, red, yellow, black or white . . . the hustling Rose . . . the irrepressible Pete Rose . . . brash, bold, and personable . . . the most talkative ballplayer I know . . . who epitomizes hustle more than any other athlete . . . and gets along best with the average fan."

The coverage was hyperbolic at times, perhaps. But it wasn't untrue. Long after the games were over and most other players had gone home, Pete would still be there at the ballpark, signing autographs for fans. He'd stay for them, win or lose, signing and signing for more than an hour at times—Karolyn and Fawn could wait—and then, the next morning, he'd be the first one back at the stadium, ready to work. Players would stroll onto the field, with their bats on their shoulders, to find Pete was already in the cage, dripping with sweat and swinging.

Leo Durocher, the manager of the Cubs in the 1960s, met hundreds, maybe thousands, of ballplayers during his career. Durocher had been in baseball since 1928; had played with Babe Ruth and Lou Gehrig on the Yankees; had managed Jackie Robinson in his early years with the Dodgers; had logged more miles on buses, trains, and planes bound for baseball diamonds and ballparks than almost anyone in America; and knew everything there was to know about the game, plus some things he preferred to keep to himself. Durocher was suspended from baseball for one year in 1947 for consorting with gamblers.

But in his career, forty years in baseball, Durocher had never seen anything quite like Pete Rose. When the Reds played the Cubs, the old manager sat in the dugout in his blue stirrup socks and eyed Pete with a mix of reverence and ire, asking himself questions that had no answers. Why didn't his players work this hard? Why didn't his guys turn ground balls into singles and singles into doubles? Why didn't they dive headfirst into third base or headlong into the outfield wall at Wrigley Field? Why couldn't he have a player who fought like Pete Rose? Why couldn't everyone be like Pete?

"We can't get him out," Durocher grumbled. "He's something."

17

In the spring of 1968, the Reds moved Pete to a different starting position, his third in six years. Instead of playing second base or left field, he'd be standing in right—a position that gave him trouble, especially on the road. At times that year, he got turned around chasing fly balls.

But at the plate, Pete kept hitting. In April, he batted .412, the best average in the National League. In May, he appeared on the cover of *Sports Illustrated* for the first time, a signature achievement for any athlete, and in June he received more All-Star votes than any other player in the league, appearing on 236 of the 258 ballots cast by his peers. Gone were the days of Mickey Mantle and Whitey Ford laughing at Pete from the dugout at spring training. Gone were the days of Mantle and Ford—period. Ford had retired during the 1967 season, his throwing elbow ground to dust and his spirit broken. Ford cried at his farewell press conference, dabbing his eyes with a handkerchief, and Mantle was about to join him in the quiet pastures of retirement. It was his last year in baseball, and he was struggling.

At the All-Star break in 1968, Mantle, the great Yankee slugger, was batting .229, a hundred points below Pete. Mantle was an All-Star in name only, coming off the bench to strike out in the game, while Pete was going to be starting in the outfield. He was the future, and he planned to show up at the game in style. A local clothier had gifted him an outfit for his appearance there: a mod, tailored eight-button jacket and snug, tight-fitting pants.

A hairline fracture in his left thumb kept Pete out of the game—his worst stroke of luck in years—and he had only himself to blame for it. Just four days before the All-Star Game, he lost a ball in the lights at Dodger Stadium and fell awkwardly on his glove hand as he dove at the last moment. Karolyn was crushed for him. It didn't seem fair that Pete couldn't play in the game or that, in his absence, the local papers showered the Reds' other All-Stars with attention. Tony Pérez, Tommy Helms, and Johnny Bench were all on the National League squad that summer, and Bench had been selected to the team as a rookie, an achievement that eluded most first-time players, including Pete. He hadn't become an All-Star until his third year with the Reds—and now here was Bench, making the team at twenty years old, an age when Pete had still been stuck in the minors, playing for the Tampa Tarpons. It was hard for Pete to sit out when Bench and the others were playing.

But the beat writers wondered if a little rest might be good for Pete. He had been nursing a groin injury for weeks, and under normal circumstances he refused to take a day off. The broken thumb would force him to sit, and when he returned near the end of July, Pete played like a man making up for time lost. He batted .354 in his first week back, hit .347 in the month of August, and started September with the highest batting average in the league, .346—thirteen points better than the next-best hitter in the race for the National League batting title.

At the house on Braddock Street, Big Pete was thrilled. He was fifty-six years old that summer, fully gray, excited to read the box scores in the newspaper every morning before going to work at the bank, and seemingly interested in little else. He took no joy in being a father-in-law to Karolyn or a grandfather to Pete's daughter, Fawn. The little girl found him to be so cold that she didn't like to visit the house in Anderson Ferry. And Big Pete seemed equally detached from his younger son, Dave. The young man had signed a minor-league contract with the Reds the previous summer and was playing in the Gulf Coast League down in Florida, following his older brother's path. But with the *Sports Illustrated* reporter, Big Pete went out of his way to complain that Dave didn't have Pete's "go-go spirit." Dave didn't hustle. The father had praise only for Pete—and his .346 average—and corporate executives felt the same way about the Reds' young star.

Excited about the opportunity of working with Pete Rose, they began setting up meetings late that summer to discuss sponsorship deals, business contracts, television commercials, speaking engagements, and money—good money. Yet the offers all came with a caveat: he had to win the batting title. And with the pressure on, Pete began to fade after Labor Day. He had stretches where he went 0 for 12 and 2 for 20. He lost sixteen points on his average in just a few weeks. He walked into the clubhouse in Cincinnati with three games left to play in the season to find that his once-insurmountable lead in the race for the batting title had shrunk to mere decimal points. Pete was just .0007 ahead of the Pirates' center fielder, Matty Alou, and Alou was loose and smiling in Pittsburgh. He'd been here before. Alou had won the title two years earlier in 1966.

For the next two games, Pete and Alou matched each other almost point for point. Under the lights at Crosley Field in the third-to-last game of the season, Pete gave one of the worst performances of his life. He went 1 for 7 in a fifteen-inning affair, struck out looking in his last at bat, and watched good pitches go by. Had Alou done anything that day, the batting title would have been his. But Alou went 0 for 4 in Chicago that afternoon, squandering his chance. Then, in the second-to-last game of the season, both men were perfect at the plate. Pete went 5 for 5 and Alou went 4 for 4, meaning it would all come down to the last day of the season—one last game.

Pete stayed up late that night in his apartment at Hilltop Garden, watching old movies on television and running numbers in his head. He knew that just one at bat the next day, just one hit, just one swing, could determine the batting champion, and with so much at stake he couldn't rest. He couldn't close his eyes. It was three o'clock in the morning before he nodded off and daybreak before he knew it. He awoke to the smell of sizzling fat in the kitchen. Karolyn was broiling a steak for his breakfast, the same meal he'd had the day before when he had gone 5 for 5. He scarfed it down and reported to the ballpark.

On the field, before the game, Pete's teammates tried to stay out of his way. They had never seen someone want something so badly. Dave Bristol could feel it radiating off Pete like steam, and the fans at the ballpark could feel it, too. They cheered every time he came to the plate that day. But in the end, it was the first at bat that mattered most.

Pete worked the count to two balls and two strikes and then sliced a curveball into right field. It wasn't a well-struck ball—he almost stabbed it with the end of his bat—but it found the grass and rolled into the bullpen for a double. As he stood on second base, with the crowd cheering, Pete could almost feel the tension wash away, and as the game went on, the reports that fans gave him from the bleachers made him feel even better. In Chicago, Alou was going hitless, 0 for 4. It was over.

The Reds finished fourteen games out of first. But Pete Rose was the best hitter in the National League.

Pete lingered in the clubhouse that evening, long after most players had left, regaling reporters with the story of his conquest: how he had doubted himself, how he had battled, how he had prevailed, and how the people had loved him for it. For a long time, he didn't even take off his uniform. It was as if he didn't want it to end. Eventually, he got undressed and drove home to Karolyn in the apartment at

Hilltop Garden, a new man with new prospects. In the weeks ahead, Johnny Bench was named Rookie of the Year. But Pete Rose was everywhere.

He filmed new commercials for the sponsors that wanted him and hit the speaker circuit across the Midwest and beyond. He was in Dayton, Chicago, and Wabash, Indiana. He was in Washington, Philadelphia, and Houston. Then he went back to Dayton, and back to Houston, and on to Columbus and Atlanta. Full houses everywhere, Pete boasted. Yes, the people loved him. And if they missed him in person, they didn't need to worry. They could catch him that winter on their radios and their televisions. He was the subject of a new documentary: *Cincinnati Kid: Pete Rose.* He was in advertisements for Gatorade. He had his own baseball glove, the Pete Rose model, that was produced and sold by MacGregor. He was hired to stump for a downtown store with an East Side name, Hyde Park Clothes—"Get the look of a winner!"—and he was returning to the Reds in 1969 with the largest contract ever given to a Cincinnati ballplayer: a one-year deal worth $85,000.

It wasn't the $100,000 contract that Pete had wanted, but he couldn't do anything about it. The Reds—and general manager Bob Howsam—owned him. Under baseball's reserve clause, Howsam had the right to bring players back, year after year, for the same money, regardless of the player's talents, stats, desires, or needs. Pete couldn't walk away. He couldn't bargain with other teams even if he wanted to, and by March 1969, Pete felt compelled to take whatever Howsam was offering. Karolyn was pregnant again, and they were leaving Hilltop Garden to buy a house.

The one they ultimately chose wouldn't be considered notable by today's standards. The place was just twenty-two hundred square feet. But it was a new house, with four bedrooms and half an acre of land in the rolling hills of the West Side, not far from the Western Hills Country Club, and Karolyn closed on it in September 1969 at a moment when she was round and heavy with the new baby, Pete was in the middle of a West Coast road trip, and baseball was changing yet again. For years, a respected poll had been asking people to name their favorite sport, and for the first time in 1969, baseball didn't win. Thirty-one percent of people chose football, making it slightly more popular than baseball, sitting at 28 percent.

Baseball owners were alarmed. Their sport had long outperformed football. Now the last two Super Bowls had earned higher television ratings than the World Series. The most recent Super Bowl—with Joe Namath and the underdog New York Jets stunning the heavily favored Baltimore Colts—had transcended sports. Everyone was still talking about the game, even after baseball season started in the spring of 1969, and it was clear to baseball owners that Namath was just the beneficiary of a trend, not the reason for it. In the fall of 1968, more people had watched *college* football than ever before.

The answer, baseball officials decided, was a set of sweeping changes, implemented before the 1969 season. First, owners voted to add more teams. Montreal, San Diego, Seattle, and Kansas City all got their own franchises by paying $10 million for the privilege, spoils to be divided up among the existing franchise owners. Next, owners decided to split the teams in each league into two divisions. In order to advance to the World Series going forward, a team would have to win its division, and then a five-game championship series against the other division winner in their league. With more games and more teams there'd be more revenue. Teams were projected to make a record $37 million that year off broadcasting rights alone, including a historic figure paid by a single network. NBC was putting up more than $16 million to air the newfangled playoffs, the World Series, the All-Star Game, and twenty-eight nationally televised "Games of the Week." Finally, to generate more runs and make the product more interesting on NBC, a committee voted to lower the pitcher's mound and shrink the strike zone, giving hitters an advantage.

Howsam was excited about what it meant for the Reds. Cincinnati—assigned to the NL's new western division—would now have a greater chance of making it to the postseason every year. But the growing pot of money helped create a bitter dispute between the increasingly wealthy owners and the newly unionized players, led by a man with a neat mustache, sharp features, and a history of organizing steelworkers: Marvin Miller.

Miller questioned if NBC even had permission to show the players' pictures on TV, given that no one had negotiated the new television deal with the players themselves. Labor stoppages seemed likely in the future—almost certain, in fact. Among other things,

Miller was intent on fighting baseball's reserve clause. Just days before Pete signed his $85,000 contract with the Reds in early 1969, Miller called the clause both unconstitutional and un-American, and despite the easier path to the postseason the Reds ended the year in their usual fashion: they finished third in their new division and went home early. The only thing to cheer in Cincinnati in October was Pete Rose. Like the year before, he won the batting title on the last day of the season, edging out Roberto Clemente for the honor by dropping a bunt down in front of the pitcher's mound in Atlanta in his last at bat.

One typically didn't bunt in the situation Pete found himself in that afternoon. With two outs and runners in scoring position, it was time to swing away. But the Reds were already eliminated from the playoffs. The game didn't matter. Just the batting title. And with the bunt, Pete claimed it. He was safe at first, batting .348 for the season and becoming the first back-to-back batting champion in Cincinnati Reds history.

It was an achievement worth celebrating. The governor of Ohio declared November 1 Pete Rose Day across the state. Business leaders in Cincinnati presented Pete with a diamond ring encrusted with his initials, and the city named a West Side landmark after him. They rechristened Bold Face Park—the baseball diamond from his youth—as Pete Rose Playground. It was arguably the greatest honor of his life and possibly the best time in his marriage. Amid all the accolades that offseason, Karolyn gave birth to a son—Peter Edward Rose Jr., "Petey." They had it all: a boy, and a girl, and a new house in the new suburbs of the West Side.

But at the peak of his fame and happiness that winter, Pete struggled to win over at least a few fans in Cincinnati. When the city announced that local officials were renaming Bold Face Park for him, five hundred people signed a petition opposing the change. They didn't think Pete Rose was worthy of a local landmark, perhaps because there were growing questions and rumors about him—questions and rumors that even West Siders couldn't ignore.

18

One of the rumors circulating about Pete concerned gambling. He seemed to do a lot of it.

At spring training in Tampa, baseball games were typically over by the late afternoon, leaving the nights wide open for the players, and many of them enjoyed filling the time by doing "doubleheaders." They would catch the last horse races of the day at Florida Downs, a track in nearby Oldsmar, and then they would shoot across the bay on the causeway to the Derby Lane dog track on the edge of the marsh in St. Petersburg. Some of the biggest stars in baseball could be found there at night, lounging at private tables and betting on the greyhounds under the lights.

But doubleheaders weren't enough for Pete. He preferred what the guys called triple-headers. At spring training, he'd hit three gambling locales in a single day: the horse track, the dog track, and a late-night jai alai establishment not far from the Reds' hotel with attractive tele-wager girls ready to take his bets while he relaxed in a new restaurant called the Cancha Club. He'd go for hours, if possible, and during the regular season in Cincinnati he tried to replicate the thrill of Florida's exciting triple-header circuit by driving out to River Downs to bet on a few races before reporting to Crosley Field for games.

Pete wasn't doing anything illegal. He wasn't breaking the rules of baseball or even violating Bob Howsam's many edicts designed to make players appear "wholesome." It was his free time. He could go to the track if he wanted, and he was joined there in the afternoon by plenty of others, including Scoops Lawson. But Pete didn't have to break the law, or the rules, to upset some Cincinnatians.

In this city—"a citadel of conservatism," Howsam called it—upstanding citizens didn't want their icons wearing their hair long, they didn't want them protesting the war in Vietnam, they didn't want them driving flashy cars, and they didn't want them gambling at the track before work. And since Cincinnati was a small town in comparison to other major-league cities, people knew Pete wasn't just hanging out there with Scoops Lawson. They heard he was mingling with tavern owners, downtown jewelers, shadier characters, and at least one well-known West Side bookie. He was running with gamblers, which made him a gambler. The workers at the betting windows marveled at the amount of money Pete bet on horses—and lost—before he packed up and drove to the park, as if nothing had happened, as if everything were fine, and inevitably, the stories got back to Howsam. Fans called the Reds' front office to lodge official complaints that Pete was gambling his life away at River Downs.

Pete laughed it off. What did people expect him to do in the afternoon? "Stay home," he said, "and cut the grass?" He could bet on the horses if he wanted, he said, and he told people that the most important person in his life understood. Karolyn got it. But Karolyn was good at playing down her disappointments, especially in front of sports reporters and, increasingly, newspaper feature writers, often young women, whom editors dispatched to write cute pieces about Pete Rose's bombastic wife cheering in her seat near home plate.

Karolyn joked about where she ranked in comparison to baseball in Pete's life. (Much lower.) She laughed that Pete's idea of a romantic surprise was getting season tickets to the Cincinnati Royals basketball team. ("I thought we were going on a vacation.") And she cast herself in the role of the good wife, raising the kids, Fawn and Petey, while Pete was on the road. ("My daddy is a superstar," Fawn told one reporter.) But in the house on the West Side or the family's motel room at spring training in Tampa, life was harder on Karolyn than she allowed herself to admit. She was often lonely. She felt isolated, and she couldn't stop worrying about what Pete was doing on the road. There were other women around—the groupies or, as Karolyn called them, the Baseball Annies. The Annies were always young and available, with no kids in tow. They were everything Karolyn was not.

On one occasion, not long after they were married, Karolyn took a phone call from a woman at their motel at spring training. As Karolyn pretended to be the housekeeper, the woman left a message for Pete, saying she was free that night if he wanted to drive over and meet her in Miami. On another occasion, Karolyn watched two of the Annies approach Pete outside Crosley Field. Karolyn was walking right next to him that day, but that didn't stop one of the two women from passing Pete her phone number on a slip of paper as they crossed paths.

Pete dropped the paper "like it was on fire," Karolyn recalled later. Still, the two women stuck around. The next day, Karolyn spotted them in the stands at Crosley Field watching her husband play ball. They followed Pete around in their miniskirts and hot pants while Karolyn was relegated to sitting with the kids, an afterthought. At spring training in 1968, she learned exactly how much Pete thought about her when he was on the road.

That March, he flew alone to Tampa after a two-week stint with the army reserves, and he was in a hurry, as usual. He wanted to get to the ballpark and into the batting cage, and in his rush to play ball, he forgot that he had sent Karolyn and Fawn to Florida in advance. They were waiting for him at a motel there, but Pete didn't show up that morning and he didn't call them, either. Karolyn finally had to track Pete down. She ran over to the ballpark in a panic around one o'clock that afternoon and felt relieved, if perhaps a little silly, when she spotted him in the cage with the guys.

"That's my Pete," Karolyn said. "It's baseball first, family second."

Howsam was well aware of Pete's problems—his shortcomings, Howsam liked to call them. But lots of players slept around on the road. In his famous baseball book *Ball Four,* written in the late 1960s, the Yankees' pitcher Jim Bouton said that everyone—the wives, the girlfriends, the reporters, and the front-office executives—understood the arrangement, and as a result, most players didn't worry about getting caught fooling around with another woman. "Our biggest concern," Bouton wrote, "was getting the clap." Bottom line: if fidelity were a prerequisite for playing time, Howsam would have struggled to field a squad. He had bigger issues on his mind.

At the end of the 1969 season, Howsam was disappointed that the Reds kept missing the playoffs despite having a roster that included Rose, Bench, Pérez, and Helms, and he was ready to make a change.

One week after the season ended, Howsam fired Dave Bristol as manager and replaced him with George "Sparky" Anderson.

Almost everyone hated the decision. Bristol had known players like Rose, Bench, Pérez, and Helms since their earliest days in the minor leagues. One player cried when he heard that Bristol had been fired, and almost everyone in the clubhouse mourned Bristol's departure, knowing how much he loved this team, his team—the "Big Red Machine," Bristol called them. Sparky, by comparison, was unproven and unknown. Thirty-five and prematurely gray, he had never run a major-league ball club. He had struggled at times managing bad teams in the lowest rungs of baseball. One winter, in the Venezuelan league, Sparky had been fired as the manager of the Magellan Navigators after losing thirteen games in a row, and just months later he had grabbed an umpire around the throat during an argument while managing the Rock Hill Cardinals in the Western Carolinas League—an incident that ended when he was escorted off the field by two police officers. He thought he was destined to be banned from baseball forever, not promoted, and given his lack of success—his lack of anything—*The Cincinnati Post* had to ask, "Who's Sparky Anderson?"

But Howsam was trusting his instincts. Sparky had a winning record in the minors as a manager in Toronto, St. Petersburg, Modesto, and Asheville. Howsam liked him. "My conscience is clear," he said, and Sparky knew his role. Managing this team, he thought, was going to be like being chief executive at General Motors. He just needed to stay out of the way and let the machine—the Big Red Machine—do its thing. His first order of business was naming Pete Rose team captain, and his second was making sure that Pete was happy. In early 1970, just before spring training, the Reds' star finally got his $100,000 deal, the first one in Reds history, plus a little extra that reportedly brought the sum up to $105,000.

It was what Pete had long wanted. "*Good money . . . A lot of money.*" But if he was looking to get a celebratory press conference standing next to Bob Howsam, Pete was going to be waiting a long time.

Howsam didn't feel great about Pete's contract or much else that was happening off the field that winter. While he was negotiating with Pete in Cincinnati—often in the newspapers and sometimes with Scoops Lawson acting as a de facto intermediary—a player who had been traded from the Cardinals to the Phillies informed the union chief, Marvin Miller, that he wanted to fight. Curt Flood was a speedy center fielder, a three-time All-Star, a two-time World Series champion, a seven-time Gold Glove winner, and a Black player from a segregated neighborhood of West Oakland that he once described as "99 percent Black, and 100 percent poor." Flood told Miller that he was tired of being treated like a piece of property that could be bought and sold. Miller helped get him a lawyer, and then Flood wrote to the commissioner, Bowie Kuhn, to explain that he wouldn't be reporting to Philadelphia for spring training in 1970. Instead, he was filing a lawsuit to challenge baseball's reserve clause, a lawsuit that Flood knew could cost him everything, even if he won. He was a young Black man suing twenty-six white millionaires—the team owners. "Really powerful men," Flood acknowledged.

The establishment revolted immediately. August Busch, the owner of the Cardinals, railed against Flood, mourning the state of both baseball and America. "I don't understand what's happening all over our great country," Busch cried, "on the campuses and everywhere." Bob Howsam agreed. He saw the reserve clause as the foundation of the sport. If players were free to negotiate with multiple teams, choose the contract of their liking, and sign with the highest bidder, executives like him could be forced to overpay for talent, signing stars to long-term agreements. Teams would have no incentive for developing young prospects, he argued. The wealthiest owners would end up with the best players. There'd be no parity in the sport, and Howsam didn't understand how Flood could argue that he was being treated like a piece of property. In St. Louis, Flood had made $90,000 the previous year, more money than Pete Rose.

"Curt Flood should get down on his knees," Howsam said that winter, almost seething, "and thank the Lord that he has had the opportunity to be in baseball."

Many fans felt the same way. Flood received so many angry letters in the days after announcing his intentions that he confessed to having second thoughts about the suit. Maybe he should have just taken his $90,000 and kept playing. And the reactions of some of his fellow players didn't help. Old Hall of Famers accused Flood of trying to ruin the game. Willie Mays snorted at the possibility of the players' union paying Flood's legal bills. Carl Yastrzemski, the highest-paid player for the Boston Red Sox, publicly announced his opposition to Flood's lawsuit, and Pete Rose did as well, though for once Pete chose his words carefully, more carefully than Yaz did, anyway. "I think Curt's a helluva outfielder," Pete said. He just preferred to keep baseball the way it was. At most, Pete said, he'd support tweaking the reserve clause to give players more freedom.

It was a position that most star players chose to take that winter. They stood with Curt Flood, but not next to him. They supported "reasonable modifications" to the reserve clause but steered clear of his inflammatory lawsuit as it slogged through the courts—for weeks, at first, then months, then years. No one wanted the hate mail that Flood was getting, especially the young stars who could gain the most if Flood prevailed in court. Tom Seaver, the National League's best pitcher, playing for the Mets in New York, figured there were three up-and-coming stars who stood to benefit most of all: Reggie Jackson in Oakland, Bobby Bonds in San Francisco, and Pete Rose's young teammate in Cincinnati, Johnny Bench.

In just two years in the game, Johnny had proven himself one of the most talented catchers in baseball and one of the most beloved stars in Cincinnati, maybe even more beloved than Pete. Advertisers and corporate sponsors couldn't get enough of Johnny, and fans wanted to know everything about him. "Like when is his birthday?" one woman wrote in a letter to one of the local papers. "Where was he born, and where does he live, how tall is he, and does he have a steady girlfriend?" He did not. Johnny was just twenty-two years old, and the joke that winter in Cincinnati was that he was staying in shape by dancing at nightclubs downtown and dating airline stewardesses who found him dreamy. "Everything about him is fantastic," one of the stewardesses said.

If Pete could get $105,000 in 1970, then Johnny figured he could squeeze even more out of Howsam in the years ahead. Maybe even twice as much. Pete had hardly signed his name to the contract when people started saying that Johnny would be the Reds' first $200,000 man. In the meantime, Pete and Johnny were going into business together. In February 1970, Hy Ullner, a successful businessman and the owner of Hyde Park Clothes, persuaded the two baseball stars to slap their names on a car dealership located on South Dixie Highway near Dayton. Pete and Johnny each got a 25 percent share of the enterprise; Ullner and another businessman owned the rest, and they'd do most of the work. But Pete made it clear that he wanted to hustle for Ullner, too. He showed up at spring training in March driving a brand-new black-and-gold Mercury Cougar hardtop and ready to sell.

"Wanna buy a car?" Pete asked people.

He sounded serious—as if he were really trying to move product off the lot. And by the end of the spring, he was peddling something else: his first book—*The Pete Rose Story: An Autobiography.* It was a breezy paean to himself. A love story, really. He reminded readers twice in the first two pages that he earned $100,000 a year. He wrote pages and pages about his father—"the most important guy in my life." He preached the gospel of hustle: how he had to hustle, how he was nothing without hustle, how his father told him, "Don't forget to hustle." And Pete ended the book by saying that he disagreed with the clichéd line that people always used in sports: it's not whether you win or lose, but how you play the game.

"My dad never believed that," Pete wrote, "and neither do I. Winning is what counts and don't you ever forget it. What I mean is, it doesn't matter what you're trying to do—play Little League, be a good father, put in a day's work for a day's pay, raise your kids so they grow up right, or get the right girl to marry you—they don't pay you to lose."

It was classic Pete Rose, and so was this: in a book that was more than two hundred pages long, the story of his life written in his own words, he barely mentioned Karolyn and his children, Fawn and Petey. It was almost like they weren't there. They didn't exist. It was a feeling that Karolyn had learned to live with, but that the kids would have to navigate, too, especially Fawn. That spring, she was five years old, and she loved her daddy. She wore a little Reds uniform with her dad's number on it and couldn't wait for him to get home from road trips. She wanted to talk baseball with him or throw the ball in the yard. She said she was going to be a switch hitter just like him, and even after her little brother was born, Fawn walked around telling people that her name was "Pete Rose Jr."

Pete liked throwing the ball with her, but he was often gone. He was busy selling cars and books, going to the racetrack, reporting to the stadium, trying to win, hustling for his father, and fending off critics who believed that Sparky Anderson should have chosen Johnny Bench to be team captain. One fan complained in a letter to the *Enquirer* that Pete seemed distracted calculating his batting average, counting his money, rehearsing his pithy lines for reporters, and trying on new clothes. But the beat writers at the *Enquirer* defended Pete. The fan had it all wrong. If Pete was distracted in the spring of 1970, it was because he was saying goodbye to an old friend.

In late June that year, the Reds played their last game at Crosley Field. They were abandoning the ballpark near the railroad tracks for a circular fortress built on the shores of the river across town, just as the new owners had promised when they bought the team four years before in 1966, and this fortress was better than anyone could have imagined at the time. The new stadium had fake grass and plastic seats.

At the end of the last game at Crosley Field, a small crew of groundskeepers unearthed home plate from the dirt, strapped it beneath a helicopter, and flew it downtown. Then they shut off the lights at the old park, let the grass grow thick with weeds, and allowed the city's beloved baseball diamond to slip into quiet ruin. By the end of the year, Crosley Field had become a city impound lot. It was filled with the wreckage of lost and broken-down cars.

19

ARCHITECTS TODAY, TASKED with building a baseball stadium, would go to great lengths to replicate the charm and character of Crosley Field: its cozy confines, its old-fashioned scoreboard, its walls adorned with advertisements for Hudepohl beer and Partridge Whoppers—"Cincy's Favorite Frankfurter"—and its unique, terraced outfield. About twenty feet before the wall, the grass sloped upward, forcing outfielders chasing down a deep fly ball to climb a low hill, a quirk from the past that caused visiting fielders, even great ones, to stumble at times and gave the Reds a real home-field advantage. Their players knew how to navigate the slope.

But the field also had its share of issues, and the Reds' ownership had been complaining about these problems for years. Crosley Field was too small, they said, with only thirty thousand seats. It was about half the size of newer ballparks that had sprung up in Los Angeles and San Francisco, and there was no good way to get to it. The field was located in a maze of tiny streets on the western edge of downtown, and because it had been built in 1912—when most people didn't have cars—there was almost no parking nearby. Vehicles clogged the neighborhood on game days, and infrastructure developed in the 1960s only made things worse. In 1964, a new federal highway, Interstate 75, went in just beyond the right-field wall, turning Crosley Field into an island. It was close to everything and just out of reach. On at least one occasion, the Reds had to delay the start of a game because many fans were trapped outside the ballpark in traffic—in their cars.

The new stadium downtown along the river was going to change all that. For starters, the architects, two men from Atlanta, set aside huge chunks of real estate for parking lots and erected a four-story garage, reportedly the world's largest. Fans would be able to drive in on freshly paved roads or walk up over new pedestrian bridges, and once inside they would find themselves encased in a perfect orb of reinforced steel and concrete, where everything was bigger and better.

To accommodate the fan who was perhaps drinking too much Hudepohl beer and eating too many of those Partridge Whoppers, the seats in the new park would be three inches wider than those at Crosley Field, with five additional inches of legroom. No one would have to complain about an obstructed view or a long walk to the concession stand, because there would be more concession stands, too. Forty kiosks lined the concourse, capable of serving a capacity crowd of about fifty-two thousand people, and the wealthiest fans, the corporate executives at Procter & Gamble and big downtown banks where Pete's father worked, would have even more options for drinking and dining. They could lounge in an array of private boxes, outfitted with fully stocked bars, air-conditioning, and plush, wall-to-wall carpets.

But without question, the most exciting carpet was on the field itself. Instead of seeding the new diamond with grass, the architects arranged for another option. They laid down a thick layer of crushed rock, had it coated with blacktop and foam, and then covered it with nearly four acres of a synthetic field surface originally called ChemGrass and then rebranded as AstroTurf. Monsanto, the manufacturing giant behind the turf, had first used this surface to make the field inside the Houston Astros' new stadium, the Astrodome, and this name, AstroTurf, just sounded better. ChemGrass smelled of *toxins;* AstroTurf was the *future.*

Really, though, it was the same, no matter what they called it. It was just a stew of chemicals—boiled down, dyed green, rolled out in two-hundred-foot strips, and guaranteed to last forever. Or at least, Monsanto said, ten good years.

This was Riverfront Stadium, the new home of the Cincinnati Reds.

Pete was excited about the size of the new ballpark in the days before the Reds moved in. "They got fifty-two thousand seats sold," he told reporters after the last game at Crosley Field in June 1970. "That's going to be spectacular—just to see fifty-two thousand people at one time." He believed that playing there could help him personally. He thought that hitting balls on AstroTurf might add anywhere from ten to thirty points to his batting average as the ball skipped and rolled, and like everyone in Cincinnati he was thrilled about the season that the team was putting together. At the end of June, the Reds had the best record in baseball, all alone in first place in the National League western division, nine and a half games in front of the Dodgers.

But he was also sad about leaving Crosley Field. For him, the place was filled with memories going back to his childhood: the games he had attended there with his father; the time he had caught a foul ball there as a boy; his winter in the rail yard, dreaming of playing in the ballpark over his shoulder; his rookie season; Hutch; his mother and father smiling in the crowd; success; and finally the batting titles in 1968 and 1969. It had all happened here, at Crosley, and he was losing it while so many other changes were afoot.

After collecting more than two hundred hits in four of the past five seasons—and winning his back-to-back batting titles—Pete was barely batting .300 at the end of June. He wasn't meeting the high standards he had set for himself or earning the $105,000 the Reds had paid him. Meanwhile, Johnny Bench was establishing new standards and then blowing right past them. In just his third year in the majors, Johnny was on pace to hit fifty home runs—a mark that in the previous twenty years only Willie Mays had achieved in the National League—and it was helping to make Johnny even more of a fan favorite in Cincinnati. Just that month, he replaced Pete in right field for a couple of nights, and when Pete returned to his regular position, some fans chanted, "We want Johnny."

Pete laughed it off, but he found the chants embarrassing, and Johnny wasn't the only player having a better year than him. Tony Pérez was batting .356 at the end of June—forty-seven points higher than Pete—and Pérez was managing to do it while also hitting for power, something Pete never did. Pérez had more home runs than anyone else in the league, including Bench. Reporters were writing that Pérez was a threat to win the triple crown, one of the most elusive records in sports. He could finish the season with the highest batting average, the most RBIs, and the most home runs in the league.

Pérez shrugged off the idea, quiet and modest. It was still only June, and he had never hit the ball this well before. "I just think about winning the pennant," he said, his English improved since his days in Geneva. But even opposing pitchers admitted it was possible for Pérez to hit for the triple crown. Sometimes, that spring, they stood on the mound and watched his towering home-run balls sail out of the park.

In the dugout, the Reds' new manager, Sparky Anderson, felt spoiled by it all. He had never been affiliated with a team like this one. He loved the new stadium—"Everything is beautiful," Sparky said after moving in—and he was excited that his players wouldn't have to travel for the All-Star Game two weeks later in mid-July.

For the first time in nearly two decades, Cincinnati was hosting the big game. It would be held at Riverfront Stadium, and it would be a historic night in many ways.

The game, including the coaching staffs, would feature twenty-four future Hall of Famers. Bench would start at catcher, Pérez at third base, Rose would get invited to come as a reserve, and every baseball fan, including Richard Nixon, the president of the United States, wanted to be there. Down at Riverfront, fuses blew inside the new call center in late June as operators tried to answer phone calls for tickets, until there were no more tickets left to sell. The stadium was sold out, fifty-two thousand seats gone. And there was one more reason why it was important, one more reason why people would never forget the 1970 All-Star Game. It would change Pete Rose's life forever.

20

AS THE REIGNING two-time batting champion and a Cincinnati native, Pete could have gone to dinner with almost anyone the night before the All-Star Game that July: his teammates Johnny Bench and Tony Pérez; his old friend Frank Robinson, now with the Baltimore Orioles and back in town for the first time since he was traded away; or even the great New York Yankee who seven years earlier had helped coin his nickname, Charlie Hustle. Mickey Mantle, now retired, had moved into the broadcast booth, and like the rest of the baseball world he was going to be there in Cincinnati that week, calling the game for NBC. Instead, Pete extended a dinner invitation to a player on the Cleveland Indians, Sam McDowell.

McDowell was the opposite of Rose in many ways. He was a towering left-handed pitcher with a fastball that topped out at around a hundred miles per hour. The Oakland A's slugger Reggie Jackson called him "Instant Heat," and everyone else called him "Sudden" Sam—Sudden Sam McDowell—because his pitches were suddenly there, suddenly on you, and you were suddenly swinging, and you were suddenly out.

That alone made McDowell an odd friend for Pete Rose to choose. Pitchers were his enemies, and American League pitchers were the worst kind. In 1970, the National and American Leagues were true rivals that played only twice a year—at the All-Star Game and in the World Series—and players approached the midsummer contests as if they counted, even though the All-Star Game itself meant nothing. "This is *not* an exhibition," the National League president, Warren Giles, would snarl in the locker room, wherever the game was being played, the veins bulging in his ample neck. "You are here to win." And Giles didn't need to ask Pete twice. Pete would sit in the dugout and curse the AL players beneath his breath.

But it was hard for anyone to curse Sudden Sam. He was one of baseball's good-time guys, with stylish sideburns too long for Bob Howsam and the Cincinnati Reds, gorgeous hair combed up into a pompadour, and a fondness for Chivas Regal. The drinking would hasten the end of Sam's career in the years to come and force him to later concede that he was probably, in his words, "the biggest, most hopeless, most violent drunk in baseball." In the meantime, for now, everyone thought it made him a good bit of fun on a road trip. And so, even though Pete didn't drink, he liked Sam. The pair had become friendly during previous All-Star Games. Pete invited Sam and his wife to have dinner with him and Karolyn the night before the game in Cincinnati, and Sam accepted with one caveat: He had already made dinner plans with the other All-Star from the Cleveland Indians, his catcher Ray Fosse. Sam would come, he told Pete, if he could bring Fosse with him.

Fosse could barely believe his good fortune. He was twenty-three, newly married, playing in his first All-Star Game, and coming off a disappointing rookie year. In 1969, he had batted just .172 in limited playing time with the Indians, and he remained such an unknown in 1970 that his name didn't even appear on AL All-Star ballots. But the Indians had been counting on Fosse for years. They had made him the seventh pick in the 1965 draft and the first catcher off the board, impressed both with his size and with his arm. They were so impressed that they had taken him twenty-nine spots in front of Johnny Bench, and they were thrilled in 1970 that their faith in

Fosse finally appeared to be paying off. Heading into the All-Star break that year, Fosse was batting .312 with sixteen home runs—not Johnny Bench, but getting there. In McDowell's estimation, Fosse was the best catcher he'd ever seen and maybe the toughest one, too. Ray had once refused to come out of a game after a foul ball hit him in the ear and ripped off a piece of it. He was bloodied and hurting that day, but he was staying in.

The night began at Pete and Karolyn's house. The players and their wives made small talk over cocktails and soft drinks. Dinner followed at a popular restaurant on the river not far from Pete's childhood home on Braddock Street. Then they returned to Pete's house for a nightcap or two, with Sudden Sam playing the guitar that Pete never used. Everyone was having a good time. Fosse had lots of questions for Pete about Johnny Bench, and Sam behaved himself. He kept the Chivas Regal to a minimum, knowing that the AL manager, Earl Weaver, would be giving him the ball the next day. The stakes were too high.

The American League hadn't beaten the NL since 1962, the longest losing streak either league had ever endured. That needed to change; Weaver was public about it. But the National League players were equally determined to keep the streak going, and as usual Pete found a way to gain an edge the night before the game. He went to bed first, leaving it to Karolyn to get Sam, Ray, and their wives back to their hotel downtown.

Fifty-two thousand fans filled Riverfront Stadium the next night, and fifty million viewers tuned in to NBC to watch—the largest audience in All-Star Game history. Roughly half of American households had the game on, making it the single biggest show of the summer and the first seminal moment of the 1970s. People wanted to see the stadium's new AstroTurf, which looked oddly blue on their television screens. They were excited to catch a glimpse of President Nixon, who had a reserved seat near home plate amid a clutch of Secret Service agents, and everyone from the Secret Service agents to the fans was on alert for one particular threat—a stripper from the little town across the river where Cincinnatians liked to commit their sins: Newport, Kentucky.

Morganna Roberts wasn't just *any* stripper. She was twenty-three, bore a striking resemblance to Karolyn Rose, claimed she had been stripping since she was thirteen, and boasted that she was the highest-paid exotic dancer in the country, making $1,000 a week. In the previous year, she had started running onto baseball fields to kiss players in the middle of their games. Pete Rose was her first. "He cussed a lot," she reported, but not enough to dissuade her from kissing him that day or other players on the Braves, Dodgers, and Senators in the months to come.

Everyone knew she would be making an appearance at the All-Star Game in Cincinnati. Her employer in Newport across the river, the Galaxie Club, had been taking out ads in the local papers, promoting the scheme for weeks. The only question was, who would it be—the president; the commissioner of baseball, Bowie Kuhn; Johnny Bench; someone else? Stadium officials, Reds management, and Cincinnati police officers weren't inclined to find out. If Morganna was spotted on the premises, she was to be detained preemptively—an edict that stirred up even more publicity, pleasing Morganna. No matter what happened at the stadium, she was going to have another profitable night onstage at the Galaxie Club.

From the start, everything went poorly—for both security and the National League. Agents stopped the wrong woman at the gates of the stadium. Instead of apprehending Morganna, they detained Karolyn Rose, an embarrassment for everyone involved, and Morganna, who came in disguise wearing pants and dark Jackie O sunglasses, made it onto the field just as she had planned. In the top of the first, with Bench crouching behind the plate and Carl Yastrzemski batting, she leaped the wall halfway down the third baseline and sprinted toward them. But she never made it anywhere near Johnny or Yaz. An officer tackled her in foul territory.

Fans booed the police for interfering with the fun, and then, for two hours, people sat in their seats with little to cheer—or boo. For the bulk of the game, Morganna's failed kiss was the most exciting thing that happened. Sam McDowell pitched three scoreless innings. Ray Fosse scored the first run of the game in the sixth. The NL hitters were stymied all night, and in the ninth the American League was winning 4–1, needing just three outs to break its losing streak.

McDowell was done playing—showered, dressed, and sitting in the clubhouse, ready to fly home to Cleveland, when the comeback began. Jim "Catfish" Hunter, of the Oakland A's, gave up a home run to start the ninth and then a pair of singles. With the score now 4–2—and two men on—Earl Weaver pulled Hunter from the game and proceeded to trot out two more pitchers in the inning. But another run scored, and Roberto Clemente did the rest for the National League. He hit a sacrifice fly to tie the game 4–4.

In the visitors' clubhouse, McDowell and the other AL players who were out of the game and ready to leave were devastated. They had squandered their lead. The game was going to extra innings, and it showed no sign of ending anytime soon. The tenth was scoreless. The eleventh was, too. The American League stranded Yaz on second to end the top of the twelfth, and the National League seemed poised to go quietly in the bottom of that inning. Clyde Wright—a young pitcher for the California Angels with a southern accent, uncanny control, and a no-hitter to his name—induced groundouts from Clemente and the Cardinals catcher Joe Torre. There were two outs, and Pete Rose was up.

Pete was having a terrible night. In front of the hometown fans, the sold-out stadium, President Nixon, Karolyn, his parents Big Pete and Laverne, and the fifty million viewers watching at home on NBC—by far the largest crowd that had ever watched Pete play—he sat on the bench until the fifth inning, not playing at all, and once he got in the game, replacing Hank Aaron in the lineup, he did nothing. He walked in the sixth, struck out in the eighth, and struck out again in the ninth to end the inning, stranding Clemente on first. He dropped his bat in disgust, and when he got his chance in the twelfth, he turned to Fosse behind home plate and jokingly made a request. He asked Fosse to call for a pitch that he could at least foul off.

Wright fell behind in the count, two balls and no strikes. Then the Angels pitcher delivered a fastball inside, and Pete turned on it, slapping it to center field for a low, line-drive single. Pete was safe at first base, and it could easily have ended right there. The next batter, the Dodgers' infielder Billy Grabarkewitz, hit a ground ball toward third base, where Brooks Robinson was standing for the AL. It was a mismatch for the ages. Grabarkewitz was playing in his first All-

Star Game and would never be back again, and Robinson was the greatest third baseman to ever play the game. Bouncing balls didn't get past him. This one did. Robinson was playing Grabarkewitz off the line. The grounder slipped past his outstretched glove for a single and Pete moved over to second. He was now the winning run, 180 feet away, with two outs and the Cubs' Jim Hickman coming to the plate.

Hickman thought there was more to life than baseball, and his statistics proved it. He had a lifetime batting average of just .236 entering the 1970 season. He would play in just one All-Star Game in his career—this one—and he nearly missed it. Hickman had opted to fly in from Chicago that afternoon. The plane was delayed, beset by mechanical problems, and Hickman arrived so late that he couldn't even take batting practice. He was nervous under the lights at Riverfront and possibly better suited for his next job. Within a few years, Hickman would be growing soybeans in Tennessee. But when Wright served up yet another fastball inside, Hickman swung, and off the bat it was clear that the ball was going to fall for a hit in shallow center field.

On second base, Pete never saw it land. He did what he was supposed to do: he took off, running. With two outs, he was moving on contact. He locked in on his third-base coach—the Cubs' manager, Leo Durocher—and by the time Pete reached third base, he could see that Durocher wasn't just sending him home. The old manager was almost running there with him. Durocher was leading Pete down the line, waving his arms, and shouting.

"You gotta go. . . . You gotta go."

Pete had to score.

In the AL dugout, Earl Weaver thought it was all over. Pete was too fast, and his jump was too good. There seemed to be no way for anyone to throw him out at home. But the baseball skimmed across the stadium's new artificial turf like a skipping rock on a quiet lake—smooth and fast and true. Three perfect bounces into the waiting glove of Kansas City's center fielder Amos Otis, and Otis didn't hesitate. He came up firing.

Everyone in the stadium now realized that the play was going to be close: Karolyn; Pete's parents; Fosse's young wife; Richard Nixon; Sam McDowell; and Pete himself. He stole a quick glance over his left shoulder just as Otis collected the ball and then turned back toward the plate. He was halfway between third and home now, running flat out, fully committed. The throw was coming, and Ray Fosse, Pete's dinner companion from the night before, was straddling the third baseline a few feet in front of home. The young catcher—the next Johnny Bench, with millions of fans watching on TV and his peers, the future Hall of Famers, counting on him to make the tag—wasn't about to get out of the way. He stood his ground, placing his 215-pound frame between Pete and the plate. If Pete slides feetfirst, he takes Fosse out at the legs or never makes it home. If he tries to go around him, hook sliding, he could be out. The throw could beat him. And if he slides headfirst—Pete's signature move—it's probably the worst possible outcome. Pete breaks a collarbone. Maybe both collarbones.

Still, instinctively, Pete almost does it. Four steps before the plate, he begins to lean into his headfirst slide, chin going down, hands coming out. Then, seeing Fosse up close, he hesitates, thinks better of it, plants his right foot in the turf, changes course, and makes a different choice, the only choice left for Pete to make as he's bearing down on Fosse. He decides to lower his shoulder and barrel into Fosse standing up—a human spear, unleashed in the hot summer night. Both men fall to the ground, and Fosse rolls over. But since Otis's throw never lands in Fosse's glove, the call is easy for the umpire to make.

Pete is safe.

21

In the visitors' clubhouse, what McDowell would remember most was the silence that followed—ten seconds of silence while the American League players wrestled with the truth: they had lost to the NL again, their eighth loss in a row, and Fosse appeared to be hurt. The big catcher was slow to peel himself off the ground.

In the stands, Karolyn couldn't believe it. Pete had injured the nice man they'd had dinner with the night before, laying him out on his back on national television. Fosse's wife hurried down from the cheap seats to check on her fallen husband, and McDowell knew in an instant that something had to be wrong. Fosse wasn't the sort to seek extra attention by playing up an injury, and there he was at home plate, reaching for his left shoulder. Finally, with help, Fosse got up. He made his way to the clubhouse, and once he was there, the debate began: Did Pete really need to hit Fosse like that?

"Could he have gotten around you?" Frank Robinson asked Fosse in the locker room after the game, still wearing his uniform.

"Yeah," Fosse replied. "He could have slid and gotten his hand in."

Pete's old friend nodded. "He didn't have to do that to Fosse," Robinson told other AL players that night. Davey Johnson—the Orioles' second baseman who would one day lead a scrappy New York Mets team to the World Series as a manager—agreed. "I don't know if it was necessary to be that aggressive in a game that doesn't really mean that much," Johnson said. Frank Howard, a home-run hitter for the Washington Senators, stood with Robinson and Johnson, disapproving of Pete, and the Angels' pitcher Clyde Wright stood with them, too. "I was right there," Wright told reporters that night, "and I don't know why he had to hit him that hard." Like Robinson, he thought Pete could have slid around Fosse and avoided the collision altogether. "That dirty S.O.B. could have slid around Ray," Wright said.

But others defended Pete, including all three Hall of Fame managers involved in the game that night. The NL manager, Gil Hodges, called Pete's slide a "bulldog play." Durocher, who sent Pete from third, praised him for slamming into Fosse. "If Pete slides, he doesn't get there," Durocher said. "He had to hit him the way he did." And Earl Weaver agreed with both of them, even though the play cost Weaver the game. Fosse had done his job, Weaver said, and Pete had done his, too. Fosse was just exposed, the Cardinals' catcher Joe Torre said after the game, in the way catchers often are. "The catcher is vulnerable," Torre said. "He's waiting for the ball."

Even the Cleveland *Plain Dealer,* Fosse's hometown paper, sided with Pete. In an editorial that ran thirty-six hours after the game ended, *The Plain Dealer* wrote that Fosse was a local hero, but the paper said he invited the encounter by blocking the plate. "This left Rose with little alternative," the paper concluded, "but to run into and over the Cleveland catcher since the baseline belongs to the runner, and others infringe only at their own peril."

Perhaps most important, Fosse himself didn't seem to blame Pete for the play, at least not at first. Yes, he thought Pete could have slid around him. And yes, he was injured. His left shoulder hurt so much that he couldn't put his hand over his head. But X-rays that night at a Cincinnati hospital found nothing broken. Fosse was cleared to play when he returned to Cleveland, and in multiple interviews both after the game and in the days that followed, he indicated that Pete did the right thing. "If he had tried to slide," Fosse said in one interview, "I would have had the ball and had him." Pete would have been out. It just hurt, getting run over like that. "I tell you," Fosse said, "I've never been hit like that before."

It was only later that opinions began to shift on the matter. At least part of the reason for the change was that baseball itself was evolving into something different. In twenty years, by the 1990s, the All-Star Game would become so meaningless that multimillionaire players would leave early and fly home on private jets as soon as they were removed from the game. Managers now managed not to win but to get every player onto the field, and the game itself became a farce, with the low point coming in 2002. That July, the All-Star Game ended in a tie after the teams ran out of pitchers. In this new world, players, fans, and writers could not imagine why Pete Rose would have ever slammed into Fosse back in 1970, unless it was because of a character flaw. The play became evidence that something was wrong with Pete. He wanted to win too much.

Then, in 2011, another young promising catcher was injured after trying to block the plate during a regular season game. Buster Posey, the reigning Rookie of the Year for the San Francisco Giants, couldn't even walk off the field that night. He had a broken leg and three torn ligaments in his ankle, and before anyone even knew the extent of the injury, Posey's agent was calling for a rule change, directing his complaints to a man who'd seen the Rose-Fosse collision up close: the former Cardinals catcher Joe Torre.

The leader of on-field operations for Major League Baseball at the time, Torre was slow to implement any rule changes. He had defended Pete back in 1970, and he was not inclined to eliminate home-plate collisions now. With the game on the line, Torre said, nobody wanted to see a runner "politely slide" into home. But Torre was increasingly in the minority, and within a few years, he helped usher in a new rule. Going forward, no catcher could block the plate without the ball and no runner could deviate from his course to initiate contact with the catcher. To protect players and reduce the likelihood of concussions, the Rose-Fosse collision had been nearly litigated out of the game.

But the biggest reason why people began to change their minds about the play that ended the 1970 All-Star Game had to do with the men themselves. Both Pete Rose and Ray Fosse grew old in the public eye, and neither could ever outrun the moment. It was always at their heels, forever defining the two men, because of the fifty million people who watched the game that night and legions more who watched the replay again and again in the years to come. It was almost as if they were suspended in amber, tumbling into the dirt at home plate at Riverfront Stadium, inextricably linked and forever changed by one of the most iconic plays in baseball history. Nothing was the same for Pete or Fosse ever again.

Initially, Fosse received just as much praise as Pete. In the days after the All-Star Game, *The Sporting News* ran a long feature about the young catcher for the Cleveland Indians. *The Plain Dealer* declared, "A star is born . . . Fearless Fosse," and Indians fans predicted that one day baseball writers would be comparing Johnny Bench to Ray Fosse—not the other way around. But Fosse struggled for the rest of that season and, arguably, for the rest of his career. Having hit sixteen home runs before the break in 1970, he managed two more for the rest of the year, and he never hit more than twelve home runs in a single season ever again. Doctors had misdiagnosed his injury from the start.

Fosse admitted later that a second medical evaluation the following spring found evidence of a break and a separated left shoulder. He played through it because his manager wanted him on the field. Yet Fosse couldn't swing as he once had. The shoulder injury altered his follow-through, and it probably cost him his job in the end. The

Indians traded Fosse before the 1973 season. He was batting below .200 by 1974. He was out of baseball by the end of the decade, and by the 1990s he was upset with Pete Rose.

Fosse could have lodged any number of grievances against him. He could have been angry that Pete profited off the collision, growing his name recognition and brand on the merits of the play; that Pete worked autograph shows, getting paid to sign photos of him taking Fosse down; or that Pete made crass comments at times, like his statement that he had crashed into Fosse because he wasn't playing "girls' softball." But what irked Fosse the most was a different remark. In the late 1980s, Pete said he had hit Fosse because his father was in the stands that night and he didn't want to play "like a sissy" in front of him.

Fosse didn't get it. He didn't understand why the presence of Pete's father had anything to do with the collision at the plate in 1970, and his view of the play seemed to be changing with the times, too. At the twenty-fifth anniversary in 1995, Fosse called Pete's slide "uncalled for." At the thirty-fifth anniversary in 2005, he questioned why Pete had hit him at all—"I did not have the ball," Fosse said—and in 2015, the forty-fifth anniversary of the night in Cincinnati, Fosse remained upset.

It wasn't bitterness. Fosse had gotten the chance to play the game that he loved, and he had remained a part of it after he retired, working as a broadcaster for the Oakland A's for thirty-five years.

But he did have questions. Among other things, Fosse wondered how many home runs he might have hit if he had never met Pete Rose.

"Could I have hit thirty?" Fosse asked in 2015. "Could I have hit thirty annually?"

He'd never know.

For Pete, the opposite was true. Until the moment he knocked Fosse down, most Americans had never seen him swing a bat or run the bases. He was a star only in Cincinnati who elsewhere existed only in theory, in box scores, in sports magazines, and in the occasional newspaper story—especially in American League cities where the Reds never played. But this game was nationally televised, and the ending was exciting, so almost every fan saw the collision at home plate, either live or in replays. It became part of the American conversation in a way that's hard to appreciate today in a fractured media landscape where people rarely watch the same thing at the same time. It proved that Pete Rose always played hard. It made him relevant, a sensation, even. It *made* him Charlie Hustle, and it overshadowed everything else, including the great season the Reds put together in 1970.

Powered by Johnny Bench and Tony Pérez, Cincinnati ran away with its division that year. The Reds swept the Pirates to win the NL pennant, Pete's first, and then lost to the Orioles in the World Series in five games—a disappointment, but not a surprise. The Orioles were heavily favored to win, and Pete limped off into the winter, saying all the usual things. They were a good team, and they would be back. But if and when that happened, Pete wouldn't be the same person. The 1970s version of the man was coming into focus, and this version of Pete Rose was letting his hair grow. Instead of his crew cut, he had bangs, sideburns, more trouble off the field, pain, and a sense of his own mortality that crystallized in a single moment that December.

Pete was at his barbershop one morning getting his hair trimmed, when the phone rang. It was one of his sisters calling. She had tracked him down because she had news that couldn't wait and she needed to tell it to him now. Their father had felt ill at the bank and had gone home to the house on Braddock Street. He got on a city bus. He walked up the hill to the house. He climbed the steps to the porch and then crumpled to the wooden floorboards just inside the door. Big Pete was dead of a heart attack at age fifty-eight.

Pete spun across town, not believing the news. There was no way his father could be gone. He had just seen him. They were just talking. His father was the strongest man he knew, never a sissy, always there. But inside the house, Pete found only his mother, and she was sobbing. Authorities had already taken his father away, and the next time that Pete saw him, he was just a body laid out inside a casket in a funeral home on the West Side.

It was a Friday night, cold and cloudy, and Pete Rose could feel it.

A storm was coming.

ACT III
FAME

22

On Sundays in the fall, Alphonse Esselman's little brick ranch on Beechmeadow Lane on the West Side of Cincinnati appeared, to neighbors, like a tiny battleship. The rooftop was dotted with a forest of antennas. A tangle of wires stretched over the shingles and into the house, and the living room inside glowed with the flickering light of three different televisions. The TVs beamed in football games from across America, and Esselman watched in intense and almost mandatory silence. This was not fun; this was not relaxing. This was big business. Al Esselman was one of the best-known bookies on the West Side, with thousands of dollars riding on the games and a host of prominent clients to pay off, or collect from, on Tuesday morning, depending on how the games played out.

Settle-up day, as gamblers call it, is, for bookies, the most precarious day of the week. They need to track clients down, collect debts, pay off winnings, skim their 10 percent off the top, and somehow, in the end, come out ahead—a challenge for anyone and maybe especially Esselman. He was the son of German immigrants. His father died before he was born in the early 1920s, and he dropped out of school after eighth grade. But Esselman didn't need high school calculus to run his schemes. He had a natural affinity for numbers and a handsome swagger about him. When he smiled, his gray-green eyes twinkling, the man oozed confidence, because he knew he was beautiful and he knew what he was doing. For at least twenty years, he had been running illegal gambling operations in Cincinnati.

Esselman was probably first exposed to the practice in his childhood neighborhood, a small cluster of brick townhouses, hemmed in between the rail yards next to Crosley Field and the river on the edge of the West Side. Nick Grippo, a stocky Italian, ran a pool hall there at the corner of Eighth and State, and young Alphonse could be at the door of the establishment in a matter of moments, running from his home on St. Michael Street. It seemed as if nothing good ever happened at Grippo's. There were burglaries, fires, arrests, and bar fights of almost every variety, sometimes involving Grippo himself. He once stabbed a man in the abdomen on the streets of Cincinnati and got away with it.

Most important perhaps, Grippo's pool hall was crawling with gamblers, and it was here, more than likely, that Al Esselman wormed his way into the Cincinnati underworld. He learned how to run a sportsbook and other games of chance. He made connections with bettors as far away as Chicago, and by the early 1950s Esselman was running schemes for these bettors out of a series of local taverns that he owned or operated—the Lakewood Grill, the Turf Club, and the Jai Alai Piano Lounge. Esselman had become Nick Grippo—only he had style.

Esselman bought the finest suits; drove the newest cars; outfitted his wife in expensive furs; lavished his children with gifts; and held court at the Western Hills Country Club, where he was a member—a true sign of local status, though it was confusing for his oldest daughter, Jackie. If questioned at school about what her father did for a living, Jackie was supposed to say that she didn't know. And yet, if she got in trouble, she was told to make it clear that she was Alphonse Esselman's daughter. She could wear his name as a protective cloak. He'd always ask her, "Did you tell them who you were?"

By 1953, the Cincinnati vice squad was on to Esselman and raided his house on Beechmeadow Lane, storming in at the very moment Esselman was on the phone taking bets from a caller.

"What's all the fuss about?" he protested. "I'm just a small fry."

According to documents strewn across the room—and the vice squad's calculations—Esselman's business wasn't as small as he wanted them to believe. He was handling as much as $1,000 in action every day, and his conviction in 1954 apparently wasn't enough to stop him. He pleaded guilty, paid his fine, and was soon under surveillance again. Just seven years later, authorities were tailing Esselman once more, only this time it was undercover FBI agents in his rearview mirror, and this time, he was going away to federal prison for about eight weeks.

Esselman's wife, who played golf in the ladies' league at the Western Hills Country Club, was not pleased, and his daughter, Jackie, wasn't pleased, either. Her father's second arrest had come during the spring of her senior year in high school, and one of the nuns at her all-girls Catholic school had used the news to embarrass her, to shame Jackie in front of the class. *Look at Alphonse Esselman's daughter now.*

But Pete Rose didn't mind. Right around the time that Esselman returned from his stint in federal prison, Pete began hanging out with him at River Downs, betting on horses. Pete liked Esselman because the man knew his horses and, seemingly, every other sport, too. Esselman could talk about sports for hours, and sometimes when Pete had nothing better to do, he'd sit with Esselman at his office at a used-car lot on Glenway Avenue, across the street from a popular burger joint not far from West High.

The lot was Esselman's latest business venture, and possibly his newest front. At the car lot, Esselman took bets from his clients, and by the early 1970s, he had a new one: his friend Pete Rose. During football and college basketball seasons, Pete might bet with Esselman almost every night and certainly on Saturdays and Sundays in the fall, after baseball season was over. Pete was always more excited about watching games if he had a little action on them, and Esselman was happy to oblige. He could give Pete that thrill.

At home, especially on big football weekends, Pete disappeared into a room and watched games all day. Karolyn saw him when he emerged for snacks from time to time or for dinner, and throughout the day, she could hear him in there, shouting. "Plenty of time," he'd say, figuring spreads and probabilities in his mind. But it was almost as if he were gone, lost inside a world of his own making, a world that could destroy him. By consorting with Al Esselman and placing bets with him, Pete was violating a rule of baseball known by every player.

The gambling decree, known in baseball as Rule 21(d), wasn't adopted after the 1919 World Series when several members of the

Chicago White Sox took money to throw games to the Cincinnati Reds—the notorious Black Sox Scandal. The rule was first codified in 1927, after two new gambling secrets emerged about a pair of baseball icons and future Hall of Famers: Tris Speaker and Ty Cobb.

The first of these allegations was leveled by Cobb's former teammate Dutch Leonard in late 1926. Leonard claimed that Speaker, Cobb, and other players had met under the grandstand in Cleveland at the end of the 1919 season, agreed to fix the result of the next day's Tigers-Indians game to have the Tigers win, and then made a plan to bet on it. Leonard even produced a letter from Cobb that seemed to corroborate the shady deal—or, as Cobb called it in the letter, "our business proposition." A second allegation, made at the same time by a different player, suggested that fixed games might be more widespread than fans knew. This player claimed that in 1917, Cobb's Tigers had lost the final four games of the season to the White Sox in exchange for small, individual payments of $45 per man.

Cobb, baseball's all-time hit leader, and Speaker, the man who would soon claim the second spot on that list, resigned from their posts as player-managers in Detroit and Cleveland just weeks before the allegations made the newspapers, as if they knew something was coming. Then they denied everything. Cobb said his reference to the "business proposition" referred to Leonard's bet, not his own, and other players stepped forward to say the $45 payments in 1917 had nothing to do with throwing games, but with defeating the White Sox's rival, the Boston Red Sox, to win the pennant that year.

The money was a gift to the Tigers, the players said, not grift. They were rewarding Detroit for helping Chicago claim the AL crown. Either way, it looked terrible for baseball, and in defending himself, Cobb managed to make things worse. He said that while he himself didn't bet on the game in 1919, he was aware of Dutch Leonard's attempt to get a bet down. He said he helped connect Leonard with a team official who Cobb believed had connections with bookmakers. Cobb then added that it wasn't unusual for players to bet on themselves to win. "This isn't the first time," he said, "that there has been evidence of betting by baseball players."

Commissioner Kenesaw Mountain Landis—a former federal judge who had publicly committed himself to removing corruption from baseball—had to do something. But when Landis arranged to hold a series of hearings in Chicago in late 1926, Leonard declined to attend. And without Leonard's testimony, Landis went soft. He found a way to save Cobb, Speaker, and the other men implicated in the new allegations. Since they were seemingly already out of baseball—and since these allegations were nearly a decade old when they came to light—Landis said he was taking no action against them and instead used the opportunity to introduce a new gambling rule that would apply going forward. Under this rule—later known far and wide as Rule 21(d)—players faced suspensions if they bet with bookmakers and permanent banishment if they bet on games in which they played or managed.

Cobb and Speaker returned to the field weeks later. Both would play again in 1927, as if nothing had happened. But others wouldn't slip away so easily. In 1943, Bill Cox, the owner of the Philadelphia Phillies who had made his fortune in lumber, was the first to feel the sting of baseball's new gambling rules. Landis banished Cox for life after Cox admitted to placing fewer than two dozen "small, sentimental bets"—somewhere between $25 and $100—on the Phillies to win games that season. Landis died a year later, but his successor, A. B. "Happy" Chandler, a former U.S. senator from Kentucky, was similarly determined to keep the game clean. Chandler said he wanted to protect baseball "from hoodlums and hoodlumism," and one of his first acts was to suspend Leo Durocher, the man who would later wave Pete around third base at the end of the 1970 All-Star Game, because of Durocher's long-standing relationships with gamblers and mobsters.

Every spring, baseball officials gave presentations inside major-league clubhouses about the dangers of gambling. Players were told not to speak with bookies, not to hang out with them, not to be seen with them, and not to drink in bars with them, if they could avoid it, because a bookie with access put the game at risk and threatened all their livelihoods. A ninety-day suspension of yet another star in 1970—the Tigers' pitcher Denny McLain, the 1968 Cy Young Award winner and MVP—made it clear to current players that baseball remained willing to punish those who broke these rules, and the rule itself was plain for everyone to see, including Pete.

Rule 21(d) was posted in bold lettering on the door to the Reds' clubhouse at Riverfront Stadium. To get to his locker, Pete had to look at it every single day.

But Pete was convinced he would be fine. Sure, he was betting on basketball and football, but didn't everyone? Pete thought so. "Hell," he said later, "everybody bet on that." And anyway, Al Esselman was his friend. When Pete got behind on payments, Esselman carried him. He wasn't dogging Pete all over town, asking for his money, and he wasn't outing Pete for his transgressions, even though Esselman would have his chances to do just that.

In the early 1970s, the FBI began using informants to expose a bookmaking operation being run out of a bar in downtown Cincinnati that ultimately led to the arrests of seventeen men, including Esselman. He was going down again: arrested, arraigned, and facing yet another stint in federal prison. It was a moment when Esselman could have given up others to save himself, especially a famous client like Pete Rose. But such a thing would have been unlikely to happen back at Nick Grippo's pool hall in the 1930s, and it wasn't going to happen now on Beechmeadow Lane.

In late 1973, Esselman kept his silence. He pleaded guilty to the charges, as usual, and took his punishment without a word of complaint—five years' probation and a $10,000 fine. They couldn't stop him. He was going back to the underworld and to his used-car lot on the West Side. He was going back to taking Pete Rose's phone calls and taking his bets.

23

PETE SEEMED OBSESSED with money going into the 1971 season. He had gotten his $105,000 contract the year before. He wanted more, and for the first time, he brought help to the negotiating table to secure it. He showed up at the Reds' front office that February with Hy Ullner, his business partner from Hyde Park Clothes and the car dealership he shared with Johnny Bench near Dayton. Ullner, a shrewd negotiator and a likable man, explained that Pete wanted a multiyear deal and a 19 percent raise. He was asking for two years and $250,000.

Pete thought it was a reasonable request. After his slow start in 1970, he had helped lead the Reds to the World Series. He had batted .316 for the year; had led the league in hits; had compiled two hundred hits for the third season in a row; had earned his fifth All-Star selection; had knocked down Ray Fosse to win the game; had left Fosse there in the dirt, clutching his shoulder, hurt; had put fans in the seats at the new stadium; and had hustled. He was worth it, Pete thought, and he needed the money.

A hundred thousand dollars wasn't as much as most people thought. "You make $100,000," Pete said, "and you take home about $55,000." After bills, Karolyn's needs, and the kids, Pete figured he had just $20,000 in spending cash—less than $400 a week. Apparently, not enough. But this wasn't just about money; it was about principle. Carl Yastrzemski was getting a multiyear contract that month—three years and $500,000. If Yaz was worth half a million, then Pete believed he was worth at least $250,000. In fact, if anything, Ullner was offering Bob Howsam a bargain.

On any given day, Howsam ambled through the concourse of the stadium like a gentle bear, but he hadn't gotten this far in life making poor personnel decisions, and he wasn't about to start now. Simply put: there was no way he could pay Pete $250,000. For starters, Howsam had to pay Johnny Bench and Tony Pérez, two players who were arguably more important to the Reds' success in 1970 than Pete, and both of those men were demanding six-figure contracts. Bench, the National League MVP in 1970, wanted Yaz money—three years and $500,000—while Pérez was asking for $110,000. Howsam couldn't pay them and also Pete. He also wondered if Pete even deserved a raise at all.

Howsam didn't like that Pete played basketball all winter, barnstorming across the city and the Ohio River valley to play games in small arenas for extra money with a hand-selected group of teammates who included Johnny Bench; Tommy Helms; the Reds' starting center fielder, Bobby Tolan; and their starting first baseman, Lee

May. Sooner or later, Howsam thought, one of them was going to get hurt, and it seemed as if it could be Pete.

In early negotiations with Ullner that winter, Howsam used the word "plateaued." He said that Pete had "plateaued," and a second front-office executive suggested in the press that Howsam was being too nice about things. This executive hinted that maybe Pete was already in decline and suffering "down" years. After all, .316 wasn't a great average for the Reds' leadoff man. It was nineteen points lower than what Pete had hit in 1968, and thirty-two points lower than his average in 1969. By baseball definitions Pete wasn't even young anymore. That spring, he was turning thirty.

Neither Pete nor Karolyn could believe what they were reading in the papers and what they were hearing reported back to them from Ullner. The Reds had put their son, Petey, just fifteen months old, on the cover of the team media guide that winter—and now they were taking shots at his dad in the papers? Karolyn joked that she wanted residuals for Petey while Pete simmered and boiled. He had bickered with the Reds over his salary in the past, but this felt different. In the span of a few months, he had lost the World Series and he had lost his father, and now he was just lost—genuinely hurt by Howsam and the Reds. While Pérez finally signed for far less than what he wanted that winter and Bench did too, Pete held out for more money deep into March, stewing inside his house on the West Side and threatening to stay there forever.

He didn't understand how Bench could get a pay increase while he got nothing. "You figure that out," Pete told the press. He couldn't process the notion that anyone might think he was in decline, and he wasn't going to apologize for batting .316. "Sure, my batting average dropped thirty-two points—like they keep telling me," Pete said that winter. But .316 was still good enough for the ninth-highest batting average in the league. That sort of play deserved to be rewarded, Pete believed, and it demanded more than $105,000. He vowed, again and again, not to report to camp unless Howsam came to him with a better deal. He would stay home, Pete said, and stay busy with other work: at Ullner's clothes company, at the car dealership, or at a new and popular bowling alley he also shared with Bench in the suburbs.

"I'll sit here," Pete said, "and I'm serious."

No one believed him—least of all Karolyn. At home in Cincinnati, she made plans to pack up the kids and go to spring training without Pete. Long gone were the days when she was socially ostracized by the other players and their spouses. She was the leader of the wives now, their "Big Momma." She wasn't going to miss out on all the fun on the pool deck at King Arthur's Inn, the Tampa motel where the Roses and other families stayed every year. She wasn't going to cancel the trip because Pete was sore over Howsam's offer, and finally around mid-March, Pete crumbled. He flew to Florida in a slick green suit he'd picked up at Ullner's shop and signed a contract with a token raise of about $1,400. It was yet another insult, nickels and dimes thrown on the floor to appease a recalcitrant star, but at least it was over. Pete was back with the team. Bruised and bitter, but himself again. He was even gambling.

Just before his first spring training game against the Kansas City Royals in Fort Myers late that March, Sparky Anderson offered Pete a friendly wager. He bet him a steak dinner that he wouldn't get a hit in his first at bat. Pete had missed too much time. He was a little overweight, and he was wearing a tight rubber slicker beneath his uniform to help him shed the extra pounds in the Florida heat. None of this would seem to help Pete swing. Still, he accepted Sparky's wager, strolled to the plate to start the game, and stepped into the box to face a right-hander whom the Royals had acquired in the offseason, Bruce Dal Canton.

Dal Canton had enjoyed some success against Pete while pitching for the Pittsburgh Pirates in recent years. But he had struggled the previous season especially with his curveball, and he quickly fell behind in the count to Pete—three balls and no strikes.

Pete stepped out of the box to shout something at Sparky in the dugout.

"The bet's off if I walk," he cried.

Then he stepped back in and crushed Dal Canton's 3-0 offering to center field for a single. The steak dinner was his, and Pete had hardly rounded first base when he demanded that Sparky buy the meal with his own money.

"None of that expense-account stuff," Pete said.

—

The moment seemed to bode well for the Reds. The star players were all back, and Pete was angry. His goals in prior seasons had been to collect two hundred hits, hit .300, and score one hundred runs. Now, feeling spurned by the front office, he wanted more. "I've got to get two hundred and twenty-five hits, hit .350, and score one hundred and thirty runs," he said. Even Sparky, who was prone to dark bouts of pessimism, felt good. The baseball writers had picked Cincinnati to return to the World Series.

Instead, the team struggled from the first pitch. At the end of April, Pete was batting .238, and Bench and Pérez were doing even worse. At Riverfront, fans began to boo, and Bench antagonized them by tipping his cap sarcastically when their ire rained down on him.

Then, in early May, it got worse: Bobby Tolan—the Reds' center fielder and the league's stolen base leader in 1970—suffered an Achilles tendon injury while warming up before a game at Dodger Stadium. Tolan had first tweaked the tendon over the winter while playing on Pete Rose's basketball team—the team that Howsam wanted to disband—and now Tolan was out for the year as a result. To replace him, Howsam sent two minor leaguers to San Francisco for a young outfielder from Alabama named George Foster—a move that Howsam appreciated in the moment, but that almost no one noticed as the offense continued to sputter all summer.

"I can feel my stroke coming," Pete muttered to himself during one batting practice in late July. He must have seen two hundred pitches that day as he tried to get things right, swinging and swinging, until his hands blistered and almost bled.

"I can feel my stroke coming," Pete said again.

Only this time, it never did. He finished the season with one of the lowest batting averages of his career—.304. He fell eight singles short of two hundred hits, didn't score one hundred runs, and, worst of all, didn't make the playoffs. The Reds finished in fourth place in their division, four games under .500 and eleven games out of first.

In his office overlooking home plate, Howsam sat in a massive chair behind a big wooden desk with a lot to think over: the troubled offense in 1971; the lack of power and hits; and the state of his star players—Rose, Bench, Pérez, and Helms. It was fair to wonder if perhaps Pete and Johnny had too much going on off the field. The pair had their car dealership and their bowling alley, and Bench seemed to be adding more by the day. He was appearing in new commercials for Gillette razors and had started hosting his own weekly television show, *MVP: Johnny Bench.*

"TV, glamour, all that stuff can take a young man's mind away from his business," one National League manager speculated that year. Howsam agreed. But the team's struggles in 1971 gave Howsam one thing that he liked: leverage. He signed his stars to discount contracts that offseason; there'd be no holdouts going into 1972. He got Pete to agree that he'd stop playing basketball all winter on his traveling Reds squad; from now on, Pete would only coach the team. Howsam cut Bench's salary, and Pérez's too, and neither man complained. The Reds' general manager then oversaw the creation of new rules that would be enforced by Sparky Anderson in the spring: any player reporting to Tampa overweight would be docked $50 per pound. He dispatched nearly one-third of the roster to play winter ball and convened an emergency meeting with Sparky to find out if he had any other suggestions that could help return the team to the playoffs.

Sparky told Howsam that the Reds needed a healthy Tolan in the lineup next year; the best version of Johnny Bench; more relief pitching; and a philosophical overhaul. It was as if they had been built to win at Crosley Field, not Riverfront Stadium. Home runs in the old park had become fly-ball outs in the new one, and Sparky thought his players were too slow for the AstroTurf. In order to compete, he wanted more speed, and he had an idea where Howsam might find it. Houston, Sparky said. The Houston Astros.

It was time to make another trade.

24

Joe Morgan had come to loathe almost everything about being a Houston Astro.

He hated losing, and the Astros lost a lot. He hated the fact that a prominent country club in town refused to let him play golf with one of his white teammates, because Morgan was Black. He hated the idea that he was wasting his talents playing for a lackluster team in a dome stadium that was nearly empty most nights, and he hated his manager most of all. Harry Walker—a former NL batting champion and a white southerner with a brother named Dixie—had once been a member of the 1947 St. Louis Cardinals squad that had allegedly threatened not to play if Jackie Robinson stepped on the field at Sportsman's Park.

Morgan's simmering feud with Walker was hardly a secret, and it hurt Morgan's reputation around the league. Some sportswriters called him "a troublemaker," and this term, along with Morgan's .263 career batting average, would have been enough to scare away most teams, including the Reds. Cincinnati hardly had a reputation for diversity and inclusion—a lesson that Frank Robinson had learned in the 1960s and that Bobby Tolan, another Black player, would soon learn. The Reds traded him away in 1973 because they thought him disgruntled and angry, too radical. Tolan was growing a beard.

But Sparky was willing to take a chance on Morgan. The Astros' second baseman swung left-handed, and Sparky needed another lefty in the lineup. Morgan had the speed the Reds wanted; in the past three years in the National League, only Lou Brock, a future Hall of Famer, had taken more bags than Morgan. He also had power. For a man who was just five feet seven and 155 pounds, Morgan hit a surprising number of home runs, and recency bias probably played a role in Sparky's thinking. That September, in six meaningless games against the Reds, Morgan batted .369 and hit a walk-off home run to win the final game for the Astros. Almost nobody in Houston saw it; the Astrodome was nearly empty that night, as usual. But Sparky certainly remembered it. With the victory that night, the lowly Astros had managed to pass the Reds in the NL West standings.

Howsam went straight to work, starting conversations with the Astros during the World Series in October 1971. While the Orioles and Pirates played the games, he worked over Houston's general manager at a Holiday Inn in Baltimore, and the two men met again a month later at the winter meetings at a resort in Scottsdale, Arizona.

By then, everyone had heard the rumors of a possible trade, the players included, and Scoops Lawson pressed Sparky for the truth that day over a cup of coffee at the resort. But Sparky couldn't tell Scoops what was really happening. He needed to tell Pete Rose first.

The Reds were about to acquire five players from the Astros—third baseman Denis Menke, pitcher Jack Billingham, center fielder César Gerónimo, minor-league prospect Ed Armbrister, and second baseman Joe Morgan—in exchange for three guys in Cincinnati. The Reds were sending the Astros a reliable utility man, their starting first baseman, Lee May, and their starting second baseman—Pete's good friend—Tommy Helms.

Helms took the news with his usual country-boy smile. Reached by the press at his home in North Carolina that afternoon, he picked up the phone, saying, "This is Tommy Helms, of the Astros." He didn't want to be traded, but he wasn't going to cry about it, either. He'd go to Houston, he said, and looked forward to beating the Reds in 1972. Almost everyone else took a different approach, railing against both Howsam and the deal.

At the local papers, mail poured in, two to one against the trade. *The Cincinnati Enquirer* called Howsam "Smilin' Bob, your friendly used player dealer," and the beat writers piled on. Statistically speaking, Helms was the best defensive second baseman in the league, and Lee May was the Reds' most consistent slugger. Over the past three seasons, May had hit more home runs than any other Cincinnati Red, including Johnny Bench. If the Reds were going to part with a power hitter and a corner infielder with defensive limitations, some people argued it should have been the third baseman Tony Pérez. Maybe the Reds just wanted to off-load salaries to save money, fans speculated. Maybe they were just being cheap again, or maybe Howsam had engineered the trade for a different reason.

"Do you realize what you've done?" Pete asked Sparky when he first heard the news. "You've just traded away two-fifths of my basketball team."

The criticism was hard for Howsam to bear that winter because he believed in what he had done. He thought César Gerónimo had the tools to be a great outfielder. He argued that the Reds had improved their infield defense with the trade. Pérez could now move to first base—his natural position—and the newly acquired Denis Menke could play third. And then there was the player he had coveted from the start: Joe Morgan. "Joe stole forty bases last season," Howsam told the press. "That's just nineteen less than the total stolen by all of the players on our club."

There was just one problem: Morgan wasn't sure how he felt about the trade. He wondered if Harry Walker had banished him to Cincinnati. He heard from a Black teammate that racial discrimination was prevalent in the city, especially on the Kentucky side of the river, and like the fans Morgan questioned Howsam's thinking. He couldn't believe the Reds' general manager had traded Lee May. "I was sorry to hear that May went to Houston," Morgan told reporters. "I had always wanted to play on the same club as him."

Sparky was worried enough about Morgan that he put in a request with the Reds' clubhouse attendant before spring training started. He wanted Morgan to get a locker right next to Pete Rose's. Sparky figured if Pete had his eye on Joe, then the Reds' new second baseman wouldn't cause any trouble.

It was an ironic concern in hindsight. Around that time, Pete was already placing bets with bookies, hanging around Al Esselman at the racetrack and at his car lot on the West Side, but it was Morgan who was setting off alarm bells in Sparky Anderson's mind. It was Morgan who was fielding tough questions from the Cincinnati beat writers that winter. He had hardly digested the news about the trade when the local press started asking him if it was true that he was difficult and if it was true that he was a problem.

No, Morgan replied. They had it all wrong.

"I'm not a troublemaker," he said.

25

PETE ROSE LET himself go that winter, doing whatever he pleased, in full revolt against Bob Howsam, the Reds, their many expectations, and their never-ending rules.

Pete hated not playing basketball on his winter squad, so he started again. On the night that Howsam dealt Lee May and Tommy Helms to Houston, Pete dug out his pin-striped, snug-fitting, No. 14 basketball jersey and took to the floor against a team of high school teachers in rural Indiana, about an hour away. Pete said he was playing only because his team needed a fifth player that night, but he continued playing basketball throughout the winter, despite what he had promised. He also made his presence known on the streets of Cincinnati by purchasing the most ostentatious vehicle possible: a gleaming white 1970 Mangusta, a rare Italian sports car, with deep-red carpeting, black-leather seats, scissor-swing doors, and sleek lines. From the road to the roof, the Mangusta was only forty-two inches tall.

Pete wasn't sure how fast the car went—"The speedometer," he explained, "is in Italian"—and he had problems navigating even basic functions. The engine was in the back and the trunk was in the front, and one day, shortly after buying the Mangusta, he opened the trunk door into his chin, slicing it wide open. It didn't matter. Pete looked good in the car. That winter, he grew his hair long, sprouted a bushy goatee to cover his facial wound, and added one more element of flair. On at least one occasion—at a party at Al Esselman's country club in Western Hills, celebrating Cincinnati sports—Pete wore round, wire-rim glasses that made it hard for Bob Howsam to recognize him in the crowd as he gave a speech in the front of the room. It was as if Pete were trolling Howsam, and the fans at the party that night were in on the gag. When Howsam asked from the podium if Pete was still out there, fans shouted no.

"He's gone to Houston," one man hollered.

"He's playing basketball," said another.

But Howsam could play this game, too. At a different banquet that winter, the Reds' general manager dangled $2 in front of Pete while he spoke in front of a packed room in Cincinnati, and told Pete to use the money to get a shave and haircut.

"I knew there was a way to get a raise out of you," Pete said.

The crowd laughed that night at the banquet, though sometimes they weren't sure if they should. On the dinner circuit that winter, there was a hard edge to Pete that felt different. At the event in Cincinnati, reporters noted that Pete took the money that Howsam dangled in front of him. He folded the dollar bills and placed them in his pocket. He was keeping Howsam's cash, and he was making jokes that cut a little too close to the truth to be funny, especially when it came to Johnny Bench.

Like Pete, Johnny grew a mustache that winter, and like Pete he had reasons to bristle at the Reds' management. Johnny thought it ridiculous that Sparky wanted him to get down to two hundred pounds by spring training. But as soon as he signed his new contract that offseason, accepting Howsam's pay cut, the Reds' catcher shaved. If he was going to be a ballplayer, Bench said, he thought he should appear like one, and the clean-shaven look was probably best for his other engagements. Bench was playing golf in Puerto Rico, Hawaii, and California in televised celebrity events that featured Bob Hope, Jack Nicklaus, Joe Namath, Frank Sinatra, and Dean Martin, among others. He was lowering his handicap to an impressive six, and he was developing a new philosophy for life: "Live hard, die young, and make a good-looking corpse." The emphasis was on "good-looking," because wherever Bench went, young women were there, and the lucky ones got to see him, tanned and shedding pounds for Sparky, in his new three-story condominium in a complex overlooking the Ohio River in the hipster, East Side neighborhood of Mount Adams.

The complex, called the Cloisters, was only about ten miles from the West Side establishments where Pete could usually be found on Glenway Avenue. But it felt like a distant planet, orbiting another sun. Bench parked in a private driveway; left his car with an attendant; gave interviews on a balcony looking down at the river; entertained in a designer-curated living room ensconced in velvet, shag carpet, and chrome; listened to music on a hi-fi stereo in a loft decorated with large pillows—only pillows; read *Playboy* magazine in his den in front of a wall of trophies illuminated with recessed lighting; slept in a bed covered in black fur; and took his calls on a white Princess telephone while gazing out the windows at the city—his city.

"Conceited? No, I'm not," Bench told visitors. He was still the boy from Oklahoma who had grown up pulling cotton and dreaming of one day playing baseball. He was just proud of his condo at the Cloisters. And by early 1972, Bench finally had more time to spend there. Under pressure from the Reds to eliminate his outside interests and rediscover his home-run swing, the catcher had opted to keep his weekly television show, *MVP: Johnny Bench,* and he was still going to play golf. But he would sell his stake in the car dealership and the bowling alley, the businesses he shared with Pete—a decision that effectively ended Pete's involvement, too. Just like that, it was all gone. The bowling alley changed hands. The car dealership got a new name, and Pete's attempts to joke about it one night that winter didn't go well.

"Johnny had a bad year," Pete cracked, "and it cost me two businesses."

He made the comment on a Saturday night at the end of January 1972 at a banquet at the Netherland Hilton downtown. A thousand people there, including Johnny, and the remark fell on the room "like icy rain," one reporter said. Even the newest Red, Joe Morgan, knew something was wrong when he arrived in Cincinnati that month. He felt the divide between the two men, Pete and Johnny, and he believed it ran far deeper than any concerns that Pete might have had about bowling alleys and cars. It seemed to be about ego, about how each man was perceived and received, and about how each man viewed himself.

That winter, at age twenty-four, Johnny was already talking about retiring. He'd like to make $1 million a year, he said, and then walk away, maybe even before he turned thirty. He could think of lots of things he'd like to do besides baseball. Pete, on the other hand, almost was thirty-one, and couldn't think of anything better than the game. He wanted to play forever, keep hitting forever, never grow old, never stop swinging, never go home.

Players would have to choose sides. They would have to choose between Pete and Johnny. Morgan was told he couldn't be friends with both.

26

PETE REPORTED TO spring training on the last day of February with a fresh haircut, a clean shave, and a gash over his right eye. He had suffered the injury at a racetrack in northern Kentucky a few days earlier after an evening of gambling. Leaving the track, Pete had opened a glass door into his face. The wound was an annoyance more than anything. Pete was scheduled to film a commercial in Miami that week, and a doctor would have to go to work on the gash, cleaning it up with twelve tidy stitches. It was also the first of many surprises that spring.

As soon as Pete arrived in Tampa, Sparky Anderson called him to his office to discuss a personnel problem. With César Gerónimo, acquired from Houston in the Joe Morgan trade that winter, and George Foster, picked up by Howsam the previous summer, Sparky had too many outfielders, and he wanted to know if Pete would change positions again and move from right field to left. Pete agreed. "It's okay with me," he said. "There's no problem."

But in left field, that March in Tampa, Pete struggled at the plate, batting .170, and he and Johnny Bench continued to exchange cold barbs. At one point that spring, Pete made a comment suggesting that it would be great if Johnny started hitting home runs again. Johnny turned to Pete and said, "You just get your two hundred hits." And off the field, Bob Howsam couldn't stop thinking about a different source of tension: Curt Flood, the former St. Louis Cardinal who had sued baseball in 1970 to end the reserve clause; Curt Flood, who was trying win free agency for himself and every other ballplayer; Curt Flood, who was hoping to change everything.

The Flood case had been hanging over the sport for two years now, slowly making its way to the U.S. Supreme Court. Justices in Washington would hear Flood's case in 1972, and no matter the outcome, baseball owners knew they would have to make concessions to the players. The union chief, Marvin Miller, wasn't going to quit fighting for free agency; Miller wasn't even sure he wanted *this* season to start. The players' pension plan no longer reflected the influx of big-time television money, and on the last day of March, for the first time in baseball history, player union reps voted to go on strike. The vote was 47–0.

Howsam was furious. Front offices around the league were paying players more than ever before, money that old-timers like Hank Aaron had never thought they would see. When Aaron came up with the Milwaukee Braves nearly twenty years earlier, he had hoped to one day make enough money to buy a new Pontiac. Now Pete had the white Mangusta, Bench had his lavish bachelor pad, Aaron was making $200,000 a year, and a few dozen players, including four members of the Reds—Rose, Bench, Pérez, and Morgan—were closing in on Aaron and planning to blow right past him.

With the clubhouses locked, the players scattered. Some went home, some went to Cincinnati, some stayed in Tampa, some worked out in small groups with buckets of borrowed baseballs, and others didn't. At the low point of the dispute, Pete was spotted at both the union meetings in Cincinnati and the racetrack in northern Kentucky, prompting one reporter to joke that the Reds' star was staying in shape by walking to the betting windows. Finally, after thirteen days, the two sides struck a deal: owners would add half a million dollars to the players' pension fund, far less than what the players had wanted, and the season would begin the next day with no makeup games and no back pay, either. Pete was out about $5,000—and even more if he factored in the cost to his reputation. During the strike, fans had sided with the owners, and at opening day at Riverfront Stadium in Cincinnati they let the players know it. They booed Johnny Bench and threw objects at Pete Rose. As he stood in left field, his new position, he felt two oranges come whistling past his head.

The Reds lost the opener to the Dodgers that day, 3–1, and then continued to lose, falling into last place in their division. It was early in the season—"plenty of time," as Pete liked to say—but it didn't feel like it. The locker room in Cincinnati was quiet while in Houston the Astros surged into first place, powered by the two men whom Howsam had shipped there over the winter: Tommy Helms and Lee May. In the press box early on, the reports kept coming in over the wire: *"Home run for Lee May, Houston . . . Home run for Lee May, Houston."*

Sparky Anderson was working himself into a dark cloud of doubt, and reporters were already there. They had predicted this; now it was happening. The Reds were as dysfunctional as their new $1.3 million scoreboard hanging in the outfield at Riverfront Stadium. The electronic monstrosity flickered on and off all spring—a ghost in the machine, broken. According to the manufacturer, there was "a massive malfunction in the computer." It was a perfect metaphor for the young season. But at least one man wasn't worried. Pete didn't care that the scoreboard had gone dark; that the Reds were in last place; that he was batting .240; or that fans were throwing oranges at his head in left field.

"Give me two weeks," Pete said.

In the face of all evidence to the contrary, he thought his bat—and the Reds—were about to get hot.

27

THE COMEBACK BEGAN after a Wednesday afternoon loss to the Chicago Cubs around the middle of May, the Reds' fourth loss in a row.

While other players showered, dressed, and prepared to leave for the night, Pete asked Sparky for permission to do some extra hitting on the field. The next day, the Reds were off and Sparky had already scheduled a mandatory workout for the morning. But Pete didn't want to wait. The weather was good right now. Sparky waved him out of his office. Groundskeepers rolled the batting cage out to home plate, and Pete ducked his head out of the clubhouse to tell Karolyn that she should go home without him.

"I'm gonna do some hitting," he informed her.

In the cage, as he swung, Pete talked to himself.

"That's outta here. . . . Base hit. . . . Double. . . . I seen that one. . . . C'mon." If he thought he missed on a pitch, he was hard on himself. "Habits, bad habits." And when the coach on the mound exhausted his washtub full of baseballs, Pete called for more and it started all over again. "Gotta stay aggressive," he said. "C'mon, get the top of the ball."

By this time, Pete had a small audience. The groundskeepers, who couldn't do their jobs until Pete went home, sat in the dugout. An assistant coach stood on the first baseline, and George Foster had returned to the field, too. Foster was playing cutoff man in the outfield and bringing baseballs back to the mound. More washtubs, more time. Pete hit and hit until the coach couldn't throw anymore. Then, since Foster had helped him, Pete offered to assist Foster. Pete could stay, he said, and throw batting practice to him.

Foster looked at him, hesitant. As a young Black player on his former team in San Francisco, Foster had learned to stay quiet—and stay with other Black players. He didn't want to inconvenience Pete. And he knew that he and Pete were different in ways that went much deeper than the color of their skin. Foster liked to hold Bible study classes in the stadium on Sundays, small gatherings that never interested Pete Rose. But Pete was serious about throwing to Foster. Foster accepted the offer. Pete started throwing pitches to the young outfielder and began talking to Foster as he had just talked to himself.

"Attaboy," Pete said, as Foster swung. "Go get it. . . . Bye-ah."

Fifty years later, Foster would still remember the day because no star had ever treated him like that before, especially not a white star. Foster was hitting home runs, and Pete's washtub was soon empty. They needed more baseballs, and the groundskeepers were still just sitting there, waiting. But Pete wanted Foster to know that he was in no hurry to leave.

"Want another bucket?" he asked Foster.

"If you got it," Foster said.

"If it will help you," Pete said, "I got it."

The Reds beat the Cardinals that Friday night; swept the four-game weekend series from St. Louis; reeled off five more wins; put together a nine-game winning streak; and began to climb in the standings, gaining ground on the Astros.

Once anxious to start the season, the newly acquired Joe Morgan began to hit. By the end of May, Morgan had seven home runs, and Bench was right there with him. Sparky could see it: Johnny was returning to his old MVP form while Pete was finding new ways to win. In one close game in San Francisco that month—with a man on second base and the Giants trying to issue Pete an intentional walk to set up a double play—Pete realized the pitcher was leaving the ball too close to the outside corner and made a snap decision on the fourth intentional ball. He reached across the plate and slapped the ball toward the unsuspecting third baseman, who had just been called up from Triple-A. The young man was stunned. The winning run came around to score, and the Reds were on their way to Houston for a four-game series that suddenly felt like everything. With a sweep, Cincinnati could tie Houston for first place—a fact that everyone on the team plane that night understood, but no one dared say out loud. All Sparky would concede was this: "I think we can beat them."

Over the next four nights, the Reds outscored the Astros 40–15, won all four games, claimed their share of first place, and proved they were willing to fight for it. With two outs and nobody on in the last inning of the last game in Houston, a Cincinnati reliever walked an Astros batter by firing a fastball at his head. The benches cleared twice, and police officers finally had to intervene to clear the field.

The Houston players had misjudged the moment and themselves. They weren't beating Cincinnati. They weren't beating Pete Rose. They couldn't compete with a team that had Rose, Bench, Pérez—and Morgan. "This *must* be a Big Red Machine," Morgan said in Houston. The Reds pulled away from the Astros all summer, won the division, and defeated the defending-champion Pittsburgh Pirates to claim the NL pennant that fall. Pete Rose batted .450 against the Pirates in the playoffs. Johnny Bench hit an opposite-field home run in the ninth inning of the decisive game five, when the Reds were trailing by one and the season felt like it was slipping away, and George Foster scampered home minutes later to win the game—and the pennant—in the unlikeliest of fashions: on a walk-off wild pitch.

In the postgame celebration on the turf at Riverfront Stadium that night, Pete jumped up and down like a little boy in his black cleats. He was going back to the World Series, and Major League Baseball was intent on doing everything it could that October to keep the focus on the games. When it emerged that month that federal agents had raided the home of a popular maître d' in Baltimore's Little Italy—and discovered betting records in his house, including a notebook containing the names of eleven American League umpires—baseball officials and local authorities buried the story.

It was a minor item, they said. A closed case.

Nothing would come of it.

28

TELEVISION EXECUTIVES WEREN'T sure how they felt about the still new and expanded baseball playoffs. Into the early 1970s, NBC didn't even televise every game, often choosing to air a regular-season Sunday afternoon football game over playoff baseball. With the Reds-Pirates series in 1972, that began to change.

Nearly a quarter of a million people attended the games in Pittsburgh and Cincinnati—a new playoff record—and in Cincinnati, after the Reds' victory in game five, most fans didn't even go home. They gathered on Fountain Square, two blocks north of the stadium, and shut down city streets. For hours, no cars could pass between Fourth and Sixth, Race and Walnut—not even the Pirates' team bus parked outside the Netherland Hilton. Fans sat on top of the bus, drinking beer and dreaming. They wondered whom the Reds might play in the World Series—the Detroit Tigers or the Oakland A's—and finally decided it didn't matter. The Reds would win, either way.

Pete Rose agreed, and so he didn't care when the A's won the next day in Detroit and hopped directly onto a plane to Cincinnati. He couldn't wait for them to arrive. "We want people to see how good we are," he told reporters. In Pete's estimation, the Reds had the stronger hitters, the faster runners, the bigger stars, and the better stats, and they had compiled those stats while playing in the superior league. The AL had lost six of the last nine World Series and ten of the last twelve All-Star Games—and this particular collection of American Leaguers, the A's, looked more like a beer-league softball team than a major-league franchise.

They wore awful white cleats, garish yellow jerseys, bright green hats, and long hair—the antithesis of what Bob Howsam had been building in Cincinnati in every way. To Howsam's horror, the A's owner, Charlie O. Finley, had even encouraged his team to sprout bushy mustaches. Finley had offered each player $300 to grow one that season so that he could hold "Mustache Day" at Oakland Coliseum in June. Under the promotion, mustachioed men attending the game with a friend got in for free. This was not a serious ball club or a legitimate threat to win the World Series. When the A's landed in northern Kentucky and the door of their team plane opened onto the tarmac, the smell of champagne wafted out into the night. Oakland was still partying.

But Finley was a wily character, much smarter than anyone wanted to admit. In the last month of the season, he had dispatched an old scout to follow the Reds everywhere, sit behind home plate at games, gather intelligence on the team, and come up with a plan to beat Cincinnati—just in case. The night before the series started, this scout met with Finley and the A's manager, Dick Williams, inside Finley's hotel room near Fountain Square and delivered a treatise on how to defeat the team that everyone was picking to win the World Series. Keep Pete Rose and Joe Morgan off the bases, the scout said. Don't let them bunt. Make them swing. Then frustrate the Reds' top of the order with good pitches—up and away, low and in. Finally, no matter what, don't pitch to Johnny Bench. When in doubt, walk Johnny.

Finley thought it was the greatest scouting report he had ever seen and went to bed that night feeling loose. He liked that the Reds were confident. He liked that Pete Rose was running his mouth. He liked the sign that one business had strung up on the square.

BRING ON THE MUSTACHES, it said.

Karolyn and the kids were excited to attend the World Series. Fawn was now almost eight. Petey was almost three, and the boy had become something of a mascot to Reds' fans. Sometimes that fall, when good things happened on the field, people sitting near Karolyn in the stands picked up Petey and swung his body in the air. But during the first two games at Riverfront, the kids had little to cheer. The Reds lost both games by a run, falling behind in the series 2–0 before they even boarded their plane for the West Coast, and Pete was struggling.

"How's your daddy doing?" a reporter asked Petey in the Reds' clubhouse.

"Say horse spit," Pete instructed his son.

He was just 1 for 8 in the series so far. He grounded out to end game one, stranding the tying run on third base. He was equally quiet in game two facing Oakland's mustachioed starter, Jim "Catfish" Hunter, and he didn't like that Hunter gave interviews afterward, crediting the win to his "super fastball."

Pete disagreed. He didn't think Hunter's fastball was "super." He refused to even say Hunter was great. Pete called him a good pitcher with a "nothing fastball" who had managed to pitch a "super ballgame," but wasn't anything like the National League's best pitchers—Tom Seaver and Bob Gibson. Pete compared Hunter to an average starter in the middle of the Mets' rotation who had gone 11-8 in 1972. "He throws like Jim McAndrew," Pete said.

The Reds flew to Oakland, and Sparky Anderson immediately pronounced the field there awful and the stadium ugly. The reception the team received probably didn't help. The Reds stepped into the visitors' clubhouse to find an arrangement of yellow mums in the shape of a cross and adorned with three words: "Rest in Peace." Heavy rains then moved across the East Bay, flooding the Reds' dugout, turning the outfield into a swamp, and giving Finley another zany idea. The A's owner sent in a helicopter to fly over the grass and hasten the drying process. It didn't work. Commissioner Bowie Kuhn had to postpone game three, and when play finally started in Oakland one day later, Pete found himself under siege in left field. A's fans tried to pelt him with tomatoes, apples, oranges, and eggs.

Amid it all, the Reds won game three 1–0, clawing their way back into the series. But Sparky thought it was their worst game yet. Pérez, who scored the only run of the night, nearly didn't make it to home; he slipped and fell in the grass rounding third. Bench struck out looking three times, and Pete went hitless at the top of the order. For the series, he was now batting .091, and the media accounts of the abuse Pete endured in left field during game three turned him into a sideshow by the following night. While he dodged flying objects, Karolyn left her seat near the Reds' dugout to argue with Oakland fans in the bleachers.

"Don't you people know that's a big-league ballplayer out there?" she cried.

A's fans just laughed at her. "He's a bum," someone yelled.

The Reds lost again, and the A's now held a commanding 3–1 lead. With a victory in game five, they could celebrate a world title on that awful field in their ugly ballpark. Their game two ace, Catfish Hunter, was returning to the mound—with a score to settle against Pete Rose.

He knew he wasn't Tom Seaver or Bob Gibson, the "super" pitchers whom Pete had mentioned after game two. But he wasn't Jim McAndrew, either. Hunter was in the middle of one of the greatest runs any pitcher would have in the 1970s—five consecutive years of recording at least twenty wins, with an earned run average of 2.65. And yet here was Pete, calling him out. Hunter didn't get it. He didn't understand how Pete could talk like that and get away with it, and going into game five, Hunter crafted a plan. If the A's got a lead and it wouldn't hurt the team, he might leave a fastball inside and drill Pete in the back. "I think Rose is a good ballplayer," Hunter told the press before the game. "But he pops off too much. He doesn't show me any class at all."

Pete just shrugged. He wasn't trying to be classy; he was trying to win. Over breakfast at the Oakland Hilton on the morning of game five, Pete told Scoops Lawson that he was ready for Hunter.

"This guy," Pete said. "*Jim* Hunter . . . I just can't believe he is going to stop me."

In the NBC broadcast booth, Curt Gowdy welcomed fans across the country that afternoon as they tuned in to watch him and his partner Tony Kubek call game five. Kubek, NBC's color commentator, was a former infielder for the Yankees, while Gowdy, the network's play-by-play announcer, was a television star, with more than twenty years behind the microphone. Gowdy had white hair and a smooth voice, and he started the telecast that day by addressing the obvious. The A's were better than people thought.

"Call them what you want, from the owner on down," Gowdy said. "Loose. Wacky. A very colorful team with their mod hairstyles—the Oakland A's have been doing it in the World Series." And they seemed poised to end it today, Gowdy said. "They have their best pitcher, Jim Hunter, slated to start."

The crowd roared when Hunter took the mound moments later and then booed when Pete Rose stepped into the batter's box to start the game. They didn't have time to do much else. Hunter's first pitch was a fastball, belt high right down the middle of the plate. To Pete, it looked about the size of a basketball. "About this big," he said later, spreading his hands wide. He swung hard, made good contact, and began to run.

"A high drive into deep right," Gowdy said.

"Way back . . .

"And it is . . . GONE!"

With a flick of his wrists, Pete put Hunter's first pitch of the afternoon over the right-field wall and then ran around the bases like a man who was late for his train. He clapped his hands as he crossed home plate and bounded into the dugout, shouting. Pete was alive and the Reds were, too. They won game five in Oakland; flew east in the night to Cincinnati; hardly slept on the plane; blew out the A's just hours later in game six; and went into game seven at Riverfront Stadium the following afternoon with the series tied

3–3 and the team feeling confident again with Pete getting hot at the top of the order. After his terrible start, he was now six for his last thirteen, and the Reds were once again favorites to beat the A's—both at the sportsbooks in Nevada and in the home clubhouse in Cincinnati.

"Hey, hey, hey," Pérez crooned after game six. "They don't have a chance."

But there would be no miracle against Oakland. No late-inning heroics or Pete Rose home runs. The Reds lost game seven the following night 3–2 and had to sit there and watch while the A's celebrated on the turf with their long hair and their mustaches—a moment that was especially hard for Pete to swallow. He had come up with two outs and a man on first in the bottom of the ninth, the Reds' last chance, and hit the first pitch he saw to deep left field.

It was a line drive, well struck, almost to the warning track, and tailing away from the A's left fielder, and for a moment the crowd shrieked—Pete was going to do it. He would spark the comeback. He would refuse to fail. But Oakland had him played perfectly. The left fielder moved under the ball and made the catch.

Pete Rose was out, and the A's were world champions.

29

AFTER THE LOSS, Pete sat in the locker room with his arm draped over Petey's shoulders. The boy had lots of questions. Pete had questions, too.

He couldn't understand why he had struggled so much in the World Series, batting just .214. He couldn't believe the A's had won, and, worst of all, he couldn't even go home. Before game seven, the team had booked a postgame victory party at a country club in northern Kentucky, and even though the Reds had lost, the party was still on. Pete picked around the dinner spread that night with the other players and their wives. He watched while one of the beat writers tried to take the edge off the room by doing comedic impressions at a microphone, and he sat in silence while Johnny Bench gave a short speech.

Johnny had struggled against the A's, just like Pete, and he felt as if he had to say something about it. At the microphone, he thanked Sparky Anderson for a great season and called out one other important person by name. "I want to say what a privilege it has been the last five years to play on a team with a man like Pete Rose."

To the room, subdued and quiet, the words felt like a peace offering. That season, Johnny had led the league in both home runs and RBIs. In a matter of days, he would win his second MVP award. With the award in hand, he was going to get paid that winter. Howsam would have no choice but to give Johnny a $115,000 contract—more than Pete had ever made—and Johnny continued to eclipse Pete in other ways. He was dating a blond model, but not exclusively. He wanted the freedom to do what he wanted, when he wanted. One day, Johnny might be on a yacht in the Caribbean. The next day, he might be in a television studio in Los Angeles or a golf course in Palm Springs. And whenever he was in Cincinnati, he was almost never home, in his condo at the Cloisters. Johnny had to tape his television show, which was moving into national syndication, or appear at events selling his new book, *From Behind the Plate.* According to advertisements, the book told the story of Johnny Bench—*"A bachelor swinger. A true superstar. Now, in his own words."*

With his speech at the after-party, Johnny seemed to be saying that despite all this, Cincinnati was still Pete's town. But Howsam himself didn't seem convinced of that anymore. At the winter meetings in Hawaii in late 1972, rumors circulated that the Reds' general manager would be open to trading Pete Rose. He was going to be thirty-two in the spring, old by baseball standards. If Howsam was ever going to trade him, now was the time to do it. And there was nothing Pete could do to stop him. The Supreme Court had recently ruled against former St. Louis Cardinal Curt Flood, upholding baseball's reserve system and delaying the dawn of free agency by at least a couple more years. The Reds still owned Pete, a reality that put him in a dark mood that winter while Johnny signed his big contract, smiled on TV, and drove his blue Lincoln Continental around town with beautiful women at his side.

"This year," Pete vowed, "I'm not giving in."

He wanted to get paid. But everyone had seen this soap opera before, and it ended the same way it always did. After a brief holdout in March, Pete cracked. He couldn't tolerate life without baseball. He flew to Tampa; checked into his usual room at King Arthur's Inn with Karolyn and the kids; accepted Howsam's best offer, roughly $118,000, a little more than Johnny, a symbolic gesture, perhaps; requested extra batting practice, swinging and swinging in the cage; and asked for a short reprieve from Sparky Anderson's haircut mandate. Pete was scheduled to shoot a hairspray commercial inside the Reds' locker room that month with an actress whose lines called for her to flirt with him, and he was hoping to keep his hair long until then.

The commercial took almost the entire day to film—six and a half hours—and later, if the actress was being honest, she had to admit that she found the Reds less sophisticated than athletes she had worked with in the past. Pete and his teammates, she said, were "a little earthy." But for the camera, she disguised her true feelings, gazed into Pete's eyes, delivered her lines, and ended the spot by playfully slapping Pete on his bare chest while his teammates laughed on cue. The tagline was "Come on, girls."

The Reds entered the 1973 season as favorites to win the NL pennant and return to the World Series. Baseball writers, oddsmakers, and even other teams were all picking Cincinnati. The Reds should have won it all the year before; they'd finally win it now. And early on, Pete did his part. He batted .320 for the first two months and bragged to the press about it. "Every summer," he said, using the third-person voice, "two things happen. The grass turns green and Pete Rose hits .300."

Still, the Reds struggled. At the start of July, they found themselves ten games behind the first-place Dodgers in the NL West, with the lowest team batting average in baseball and a lineup in disarray. George Foster was back in the minors, and he was angry about it. César Gerónimo was playing so poorly that he was in danger of joining Foster there any day. Gerónimo was batting .172 for the year, and Johnny Bench wasn't doing much better. His average was languishing in the .230s.

An aerial view of downtown Cincinnati in the 1940s. The city was the world headquarters of the Procter & Gamble Company and a proud bastion of conservative politics. *(Courtesy of Getty Images)*

As a boy growing up on the West Side, Pete spent his weekends in the fall going to his father's semipro football games. Big Pete (*far right*), wearing jersey No. 68, kneels in the front row. Little Pete (*front row, center, in helmet*) kneels and smiles with his arms crossed. It was 1947, and Little Pete was six years old. *(Courtesy of Delhi Historical Society)*

Young Pete Rose (*second row, second from right*) loved playing baseball and in 1956 won a city championship with a team of West Side kids playing for the S&H Green Stamps. Star pitcher Art Luebbe stands behind Pete. (*Courtesy of Tom Luebbe*)

Crosley Field, the home of the Cincinnati Reds in the 1950s and 1960s, was almost sacred ground for Pete. He went to games there with his father and dreamed of one day playing on the field. (*Courtesy of Getty Images*)

Cincinnati Reds manager Fred Hutchinson took an interest in Pete after the Reds signed him out of high school in 1960 and then gave him his first real break in 1963. Hutch believed in him. *(Courtesy of Getty Images)*

Pete became a fan favorite in Cincinnati right away, impressing people with the way he hustled. (© *Ken Stewart, Courtesy of ZUMA Press*)

During his rookie year, Pete met Karolyn Engelhardt one afternoon at the racetrack. They were married within a matter of months, in January 1964, in front of a massive crowd at a church on the West Side. (© The Enquirer–*USA TODAY NETWORK*)

In 1968, Pete won his first batting title, hitting .335. He then replicated the feat the following year, becoming the first Cincinnati Red to win back-to-back titles. (*Courtesy of Getty Images*)

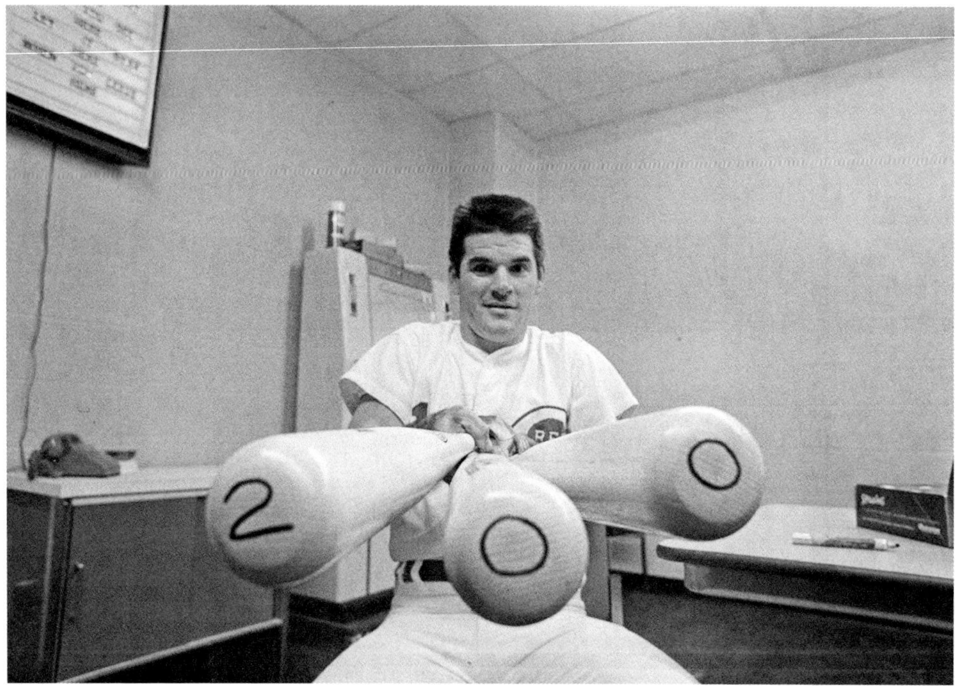

Pete's goals every year were simple: bat .300, score a hundred runs, and compile two hundred hits—an accomplishment he achieved ten times over the course of his career, a major-league record. (*Courtesy of Getty Images*)

Pete's father was thrilled with his son's success. He had pushed the boy to be great—sometimes at the expense of his other children—and Pete had proven him right. *(Courtesy of Getty Images)*

In 1970, the Reds hosted the All-Star Game at their new home, Riverfront Stadium. Roughly fifty million people watched the game on television, and President Richard Nixon watched from a seat near home plate. Nixon threw out the ceremonial first pitch, with baseball commissioner Bowie Kuhn (*right, pointing*) and National League manager Gil Hodges (No. 14) looking on. *(Courtesy of Getty Images)*

Pete won the 1970 All-Star Game for the National League in the bottom of the twelfth inning, when he scored the winning run by knocking down Indians catcher Ray Fosse at home plate. The play cemented Pete's reputation as "Charlie Hustle" and forever altered Fosse's career. Fosse was never quite the same. *(Courtesy of Associated Press)*

The dawn of the 1970s brought a new manager to Cincinnati: Sparky Anderson. He loved Pete and immediately named him team captain. (*Courtesy of Getty Images*)

By then, Pete was no longer the best player on the Reds. Catcher Johnny Bench won the National League MVP award in 1970 and 1972, and he won over fans as well. Johnny was younger than Pete, better looking, more sophisticated—and single. (*Courtesy of Getty Images*)

The Reds lost the World Series twice in the early 1970s and then fell short again in 1973, when the underdog Mets stunned the Reds in the playoffs. It was a result that Pete refused to accept, and he tried to find a way to spark his team. During game three, Pete fought with Mets shortstop Bud Harrelson. Both benches cleared. Fans threw objects at Pete, and the umpires had to stop the game twice. (*Courtesy of Getty Images*)

In 1975 and 1976, the Reds finally broke through, winning back-to-back World Series titles and proving they were one of the best teams to ever play the game. On opening day 1976, pitcher Gary Nolan (No. 38), stood with the team's eight starting players, the core of the Big Red Machine. (*From left to right*) Pete Rose, Joe Morgan, César Gerónimo, Ken Griffey Sr., Nolan, Davey Concepción, Tony Pérez, George Foster, and Johnny Bench. (© The Enquirer–*USA TODAY NETWORK*)

Baseball fans would flock to Fountain Square in downtown Cincinnati to celebrate the team in the mid-1970s, like this event in October 1975. Reds broadcaster Marty Brennaman (*left*) introduced Pete to the crowd, and the people went wild, chanting his name, "*Peeeeeeeete.*" (© *Ken Stewart, Courtesy of ZUMA Press*)

In January 1976, the S. Rae Hickok foundation named Pete "Professional Athlete of the Year," and Pete collected his spoils: a diamond-encrusted belt worth at least $10,000. (*Courtesy of Getty Images*)

In February 1976, Pete's alma mater, Western Hills High School, named the street outside the school in his honor. But there was trouble for him both at work and at home. *(Courtesy of Associated Press)*

In March 1976, the owners locked out the players, fighting over free agency and money. Instead of driving his Rolls-Royce—license plate PETE—to the Reds' complex in Tampa every morning, Pete practiced on Little League fields in West Tampa, and he didn't always go home to Karolyn at night. *(Courtesy of Associated Press)*

After twelve years of marriage, Pete and Karolyn were struggling. She was raising their two kids, and he was gone: playing baseball, gambling at the racetrack, or hanging out with other women. *(Courtesy of Associated Press)*

Maybe Johnny had too much going on between his television show, his girlfriends, and the rumors that he was getting engaged. By late summer, the local papers were getting more letters about Bench's marital status than almost anything else. Pete, on the other hand, couldn't stop talking about baseball, in part because he was having the greatest season of his life. In July, he batted a scorching .417. The Reds won twenty-three out of thirty, and suddenly they were just three and a half games behind the Dodgers, with two months to play.

"This isn't over yet," Pete declared.

Cincinnati was coming, getting deeper and stronger by the day. Howsam brought Foster back from Triple-A and called up another outfielder who seemed to have promise: Ken Griffey. Pérez and Morgan hit well all summer. Bench finally found it again, hitting almost .300 over an eight-week stretch, and on Labor Day, Cincinnati was just one game behind Los Angeles—with the gap closing by the minute. That night in Houston, the Reds came from behind to beat the Astros 4–3. Then they retired to the visitors' clubhouse inside the Astrodome, slugged back a few beers, ate some postgame chicken, and turned on a television mounted on a shelf to watch Curt Gowdy and Tony Kubek call the end of the Dodgers-Giants game on NBC.

At one point that night at Candlestick Park, the Dodgers had been up 8–1. But by the time the Reds tuned in to the game, the lead had shrunk to one. The score was 8–7. The Giants had the bases loaded in the bottom of the ninth, and Pete Rose and the Reds were shouting at the television because the Giants' best hitter was coming to the plate: Bobby Bonds.

"Can you imagine this situation?" Pete said, turning to his teammates.

Bonds had hit thirty-six home runs that year, including two just the day before, and all Bonds needed now was a little shot in the gap. Two runs would score. The Dodgers would lose and the Reds would move into a tie for first. It felt like the season was on the line—and maybe it was. When Bonds got a hanging screwball—"a hanging scroogie," Bonds called it—the Reds' players shouted and screamed until they couldn't hear Gowdy or Kubek anymore. Bonds had hit the pitch over the wall for a walk-off grand slam.

In San Francisco, the Giants mobbed Bonds as he touched home plate; Cincinnati might have celebrated even more. As the ball settled into the left-field seats at Candlestick Park, the Reds jumped around inside the visitors' clubhouse in Houston, bouncing up and down until the television rattled off the shelf and crashed to the floor.

"Bye, bye, baby!" Morgan hollered.

The Dodgers were done, and everyone knew it—the Reds most of all. They ran away with the division title for the rest of the month and returned to the playoffs, as predicted.

30

The Reds' opponent this time was the New York Mets, and no one feared the Mets. Not in 1973, not ever. Before the season had started, Pete had dismissed them, telling a reporter for the New York *Daily News,* "I don't think of the Mets as contenders."

Pete was just being honest. In their short, twelve-year history, the Mets had finished last—or second to last—in the National League seven times. When they weren't finishing last or almost last, they were just average. Their one great season, 1969—when the Mets won a hundred games and the World Series—felt like a distant memory, and New York did not seem destined to recapture this magic in 1973. Despite winning the NL East, the Mets were just three games above .500, seventeen games behind the Reds in the win column, and heavy underdogs as a result.

But they did have one asset that the Reds did not: Tom Seaver. He was the league's most dominant pitcher, and the Mets' manager, the former Yankee Yogi Berra, was using Seaver to play mind games with the Reds. Berra suggested that Seaver probably wouldn't start game one at Riverfront Stadium, due to persistent shoulder soreness. Then, after an off-day workout at Shea Stadium in New York, Berra changed course and said Seaver would start—an announcement that sparked Seaver-mania among the press corps.

"Tom Seaver, Tom Seaver—that's all I hear," Pete complained to the press.

He knew he could hit Seaver. He believed he could hit anyone.

"You just bear down harder," Pete said, "against a Seaver."

The first pitch for game one was at four o'clock that Saturday afternoon, a terrible time to hit a baseball in most stadiums, including Riverfront. Between the setting sun and the long shadows, batters typically struggled at this time of day, and now Tom Seaver was on the mound, high kicking in his blue stirrup socks and firing ninety-five-mile-per-hour fastballs at the Reds' knees. It didn't go well.

For seven innings, Seaver shut out Cincinnati and struck out eleven, including Pete to end the fifth. With a full count, a runner on second, and the Reds trailing 1–0, Pete did something he rarely did: he looked at the third strike on the outside corner, a fastball tailing away from him, and didn't even argue the umpire's call. He knew it was a strike, and the fans at Riverfront knew the Reds were in trouble. The sold-out crowd, fifty-three thousand people, the largest crowd in playoff history, sat there in silence.

The eighth inning for the Reds started with more of the same. Seaver logged another strikeout, his twelfth, and Cincinnati's top of the order came back around, with Pete Rose striding to the plate, deep in thought. Pete was still thinking about the fastball he had missed three innings earlier, but he was also thinking about something else, something Seaver had said in a sports column that appeared in that morning's *New York Times.*

Seaver said that many batters were easy for him to solve. They came to the plate every time looking for the same pitches and, consequently, he knew how to get them out. But Pete was different.

"Rose remembers things," Seaver said.

It was a single line—in the ninth paragraph of a short column, deep inside a paper that was not known for its sports coverage and that most people in Cincinnati, including Pete, never read. But looking for an edge, Pete had combed through the out-of-town papers that morning. He had found the line. He had latched onto it, and he was using it now as he stepped into the batter's box with one out in the bottom of the eighth. Seaver had struck him out on the outside corner the last time, Pete thought. He'd probably try to do something different this time—since Seaver knew he would remember.

Seaver started him with a high fastball, sizzling with movement. Ball one. Then the Mets' ace turned back to the outside corner. For the next three pitches, he painted and Pete watched. He didn't swing at anything outside, until the count was even—two balls and two strikes. At that point, Pete had no choice. So when Seaver went back to the outside corner yet again, Pete fouled off the pitch.

In Cincinnati, the crowd remained fatally quiet. No one was standing; no one was cheering. Seaver had struck out five of the last seven batters, and he was on the cusp of striking out Pete now, too. But Pete figured that Seaver wouldn't go back to the outside corner to do it. He thought Seaver would go inside with his next pitch, and when Seaver put a fastball there a moment later, Pete hit it to deep right-center field, stunning everyone, including Gowdy and Kubek, who were calling the game for NBC in a booth above home plate.

"There's a long blast," Gowdy cried.

"Going . . . Going . . .

"It is . . . GONE!"

Pete, who had hit only five home runs all year, had just taken Seaver's best shot and crushed it over the wall.

Tie game.

As both a player and an announcer, Tony Kubek had seen some of the greatest moments in recent baseball history. He had watched Bill Mazeroski hit a walk-off home run to win the 1960 World Series for the Pirates at Forbes Field in Pittsburgh; been teammates with Mickey Mantle and Roger Maris; had a front-row seat to their epic home-run chase in 1961; played in six World Series, four of which went seven games; won three of them; and called the last four for NBC. But Kubek had never seen fans react the way they did when Pete hit his home run that day. For thirty seconds, it felt like the stadium was shaking on its foundation, as people stood up and cheered as loud as they had ever cheered for anything. The score was just tied. Seaver was still Seaver, and yet, this one was over. In the bottom of the ninth, Johnny Bench hit his own home run off Seaver to win it for the Reds, 2–1.

Pete suddenly felt great about the Reds' chances of making it back to the World Series. They had stolen the game against Seaver; the hard part was over. But in game two the next day, the Mets blanked the Reds, 5–0. Then the series moved to Shea Stadium in New York, and the Mets jumped out to an early lead in game three as well. They were up 6–0 to end the second and 9–2 to start the fifth, when Pete singled and Joe Morgan hit a weak ground ball to the Mets' first baseman, John Milner, that seemed set up to end the threat—and the inning. All Milner had to do was collect the ball, throw to Bud Harrelson at shortstop, get the lead runner, Pete Rose, and wait for the ball to come back to him for the double play. Something had to change, and Pete had a plan. If he couldn't break up the double play, he was going to at least slide into Bud Harrelson. He was going to knock Bud clear into left field, if he could.

Bud and Pete had a good relationship. Over the years, Pete had offered Bud support whenever he was struggling at the plate, and at one point Pete even suggested that Bud might play better defense if he used a smaller glove—advice that proved correct. Bud hadn't forgotten it. He considered Pete one of the best players he'd ever seen, and if not a friend, then at least friendly. But after the Mets' 5–0 victory in Cincinnati in game two, Bud said something that rankled Pete. He said he thought the Reds were swinging from their heels.

"What the hell does Bud Harrelson think he is?" Pete asked. "A hitting instructor?"

Bud was a wisp of a man, fifty pounds lighter than Pete, and a lifetime .240 hitter. Pete couldn't let him talk like that. With Morgan's ground ball bouncing toward first base, Pete had his chance to let him know—and an opportunity to awaken the Reds' offense at the same time. He slid hard—right at Bud's knees, as Bud turned the double play—and threw an elbow, Bud claimed, as he hopped back to his feet. Bud knew the hard slide was coming; the elbow was unexpected. Bud said later that it nearly caught him in the chin, and he let Pete know that he didn't appreciate it. In the heat of the moment, Bud called Pete a "no-good motherfucker," or something like that, and in response, Pete grabbed Bud around the collar and threw him to the ground. Both men tumbled into the dirt, and the benches cleared. The fight was on. For the next ninety seconds, the Reds and the Mets threw wild punches at each other in a melee on the field.

Had this happened a few years later, the umpires would have

ejected multiple people that afternoon, starting with Pete and Bud. But at Shea Stadium that day, the game just resumed, with the Mets coming to the plate in the bottom of the fifth and Pete running out to his position in the outfield. There were no ejections, no ramifications. Just chaos. As Pete set up in left field, Mets fans pelted him with garbage, bottles, and beer cans, and at least twice Pete picked up the objects that had been thrown at him and seemed to hurl them back at the fans.

It was dangerous for everyone involved, especially Pete, and the umpires had no choice but to stop the game. Groundskeepers needed time to collect the debris, and the public address announcer at the stadium needed to issue a warning. If New Yorkers continued throwing items onto the field, the Mets would have to forfeit—a warning that seemed to work and then didn't. A couple minutes after play resumed, a whiskey bottle nearly hit Pete in the head. The umpire positioned closest to Pete on the left-field line was stunned. In his estimation, the bottle could have seriously injured Pete—or worse. "It could have killed him."

Sparky Anderson shook his head and pulled his team off the field. "Let's go," he said.

The crowd booed, and for a moment the outcome of the playoff game seemed to be in question. Umpires huddled near home plate discussing the situation while Yogi Berra, Tom Seaver, and a handful of other Mets ran out to left field to plead with the fans to stop throwing things. Finally, after several minutes, the people listened. The Reds returned to the field and play resumed without incident—and without any more action, either. The score remained 9–2 the rest of the way, and the Mets won it easily. It was as if the fight and the aftermath had sucked the life out of everyone—except for the New York fans.

Every time the ball came anywhere near Pete Rose, they booed him.

31

After the game, Howsam advised Pete to take a forty-five-minute time-out in the trainer's room before going to his locker to meet the press. Howsam didn't want Pete saying something to reporters that might inflame the situation; the Reds had to play at Shea Stadium again in less than twenty-four hours—with the season on the line. The Mets were one win away from going to the World Series.

Pete did as Howsam instructed. But when he emerged from the trainer's room to face the media, he refused to censor himself, and instead channeled his dead father. He wasn't going to play like a sissy out there, he said. "I'm no little girl," Pete told the press. He was going to play hard—and that meant barreling into second base to break up a double play in any scenario, especially in the playoffs. "I'll slide the same way tomorrow," Pete said. He paused and smiled. "I might slide harder tomorrow, if that's possible."

The press ate it up, loving the fresh storyline and Pete in general. "A Rose Is Not a Rose Unless He's Battling," one headline declared. Those closest to Pete had a different reaction: they were worried about him. Despite his public persona, Pete hated confrontation. He avoided face-to-face arguments whenever possible. He chose silence over bickering with Karolyn at home and he preferred sarcastic barbs over fighting in the locker room. Most of all, he cared about how he was perceived—and now he was the enemy. He needed a police escort just to walk to the team bus, which was mobbed by two hundred angry New York fans as it pulled away from the stadium. They banged on the windows with their greasy fists—all because of Pete.

Back at the hotel that night, Joe Morgan had never seen him so miserable. Pete barricaded himself in his room for most of the night, picked at his dinner, sat in silence, and didn't even want to talk about baseball. "He was like a person on the run," Morgan said later, "a guy with a price on his head." Karolyn wasn't even sure she wanted him on the field the next day. She called Sparky in his hotel room to find out how the Mets were going to protect Pete in game four—a question that the Mets were asking themselves, too. Overnight, they hired more than two hundred police officers to stand post at the stadium.

In the morning, the Mets' president, Donald Grant, awoke with an idea that he believed could stave off problems for everyone involved. He wanted to get Bud Harrelson and Pete Rose together at home plate before the game and stage a "no-hard-feelings handshake" that could be broadcast to the fans in the stadium, shown to everyone watching at home on NBC, and featured in every newspaper the next day.

"Photographed," Grant said, thinking big, "for all the world to see."

Two hours before the first pitch of game four, Grant presented the plan to Harrelson from his box seats near the Mets' dugout, and Harrelson begrudgingly agreed to it. If Pete went to home plate before the game, Harrelson said, he would meet him there and do what Grant wanted. It was a harder sell with Pete—even after his long night in the hotel room. He couldn't bring himself to apologize or even appear like he was apologizing because he still felt like he had done nothing wrong. Pete looked at Howsam and rejected Donald Grant's plan.

"That's not the way I compete," he said.

He wasn't upset at Harrelson, he explained, and he knew Harrelson felt the same about him. But he wasn't going to agree to a fake handshake at home plate to make front-office executives feel better about the situation—even if it might make life easier for him. He wasn't going to shake the hand of the guy he needed to beat that day.

"I just don't think that's how it's supposed to be done," Pete said.

The abuse that afternoon at Shea Stadium was unlike anything Pete had ever experienced before. He received a standing "boo" ovation during warm-ups; sparked a raucous celebration in the top of the first when he grounded out to start the game; trotted out to left field in the bottom of the inning to find the stadium wallpapered with signs attacking him—ROSE IS A WEED . . . ROSE IS A PANSY . . . ROSES

DIE—BUDS BLOOM; lived for two hours in a cloud of obscenities; and had to dodge the usual flying contraband—eggs and tomatoes, mostly. It would have been enough to derail or distract most players. Not Pete. At the end of nine innings, he was 2 for 4 and the game was tied 1–1.

In the box seats near the Reds' dugout, Howsam almost felt sick to his stomach. He didn't want to lose to the Mets, in a walk-off in extra innings at Shea Stadium with all the troublemakers in the stands—the hoodlums, as Howsam called them. He was worried about his team's safety—and his own. But the Mets went down in order in the bottom of the tenth. No walk-off win. They went quietly in the eleventh, too. No champagne celebration. And by the top of the twelfth, with the game still tied, the crowd was now anxious. They should have won this game forty-five minutes ago, and yet here they were, facing Pete Rose for the sixth time that day.

By then, the Mets had exhausted both their starter and their closer, and Yogi Berra had handed the game off to his next-best option: Harry Parker, a tall right-hander who threw hard. Parker quickly had Pete off-balance. With a 2-1 count, he fired a high fastball out of the zone, and Pete chased. Then, on the next pitch, Parker got him to chase again, and Pete barely fouled it off. In the Reds' dugout, Johnny Bench motioned for Pete to relax—hands outstretched, palms down. Johnny thought Pete was trying to do too much. Pete got back into his crouch, his bat cocked over his left shoulder, and awaited the next pitch. It was yet another high fastball—Parker's third in a row—and this time Pete didn't miss it: he punched it over the right-field wall for a home run.

Pete ripped around the bases. He wasn't going to embarrass Harry Parker with a slow, self-congratulatory jog. But he couldn't restrain himself from sticking it to the fans at Shea Stadium just a little. As he ran, Pete held up a fist in the air and jumped on home plate with two feet for emphasis.

Even New Yorkers were impressed. It made no sense. It couldn't be, and it was.

The Reds beat the Mets 2–1, forcing a game five.

"I don't have a Johnny Bench swing, or a Tony Pérez swing, or a Joe Morgan swing," Pete told the press after the game, savoring the moment. What he had was intangible. "If they ever cut Rose open,"

Sparky Anderson said after that day, "they'll find three hearts and three stomachs." The home run proved to Sparky that some players *did* want to win more than others—the cliché, Sparky said, was true—and Pete's teammates agreed. They couldn't explain what they had just witnessed. Pete had appeared broken at the hotel and whole at the field, one man away from the ballpark and a different man when he was inside of it, competing.

But he was only one man, and the next day, with Tom Seaver on the mound again, it wasn't even close. The Mets won 7–2. Hundreds of New Yorkers stormed the field to celebrate the pennant, and the Reds ran for their lives. Pete, who was on second base when the game ended, felt as if he were back on the football field at West High, eluding tacklers. He was scampering for the dugout through a sea of long-haired Mets fans, and Howsam felt the same way. From his box seat, the Reds' general manager ran for the dugout too—afraid and disgusted.

In a changing world, filled with hippies, anti-Nixon protesters, antiwar peaceniks, angry fans in the bleachers, and high-paid, union-organized professional athletes on the field wearing mustaches on their faces, the Reds had done what they always did.

They lost in the postseason again.

Karolyn drove to the airport in Cincinnati that night to be there when the Reds landed in their Ozark Air Lines DC-9. It had been a frightening week for her and the kids. Little Petey had loved watching his daddy fight Bud Harrelson on television. "Daddy fights just like Joe Frazier," Petey said. But Fawn had cried during the brawl, and Karolyn had been convinced that someone was going to kill Pete in the stampede after the Mets won the series. She wanted to shower him with kisses and take him home to the house on the West Side.

She would have to wait. More than two hundred people had gathered at the gate to greet the team—supportive fans, autograph seekers, groupies, young women squealing as they touched Johnny Bench, and people chanting, "We want Pete."

Finally, Karolyn and Pete met in the crowd. Karolyn took his head in her hands and Pete leaned into her, his travel bag slung over his left shoulder. But as a photographer snapped away, capturing the husband-wife reunion, Pete's eyes moved about the room.

"I'm tired," he said.

At least he was home safe, and at least he was getting the recognition he believed he deserved. A few weeks later, Pete picked up the phone at his house to learn that the baseball writers had voted him MVP of the National League, the one accolade that had eluded him all these years.

He had joined the likes of Mantle, Mays, Aaron, Clemente, DiMaggio, Gehrig, Ruth, and Bench. He was inching ever closer to becoming an Immortal, and his pending membership in this club came with certain privileges. It put Pete on the cover of *Sports Illustrated*, again. It gave him leverage for his annual salary dispute with Bob Howsam. It cleared a path for Karolyn to buy a new and larger house a half mile away on a street called Countryhills Drive. It helped Pete open a new restaurant not far from Al Esselman's car lot, and it made that restaurant a West Side destination. People didn't come for the homemade Goetta, or the sauerbraten dinner. They came because Pete might be there and Karolyn might be, too. In Cincinnati, she was almost as famous as Pete and just as recognizable, with her blue eye shadow, her long fingernails, her smoky voice, her big smile, and her diamond-encrusted jewelry, sparkling with her initials—"KR."

But increasingly, in interviews, Karolyn stripped away the glossy veneer of their lives and discussed what it was really like to be married to Pete.

"I think it's hard for a wife," Karolyn said in one interview.

"It's not an easy life," she said in another.

"I have the shit detail," she joked.

She had to be everything—the wife, the mother, the cook, the cleaner, the carpool driver, and the loyal cheerleader—while Pete was gone, playing baseball. Karolyn had started to say that maybe the secret to their success as a couple was that she rarely saw him. But the line was yet another way to conceal her disappointment, the tension in the house on Countryhills, and the destructive choices that Pete was making when he was away from home.

In 1974, the year after the playoff loss at Shea Stadium, Pete had one of the worst seasons of his career. He batted .284. The Reds missed the playoffs for the first time since 1971, and Pete and Karolyn had begun to argue, Karolyn said, especially during the offseason.

"You gonna tell me what you fight about?" asked one female television host during a live taping of a popular local morning show.

"Everything," Karolyn told the host. "I'm a jealous woman."

The host seemed surprised by Karolyn's answer and tried to give her a chance to clean it up. Pete surely wasn't like that, the host clarified.

"I mean, he's not the type to be jealous of, is he?"

"Well," Karolyn said, "wouldn't you be jealous?"

The host didn't get it. Once again, she tried to guide Karolyn to the correct answer. What the host was trying to say—or get Karolyn to say—was that Pete was faithful. A good husband, overall, despite whatever problems they had.

"I mean, it's not like he runs around," the host said.

"*Wellll,*" Karolyn said, hesitating. She didn't know how to reply. "No . . . yeah . . . well . . ."

Nervous laughter broke out on the set, saving Karolyn. People didn't want to know the truth. Around this time—exactly when remains unclear and a subject of debate—Pete began having an affair in Cincinnati with a young woman. A teenager. A girl who was still in high school.

Pete said later that he believed she was sixteen, the age of legal consent in Ohio when he began having sex with her. But the girl remembered it differently. She said Pete started calling her as early as 1973 when she was fourteen or fifteen years old. She said they began having sex in Cincinnati sometime before her sixteenth birthday in late 1974, and she said the relationship lasted for years. Whatever it was, it was a bright red line and Pete had crossed it.

He was cheating on Karolyn with a woman who was half his age.

32

JOHNNY BENCH'S WEDDING in late February 1975 was the social event of the year in Cincinnati. It led the eleven o'clock news; drew crowds to the church downtown so thick that police had to clear the sidewalks; featured nine hundred guests, including the mayor and the quarterback of the Cincinnati Bengals; and ended with a reception at the Netherland Hilton that had guests in awe. Inside the hotel's Hall of Mirrors that night, there were ice sculptures, four different bars, and enough booze to float a barge down the river.

The bride's name was Vickie Chesser, and the press portrayed her as the perfect match for Johnny. She was blond and glamorous. A winner of swimsuit competitions. The former Miss South Carolina, who lived in New York now and had earned a measure of fame doing television commercials for Ultra Brite, "the sex appeal toothpaste." Bench had wanted to meet her in the winter after the 1974 season, and he made it happen in a way that only a megastar could. He got her number from someone in New York, called her around the holidays, and invited her to go to Las Vegas with him for New Year's Eve—an improbable ask that worked.

Within three weeks, they were engaged, and within a month Vickie had moved into Johnny's condo at the Cloisters. She was dusting his trophy case and answering his phone calls. Now, less than two months after they had first met, they were married—a whirlwind, yes, and certainly too fast for some. Karolyn didn't understand what Vickie, a sophisticated New Yorker, could possibly have in common with a ballplayer in Cincinnati. Vickie didn't know a thing about baseball.

But Johnny brushed off any concerns about his bride. It felt good to be married, he said, and Vickie had plenty of time to learn the game, just as Karolyn had. She could start right away, in fact. The day after the wedding, she and Johnny flew to Tampa for spring training, where there was baseball to play and a new feeling of urgency after the Reds' failures in 1973 and 1974.

"We need to win soon," Johnny said as he landed in Florida.

The Reds were getting older—Pete especially. He was turning thirty-four that spring and in desperate need of a comeback year. Specifically, Pete said, he wanted to bat .320 in 1975, because his career average was .309 and he didn't want it to dip any lower.

Pete came north after spring training in April 1975 with a new friend: Mario Núñez, the maître d' in the clubhouse dining room at his favorite racetrack in Tampa, Florida Downs.

Mario was a portly, middle-aged man with glasses, a loud, high-pitched voice, a staccato laugh that was almost maniacal, gambling associates across Tampa, and a thirst for action that rivaled Pete's. "He'll bet you tomorrow is not Friday," Pete liked to joke, "if you'll lay him two to one. But he'll only bet you two dollars."

Mario didn't have much money. What he had were connections. He always seemed to know a guy who knew a guy who could handicap the races in Tampa, predict the winners. Pete would often pick Mario up after spring training games, and together they would run the old triple-header circuit: the horse track, the dog track, jai alai. Like Pete, Mario could go all night. Now he was staying at Pete's house on Countryhills Drive, with Karolyn and the kids, and growing close enough with the Reds that Sparky Anderson let him hang out in the clubhouse. Pete called him the Cuban.

The Reds got off to a slow start that spring. They finished April just one game over .500. Then, in the first game of May, they lost to the Atlanta Braves, one of the worst teams in baseball. Sparky didn't see reason to panic just yet. But he did see a problem. He had too many great outfielders—Gerónimo, Foster, Griffey, and Rose—and no real third baseman. The opening day starter there, John Vukovich, had a career batting average of .157. In order to put his best team on the field, Sparky needed to bench Vukovich. He needed to play one of his outfielders at third, and there was only one possibility.

On the day that the Reds lost to the Braves, Sparky asked Pete if he'd be willing to try it—a proposal that many established stars would have rejected, and one Pete had specific reasons to resist. Nine years earlier, in 1966, the Reds had put him at third to start the season to make room on the infield for Tommy Helms, and the experiment had lasted just sixteen games. While playing third, Pete struggled both at the plate and in the field. He was uncomfortable, and he felt the same uneasiness about third base now. Pete hadn't started a game on the infield in years. But he was older now and starting to think like a manager. He told Sparky he would do whatever he wanted.

Sparky didn't waste any time. He started Pete at third the next day. The Reds beat the Braves, won five of the next six, lost only nine games the rest of May, only seven in June, and woke up on the Fourth of July to find themselves twenty-three games above .500 and in first place. No one in the National League had a chance. With Bench behind the plate, Pérez at first, Morgan at second, Rose at third, a young Davey Concepción at shortstop, and Gerónimo, Griffey, and Foster starting most games in the outfield, the Reds were almost unstoppable.

They nearly won the division before Labor Day; crushed the Dodgers by twenty games; put up the best record in the National League in more than six decades; swept the mighty Pirates in the playoffs to claim the pennant that October; sprayed champagne all over Pete's friend, the Cuban, in the locker room afterward; gave speeches on Fountain Square in Cincinnati that night in front of twelve thousand fans; swaggered into the World Series in 1975 against the AL champs, the Boston Red Sox; and invited the Cuban to join them in Boston for the series because it was believed that Pete's funny little gambling buddy brought them good luck.

"They cannot lose," the Cuban said, "when I am there."

It was Pete's third World Series in six years and the most important one of his life. At thirty-four years old, he was running out of time to win. But winning this one would have implications that no one could fully appreciate at the moment. The fortnight to come would be unlike any other in baseball history. It would change the lives of players in both dugouts and fans in both cities. Pete Rose was about to play in arguably the greatest World Series there ever was.

33

It was a beautiful time to be in New England. The trees had reached peak autumn color, glowing orange, yellow, brown, and red. Apple festivals and harvest fairs filled the weekend calendar. There was a chill in the air, and fans still had a reason to go to Fenway Park. The Red Sox were playing in their first World Series since 1967.

Boston had two great starters at the top of its rotation: Luis Tiant, a potbellied Cuban pitcher who smoked cigars in the locker room, chewed giant wads of tobacco on the mound, and contorted his body like an acrobat with each pitch; and Bill Lee, whose whimsical approach to life was almost as befuddling as his changeup and had earned him a memorable nickname. Everyone called Bill the Spaceman.

Tiant had six pitches he could throw from impossible angles. The Spaceman dropped in breaking balls that moved so much, it was said, they changed time zones, and around the two strong pitchers the Red Sox had built an impressive roster. They had Carl Yastrzemski at first base; a native-born New Englander behind home plate, the catcher Carlton Fisk; and youth almost everywhere else. The center fielder Fred Lynn was just twenty-three years old that fall and about to become the first man to ever win Rookie of the Year and MVP honors in the same season.

Still, Pete wasn't worried. "We won 111 ballgames this year," he told the press. Thirteen more than Boston. He'd been studying their pitchers. "I know what they throw." He walked into Fenway Park before game one like he owned the place, choosing a seat behind home plate to watch the Sox take batting practice and picture in his mind all the fly balls he was going to hit off the Green Monster in left field, Fenway's towering thirty-seven-foot wall, barely three hundred feet away. Pete loved the sight of that wall. All the green, all the potential. "I lead the league," he said, "in 370-foot fly balls."

And now, those fly balls would be doubles or singles. He was going to bang them off the wall and hit forever.

The Red Sox couldn't win.

"Boston should be just like the National League," Pete said.

Patsies, nobodies. Most beat writers agreed. Almost everyone was picking Cincinnati.

Luis Tiant dominated game one for Boston. He pitched the full nine innings, surrendered just five hits, shut out the Reds 6–0, and shut down Pete Rose while fans heckled his wife in her seat near the visitors' dugout. Karolyn had never heard such abuse; Pete was equally mystified. After the game, he refused to give Tiant any credit for holding him hitless.

Tiant wasn't great, Pete told the press. He was lucky. In his first time up that day, Pete put together an eight-pitch at bat, fouling off balls until he finally grounded out. His second time up, he hammered a fastball, but right at the Red Sox second baseman, and in his final two at bats of the day, Pete ripped first-pitch curveballs to the outfield—right into the waiting gloves of Boston's fielders. He called Tiant's gem in game one "the weakest five-hitter I've ever seen," and then set his mind on solving Boston's game two starter: Bill Lee, the Spaceman, with his big, looping curveballs.

This time, Pete produced. He went 2 for 4 in game two in a cold, spitting rain. But the hits were meaningless—two singles. With his teammates struggling, Pete never advanced past first base. The Spaceman toed the rubber in the ninth with a 2–1 lead, and even after giving up a leadoff double to Johnny Bench, the Sox seemed poised to get out of the inning and win.

Boston's manager, Darrell Johnson, pulled the Spaceman, and the new pitcher, Dick Drago, retired both Pérez and Foster. Bench was now on third base, ninety feet away from scoring the tying run, and the Sox were one out away from taking a 2–0 advantage in the series, with Drago throwing fastballs with confidence.

Up in the broadcast booth, Gowdy and Kubek had seen this show before—Cincinnati shrinking from the moment, the Reds losing big games they were supposed to win in October. Then the ball began to spin in their favor. The Reds' next batter, Davey Concepción, hit a weak ground ball off Drago. But it was a high chopper over second base that went for an infield hit. Bench scored to tie the game. Concepción then stole second. Griffey doubled and, in a matter of just a few minutes, it all slipped away. The Reds won 3–2, and a few hundred reporters jostled for position around the Spaceman's locker after the game to ask him what had happened.

Looking out on the scrum, the Spaceman said he felt like a character in Stanley Kubrick's psychedelic film *A Clockwork Orange.* "It's like I've been injected with a drug," he explained, "and you guys want to see how I react." He didn't know what to say except that the series was tied, that he wanted some vodka and ice for his arm—"It opens the pores," the Spaceman said—and that the Sox weren't afraid of flying to Cincinnati and playing on AstroTurf at Riverfront Stadium in game three.

"We can come back in that concrete jungle," the Spaceman said.

As far as he was concerned, the stadium on the river in Ohio wasn't even real.

"Must have been made by a pharmaceutical company."

34

PETE FELT LUCKY that the series was tied 1–1, and he was thrilled to be going home to Cincinnati. He announced that his West Side restaurant would stay open until 1:30 in the morning that week, so that fans could eat there after the games. He popped into the restaurant late at night to surprise people and sign autographs in the dining room. He relaxed at home on Countryhills Drive, watching videotaped recordings of games one and two. He fast-forwarded through all the commercials, except Johnny Bench's. He joked to reporters that he liked to watch Johnny—"to see if he is going to make a mistake"—and he predicted that the Reds would celebrate on the AstroTurf at Riverfront. They'd probably win all three games at home, Pete said, and never have to return to cold and dreary Fenway Park.

For the next three nights, Pete did his part to make sure his prediction came true. In fourteen plate appearances, he reached base eight times—with four walks and four hits, including a triple that helped break open game three. *The Boston Globe* sarcastically dubbed him "the Reds Badge of Courage" and "the Protestant ethic, rounding third." Pete was always on base that week, it seemed, causing problems for the Red Sox. And still, it wasn't enough. The Reds won game three only due to a controversial call in the bottom of the tenth, and then they split games four and five, unable to beat Tiant yet again and forcing them to fly back to Boston, up three games to two—but not winners, not yet. In order to take the series, the Reds would have to win one of the last two games at Fenway.

Pete wasn't worried. Before the flight to Boston, he walked around the city wearing a T-shirt with his own face on it. He waxed nostalgic with reporters, telling stories about his childhood on the West Side. He marveled at how raw he used to be. "Just a raw kid from Cincinnati." He hung out with his gambling pal, the Cuban, in the clubhouse, in his restaurant, and at home on Countryhills Drive. He mourned that the season was almost over. "I'm mad," Pete said. "I won't have anything to do." And then with Karolyn, and the Cuban, and Bob Howsam, and the team, he flew east, ready to finally win.

"This is the kind of pressure I like," Pete said. "We can completely foul up and still play a seventh game. They have to sweep. Let's see how their kids react under that pressure."

It rained for the next three days in New England, a cold and persistent rain that washed out roads, derailed trains, capsized boats, dumped three inches of precipitation in Boston, turned Fenway Park into a swamp, and postponed game six—three times.

The first day, the players barely left their hotel rooms at the Howard Johnson's; it was raining too hard. The second day, with the Reds growing restless, Sparky Anderson forced the players—or at least as many as he could find—to assemble in the lobby of the hotel and board a charter bus together. They were headed to a gymnasium at Tufts University north of the city, but that almost didn't happen, either. The bus driver got lost on the way, forcing Sparky to step out at a gas station to ask for directions in his full uniform.

Sparky didn't mind that the players thought he looked ridiculous—or that the workout at Tufts turned into an autograph session with college students. He was just trying to keep the players busy. Pete, in particular, was losing his mind. While Karolyn got dolled up in short skirts and mini-jumpers and entertained the press in the lobby, Pete paced the room, wanting to play, needing to play, and giving interviews to fill the void.

He spoke to reporters from his bed, tucked under the covers. He helped them write retrospective columns on his career. He happily rehashed everything—West High, his father, Uncle Buddy, his first season in Geneva, Hutch, whatever reporters wanted to discuss—and he was the only Reds player to make himself available for a press conference during the first rainout, appearing with Fred Lynn of the Red Sox.

Just like Pete, Lynn was anxious to play. While the Reds swung their bats at Tufts, Boston's popular young rookie spent hours in the primitive batting cage under the bleachers at Fenway, swinging alone in the cold. But as Lynn sat on the same stage with Pete at the press conference, the differences between the two men were made plain for all to see. Lynn was polite and declined to say anything negative about anyone, while Pete took a different approach. He said he was happy that Lynn was batting just .263 in the series, and he added that no one would be there to listen to Lynn, were it not for a great catch that Lynn made in the ninth inning of game four in Cincinnati. Pete was joking—this was all just a show to him—but it didn't make it any less absurd. Lynn was the golden boy of Boston that summer. Local fans loved him—and local reporters did, too.

In the newsroom of the *Boston Globe* that afternoon, the columnist Leigh Montville sat at his typewriter and wrote that there were two reasons why he couldn't tolerate the Reds winning the World Series. First, he said, Red Sox fans deserved this. Boston hadn't won a series in fifty-seven years. For once in their miserable lives, Montville wrote, people needed to know what it felt like to celebrate. Second, he couldn't bear the thought of Pete Rose winning:

> You know he won't be graceful. You know he won't be content to just sit back, light up a philosophical cigar and calmly savor what has happened. Nope, you know he is going to rip out his piece of the Reds' triumph and hold it over his head and laugh

and go running away like he had just captured part of the goal posts on a Thanksgiving morn.

Pete Rose. Let's face it. You hate him.

The column appeared in the next morning's *Globe,* landing on half a million doorsteps across New England and reframing the fight in game six as the Red Sox versus Pete. But if Pete cared, he didn't show it. By then, he seemed more concerned about what the rain might do to his schedule. He had a speaking engagement slated for Wednesday night in Louisville, which he would have to cancel if the series wasn't over before then, and personal plans for Monday, which he would have to scrap if game six got played then.

He was hoping to watch *Monday Night Football* on television.

"I want to watch Buffalo," Pete said, "and the New York Giants."

The game finally went off on Tuesday night, with sixty-six million fans watching at home on NBC—the largest television audience in baseball history—and a raucous sellout crowd packed shoulder to shoulder at Fenway. People were there to watch Luis Tiant toe the rubber for a third time in the series. Boston fans expected him to win again—and Fred Lynn gave the local faithful reason to cheer right away, hitting a three-run homer in the bottom of the first to stake the Sox to a 3–0 lead. Tiant couldn't blow this. He was cruising.

But with one out in the top of the fifth—and a man on first—Pete put together an at bat that helped spark the rally. He worked the count full against Tiant, fouled off two nasty strikes high and outside, saw seven pitches, and roped the eighth pitch to straight-away center field for a line-drive single. Griffey followed with a triple, scoring two runs. Bench drove in Griffey to tie the game, and the Reds started to pile on.

By the bottom of the eighth, they were up 6–3—just six outs away from a World Series title—and they weren't even worried when Lynn led off the frame with a single and the next batter walked. Their best reliever, Rawly Eastwick, was coming to the mound. He retired the next two Red Sox batters, without any drama, and then prepared to face a pinch hitter who scared no one: Bernie Carbo.

Bernie had once been a Cincinnati Red, and a hot prospect. The team had selected him in the first round of the 1965 draft, twenty picks before Johnny Bench. The Reds believed in his left-handed swing, his power, and his understanding of the strike zone, and Bernie proved them right, at least for a while. In 1970, his first year in the big leagues, he batted .310 and helped Pete make it to his first World Series against the Orioles.

But Bernie made a baserunning mistake in game one of that series that cost the team, running into an out at home plate. Even years later, Pete would talk about Bernie's gaffe, saying, "It was a play that couldn't happen." More problematic for Bernie's career: he argued with Howsam over his contract. The arguments got him benched in 1971. Bernie began to drink and smoke marijuana, and in 1972 the Reds traded him away in the middle of a West Coast road trip. He had become expendable by crossing Howsam, batting .210, and proving himself not very useful on the bench. Sparky didn't think much of Bernie as a pinch hitter.

Standing on second base in the bottom of the eighth inning now, Lynn knew that Sparky's critique wasn't necessarily accurate. Just a week earlier, in game three, Bernie had hit a pinch-hit home run. But even Lynn believed things looked bleak now. From where he was standing on second, Lynn could see what Eastwick was throwing better than almost anyone, and he could tell that Bernie was overmatched.

Bernie looked at strike one. He swung and missed for strike two. He fouled off a juicy fastball that he probably should have hit, but didn't, and then he nearly struck out on Eastwick's next offering, fouling off the pitch at the last possible moment with a hesitant swing. "The worst swing you'd ever seen," Pete said later. Bernie was lost—and no one knew it better than Bernie himself. At this point, he was just hoping not to embarrass himself.

Eastwick kicked and fired. Another fastball. But this time Bernie was looking for it—and this time the pitch drifted over the middle of the plate. Bernie swung hard. The crowd roared, and then the world went silent. Bernie Carbo heard nothing, felt nothing, remembered nothing.

It was 11:18 p.m. on the East Coast, and he had just tied the game. Home run.

35

BERNIE RAN AROUND the bases as if he had been shot out of a circus cannon, pumping his fists in the air, holding his arms out at his side like wings, and hollering in the night. "Don't you wish you were this strong?" Bernie said as he rounded second base and saw Pete Rose.

On the infield, Joe Morgan blacked out. Later, he'd have no memory of seeing Bernie run past. Only one thought was clear in his mind: the Reds were cursed, all of them cursed. They had lost to Oakland in 1972 and New York in 1973, and it looked as if they could lose again now. But across the diamond at third, Pete remained optimistic, even as Bernie shouted at him. In Pete's mind, the Reds weren't cursed; there was no such thing as a curse. They were blessed. The game was tied, the Reds had blown it, and Pete felt blessed. He realized in the moment that he was suddenly part of something special, a great game, a historic game. He savored it.

For the next hour, the two teams battled, exchanging blows like bloodied boxers in a ring, starting with Boston. In the bottom of the ninth, the Red Sox loaded the bases with nobody out. Fred Lynn was coming to the plate, and all Lynn needed to win it was a deep fly ball. Denny Doyle would have tagged up at third and Boston would have won. But Lynn's hit was a high pop-up to shallow left field. George Foster caught it near the foul line with fans screaming in his face. Boston's third-base coach told Doyle *not* to tag up, *not* to go. "No, no, no," he said. But amid the crowd noise, Doyle heard, "Go, go, go." Foster threw a one-hop laser to home plate, and Bench laid down the tag. Doyle was out, double play. The Reds were still alive—and threatening.

In the eleventh, Morgan hit a shot to deep right field, with one out and Griffey on first. It appeared to be a double off the bat—maybe even a home run. But Dwight Evans made a leaping, one-handed catch near the wall, robbing Morgan and doubling up

Griffey, who was running on the play. Evans threw to first base to end the inning, and the game kept going—on and on, past children's bedtimes, beyond midnight, and deep into the twelfth. By then, the Reds were into their eighth pitcher, Pat Darcy, a rookie, and Carlton Fisk couldn't wait to get to the plate.

In the on-deck circle during the commercial break before the inning started, Fisk turned to Lynn and told him that Darcy didn't have it. Fisk was going to get on base, he said, and then Lynn could drive him in to win the game. Now Fisk stood at the plate with his bat in his hands, limbered up, stared into the grain of his bat, shook his head, eyes wide open, and turned on the second pitch he saw: a fastball low and inside.

What happened next took roughly three and a half seconds. The ball soared into the night sky, hugging the left-field line—maybe fair and possibly foul. The crowd rose to its feet, transfixed. Sixty-six million people watched on their televisions at home, wondering. Lynn froze in the on-deck circle, waiting. Pete turned to watch on the infield, and Fisk dropped his bat and side-hopped toward first base, guiding the ball with two hands.

He was directing it fair . . . fair . . .

It banged off the foul pole—gone.

Fifty miles away in Fisk's hometown of Charlestown, New Hampshire, church bells rang out in the dark. There would be a game seven, and Sparky Anderson felt sick about it. He couldn't sleep in his hotel room that night, and after a while, he stopped trying. He called a scout to his room and talked to him until four o'clock in the morning. But once again, Pete had a different reaction. Late in game six, he turned to Fisk and said, "This is some kind of game, isn't it?" And in the aftermath of the loss, he didn't feel any different. Pete told Sparky to relax.

"We're going to win," he said.

Seventy-five million people tuned in to watch the next night on NBC—the largest audience in American sports history to date. Roughly, one out of every three people in the country were sitting in front of their televisions, and to Sparky's horror Cincinnati fell behind early. The Sox jumped out to a 3–0 lead with the Spaceman on the mound. Pete went hitless in his first two at bats, and he was running out of chances to make good on his promise to deliver Sparky a victory when he stepped to the plate to lead off the sixth.

It was a moment when many hitters, even great ones, would start to press, try to do too much, swing for the fences, give in to anxiety. Not Pete. He took the same approach as always. He looked at a first-pitch strike because, as the leadoff man in the inning, it was his job to make the Spaceman work. He then laid off the next two pitches, both balls, and when the Spaceman threw his fourth pitch on the outside corner, Pete didn't try to do anything special with it. He poked the ball where it wanted to go: right between first and second base. A ground ball single.

With a 3–0 lead, the Spaceman didn't spend a single moment worrying about the runner on first base, Pete Rose. He induced the next batter, Joe Morgan, to hit an easy fly ball for an out, and he believed he could get Johnny Bench to hit into an inning-ending double play by enticing Johnny to swing at one of his off-speed pitches or his sinker ball, tailing down and away. "Bill Lee loves it when the big right-handers come up," Kubek told Gowdy upstairs in the NBC broadcast booth. "Usually, he can get the ground ball to the left side."

Kubek sounded like a prophet. Just moments later, Bench slapped an easy two hopper to shortstop Rick Burleson and Burleson prepared to flip the ball to Denny Doyle at second. The Red Sox were going to get out of the sixth, clean.

But Doyle was playing deep in the hole to protect against Bench going to the opposite field. He was late getting to the bag, and that gave Pete time to get there, too. By the time Burleson flipped the ball to Doyle at second for the force-out—"They got *one*!" Gowdy cried in the broadcast booth—Pete was bearing down on Doyle like a runaway truck on the Massachusetts Turnpike. He slid high at Doyle's knees and threw an elbow at the end for good measure, like he was known to do, and Doyle, under pressure, airmailed his throw to first—several feet over Yaz's head. "Up, up, away," Doyle said later.

The Spaceman was fuming. Instead of the inning being over, it was now Bench on second and Pérez at the plate, though Pérez wasn't going to be there for long. He was waiting on one of the Spaceman's looping curveballs, and when he got one, Pérez hit it out of the park.

Boston's lead had shrunk to one. The Spaceman was soon pulled from the game, and the Reds weren't finished. In the top of the seventh, with two outs and Griffey on second, Pete returned to the plate for arguably the biggest at bat of his life. With a single, he could tie the game.

Gowdy and Kubek could sense the tension in the night. "The Boston fans," Gowdy said, "are becoming uneasy." Pete had nine hits in the series, more than anyone else on the Reds, and Boston's new pitcher, the high-kicking Roger Moret, started him with a fastball on the outside corner. Then Moret made a mistake: he went back to the outside corner again, and Pete scalded the pitch into center field for a base hit. Griffey scored. Tie game, 3–3.

The fans at Fenway tried to rally their team, chanting, "Go, Sox, Go." But Pete was almost chanting, too. From third base in the late innings of the game, he exhorted his teammates to find a way to win, pounding his fist into his glove and shouting like a Little Leaguer in a grown man's body. Cincinnati's bullpen stifled Boston's hitters. Griffey walked to start the ninth. The Red Sox pitched around Pete, walking him to get to Morgan, and with two outs and two men on Morgan hit a little flare to center.

If they had been playing on the AstroTurf in Cincinnati, Fred Lynn was sure he could have reached the ball before it hit the ground. But the outfield grass at Fenway was still soft and spongy after all the rain. Lynn could feel the water in his shoes, and he had no choice but to field Morgan's hit on one hop. Griffey scored, and the Reds' bullpen held on in the bottom of the ninth to win it.

Cincinnati 4, Boston 3.

Pete Rose was finally a World Series champion.

Network executives were giddy with excitement. NBC and ABC had recently signed a new, record-breaking $93 million deal to televise baseball games starting in 1976, and the Reds and the Red Sox had proven that the networks were going to make money from it. People would tune in to watch players like Pete Rose.

"He got all the clutch hits," Morgan said in the champagne celebration after the game, "every time we needed one."

Bob Howsam credited Pete, too. The key to the entire season, Howsam said on NBC, was Pete agreeing to move to third base so that Griffey and Foster could play every day in the outfield, and Sparky Anderson reminded people of one more contribution that Pete had made: his hard slide into Denny Doyle in the sixth inning that broke up the double play and brought Tony Pérez to the plate. "That won the ballgame for us," Sparky said. Without it, Bench gets doubled up and Pérez never hits his home run.

The writers voted Pete MVP of the series, and he collected all the spoils of victory. Customers at his restaurant on the West Side gave him standing ovations in the dining room; *Sports Illustrated* voted him the "Sportsman of the Year"; the S. Rae Hickok foundation named him the "Professional Athlete of the Year" and presented him with its famous, diamond-encrusted Hickok belt at a black-tie ceremony in New York; and *Sport* magazine gave him a new car: a two-door Pacer from American Motors.

Pete had no use for the Pacer in his garage on Countryhills. He had started driving a Rolls-Royce—deep red, license plate PETE—and he had a Porsche, too. But he was thrilled to have the Hickok award—a heavyweight belt worth at least $10,000—and he couldn't wait to play baseball again in 1976. In the champagne-soaked locker room in Boston, he asked with boyhood innocence if maybe they could start right now.

"I wish opening day was tomorrow," Pete said, sounding almost sad. "I really do wish we started all over again tomorrow."

The beat writers thought the comment to be just one more example of how Pete was different. Who else would sit in the clubhouse after winning his first World Series and say he wanted to start all over again? But Pete's need to play—his desire to swing and keep swinging—went deeper than the joy it provided him. The game focused his energies and kept Pete away from the racetrack and all the characters who lived there in the shadows: the railbirds, the bookies, men like Al Esselman, and friends like Mario Núñez, the Cuban—characters who worried Pete's teammates. At least one teammate was worried, anyway.

At the World Series against Boston that fall—the greatest moment in Pete's life—Johnny Bench approached Curt Gowdy on the field one day. The two men had plans for the winter; Bench was supposed to go quail hunting with Gowdy in Arizona for Gowdy's television program, *The American Sportsman.* But what Bench wanted to discuss now had nothing to do with birds, buckshot, or even baseball. As Gowdy recalled it later, Bench was looking for an intervention of sorts—with Pete Rose.

Gowdy was confused; he didn't know Pete that well. Johnny said it didn't matter. Pete liked Gowdy, and Johnny believed that the NBC announcer might be able to talk some sense into him. Johnny was worried, he said, about the company Pete was keeping. The term Gowdy remembered was "bad guys."

Pete Rose was hanging out with "bad guys."

ACT IV
FALL

36

Ralph Evaristo Rubio Jr. treated his wives the way most people treated cars. Every few years, he traded in his old model for a new one.

By late 1975, Ralph was forty-four years old, and he had been divorced no fewer than seven times. He had left Sylvia, Kathleen, Mary, Barbara, Carmen, Gloria, and Nora—and his newest bride, his eighth wife, Rosemary, who was almost twenty years his junior, wouldn't last, either. Ralph—a first-generation Cuban American from Tampa with a pretty face and deep connections to the city's underworld—was always moving on to the next-best thing: a new tavern to run, new go-go dancers to recruit, and new illegal schemes to cook up. Crime ran in the family.

Ralph's favorite uncle, Tito, was a mobster who had built a gambling empire in Tampa's Ybor City neighborhood in the 1930s, before getting gunned down on his porch in a coordinated hit in 1938. Tito's alleged infraction was opening a gambling den in a rival mob's territory. His assassination would never be solved, and it gave Ralph a certain aura in Tampa. He was a *Rubio.* He could do anything he wanted. He bragged that he owned local judges who could get him out of trouble, and he ran an illegal sportsbook out of his house.

It was in this world that Ralph's children grew up, including Terry, the first child of his third wife, Mary. Terry wasn't the most popular girl at Leto High School in Tampa in the early 1970s, but she was hard to forget. She had a big, mischievous smile, dark hair that flowed off her shoulders, and access to a life that eluded most teenage girls. Even when she was underage, Terry could get into any club in town, because she was Ralph Rubio's kid. Doors opened for her. Velvet ropes came down, and men she didn't know came to her defense. Once, she recalled later, when a boyfriend hit her in anger, the young man ended up in the hospital with two broken legs.

Terry dreamed of being Annette Funicello, the bikini-clad star of 1960s beach movies. Instead, after high school graduation in 1971, she worked a series of unfulfilling jobs as a telephone operator, a bank teller, a cocktail waitress. Nothing lasted. Finally, in late 1975, the Tampa Sports Authority hired her to work in marketing and promotions. The authority owned the Cincinnati Reds' spring training complex around Al Lopez Field, and Terry was perfectly suited for her new position. She was to give tours to youth baseball teams, help the kids meet the big-league players, and make people feel welcome in a place called Redsland.

Pete Rose arrived at spring training in early 1976 like the king of baseball.

He was the reigning World Series MVP, the reigning *Sports Illustrated* "Sportsman of the Year," the owner of that bejeweled Hickok belt, the prize awarded to the country's best professional athlete, and one of the best-paid players in the game. In 1976, Pete was going to be the sixth-highest-paid player in baseball, and he was about to make even more—a lot more. Two days before Christmas 1975, an arbitrator ruled that two veteran players, who had played without signing their contracts in 1975, were not subject to the reserve clause. They had the right to sell their services on the open market to the highest bidder—like Curt Flood had longed to do. They were free agents.

Owners were so frustrated with the arbiter that they fired him immediately, sued for relief in federal court, and locked the players out of camp when spring training was scheduled to begin in late February. Terry Rubio had no tours to give at Redsland, and Pete decided to stay home in Cincinnati into early March. Instead of working out in Tampa, he attended a ceremony at West High, where the street outside was being renamed in his honor: Pete Rose Drive.

But he had too many plans in Florida to stay home for long. He was turning thirty-five that spring and needed only about 450 more hits to reach 3,000 for his career—an achievement that would ensure his enshrinement at the National Baseball Hall of Fame in Cooperstown, New York. He didn't want to waste a single moment because of a lockout, and he had other reasons to get to Tampa, too. The Cuban was expecting him. They needed to hit the triple-header circuit: the horse track, the dog track, jai alai.

Worst-case scenario, if the players remained locked out, Pete could spend a few weeks in Florida gambling while Karolyn and the kids lounged on the pool deck at the motel where they always stayed: King Arthur's Inn. Pete had a young Cincinnati police cadet drive his Rolls-Royce down to Florida and then hopped onto a plane. He was flying.

With nowhere to train due to the lockout, the world-champion Reds floated around for a few weeks in Tampa. They got kicked off a field at a local university. They spent a day practicing at a golf course, and they finally settled on a temporary home: the Little League fields in West Tampa.

About ten guys came to the first practice, but soon most of the team was there. Pete would pull up in his Rolls-Royce, park it on the curb, grab a handful of baseball bats out of the trunk, and go to work while fans watched, including tour groups organized by the Tampa Sports Authority, tour groups led by Terry Rubio.

The first day she saw Pete, she didn't think much of him. If she was sizing up anyone, it was Pete's younger teammates, who were in their early twenties like her. But Pete had his eye on Terry. On the fence line at the Little League park, amid a cluster of kids wearing ball caps, she stood out like a heavenly vision. Not a "perfect ten" perhaps, as the guys liked to say, but close. Terry was a "nine and a half," and the Cuban finally approached her on the fence with an offer. "Want to go to the dog track?" he asked, nodding at the ballplayers behind him to make it clear what he meant. Terry accepted, and it wasn't long before she found herself in the passenger seat of Pete's Rolls-Royce and at his table at the track, with the Cuban lining up their bets and big money changing hands. On some nights, Pete won or lost thousands of dollars, but either way he was the same with Terry: funny and attentive. *Boyfriend material.*

They hung out that week in what turned out to be the last days of baseball as everyone had known it. On March 9, a federal judge upheld the arbitrator's decision, effectively ending the reserve clause forever, and eight days later owners reluctantly unlocked the doors of their facilities. Going forward, in a deal that the owners and players finalized later that summer, players with six years of service in the big leagues could become free agents in 1977, so long as they didn't have an existing contract. And players with existing contracts had the option to play for the same money the following year, then become free agents in 1978.

Everything was about to change. Million-dollar mega-deals were about to become the norm. Spring training officially opened. Players began working out at Redsland and Terry Rubio started giving her tours on-site, though by then she was more than just another marketing girl. She was Pete's girl.

One day, shortly after the Reds returned to the park, Terry remembered how a former team official found her in the stands, pressed a key for a hotel room into her hand, and told her, with a wink, "Pete said to give this to his nine and a half." The room was at the Old Orleans Motel, a vintage roadside gem just two miles from Pete and Karolyn at King Arthur's Inn, but Terry believed it was okay because she thought Pete had an agreement with his wife: Karolyn could be Mrs. Pete Rose, and Pete could do whatever he wanted.

Terry had sex with Pete in the hotel room that night, she said, and then continued to meet him—not just for the rest of spring training, but throughout the 1976 baseball season in a relationship that was possibly the worst-kept secret in the National League. When Pete wanted Terry to join him on the road in Philadelphia, San Francisco, Los Angeles, or Montreal, she booked her flights directly through the Reds' traveling secretary. She stayed in Pete's hotel room, mingled with the other wives and the press, sunbathed next to Sparky Anderson at hotel swimming pools, and cheered Pete all the way to the World Series again. Terry was in New York that October when the Reds faced the Yankees, trying to win their second championship in a row. She was in one hotel room at the New York Sheraton while Karolyn was in another.

It was a brazen arrangement—even by ballplayers' standards. Terry was worried she would run into Karolyn in the lobby. But

Pete seemed to get off on pushing the limits, Terry thought. He was doing it in other parts of his life, too.

The night before the World Series started, he went to the racetrack in northern Kentucky, gambled, and complained that there was only one ten-dollar window open. And on the field during the series, he risked his personal safety to intimidate the Yankees. Every time their all-star leadoff man, Mickey Rivers, stepped into the batter's box, Pete played him to bunt down the third baseline. He planted his feet in the ground about fifty feet away, refused to budge, and let Mickey know it. "I ain't moving," Pete shouted.

Mickey hadn't seen someone play him this close since the ball fields of his youth, and the sight of Pete just standing there—crouched down in his ready position and glaring—left Mickey shaken. He went 0 for 9 in the first two games and 3 for 18 on the series. Pete Rose was crazy—totally crazy, Mickey said decades later—and he was also a World Series champion for the second time.

The Reds embarrassed the Yankees, won the series in a four-game sweep, and then celebrated with eight cases of champagne in the visitors' clubhouse at Yankee Stadium. But compared to the year before, the party was quiet, almost subdued—even for Pete. "I just couldn't get turned on about the World Series this year," he admitted, after winning it.

He had *expected* to win.

Karolyn flew home in the wee hours of the morning on the team plane with Pete, the other players, and their wives, and appeared next to her husband later that day at the Reds' victory parade in downtown Cincinnati. The city's first couple, Pete and Karolyn, both wore long coats, trimmed around the collar with soft pelts of luxurious fur, and waved to the massive crowd at Fountain Square, smiling and happy and telling themselves pleasant little lies. Karolyn talked about "togetherness" and Pete vowed that the Reds would win the World Series again next year.

With the death of the reserve clause and the dawn of free agency, Bob Howsam knew it was unlikely. He wouldn't be able to afford this team in the years ahead, and he decided to get in front of the financial disaster that was coming by trading Tony Pérez to the Montreal Expos in December 1976. He broke up the Big Red Machine.

On paper, Howsam could defend the move. Pérez's best years were behind him, and the Reds could pay his replacement far less for roughly the same production. What Howsam didn't know, perhaps because he rarely consorted with the players, was that Pérez had been the true leader in the Reds' clubhouse all these years, the quiet glue in a room full of loud individual stars, and without him the team would crumble.

Joe Morgan was furious. When reporters called him with news of the trade at his home on the West Coast, Morgan lashed out at Howsam and the Reds, saying, "They used Tony Pérez. . . . They used him until they used him up." Others were just stunned.

"My God," Karolyn gasped when she heard.

She and Pete were on a cruise in the Caribbean that week with the Griffeys, which left it to Johnny Bench to bear the burden of saying goodbye alone. He attended the press conference at which the trade was announced and supported Pérez, misty-eyed, despite his own troubles that winter. Johnny's marriage to Vickie Chesser was over. It had hardly lasted a year, and it was about to become a public spectacle. By spring training in 1977, Johnny and Vickie would be fighting in court and in the pages of the Cincinnati newspapers. Johnny said Vickie was a woman who never became a wife, and Vickie said Johnny was "a true tragedy as a person."

But the biggest problem brewing for the Reds was Pete Rose. That winter, he didn't try to hide Terry Rubio from anyone. He bought her expensive jewelry, took her to the racetrack in Kentucky with friends, teammates, and reporters, traveled with her on private jets to shoot commercials in New York, allowed her to appear in newspaper photographs standing next to him, and, according to Terry, wanted her even closer to him at spring training in 1977. That March, she said, she got her own room at King Arthur's Inn, for secret meet-ups after Karolyn went to sleep at night.

It was reckless behavior. It threatened to destroy everything Pete had built in his fourteen-year career, and Terry wasn't the only one at King Arthur's that spring watching Pete coming and going, waiting for him, hopeful. A young man from New Bedford, Massachusetts, had a room at the motel, too, and more than any other person this man would shape Pete's life for the next decade, until he and Pete were inextricably tangled up and going down together.

His name was Tommy Gioiosa. He was nineteen years old, and he was obsessed with Pete Rose.

37

Tommy Gioiosa always knew what he wanted to do when he grew up. He wanted to play baseball, and if he couldn't play baseball, he wanted to be a cop.

In the 1960s—in Tommy's hometown of New Bedford—there didn't seem to be many other desirable options. Tommy didn't want to work on the fishing boats in the harbor or in the seafood processing plants on the shore. He didn't want to be a scissors grinder like his grandfather, sharpening tools in town, and he was certain that he didn't want to end up like his dad. Tommy's father cut glass for a living and spent too much of his earnings on beer, Tommy thought, hanging out at a local establishment called the Panthers Athletic and Social Club. The club sounded elite, but like everything else in Tommy's life it was rough around the edges, old men at the bar and money down the drain. The Gioiosas owned half of a two-family house on Covell Street in town, and not much else. Sometimes, they didn't even have enough hot water at the house for everyone to be able to shower in the morning.

Tommy probably should have focused on his backup plan: becoming a police officer. But by the time he was at New Bedford High in 1972, he was fixated on earning fame, riches, and the validation he never got at home through baseball. For his first job, he worked the door of Carl Yastrzemski's traveling trophy gallery, a trailer full of Yaz memorabilia that parked in front of the Mars Bargainland discount store in New Bedford one weekend. In his sophomore year of high school, he earned the starting nod at second base. He made up for his lack of size with grit, discipline, and a good eye at the plate. He batted .561 his senior year and was rumored to be getting looks from the Cleveland Indians and some big-time colleges. "I have a prize for you," one scout wrote in a letter to the baseball coach at Virginia Tech that spring, "and his name is Tom Gioiosa." Instead, in 1977, Tommy joined the baseball team at Massasoit Community College in nearby Brockton.

It was a long way from Virginia Tech, but at least Tommy was still playing and doing a little traveling, too. In March 1977, Massasoit went south to Tampa to play in a college tournament at Al Lopez Field. They checked in at King Arthur's, and on the pool deck there Tommy befriended a little boy named Petey. The kid was seven years old, knew a lot about baseball, and said his father played for the Reds—a story that Tommy wasn't sure he believed until he was standing in Petey's hotel room later, meeting the kid's parents: Pete and Karolyn Rose.

Pete was watching golf at the time and shouting at the television because someone had missed a putt, and Tommy could hardly speak. He had modeled his whole game after the Reds' star, outworking and outhustling people, and now Tommy was standing in Pete's hotel room, shaking hands with his hero. It was an unforgettable moment for Tommy, and he clung to it like a raft in a storm after he returned to Massachusetts that spring. He hadn't just met Pete Rose; apparently, Tommy had made an impression. Pete liked Tommy. He remembered his name and everything—which seemed notable, given everything that was going on in Pete's life. In addition to juggling Terry and Karolyn that month, gambling at the racetrack, playing ball, and keeping secrets, he was embroiled in yet another contract dispute with Bob Howsam.

Howsam was only fifty-nine years old that March, but he suffered from chronic and debilitating back pain and was beginning to feel too old for baseball—at least this new iteration of baseball. He couldn't believe that Reggie Jackson was going to make more than half a million dollars in 1977 playing for the New York Yankees; that a lesser player like the Reds' shortstop Davey Concepción refused to report to camp that winter unless Howsam doubled his salary; or that he could lose Pete in 1978, and Johnny in 1979, unless he signed them both to new, long-term deals worth millions.

Howsam finally decided to write a letter to the fans explaining his predicament. The Reds were working to sign their big-name stars, he said. "But," Howsam added, "our ability to keep baseball as the prime family sports entertainment bargain depends on operating the club with fiscal responsibility." That meant they would not be bringing in high-priced free agents in 1977 and not overspending on aging stars like Pete Rose. The ball club and the player had always bickered over money, but that winter their fight bled into April. Spring training was over, and they were back in Cincinnati, before Pete finally worked out a two-year contract worth roughly $750,000 with his new agent, Reuven Katz, a tax lawyer with a Harvard law degree and an office on the thirty-fourth floor of Cincinnati's tallest building.

It was late, almost ten o'clock at night, when they got it done, and there were just a few witnesses in the office: Reuven, Pete, and one of Howsam's assistants, though Terry Rubio wasn't far away. To start the 1977 season, she flew north to be with Pete.

Cincinnati got off to a great start that week. Just hours after Pete signed his contract in Reuven Katz's office, the Reds beat the Padres on opening day. They won their second game, too, starting the season 2-0, and Pete seemed giddy with excitement.

He had made arrangements for Terry to stay in town. He got her set up in an empty bedroom at a friend's house in a suburban neighborhood north of the city, and Terry came to Reds games at Riverfront Stadium that spring, cheering in good seats just a couple rows away from Karolyn, in a way that made her host, Pete's friend, uncomfortable. The man was a vice president of a local shoe company and close enough with the Roses that he had spent the holidays at their house on Countryhills. He didn't want Terry drawing attention to herself by cheering so loudly. He didn't want Karolyn to start asking questions.

Fortunately for Pete's nervous friend, there wasn't much for Terry to cheer in 1977. Howsam had miscalculated by not signing free agents and trading away Pérez. The locker room was quieter without him and the lineup was, too. Thirty-nine times that year, Pete advanced to third base with fewer than two outs in an inning and didn't score—a statistic that didn't make any sense to anyone. Sparky Anderson wondered at times if his players were even trying, and Pete wondered the same thing—especially after the Reds were eliminated from the playoffs in September.

Pete was still out there hustling and refusing to take days off. He said it was important to him that the Reds finish second in the division, not third. "You're damn right I want to finish second," he growled at reporters. But the same couldn't be said for his teammates. One night, Foster gave up on a fly ball that he thought was a home run and watched it bang off the top of the wall for a triple, and other nights Morgan, Bench, and Gerónimo didn't play at all. They sat in the dugout, resting. "Did you see our lineup tonight?" Pete asked reporters after one of those games. "All of a sudden, everybody is hurt. No one wants to play."

After the season ended, Pete donned a cream-colored three-piece suit, slipped his two World Series rings on his fingers, clasped a gold bracelet on one wrist, and went to the racetrack in Kentucky to gamble. It had become a postseason tradition for Pete, and he looked good that day walking the grandstand, with his rings and his jewelry. The gold bracelet was bedazzled with gems that shimmered in the autumn sunlight and spelled out his name. But unlike the year before, Terry Rubio stayed scarce, out of the photographs, away from the press, and far from the racetrack.

She had to hide. She had to keep a low profile.

Terry was pregnant.

38

TERRY KNEW THE baby was Pete's. She hadn't been sleeping with anyone else the previous spring. She could pinpoint her pregnancy to a twelve-day stretch in June during which she spent six days with Pete in Cincinnati and then six days with him on the road in Montreal and Philadelphia, and she recalled how Pete didn't argue with her about it when she told him the news.

He seemed to know the baby was his, too. He visited Terry in Florida that winter and started sending her money to help.

The Reds had a harder time handling the situation. At spring training in 1978, when Terry was eight months pregnant, a prominent Cincinnati business executive, whom Terry had never met before, arranged to have lunch with her in Tampa to ask if she would marry Pete—a proposition that Terry dismissed as both ridiculous and impossible.

Pete had no intention of acknowledging their child or changing his life in any way. Even as Terry was about to give birth, Pete was still married to Karolyn and spending his free time at spring training doing triple-headers with the Cuban and a new gambling friend, Reds groundskeeper Arnie Metz. After games in Tampa that March, the three men would pile into Pete's latest car, a Porsche, and hit the circuit, with Arnie crammed into the backseat and the Cuban laughing in the night. There was no room in the car for Terry, no place for Terry at all. She had heard reports from friends in Cincinnati that Pete was already moving on to someone new, a blond cocktail waitress named Carol Woliung who was an upgrade over Terry in many ways, at least according to Pete.

Carol was twenty-four years old, had been a cheerleader in high school in rural Indiana, was freshly divorced from a car dealer there, was now working at a popular bar near Riverfront Stadium, and, unlike Terry, was decidedly *not* pregnant. Pete liked to brag that Carol had the "nicest ass" in Cincinnati. Bottom line: Pete didn't want to marry Terry, and Terry didn't want to marry Pete—a message that Terry delivered to the business executive over lunch in Tampa in her usual straightforward manner. The Reds couldn't make her—and her baby—go away by ringing wedding bells. She was having this baby, with or without a husband, with or without Pete.

What should have concerned people in Cincinnati was a different issue. Around this time, Terry believed she was being followed, tailed and watched. One of her father's friends at the sheriff's office in Tampa confirmed it, and the man who was doing the following later confirmed it, too. He was a former New York City cop now working as a private investigator in Florida, and his client, he said, was Major League Baseball. According to the private investigator, baseball officials hired him to monitor Pete and Terry in Tampa because of the number of phone calls that Pete placed to Terry, often just before games in 1977. They wanted to know if Pete had been placing bets with Terry, maybe even bets on baseball, who then could have funneled the action to her father, Ralph Rubio, the bookie.

Terry denied it. She wasn't even sure if Pete knew her father was a bookie. She didn't have a close relationship with the man, and she said Pete met him only a couple of times. The private investigator parked outside her apartment in Tampa seemed to be wasting his time. Still, it was unsettling—and possibly not just for Terry.

On March 1, 1978, Bob Howsam stepped down as chief operating officer of the Reds. The decision had been in the works for months: because of free agency, because of his back pain, because he had just turned sixty—because of a million reasons. Howsam wanted to spend more time out west, where he had a home in the mountains and a swimming pool fed by a natural hot spring. He wanted to float in those soothing waters and focus on his health. But the Reds' struggles in 1977—and Pete's problems off the field going into 1978—certainly gave Howsam no reason to stick around.

He walked away and handed over control to his hand-chosen successor: a no-nonsense, puritanical, hitch-yourself-up-by-the-bootstraps U.S. Navy veteran from a small town in Nebraska, Dick Wagner.

Wagner couldn't wait to get started. He had been with Howsam since their days in St. Louis in the 1960s. He believed in Howsam's approach and had long prepared for this moment while working as Howsam's top lieutenant in Cincinnati. As Wagner said on the day he took over, "You might say that I got my Ph.D. in Bob Howsamism." The Reds' new leader announced that he wouldn't change a thing.

But even as he said it, Wagner knew it wasn't true. While he shared Howsam's philosophy—and his fervor for frugality and uniformity—he was a different man. He liked to arrive at the stadium at six in the morning, roam the building with a walkie-talkie during games, and respond to problems that other executives, including Howsam, delegated to a minion or ignored altogether. Wagner had reprimanded Reds players in the past for poor posture on the bench.

He had fined players for tossing baseballs into the stands—they cost money—and he had intervened once in the middle of a game when he noticed that Pete Rose had violated the team's uniform rules by writing his number on his batting helmet so that he could easily find it in the dugout. The number needed to be erased, Wagner said, phoning the clubhouse—right away, if possible. This is what men of action did, and Wagner was nothing if not a man of action. Before one nationally televised game at Riverfront in 1976, Wagner leaped onto the field in his shirt and tie, grabbed a fire extinguisher while Howsam looked on, and used it to drive off a swarm of bees that was harassing players and fans near the Reds' dugout. Wagner realized that no one else wanted to tangle with the bees. "So," he said later, "I did it myself."

Now Howsam had gone west. Wagner was in charge, and one of his first projects was cleaning up another problem that seemingly no one wanted to touch for fear of getting stung: Pete Rose, with his gambling friends, his affairs, and his secret baby, a daughter, born on March 24, 1978, in Tampa, just three weeks after Wagner had taken control. Pete visited the little girl in the hospital, Terry recalled, but he didn't stay long. He had to get to Cincinnati, where there was baseball to play and a marriage to save.

Karolyn had tolerated a lot over the years, but Terry's baby in Florida and Pete's new, soon-to-be love interest in Cincinnati, Carol, were insults that she could not abide in silence. Their daughter, Fawn, was a teenager now—old enough to understand that her parents were struggling—and Karolyn didn't want Fawn to think that a husband could ever treat his wife the way Pete did. In front of Fawn one day around this time in the middle of a Reds game at the stadium, Karolyn confronted Carol near the concession stands and ripped a diamond necklace off Carol's neck that Karolyn suspected Pete had purchased.

By June 1978, it all came to a head: Pete moved out of the house on Countryhills. He left Karolyn and the kids, and his man cave in the basement with a pool table, a pinball machine, and trophy cases on the wall, and started staying with his friend, the shoe executive, who had provided a room to Terry the summer before. Pete took over the man's garage, parked his Rolls-Royce in one bay and his Porsche in the other, and spent his nights watching television in an upstairs bedroom. Pete and Karolyn were secretly separated, though not for long. The local newspapers were all over it. Their troubled marriage was now Dick Wagner's problem, too.

But Wagner was more concerned about Pete's gambling. He heard dark and persistent rumors that Pete was losing too much money, and not just at the track but with bookies. The new president of the Reds feared that one day one of these bookies would come for Pete, perhaps when his playing days were over. Wagner worried that they would send Pete a message by roughing him up or breaking his legs, and he knew if such a thing happened—if anything like this happened—it would bring shame upon the entire franchise. He needed to do something.

One day early in the 1978 season, players reported to Riverfront Stadium for a game and assembled around the batting cage at home plate for their usual pregame ritual: hitting, swinging, taking their cuts. It was the sort of thing that Pete loved, which is why Dave Collins noticed that Pete was missing. Collins was one of the newest Reds, a young prospect from South Dakota acquired that winter in one of Bob Howsam's final trades. He was twenty-five and didn't know much about Pete, except that he loved him. Collins had never seen a man so focused on hitting, so obsessed with his job. Some players didn't know where they were going on their next road trip, and then there was Pete. He could discuss, in granular detail, the rhythms of the Mets' or the Cubs' starting rotation and how they would stack up when the Reds played them a month later. Pete could see it all. He missed nothing. He should have been there at the cage, and he wasn't, and Collins finally asked the question: "Where is he?"

One of his teammates nodded in the direction of Wagner's office above home plate. The story around the cage was that Wagner had called a meeting to discuss gambling with Pete and possibly two others: an official from the commissioner's office and someone from the FBI. If it was true, the baseball official and the FBI agent might have been one and the same. In the 1970s, the head of security for Major League Baseball was Henry Fitzgibbon, a man who had served in the FBI in the past and had long taken an interest in Pete Rose. Pete even drove Fitzgibbon out to the West Side to have a chat with his old bookie, Al Esselman. Pete wanted to prove to Fitzgibbon that he wasn't in debt and he wasn't in trouble. Dick Wagner had it all wrong—Pete Rose wasn't going to have his legs broken—and Esselman confirmed it. He told Fitzgibbon that Pete was fine. Fitzgibbon apparently felt satisfied with that answer, and whatever happened in Wagner's office on that day in 1978, it didn't change anything. "Pete played that night," Collins recalled decades later. "Everything went on as normal. I never heard anything about it again."

But Wagner made sure that some people knew there were problems. Around that time, he urged Reds broadcaster Marty Brennaman to stop hanging out with Pete on the road. Marty shouldn't be seen with him, Wagner said, or even have dinner with him. The phrase Wagner kept using was that Marty "couldn't afford it."

Pete could hurt Marty's career, Wagner suggested. He could hurt them all.

39

PLAYERS OFTEN GOT distracted over less—not Pete. Amid the questions about his gambling, the rumors of his debts, the birth of a daughter he didn't want to acknowledge, and the unraveling of his marriage in the spring of 1978, Pete felt good at the plate, swinging and swinging.

That May, he logged his 3,000th hit in a game against Montreal in Cincinnati, becoming just the thirteenth man in baseball history to ever reach the milestone. The crowd responded that night by chanting his name. Scoops Lawson wrote his usual column, hailing Pete in the pages of *The Cincinnati Post. The Cincinnati Enquirer* unveiled a new Pete Rose picture book, on sale for $50, and one *Enquirer* columnist wrote an entire piece celebrating Pete for being a *man*, for being macho—"Strongly Macho," the headline said. "The only ERA he worries about," the piece proclaimed, "is the ERA carried by the pitcher he is facing. Equal rights for women? That's for others."

Even the commissioner of baseball was celebrating. Bowie Kuhn sent Pete a congratulatory telegram. Notes piled up in Pete's locker—from Hutch's widow, Reggie Jackson, George Steinbrenner in New York, and Tommy Lasorda in Los Angeles—and the phone rang all night in the clubhouse. Bob Howsam called to say he was rooting for Pete, and Pete's business managers tried to capitalize on his achievement by rolling out a new product. Within days of the hit, they began selling a canned, chocolate-flavored beverage called Pete.

It was important to mark the moment because, at the time, it felt like there might never be another one for him. On the night of his 3,000th hit, Pete conceded that he could never get another thousand hits or come close to passing baseball's all-time leader, Ty Cobb, who had 4,191. Cobb's total, everyone agreed, was out of reach for a player who was already thirty-seven years old. It wasn't even likely that Pete would stay healthy long enough to claim Stan Musial's National League record—3,630. That task would take at least another four years, and in the afterglow of reaching 3,000, Pete's batting average cratered, like he was already done. By mid-June, he was batting just .274.

Then, on a Wednesday in the middle of the month, Pete started to get hot again. He went 2 for 4 at Wrigley Field in Chicago. The Reds won that afternoon and came home for a three-game weekend series against the Cardinals, where Pete kept hitting. He had seven hits against the Cardinals, hits in every game. That Monday the *Post* broke the news that Pete and Karolyn had separated, and still it didn't matter. The next night, in front of a wild and unruly crowd of fifty-five thousand people at Candlestick Park in San Francisco, Pete hit the first pitch of the game for a double.

San Francisco was in first place at the time, and facing Cincinnati felt like the playoffs. Fans wanted to boo the Reds or hit the Cincinnati players with cherry bombs and firecrackers, which they nearly did at least three times. At one point, Griffey could hear a bottle rocket come sizzling over his head in right field, and at another point a smoke bomb landed at Foster's feet in left. Like in New York in 1973, umpires had to stop the game and threaten the fans with a forfeit.

But amid the chaos, Pete went 2 for 5, scored twice, nearly scored a third time when he reached base on an error, and hustled all the way to third while the ball rattled around in the outfield. The Reds beat the Giants 6–3, and Pete had a little streak going. He had hit safely in five consecutive games.

The press first mentioned the streak when it hit nine games the following Saturday. Pete didn't talk about it at all; he just kept playing.

He batted .366 out west, and the streak went to ten games. He nearly incited a brawl with the Dodgers one night at Riverfront Stadium by yelling at L.A.'s rookie pitcher—"Nothing, kid," Pete snarled at him, "you've got nothing!"—and the streak went to seventeen games. He took a three-day hiatus for the All-Star break in mid-July; flew to San Diego; played in the game; beat the American League for the fifteenth time in the past sixteen years; reunited with Karolyn for one night there—the kids wanted to see him play; and picked up right where he had left off when the season resumed. The streak kept going. It went to twenty-six games. He bunted in Philadelphia to push it to thirty-two games, and he rolled into New York in late July looking for thirty-seven games at Shea Stadium.

A hit that night would tie the modern National League record, matching Tommy Holmes's feat for the Boston Braves in 1945, and no one wanted to see it more than Holmes himself. The Brooklyn native was sixty-one years old and worked in community relations for the Mets. But people didn't know who he was. Holmes had been forgotten. Now, with Pete in New York threatening his record and the press asking for photos of the two men together, the old player felt reborn.

"Thanks," Holmes told Pete, "for making me a big leaguer again."

It was an impossible way to play baseball. Hitting was a craft best practiced when one didn't think about anything outside the game, and with a streak on the line one couldn't help but think. Holmes said it took courage to come to the plate after starting a game 0 for 2 or 0 for 3, with an entire stadium hoping for a hit, and Joe Torre, the former catcher, now managing the Mets, said it was easy to lose that courage. In 1971, Torre had started the year with a twenty-two-game hitting streak—a small number, no one cared—and still Torre felt the burden of it. "There was pressure," he said, "even on me."

In New York, this pressure built like a wave, cresting over Pete's head. At the hotel where the Reds were staying, a crank caller awoke him before dawn with a message: "You're going to choke." Before noon that day, he had at least thirty interview requests. The press followed him anytime he left his room, even when he went to grab a sandwich on Seventh Avenue, and they jostled for position around his locker before the game, eighty reporters deep. Still, Pete didn't mind. He was happy to see everyone.

"Pressure?" he joked. "What pressure?"

Only two things bothered him, he said. First, in one of the morning papers, a reporter had described his single the previous day in Montreal as "a bloop to center field." Pete needed to correct the record on that. It was a liner, he said. "You could have hung wash on that thing for a month." Second, there had been a report that he and Karolyn had reconciled. Pete wanted everyone to know that this topic was off-limits. It was the one thing he wasn't going to discuss with the press.

"Tell them," he said, "to go fuck themselves."

It was a Monday night, and no one wanted to see the Mets play. They were fourteen games under .500 and fourteen games out of first. Prior to Pete extending his streak the previous day, New York had sold only seventeen thousand seats for the game. But with Pete chasing thirty-seven, and Holmes watching in the wings, eighteen thousand New Yorkers bought day-of-game tickets at the gate and then cheered for Pete, as if he were one of their own.

Pete couldn't believe it. The same crowd that had tried to take his head off with a whiskey bottle five years earlier was now chanting his name.

"Let's go, Pete. . . . Let's go, Pete."

Everyone was sure he would extend his streak to thirty-seven games—there was no question about it—and yet he was hitless in his first three tries that night, and he probably had only one more chance. Pete wasn't superstitious, but it seemed like a good time for a change. He grabbed a different bat to start the seventh inning and walked to the plate to face the Mets' starter, Pat Zachry.

Zachry, a tall right-hander and an All-Star, knew Pete well. Until the year before, the pair had been teammates on the Reds; Pete had even kept Zachry's dog at his house on Countryhills for a while. But Zachry was in no mood to answer questions about the streak before the game, and he wasn't going to help Pete now. The Reds and the Mets were tied 2–2. Zachry was trying to win. He put two breaking balls on the outside corner against Pete to start the seventh, and then he made a mistake: Zachry went there again. Pete slashed the ball into left field for a clean base hit, and the crowd at Shea Stadium gave him a standing ovation that lasted for three minutes.

Zachry didn't retire another batter that night. The Reds won the game. Tommy Holmes shook Pete's hand in a brief ceremony at first base, and the streak went on.

Thirty-eight . . . thirty-nine . . . forty . . .

It was the story of the summer, the story of a generation. Amid his hidden problems off the field, Pete was closing in on one of baseball's most hallowed records on it—Joe DiMaggio's fifty-six-game hitting streak. He wasn't wallowing over his broken marriage. He wasn't sulking about living in the empty bedroom at his friend's house. He was focused on DiMaggio. He was coming for DiMaggio. He wanted to run his streak to fifty-six games and he wondered if he might blow right past it, too.

"I might go forever," Pete said.

40

THE PRESS TREATED DiMaggio's fifty-six-game hitting streak as if it were a pillar of America itself. There was the Constitution, the Statue of Liberty, blue jeans, apple pie—and fifty-six games in 1941. Anyone who spoke about the achievement was required to address it with quiet reverence—Joe DiMaggio had earned this respect—and now here was Pete Rose swinging a sledgehammer at his record. After Pete got to thirty-eight games, DiMaggio sent him a congratulatory telegram. But the Yankee legend kept the message short. Just four words.

"Congratulations," he wrote, "and Good Luck."

The Reds had an off day on the last Thursday of July—unfortunate timing for Pete. Many people thought that a day off would break the spell. Pete didn't care. He hit in the batting cage that Friday; went to his son Petey's first baseball game under the lights on the West Side; took Petey and Fawn to dinner at McDonald's; and opened letters, including a card signed by the concessions staff at Shea Stadium. The Mets had made a fortune when Pete was in town—an extra $215,000, according to one estimate—and the concession workers wanted to thank him for it. Then Pete went out that weekend and got hits in every game against the Phillies. The streak went to forty-three. "And have you checked the schedule?" Pete asked Scoops Lawson.

The next thirteen games were against two of the worst teams in the league—the Braves and the Padres—and everybody knew what thirteen plus forty-three equaled.

Fifty-six.

"Don't get me wrong," Pete told Scoops. "A guy can go 0 for 4 against any team. But you gotta figure your chances are better against teams like the Braves and the Padres."

The press agreed, just as confident as Pete, if not more so. That Sunday night, just a few hours after Pete extended his streak to forty-three games, Phil Donahue taped an hour-long interview with him in front of six thousand people in Cincinnati, the largest audience ever assembled for one of America's favorite talk-show hosts. ABC planned to break into regularly scheduled programming that Monday night to air each of Pete's at bats against the Braves, and the Braves couldn't wait for Pete to get to town. Team officials expected forty-five-thousand fans for the first game—almost five times what they had been averaging at Fulton County Stadium that season. People queued up outside the gates at eight o'clock Monday morning to secure tickets. The line stretched down the street for two hundred yards, and when the Reds' team bus arrived about three hours before game time, Pete shouted greetings at concession stand workers.

"You're going to love me after tonight!" he said.

The Braves' owner certainly hoped so. The man was just three years older than Pete, and he was thinking about things far bigger than ticket sales, far bigger than peanuts and popcorn. In addition to owning the Braves, he had his own television network—Channel 17, it was called at the time. He broadcast Braves games, via satellite, across the South and into forty different states, and he was excited to bring Pete Rose, and his streak, into people's living rooms, because this was a show that people wanted to see. This was good television.

"We're Pulling for You, Pete!" said a note on the chalkboard inside the visitors' clubhouse on the day the Reds arrived in Atlanta. "Go Get 'Em!"

It was signed by the Montreal Expos, the team that had just left town; Pete's old teammate Tony Pérez; and the owner of the Braves: Ted Turner.

The Braves had to push back the start of the game that night by about half an hour. Too many people were stuck in traffic outside the stadium, and television executives wanted Pete's first at bat to be in prime time. The game finally went off a little after eight o'clock, and Pete dug into the batter's box, feeling confident. He had a history of dominating the Braves. In 1977, he had batted almost .500 against them, and he knew that night's starter—the crusty knuckleballer Phil Niekro—better than almost any other pitcher in the majors. Over the course of his career, Pete had more hits off Niekro than anyone else.

Niekro disappointed fans right away. He got behind in the count, three balls and a strike; threw a fastball; missed high and inside; and walked Pete to start the game. The crowd booed—with the streak on the line, a walk was the worst—and it rattled Niekro a little. He had played his entire career for the Braves, fifteen seasons. He didn't get booed in Fulton County, and he wanted to tell the forty-five thousand people in the stands how he really felt: Niekro was conflicted. He wasn't sure he wanted to be the one to end Pete's streak. Lately, Pete's quest for DiMaggio's record had captured Niekro's imagination just like everyone else's. The first thing he did every morning was check the paper to see if Pete got a hit.

In the third inning, it almost happened. Pete hit a crisp line drive, but it was right at the Braves' shortstop. He was out, and for a moment a negative thought tiptoed into his mind. Pete started to worry about the weather. There were storm clouds above the stadium, and a heavy rain after the fifth inning could wash out the game and make it official, even if they didn't finish. He needed that hit. He wanted it in his next at bat, and when he came up to start the sixth, Pete had a plan.

With the game tied 1–1 and the fans restless in their seats, he knew Niekro wouldn't want to walk him again. He also figured Niekro would start him with a couple of knuckleballs, Niekro's best pitch. Pete decided to let the knuckleballs flutter by, hope that Niekro got behind in the count, and then sit on one of his soft fastballs. The plan worked. Niekro missed with his first two knuckleballs and then uncorked a sinker—only it didn't sink. It hung there, belt high, and Pete slapped it between first and second base, just beyond the mitt of the Braves' diving second baseman. It was a ground ball with eyes, but it was through to the outfield. A bouncing single.

Forty-four games.

The crowd roared. Fireworks exploded in the night, and a beautiful young woman in a high-cut Braves uniform showing lots of leg delivered Pete a floral arrangement at first base. The flowers spelled out the number 44.

Niekro visited Pete in the visitors' clubhouse after the game and shook his hand. "Just wanted to congratulate you," Niekro said, "and tell you to keep it going." The two old rivals entertained the media that night in a postgame press conference that had to be moved to one of the stadium's football locker rooms to accommodate the number of reporters on the story. The press contingent had grown so large by then that the Reds' media director had put the Padres on notice. In a mere twelve days, barring a rainout or a hitless night, Pete was going to tie DiMaggio's record on the West Coast. The Padres needed to be ready for what was coming. At a minimum, it didn't feel too presumptive to believe that Pete would run his streak to forty-five.

Atlanta's starting pitcher the next night was Larry McWilliams—a lanky left-hander who had spent his entire career in the minors until three weeks earlier, when the Braves called him up from Triple-A Richmond. McWilliams was used to facing batters on the Charleston Charlies and the Tidewater Tides. Pete figured he could watch the kid warm up and be just fine.

The jitters got the best of McWilliams in the first inning that Tuesday night; he walked Pete to start the game, and the crowd booed him just as they had booed Niekro the night before. Pete came around to score, and the Reds went up 1–0. But the Braves struck back in the bottom of the frame, put up two runs, and knocked the Reds' starter from the game, and McWilliams settled in. When he faced Pete again in the second inning, he threw strikes and Pete pounded one of them right up the middle—a low, screaming line drive, straight at the mound.

If McWilliams had been a right-handed pitcher, his glove would have been on the first-base side at that moment, and he never would have had a chance at fielding the ball. It would have sailed into center field for a single. But Pete's hit was on the third-base side of the mound—right at McWilliams's glove. He fell on one knee, reached out with one of his long arms, and stabbed the ball out of the air. Pete was out. He couldn't believe it, and neither could McWilliams. The inning was over, and McWilliams retired Pete again in the fifth. He was hitless on the night, and with the Braves winning 8–4 to start the seventh, their manager, Bobby Cox, decided he was taking no chances. He handed the ball to his closer, Gene Garber, a bearded man in his early thirties.

It had been a hard summer for Garber. Six weeks earlier, the Philadelphia Phillies had traded him to Atlanta, a move that felt to Garber like a sucker punch in the gut. He and his wife were raising a family in Philadelphia. The Phillies had a chance to win the pennant in 1978, and they had always been Garber's team. As a boy growing up on a dairy farm in rural Pennsylvania in the 1950s, he fell asleep at night listening to Phillies games on the radio.

But Garber reported to Atlanta and did what Bobby Cox asked of him because Garber had no other choice. It was ingrained in him to work. The cows had to be milked—"morning and evening," Garber said that summer, "three hundred and sixty-five days a year"—and he had to pitch. He was going to do his job, spinning and twirling on the mound, a little like Luis Tiant and coming right at batters with an arsenal of off-speed pitches—sinkers and changeups, mostly. If he was on, his pitches broke down and in on righties and down and away on lefties. If he was off, he fell behind and had to throw his fastball, the pitch he trusted the least. The key was staying ahead in the count—a proven approach that had worked for him in the past, even against Pete Rose. Over his career, Pete batted just .229 against Garber.

Pete jumped on the first pitch that Garber threw him in the seventh inning—a slider outside—and it was a beautiful hit. A rocket shot down the third baseline. Yet it was right at the Braves' third baseman. Pete was out again, and the game got away from the Reds after that. The Braves scored three in the bottom of the seventh and five in the bottom of the eighth to take a 16–4 lead. The only reason to stick around now was to see if Pete might extend the streak in the ninth. He would get his chance with two outs.

Cox could have removed Garber from the game at that point and under normal circumstances probably would have. There was no reason to keep a closer on the mound with a twelve-run lead. But Garber wanted this moment. If he had to play in Atlanta, at least he could have this—a battle with Pete Rose, broadcast live across America. Garber returned to the mound to start the ninth, retired the first two batters he faced, and then, with two outs, prepared to pitch to Pete one last time, with the crowd on its feet, chanting his name.

"PETE . . . PETE . . . PETE."

On the first pitch, Pete tried to lay down a bunt, but it was foul. Then Garber fell behind, missing low and inside—twice. At that point, for the first time all night, Garber became nervous as he pondered a question in his mind. What if he walked Pete?

"I'll never live it down," Garber thought.

Whatever he threw next, he knew it had to be a strike, but his knees were almost shaking, so Garber decided to stick with the pitch he could control the most: his changeup. He spun and twirled and let it fly—a knee-high pitch right down the middle, hittable. But Pete missed it. He got on top of it and hit it foul. The count was now two balls and two strikes. Pete was down to his last pitch, the crowd was screaming, and Garber was coming back with the same thing: another changeup, only this time he hoped to place it on the outside part of the plate.

As the ball left his hand, Garber regretted his choice almost immediately. The pitch was too far outside, a mistake. He had gone and run the count full, he feared, and was in danger of walking Pete yet again. But the ball held just beyond the corner, a perfect strike-out pitch. Pete couldn't let it go by; it was too close. He swung and missed, and the last thing he saw as he turned to walk back to the dugout was a bearded reliever leaping in the night, pumping his hands in the air.

Garber had struck out Pete to end the streak.

41

A WEEK EARLIER IN New York, Pete had been touched by Tommy Holmes's warmth and generosity as the old man congratulated him for matching his record at thirty-seven games at Shea Stadium. One day, Pete said, he hoped he would be so kind to whoever threatened his streak. But now that it was over in Atlanta, he felt different. He was angry.

He didn't recognize Atlanta's starting pitcher, Larry McWilliams, when he got to the postgame press conference and asked the rookie to move out of his way. He cursed several times during the interview, unaware that it was being carried live on Ted Turner's network, and he took shots at Garber all night. The man who had built his entire persona around playing hard, sliding headfirst, knocking down Ray Fosse in 1970, and fighting with Bud Harrelson in 1973 seemed upset that Garber was *trying*.

"Garber pitched me like it was the seventh game of the World Series," Pete complained. He didn't like that Garber threw him changeups to get him out—"a bastard pitch," Pete called it. He said he hoped Garber would pitch again the next day so that he could hit a line drive at the mound—"and I mean hard," Pete said—and he didn't back down from his comments even after he'd had twenty-four hours to cool off. His failure kept him up all night. He wandered the streets of Atlanta, looking for a diner that was still open, and he returned to the stadium the next day still angry—angry about Gene

Garber. "I just can't understand him bearing down in that situation," Pete told reporters the next day. He added, "Did you see him jump at the end?"

On deadline, the night that the streak ended, one local beat writer called Pete out on it: Hal McCoy of the *Dayton Daily News.* "One question, Pete," McCoy wrote in his column that night. "If Garber were throwing a perfect game with two outs in the ninth would you lie down and die, or would you try your damnedest to slam a hit?" Everyone knew the answer. But Scoops Lawson and others in the press contingent helped tell the story that Pete wanted, the story about Garber and his bastard pitches, pushing Garber into a corner.

That night and for years to come—long after he retired and returned to his family's dairy farm in Pennsylvania—the Braves' reliever had to defend the way he pitched to Pete, fielding questions from people who didn't really know what had happened or only knew Pete's side of the story. "People don't let me forget it," Garber said one cold winter night more than forty years later, "or go to sleep without remembering, you know?" What bothered him most was not the questions, the reporters, or the phone calls. It was the suggestion that Pete had humiliated him with his postgame comments after the streak had ended in Atlanta. Garber felt differently—both in the moment and later. He considered it a compliment that Pete complained about him. Of course Garber was pitching as if it were the seventh game of the World Series, and of course he was throwing nasty breaking balls to Pete Rose. "That was my job," Garber said.

It was just unfortunate that he was doing it in Atlanta. Garber spent nine more seasons there—a good reliever on a team that was usually bad—while Pete got out of town the next night, for a sort of tour. In August, the Cardinals and Padres staged ceremonies to honor him, and in September President Jimmy Carter invited him to the White House to help celebrate "Pete Rose Day in Washington," a special event that brought Pete and Karolyn back together. They reunited to take the kids to the Oval Office and shake Carter's hand. Pete and Petey both wore three-piece suits, and Fawn stood next to them in a floral dress and scarf. Then, together, as a family once more, they piled into a waiting car and headed across town to the Capitol, where the House of Representatives passed a resolution that afternoon celebrating Pete.

"I rise today to salute a man whose accomplishments on the baseball diamond amount to more than most records in National League baseball history," said Congressman Tom Luken, a Cincinnati power broker from the West Side who started the proceedings that day. "I am talking about my friend and fellow Cincinnatian and constituent, Pete Rose."

Luken congratulated Pete for setting a great example for young people. A Democrat from California lauded Pete for his "exemplary behavior, legendary hustle, and zeal." A Republican from western Massachusetts begged Pete to one day run for office on the GOP ticket. A congressman from Chicago pleaded for Pete to join the Cubs. A congressman from Kentucky thanked Pete for proving that a star athlete could also be a gentleman, and once the resolution had passed without objection, pages, interns, and the politicians themselves surged around Pete seeking autographs—a massive crowd that longtime Capitol Police officers had never seen.

"Who's in there?" one page asked upon hearing the commotion. "The president?"

"Better," an officer replied. "It's Pete Rose."

Karolyn brushed tears off her cheek that week, happy to be back together with Pete, and Pete seemed happy, too. Not long after returning home from Washington, he moved back into the house on Countryhills with Karolyn and the kids. They were going to work things out. "Thank the good Lord," Karolyn said.

But as usual, Pete's reality was less polished than the one being presented in the newspapers. In Florida, his daughter with Terry Rubio was now five months old, and he was getting frustrated about sending Terry money to cover expenses. Every month, Pete complained, Terry seemed to ask for a little bit more. And was the baby even his? Pete didn't know for sure. Soon, he decided to cut her off—no more money for Terry—and throughout the summer and into the fall one man kept his distance from all of it: Dick Wagner, the president of the Reds.

While other people honored Pete for his streak, Wagner pretended as if it didn't happen. He said almost nothing about it. Instead, he focused on the flawed product on the field. The Reds were limping to a disappointing finish in 1978, and turning on each other, too. Players complained about Sparky Anderson in the press. Bench suggested that Sparky had lost control of the locker room. Howsam jetted in from Denver for a special players-only meeting to try to save the team he had built, and he came up short. Despite winning twelve of their last fifteen games, the Reds missed the playoffs, and Pete walked out of the clubhouse on the last day, hiding his eyes behind blue-tinted sunglasses. He was a free agent for the first time in his life, and he was ready for a fight with Dick Wagner.

Pete's new agent, Reuven Katz, the tax lawyer in the high-rise building downtown, had asked for a new contract the previous spring. But Wagner had balked then, and he wasn't open to much discussion now that the season was over. The morning of the final game, Wagner made Pete an offer that he had to know he would refuse: a two-year deal worth somewhere around half a million dollars a season that, by Reuven's calculations, didn't even make Pete the highest-paid Cincinnati Red.

Negotiations fell apart immediately. Wagner portrayed Pete as an overpaid athlete who wanted to leave Cincinnati, and Pete called Wagner a liar. Pete had wanted to stay in Cincinnati, Reuven said, but he wasn't inclined to do it anymore. Reuven set up meetings with six other teams—the Pirates, the Cardinals, the Braves, the Mets, the Phillies, and even the Kansas City Royals in the rival American League—and they all made offers. Great offers, Pete told reporters, the best offers. Club owners were willing to pay him almost $1 million a year to play baseball—and they were getting creative in order to win the Pete Rose sweepstakes.

The Pirates' president, the horse breeder Dan Galbreath, invited Pete to join him at his horse farm in Kentucky on the day they spoke and offered him a prized broodmare as part of his compensation package. The Cardinals' owner, the beer man August Busch, offered Pete a starring role in Budweiser commercials and possibly his own Budweiser distributorship. The Royals' owner, the businessman Ewing Kauffman, offered up a stake in a proven oil well, and Ted Turner in Atlanta dangled in front of Pete the biggest contract of all: reportedly four years at $4 million, with an annual $100,000 stipend on the back end after he retired—just for being himself.

Turner had seen in person the effect that Pete could have on a fan base and a team's bottom line. When Pete's streak ended in Atlanta that August, Turner found him in the locker room afterward and thanked him for making more money for the Braves in two nights than any player had made for Turner all season. Now Turner wanted Pete in a Braves uniform, Gene Garber and Pete Rose on the same team together. He was just coming up a little short.

"Horses," Turner muttered to one reporter in December 1978. "We need horses."

Wins would have helped, too. In the end, Pete passed up the biggest deals and all the financial perks to go with a contender: the Philadelphia Phillies, winner of the NL East division for the past three years. The offer was four years at $3.2 million—or, as Pete said at the time, enough money that if you stacked it up, a show dog couldn't jump over it.

The media descended on Countryhills Drive on the West Side that night for reactions from Karolyn, the kids, the neighbors, the fans, the people who had known Pete all his life, and predictably a few sided with Wagner. Some conservative West Siders didn't like the idea of any ballplayer making $3 million, even Pete. But most fans detested the Reds' president. Wagner wasn't just running Pete out of town that offseason; he was firing Sparky Anderson—a decision that Wagner delivered to Sparky at an airport hotel in Los Angeles within days of the announcement that Pete was leaving. The Big Red Machine had become, as one headline writer declared, "The Big Dead Machine."

At the house, Karolyn had a good cry after the media left. It was hard to imagine moving away from Cincinnati, their home, and starting fresh in Philadelphia, a city that meant nothing to her. Would the other wives accept her there? And did Philadelphia even have the things she liked? "Does Philadelphia have a Kmart?" Karolyn asked. Then she pulled herself together and got to work. There was a move to plan; a furnished home to find somewhere near the stadium in Philadelphia; banquets to attend all winter in Pete's honor; a flurry of parties, roasts, and toasts that required Karolyn's attendance; and preparations that needed to be made at the house on Countryhills. A guest was coming. In the middle of everything that winter, for reasons that aren't totally clear, the Roses invited a young baseball player from New Bedford, Massachusetts, to come stay with them. Tommy Gioiosa was coming to the West Side.

Fawn, who was now fourteen, didn't understand why Tommy was there. To her, he seemed like the young autograph seekers who hounded her dad at the ballpark, only Tommy was at their house, sleeping in a guest room, and eating cereal with the family at the breakfast table in the morning. It didn't make sense, but Pete didn't care. He loved Tommy. He said he was going to help him with his baseball career. He took him to the racetrack to bet on the horses. He loaned him the family's Jeep to drive around town, and he gave him odd jobs that Tommy was happy to do, even when they thrust Tommy into the middle of Pete's extramarital affairs.

In Tampa that winter, Terry Rubio was so angry that Pete had stopped sending money to support their baby that she decided to come after him—legally, in court. She hired a lawyer. She filed a paternity lawsuit against Pete. She knew she would prevail because she knew the baby was his. "When you hold a strong hand," she told the press, "you play it to the hilt and don't fold." And one morning that winter, Tommy recalled how Pete asked him to go outside before Karolyn got up to remove *The Cincinnati Enquirer* from the driveway. Terry's paternity suit was finally making front-page news in Cincinnati, and Pete was hoping Karolyn wouldn't notice.

Tommy did as he was told, hiding the newspaper in the bushes. But it was mid-February 1979. There was a light snow on the ground in Cincinnati. Tommy's footsteps were obvious in the yard, he recalled later. The scheme didn't work, and Karolyn would have found out anyway. Terry's lawsuit made national news, and Terry went out of her way to make sure Karolyn learned about it from her directly. At spring training, a few weeks later, Terry decided to confront Karolyn on the pool deck at King Arthur's Inn—an incident that both women would remember decades later. Terry marched across the deck with her baby in her arms and introduced the little girl, Pete's girl, to Karolyn.

Terry felt bad about it after the fact; she didn't mean to hurt Karolyn. She just wanted to hurt Pete. She wanted him to know that she wasn't going to stay quiet, and Pete got the message. He couldn't control Terry. He couldn't dictate this narrative. He couldn't prevent her from showing up at the motel or stop his secrets from leaking in other ways that were even more public and just as embarrassing.

In the months before Pete left town, at one of the many parties held in his honor, most of the old guard gathered one last time for a black-tie roast of Pete Rose onstage in front of a sold-out dinner crowd in Cincinnati. Tommy Helms, Tony Pérez, Joe Morgan, Ken Griffey, and George Foster were all there to give short speeches, along with Karolyn and the soon-to-be-fired Sparky Anderson. It was taped for broadcast on the local NBC affiliate, and it didn't need a laugh track. People were well lubricated by the time the Reds took the stage, and they howled all night at the jokes made at Pete's expense.

Griffey, wearing a pecan-tan tuxedo with ruffled sleeves, made fun of Pete's hair. "Pete has done for bangs," Griffey said, "what he did for the crew cut. He set it back twenty years." Morgan teased Pete for being the only man onstage wearing a suit instead of a tux. "I've said a lot of things about Pete Rose," Morgan joked. "But I've never said that Pete Rose had any class or any intelligence, and I think tonight is a prime example of that. He can afford to buy a Rolls-Royce and can't buy a tuxedo." When it was Pérez's turn to speak, Morgan stood up next to him and said, "I'm the interpreter." When Karolyn's turn came, she made light of their marital problems. "Remember, friends," she said. "If I leave him, I get a whole bunch of money." And when Foster stepped to the microphone about halfway through the program, the soft-spoken outfielder kept it going with a series of quick one-line zingers. Foster made a crack about Pete being old and another about Pete making Crosley Field what it had become today. "An empty lot," Foster said, "next to a post office."

Then, with the crowd laughing, he teed up his next joke.

"In life," Foster said, "it's great to take time to help others. Pete, for example, is a great humanitarian, you know, with kids. Football, baseball, basketball, and hockey . . ."

Foster paused and delivered the punch line.

"He taught those kids how to bet on them all."

The crowd first laughed at the joke and then recoiled, groaning.

"Oh, my God," one person said.

"Oh, no," said another.

An uncomfortable silence settled on the room. Foster had cut too close to the bone. He'd hit a nerve, something resembling the truth, and everyone knew it—perhaps Foster most of all. He turned to Pete sitting next to him and whispered an apology.

"Only funny now, Pete," he said.

At least it wasn't Dick Wagner's problem anymore. In late February 1979, Pete left his house on Countryhills Drive and reported to spring training in Florida as the hottest, richest Philadelphia Phillie—with more than $900,000 due to him that year and a new friend at his side.

Tommy Gioiosa drove Pete's Porsche down to Clearwater while Pete flew.

42

THE PHILLIES HAD been an unremarkable franchise since the first Grover Cleveland administration, almost a hundred years of stubborn mediocrity.

They had never won a World Series. They had made it there only twice. The Yankees had swept them the last time they made it—nearly three decades earlier, in 1950—and what fans had seen lately was just as disappointing. Since 1976, only the Yankees had won more regular-season games than the Phillies, yet Philadelphia had nothing to show for its success. In each of the past three years, the team lost in the playoffs, making errors, with their bats gone cold and their confidence shattered. All Pete had to do to earn his $3.2 million was change all that—save the Phillies, help them win, and do it now.

The Phillies' owner, Ruly Carpenter, was about Pete's age, thirty-eight years old. He had played baseball at Yale and assumed ownership of the Phillies the old-fashioned way: he inherited the team. His grandfather had made his fortune working at an explosives manufacturer in Delaware near the turn of the century, a place that was later known as DuPont. He helped the company transition into plastics and chemicals. He married one of the du Pont girls and then used his money and connections to buy the Phillies during World War II. Ruly was now the team's third-generation owner, the third Carpenter man in charge in Philadelphia, following in the footsteps of his grandfather and his father, and he was desperate to show he wasn't just an Ivy League whiz kid in tortoiseshell glasses. He was worthy of the job.

"I really want to prove I can do it," Ruly said.

Ruly believed Pete was what he needed, and other powerful men in Philadelphia agreed. In order to pay for Pete's contract, the television network that broadcast Phillies games guaranteed Ruly a $600,000 boost in annual advertising revenue for the team, and this figure—$600,000—was just for the 1979 season, accountants pointed out. It didn't include the three other years on Pete's contract or any other form of increased revenue—like ticket sales and merchandise sales, both of which spiked after Ruly signed Pete. It was as if Pete's contract were paying for itself. Everyone was making money. Everyone was carving off a slice—Ruly, the Phillies, the networks, the newspapers, and Pete's agent, Reuven Katz—while fans turned out for Pete.

At least one demographic of fans, anyway: the white fans.

"Don't get upset that I used the term 'white fans,' either," wrote Larry McMullen, a beloved white columnist for the *Philadelphia Daily News,* in a piece published shortly after Ruly presented Pete with his new Phillies jersey. "It's okay," McMullen explained. "There aren't that many white sports heroes around."

Going into the 1979 season, many of baseball's biggest stars were now Black, including six of the last eight MVPs; the biggest home-run hitters in the game, George Foster and Jim Rice; the highest-paid player, Rod Carew; some of the most exciting players, Reggie Jackson, Willie Stargell, and Dave Parker; and almost every batting champion in the 1970s. For the decade, a Black or Latino player had won the title fifteen out of eighteen times.

"White people need someone to root for, too," McMullen wrote. And Pete Rose was the perfect someone. He'd energize white fans in Philadelphia, McMullen said.

"Rose is worth every penny."

—

As usual, Pete welcomed the pressure. If it was his job to put fans in the seats and bring a title to Philadelphia, that was what he was going to do, and he didn't want to hear from anyone that he was old or that he was going to be the same age as Ruly Carpenter that spring.

Pete entertained the beat writers in Philadelphia with familiar stories about his father. He told them how his dad had played semi-pro football into his forties, working hard, and Pete set out to show everyone that he had the same sort of boundless energy. At spring training, Pete worked out with the team in Clearwater, jetted to Las Vegas for a one-night speaking engagement, flew back on the red-eye without sleeping, arrived at the ballpark three hours before anyone else that morning, ran wind sprints, hit in the cage, and granted more interviews in a single morning than most players gave all spring. Afterward, in the evenings, he relaxed at the dog track with the Cuban, Arnie Metz, or Tommy Gioiosa. He joked that he was crushing it there, picking winners, flush with Ruly's cash. And he helped set up Tommy, like he promised. Pete made sure Tommy got a minor-league tryout with the Phillies that spring.

It was the break Tommy had always wanted, and for a moment he let himself believe that it would work out. He was going to be more than just a gofer for Pete, hiding newspapers on his driveway and bringing his Porsche down to Florida. He was going to be a ballplayer and maybe catch on with Philadelphia's rookie league team, out west in Montana. Instead, at the end of spring training, Tommy got cut and returned to Cincinnati. He got a job at Sleep Out Louie's, the downtown bar where Pete had met his new mistress, Carol Woliung, and he enrolled at the University of Cincinnati in hopes of catching on with the Bearcat baseball team the following spring. Meanwhile, in Philadelphia, the year slipped away from Pete Rose.

He transitioned to playing first base—the sixth position of his career—and collected vintage Pete Rose stats in 1979, batting .331. But the Phillies struggled all year, missed the playoffs. Ruly Carpenter had to fire the team manager, and he learned on the job what Dick Wagner knew well in Cincinnati: Pete's on-field greatness often came with off-field problems. Terry Rubio's paternity suit—still pending in Florida—was just the beginning.

Before the season, right about the time that Terry filed her suit and confronted Karolyn at King Arthur's Inn, Pete granted unfettered access to a young freelance writer working for *Playboy* magazine. The writer's name was Samantha Stevenson, and her job was to talk to Pete for the magazine's celebrated monthly interview. The list of previous interviewees included Martin Luther King, Bob Dylan, Barbra Streisand, Muhammad Ali, and Dolly Parton, and Pete was thrilled at the prospect of being interviewed, too. At the time, few things signified a person's cultural significance more than being featured in the *Playboy* interview. But after about seven hours of tape, Pete changed his mind. He told Stevenson he was done.

"So the interview's over?" Stevenson asked.

"Fuckin' right it is," he said.

Pete didn't like that Stevenson was pressing him harder than the beat writers who usually covered him. She seemed to be going after "the dirty stuff," he complained, asking him about Terry Rubio, her paternity suit, Karolyn, his marriage, and whether he took "greenies"—amphetamines that many players used to stay up and alert during the course of a long baseball season. It probably didn't help that Pete had learned too late that Stevenson wasn't popular with his new teammates. Just months earlier, she had filed a lawsuit in federal court to gain access to the Phillies' locker room as a female reporter—and won. As a result of her suit and others, women were now allowed into major-league clubhouses for the first time. Stevenson could conduct postgame interviews like her male colleagues had done for years, and many people around baseball didn't like it, especially players' wives. Even after Stevenson prevailed in court, a few wives tried to physically stop her from entering the clubhouse. Pete couldn't be seen with her, Stevenson thought, and he shut down. "He wanted so badly to belong."

In the *Playboy* interview that hit the newsstands that August, Pete was quoted bragging about the $8,000 watch he wore and how much money he was making in 1979. He asked Stevenson about her new experiences in the locker room, saying, "Tell me. How does it feel to have all those cocks staring you in the face? Does it make you embarrassed? Do you like it?" He admitted to taking amphetamines, greenies—"Yeah, I'd do it. I've done it"—and he confessed that his whiteness was at least part of his appeal. There was a reason, he said, why corporate sponsors like Swanson's Pizza hired him to do commercials instead of Dave Parker, the Pirates' right fielder, the 1978 MVP, and a Black man.

"Look," Pete told Stevenson, "if you owned Swanson's Pizza, would you want a Black guy to do the commercial on TV for you? Would you like the Black guy to pick up the pizza and bite into it? Try to sell it? I mean, would you want Dave Parker selling your pizza to America for you? Or would you want Pete Rose?"

It was going to be hard for Pete to wiggle out of this one. *Playboy* had the tapes, and Stevenson could recount in detail where and when she had asked Pete the question about corporate sponsorships. They were on a plane at the time, she said, and she remembered that Pete made the comments about Swanson's Pizza with no animosity toward Dave Parker or any other Black player. He was just stating the uncomfortable truth: companies in 1979 did see white players as more marketable than their Black counterparts.

Still, Pete denied the comment, and he denied ever taking greenies. He didn't need this crisis, not now, because another one was already brewing behind the scenes. After a terrible summer in Philadelphia, Karolyn was finally finished with Pete.

Karolyn had tried to make it work. She had moved with Pete into a luxury high-rise apartment near the Phillies' stadium downtown, and she had attempted to be what he wanted—understanding and forgiving, or as Pete said in the *Playboy* interview, "a perfect baseball player's wife." It was the role she had played, and played well, for fifteen years. But guests at the apartment in Philadelphia that summer could tell that Karolyn was only half in. She had left the family dog behind in Cincinnati and seemed to be traveling light. It felt as if all she had brought with her to Philadelphia were her hair curlers, her diamonds, the kids, and a suitcase full of regrets that was getting harder and harder for her to lug around. In an interview with a reporter that summer—another reporter sent to write another puff piece about Pete's wife—Karolyn nearly said it out loud: she couldn't do this anymore.

She loved Pete more than anything, she said in the interview, and she knew that without him she would be nothing. Yet she was tired of Pete's lies and his girlfriends, of Terry Rubio, down in Florida, and Carol Woliung, wherever she was. Karolyn knew for a fact that Carol wasn't just in Cincinnati anymore. She had come to Philadelphia, too, and was on her way to becoming a Philadelphia Eagles cheerleader, a secret that Karolyn learned when she spotted Carol near the apartment at a stoplight, driving Karolyn's Porsche.

Later, Karolyn would recount in detail what happened next: how she opened the door to her own car and punched Carol in the mouth, how the police got involved in the street, and how she demanded that Carol vacate the vehicle, *her* vehicle, even if it meant Carol had to walk. In the moment, though, with the press and everyone else, Karolyn kept her silence one last time. When the Phillies went on a road trip in mid-August 1979, she packed up her things, rounded up Fawn and Petey, returned to their house in Cincinnati, and hired a lawyer.

Karolyn was filing for divorce.

The news hit the papers in early September, another blow for Pete. His perfect baseball wife was leaving him and seeking $14,000 a month in alimony payments—more money than some people made in a year.

It was yet another sign of how much baseball had changed and how much Pete had changed with it. The player who had once inked a deal with the Reds in 1960 for $7,000 could now afford to pay his estranged wife twice that figure, every month, to live somewhere else—at least according to Karolyn. He had $37,000 in jewelry; $130,000 in cars; lucrative sponsorship deals worth even more; that massive Phillies contract courtesy of Ruly Carpenter; a net worth estimated at $2.5 million; and Karolyn was coming for her half, for her share—another sensitive topic that Pete didn't want to discuss. He was interested only in playing baseball.

On the day that Karolyn filed for divorce in Cincinnati, Pete went 3 for 4 against the Mets in New York. Over the next four games, he hit safely in fifteen out of seventeen at bats. He batted .468 for the rest of 1979 and then rolled into the offseason, collecting his usual accolades. *The Sporting News* named him the Player of the Decade. Pete finished second in a popularity poll in Philadelphia. Many fans wanted him to be the new manager of the Phillies, and CBS wanted him on television.

Three weeks after Karolyn's divorce filing, Pete was invited to appear on CBS's Sunday morning football pregame show, *The NFL Today*. His job: analyzing the baseball playoffs and filling in for the famous Las Vegas oddsmaker Jimmy the Greek, who had suffered minor injuries that week in a motorbike accident. At the end of the pregame show that day, Pete stood in front of the big board of games with the host Brent Musburger and did the handicapping.

He liked Buffalo over Chicago, Pete said, and Atlanta over Green Bay. He picked New England to beat Detroit—"This is the best bet of the day right here," Pete said—and he predicted that the Tampa Bay Buccaneers would win by at least six points over the New York Giants, even though the Bucs were road favorites for the first time in franchise history.

"Where'd you get all that stuff?" Musburger asked Pete on television, impressed by Pete's knowledge, his level of detail, and the nugget he'd thrown in about the Buccaneers.

Pete shrugged. "I follow football pretty good," he said.

Then he retired to a room filled with televisions to watch the games. A wall of televisions with every single game. A beautiful thing. A magical and unforgettable thing.

"A gambler's delight," Pete called it.

43

RULY CARPENTER GOT what he wanted in 1980: the Phillies advanced to the World Series and won. His $3.2 million bet on Pete Rose paid off.

Pete played in every game that year, never resting, and dragged the team down the stretch when it seemed as if the Phillies wanted to fail as they had in the past. With seven games to play in late

September—and Philadelphia half a game out of first place—Pete proceeded to bat .400 the rest of the way. The Phillies won six of their last seven and edged the Montreal Expos to win the NL East by a game.

In the National League Championship Series against the Houston Astros, Pete batted .400 yet again and sparked the Phillies' come-from-behind victory in the decisive game five. In the eighth inning that night, with the Phillies down by three, he drew a bases-loaded walk off the Astros' fire-throwing ace Nolan Ryan. A run scored. The game unraveled on the Astros and the Phillies won—a victory that almost didn't seem right. With champagne in hand at a celebration afterward, Pete conceded that he wasn't sure the best team had prevailed.

Then, in the ninth inning of game six in the 1980 World Series—with the Phillies on the cusp of closing out the Royals and the Royals rallying with two men on and nobody out—Pete made a play that Philadelphia fans would remember forever. He and catcher Bob Boone chased down a pop fly in foul territory between first base and home. Boone got there before Pete and settled under the ball near the top step of the Phillies' dugout—only Boone didn't make the catch. The ball bounced in and out of his glove. It should have hit the ground, and the Royals should have had new life. Instead, Pete, who was crashing toward the dugout from Boone's left, stabbed the wayward ball out of the air with his glove.

An out. A miracle. A great hustle play, Tony Kubek said on NBC. A classic Pete Rose play. The Phillies beat the Royals 4–1 to win the series, and fans in Philadelphia cheered loudest when Pete bounded out of the clubhouse after the victory to stand at home plate, holding a champagne bottle in one hand and flashing a victory sign with the other.

"Peeeeeeeete!" they chanted. *"Peeeeeeeete!"*

In the clubhouse that night, Ruly Carpenter walked around in a euphoric daze, his hair dripping with champagne. "It's the greatest thing that's ever happened to me in my life," he said, barely able to form words. "It's just the greatest thing." Philadelphians partied until dawn and then stayed out on the streets for a victory parade that shut down the city. At least half a million people were there, cheering from street corners, rooftops, and light poles. Confetti fell from the sky and Pete stood atop a flatbed truck in the middle of it all, smiling and waving in a tight V-neck sweater. Ruly had paid him to bring a World Series to Philadelphia, and Pete had delivered amid a raft of personal problems that would have derailed most other players.

In the divorce proceedings in Ohio late that season, Karolyn openly complained about Pete's girlfriends. She asked if the legal term "gross neglect of duty" included adultery, and she fought Pete's efforts to fly their son, Petey, to the World Series that October. Karolyn didn't think it was fair that Petey had been invited, not Fawn, and she didn't appreciate that Pete was swooping in to get his son after taking little interest in being a parent for months. According to Karolyn's lawyer, Pete hadn't seen his children since March.

Pete's lawyer fired back that his client didn't have the ability to watch Fawn at the World Series. She was almost sixteen and a girl. Where was she going to sleep, the lawyer asked, when the Phillies were playing in Kansas City and staying in a hotel? And Karolyn ultimately relented, allowing Petey to spend the entire World Series with his father. She didn't want to prevent her ten-year-old boy from having an amazing experience. Life was hard enough already.

Within weeks, Pete and Karolyn's divorce was official. Karolyn got full custody of the children, the deed to a new house on the West Side, the family's Rolls-Royce, monthly child support, and an undisclosed alimony payment. Pete got the rest: the Porsche, the house on Countryhills Drive, and all his trophies, including, he stipulated, the bejeweled Hickok belt that he had won in 1975, though it wasn't clear where he would keep all the stuff. Pete was almost forty years old, but he wasn't coming home anytime soon.

"Might you retire?" a reporter asked him after the World Series victory.

"What the hell should I retire for?" Pete replied.

He had a guaranteed contract for the next two years. He was only seventy-four hits away from passing Stan Musial to become the National League's all-time leading hitter. He was only 443 hits away from reaching a milestone that he himself had dismissed as impossible just two years earlier: 4,000. With a few more good seasons, he could get there. He could potentially even catch the all-time hit leader, Ty Cobb, at 4,191. Pete just needed to keep going, and according to testimony in a Pennsylvania courtroom that winter, he was getting help to make sure he could.

Under oath at a hearing in February 1981, a doctor affiliated with a Phillies minor-league team in nearby Reading testified that he was illegally prescribing and delivering amphetamines, greenies, to several star players on the Phillies, including Pete Rose.

The doctor was the only one on trial here. Not the Phillies and not Pete. By saying that the doctor had properly examined them and prescribed them the pills to treat real health conditions, like weight gain, the players could have potentially helped the doctor in court. He was facing prison time and $115,000 in fines. But Pete said he'd never even seen the man. He denied any involvement with amphetamines or greenies, just as he had after his *Playboy* interview came out in 1979. Under oath, Pete maintained that his energy was natural. "What's a greenie?" he asked in court, as if he didn't know. And every other star player issued a similar denial.

The doctor was stunned. He had considered the players his friends. Now he realized they were just using him. They wanted his amphetamines to be more engaged, less depressed, have greater "pep," and feel stronger. One Phillies player who admitted to taking greenies said the pills gave him a sense of overwhelming power, as if he could do anything. But the team's biggest stars weren't going to put their reputations on the line for the doctor. They were moving on. Pete spent the rest of the winter doing the usual.

He appeared at banquets, gave speeches, signed autographs, recorded new commercials for the *Encyclopaedia Britannica,* signed a new endorsement deal with Mizuno bats, prepared to sell the house on Countryhills, bought a condo on the West Side of Cincinnati, and asked a friend to move in with him: Tommy Gioiosa. Tommy could run errands for Pete, pick up his dry cleaning, wash his cars, place his bets on sports with local bookies, and run the money back and forth to the bookies, be the middleman. Tommy would drop off an envelope of cash every Tuesday or pick up an envelope and then bring the money back to the condo development.

It was called Chateau Estates, and Pete's place there was the perfect bachelor pad. It had three bedrooms, deep purple carpeting in the living room, and easy access to Interstate 74.

They could hear the hum of the highway outside.

—

Sometimes, Tommy thought about getting on the highway and leaving forever. His one baseball season at the University of Cincinnati had ended, and he hadn't reenrolled in the fall of 1980. He had no reason to be in Cincinnati.

But Tommy was only twenty-three years old and he couldn't escape Pete's gravitational pull. He couldn't leave. *The Cincinnati Enquirer* wrote a glowing feature about Tommy's quest to be a professional baseball player—because Tommy was friends with Pete. The *Enquirer* story appeared under the headline "Charlie Hustle Is Back in Town" and suggested that Tommy might be the second coming of Pete Rose, undersized and gritty and getting the most out of his talents on the West Side through hard work and dedication. Tommy wasn't going to get this sort of attention back home in New Bedford or anywhere else, and in the summer of 1981, Tommy's loyalty, perseverance, and presence in Cincinnati paid off. In late July, Pete arranged for Tommy to get a tryout with the Toronto Blue Jays on a field in rural Sidney, Ohio, ninety minutes north of the city.

It was a day that Tommy would never forget: how he drove to the tryout in a black Camaro that he borrowed from one of Pete's girlfriends so that he wouldn't have to pull up in one of Pete's expensive cars and draw attention to himself; how he worked out at second base and left field with a handful of other players; and how the Blue Jays scouts seemed impressed with him. He wondered if his performance at the tryout would get him an offer to play with one of the Blue Jays' rookie league squads. Tommy could have left Pete's condo on the West Side and never gone back.

But the day after the tryout, the Blue Jays' scouting supervisor, Bob Engle, gave Pete the bad news. "Thomas," Engle said, using Tommy's formal name, "is a 'pepperpot' type of player with a great deal of enthusiasm." Unfortunately—according to the Blue Jays—Tommy didn't have elite talent, and he wasn't getting invited anywhere. He was stuck in Cincinnati, working at Sleep Out Louie's downtown, living in Pete's condo, and driving Pete around that summer because Pete had nothing better to do at the moment.

For the third time in a decade, the players had gone on strike, bickering with owners over money, and for the first time they were missing almost two months of games. At least Tommy got to be there when play resumed in August. He drove Pete and little Petey all night to Philadelphia. He walked into the clubhouse at Veterans Stadium. He met Pete's teammates on the Phillies. He put on a uniform so he could get on the field, and he hung around to witness a great baseball moment—Pete Rose passing Stan Musial for the most hits in National League history: 3,631.

Pete had been chasing Musial's record for years, and he made sure to enjoy the moment after the game that night. While his girlfriend, Carol, waited for him in the wings, Pete accepted congratulations from Musial himself. He held court in a room full of reporters, and then, with the reporters watching and the cameras rolling, he stood in front of a rack of microphones and pressed a red phone to his ear. President Ronald Reagan was calling.

The line took several minutes to connect, which some players would have found excruciating. The reporters just sat there, watching Pete, who was standing onstage next to Musial, waiting for Reagan to come to the line. Pete turned it into an open-mic comedy hour.

"Maybe the operators are on strike," he joked. "Good thing there isn't a missile on the way," he said a moment later. And he didn't hold back when Reagan's voice finally materialized on the other end of the line. "We were going to give you five more minutes," Pete told the president, "and that was it."

44

The room howled that night in Philadelphia. No one talked to the president like that. Just five months earlier, an assassin's bullet had nearly killed Reagan, lodging in his upper left chest, just a few inches away from his heart.

But Pete couldn't help himself. After passing Musial on the all-time hit list, he could say or do whatever he wanted, and he seized the moment to do one more thing. He called in another favor for

Tommy. Pete asked an old scout he knew with the Baltimore Orioles to give Tommy a tryout, and the scout rewarded Tommy with an invite to Baltimore's minor-league training camp in the spring of 1982. "Congratulations on being an Oriole," the scout told Tommy. "I know a little of Pete is bound to rub off on you. Just keep hustling and working hard like Pete has always done."

Tommy practiced all winter at an indoor batting cage on the West Side of Cincinnati, knowing that this was probably his last chance. If he flamed out with Baltimore, his baseball career was over. And Pete felt a similar sense of urgency going into the 1982 season. Ownership had changed in Philadelphia. Ruly Carpenter had sold the team for a record-breaking $30 million—seventy-five times what his grandfather had spent to buy the Phillies in 1943—and the new owners of the Phillies were extending Pete's contract through at least the 1983 season with a deal that approached one million dollars a year.

It was an exorbitant sum of money for a first baseman who was about to be forty-one years old and couldn't hit home runs. But the new owners looked at Pete and saw dollar signs. Only two players stood in front of him on the all-time hit list: Hank Aaron with 3,771 and Ty Cobb with 4,191. Pete would cruise past Aaron before the end of June, and Cobb's record, once considered unbreakable, suddenly felt within reach, too. "All I need to pass Cobb," Pete told reporters that winter, "is an average of one hundred and sixty-five hits for three seasons."

This was doable, and the new owners in Philadelphia wanted to keep Pete around long enough to see if he might make it because there'd be money in it for them. "An awful lot of residual money," they said.

Pete assured them that he was worth the investment. In his mind, he wasn't chasing Cobb. This was a formality. Just a matter of time.

"I'm going to catch him," Pete promised.

At first, that March, things looked better for Tommy than they did for Pete.

Tommy hit well playing with the Orioles' rookie squad down in Miami, while Pete struggled sometimes to even get out of bed at the Phillies' training camp in Clearwater. He had tweaked his back playing tennis with his agent Reuven Katz, and the injury was serious enough that it kept Pete off the field initially. He was trapped inside the trainer's room.

"Rest in peace, Ty Cobb," Pete moaned from his bedroom.

There was going to be no catching Cobb like this. No residuals for the owners of the Phillies, and at the first hint of weakness the beat writers descended like a flock of vultures pecking at the desiccated carcass that was Pete. Maybe this was how it would end, they wrote, with Pete on his back in the trainer's room in Clearwater. Even Pete knew it was a possibility.

"Anybody'd be concerned," he told a reporter. He couldn't even tie his shoes.

But Pete had said too much that winter to give up now. In recent weeks, he had hurled barbs at people across baseball: at Johnny Bench for not wanting to play catcher anymore; at Dick Wagner for being a terrible general manager; at the Reds for trading George Foster to the Mets; and at the Mets for signing Foster to a five-year, $8.5 million deal that dwarfed any contract that Pete had ever received. Pete predicted that Foster would struggle in New York, and he issued what was for Pete the ultimate insult. Pete suggested that Foster didn't hustle, that the big slugger never got dirty.

"I used to use three uniforms a day," Pete said. "George uses three a month."

It seemed unnecessary to attack Foster in this way, especially to Foster. He didn't get it. But Pete didn't retract what he had said even when he had the chance. He doubled down on the insult. He told sportswriters to shelve their columns about his broken body. He predicted he'd pass Cobb in August 1984, and he quickly returned to the field in March 1982. Pete's back was feeling better—at almost the exact moment when things fell apart for Tommy. At the end of the month, the Orioles let him go.

The scout who had signed him was devastated. "It broke my heart when they released him," the man told Pete.

"Tommy G is sure a great guy."

He just wasn't a great *player.* He was Pete Rose's friend, not Pete Rose. And without baseball, Tommy had only one real option that spring. He returned to Cincinnati. He moved back into Pete's condo on the West Side and resumed his usual duties, plus some new ones. In addition to running Pete's errands and placing his bets, Tommy began helping Pete with his girlfriends—women Pete was seeing beyond Carol. Tommy made sure these women got off their planes and arrived at Pete's hotel rooms without any problems, and he helped procure gifts outfitted with gemstones for the women, too, deriving them from an unusual source: Pete's treasured Hickok belt.

Around this time, Tommy said, Pete instructed him to take the belt to a local jeweler named Jack Zerhusen and ask Jack to remove the diamonds in the belt, replace them with cubic zirconium, and turn the real jewels into earrings that Pete and Tommy could give to women. Jack was a West Sider and a pal from the racetrack—Pete called him "Diamond Jack"—and Jack did as he was told.

"You guys are crazy," Tommy recalled Diamond Jack saying. But Jack wasn't going to stand in the way.

Tommy knew he was headed down a dark path—this wasn't who he wanted to be—but it was impossible not to have fun when he was with Pete. They could throw ground balls at each other inside the condo, and it didn't matter if a ball punched a hole in the drywall. There were enough $10,000 bundles tucked away in the drop ceiling or stacked inside the freezer to cover any problem. "*Cold* cash," Pete liked to say, chortling with laughter at the thought of his stashes. Or he didn't have to patch any of the holes. It was his condo, his rules. Pete didn't even have to pay his bookies, if he didn't feel like it. At least once, Tommy recalled, Pete stiffed a bookie from Dayton who kept calling for his money, and Pete didn't seem to think twice about ignoring him.

Tommy wrote home to his parents in New Bedford to tell them how great things were going in Cincinnati. "P.S.," he said, "Pete says hi to you both." But amid the laughter and the frat house hijinks inside the condo, the fur coats and the fast cars, the wild nights at the racetrack and the sunny reports of what it was like to spin inside Pete Rose's orbit, Tommy was hurting.

At Sleep Out Louie's, the bar downtown, his colleagues had thrown him a going-away party when he went to spring training with the Orioles. Now he was back at the bar, working the door, a failure. He felt as if he had let everyone down by not catching on with Baltimore—Pete, most of all. He was desperate to find a way back into baseball, and a bartender at Sleep Out Louie's—a giant man with arms like cords of wood—offered him a way. He suggested that Tommy take steroids, like him.

One afternoon not long after that first conversation, Tommy leaned against the kitchen counter in the man's house, dropped his pants, placed his right foot on top of his left, bit down on a towel, and felt the sting of a long syringe entering his right butt cheek. The steroids cost $15, and the results were almost immediate. Taking shots of steroids every three days—as much as he could tolerate—Tommy began to get bigger and stronger. Instead of benching 135 pounds, he clocked in at 300, then 400. And instead of being depressed about his missed opportunities, he began to feel invincible. He bought new clothes to fit his sculpted frame and found a cheaper source of the drugs he craved: a West Side bodybuilder and former Elder High School football player named Paul Janszen.

Paul was about the same age as Tommy and just as lost. In the early 1980s, he worked in a string of local bars as a bouncer and was lucky to be employed at an industrial barrel company for a while. Yet around others, and Tommy in particular, Paul tried to project total and absolute strength. He was a big man, well built, much bigger than Tommy. He drove a white Corvette that Tommy coveted and swaggered into Sleep Out Louie's with a confidence that was impressive, too. People at the bar called him "Hercules" or "The Hulk." Sometimes, Paul ripped his shirts just by flexing his muscles and arching his back. Other times, he fought. Everyone seemed to have a story of Paul throwing a punch at someone, and they knew they could go to him for steroids—Tommy included. Paul helped Tommy get stronger while Pete grew weaker, seemingly by the day.

In 1982, Pete played every game for the Phillies, but he batted just .271, and in the spring of 1983 he finally hit the wall that stands at the end of the line for every athlete. Pete batted .221 in April, slumped for much of the summer, went hitless for days at times, got booed in Philadelphia, recorded a .245 batting average for the year, and got benched in favor of a first baseman named Len Matuszek, who until that year had played fewer than forty games in the majors and had recorded only six career hits. The Phillies' manager told reporters that he had no choice. Pete was killing them at first.

It was an embarrassment, and the worst season of Pete's life, even though his old friends Tony Pérez and Joe Morgan had joined him in Philadelphia as free agents and even though the Phillies played well. When the team made the World Series again that fall, Pete could hardly enjoy it. At times, he didn't even play. In the Phillies' pivotal game three against the Orioles that October, Pete watched from the bench, preparing himself for what was coming next—a World Series loss and his unconditional release.

He was 10 hits shy of 4,000 and only 201 hits behind Ty Cobb, but the Phillies didn't want him around anymore, not even for the residuals. They were cutting him loose. If he wanted to catch Cobb, Pete would have to do it with the Montreal Expos, the only team to offer him a contract in 1984.

The Expos had three future Hall of Famers on the roster—Andre Dawson, Gary Carter, and Tim Raines—and a young hitter who would have a long history in baseball, Terry Francona. During road trips that spring, Francona listened to Pete's stories, rapt with attention. He came to believe that he learned more about baseball listening to Pete while playing cards in the back of airplanes than he did doing almost anything else, and Francona would never forget the small act of kindness that Pete showed him on a quiet Sunday morning that June. Less than twelve hours after Francona tore up his knee in a game in Montreal, Pete showed up at the hospital to see how the kid was feeling.

Yet for Pete, life felt temporary in Canada and a little sad. On the same night that Francona injured his knee, Pete grabbed an Expos broadcaster in the clubhouse, pushed him up against a locker, and ripped the man's shirt, sparking a melee. Pete was angry about being misquoted in a radio editorial. He lived an isolated life in a hotel suite with his girlfriend Carol and almost no one else, and he struggled on the field again, hobbled by nagging injuries.

Almost every hit he managed to get was a single, and he didn't have that many of those, either. At the rate he was going, Pete would have to play until 1986 to catch Ty Cobb—an impossibility. No team was going to tolerate a light-hitting, middle-aged first baseman with limited defensive range for that long, not even the Expos.

There was only one chance left at salvation.

Maybe Pete could go home.

45

THE CINCINNATI REDS had never considered bringing Pete back during his years in Philadelphia. Dick Wagner was in charge, and everyone knew how Wagner felt about Pete and high-priced stars in general. Since 1978, Wagner had driven away almost all of them—Pete, then Morgan, then Griffey and Foster. Only Johnny Bench remained.

But by 1983—Pete's last year in Philadelphia—the Dick Wagner era was sputtering to a bitter and inevitable end. After winning the division in 1979, the Reds missed the playoffs in 1980 and 1981 and then finished last in 1982. They lost more games that year than they had in any season since 1945, and as a result attendance at Riverfront Stadium plummeted to half of what it had once been during the peak years of the Big Red Machine. No one wanted to see the product that Wagner was putting on the field. Not even the team owners—at least not one of them: Marge Schott, a chain-smoking car dealer in her mid-fifties.

Marge had deep Cincinnati roots, old German money, an undying love for large Saint Bernard dogs, a knack for being the loudest person in the room, a fondness for bright red lipstick to match the color of her team and her one-piece dresses, and a penchant for saying all the wrong things. In Marge's parlance, Jewish people were "sneaky Jew bastards," Asian people were "Japs," Black athletes were "million-dollar N-words," and Dick Wagner was a buffoon, an idiot who deserved to be mocked in the public square. He had to go.

When the Reds struggled in the first six weeks of the 1983 season—falling eight games out of first by mid-May—Marge tried to shame Wagner into doing something about it. She paid for a small plane to fly over the stadium when the Phillies came to town towing a banner that read like an SOS message to the former Cincinnati stars—Pérez, Rose, and Morgan—in their Philadelphia ball caps down on the field.

"Tony, Pete, Joe," the banner said, "Help. Love, Marge."

In June, Marge pushed for an "I Don't Like Dick Wagner" Night at the stadium—she hoped it would entice fans to buy tickets—and in July a local radio personality joined in on the fun. He hired Marge's airplane pilot with money he raised from fans and ordered up a new banner to appear in the sky during the Phillies' next visit to Riverfront. This banner said, "Pete Rose Forever, Dick Wagner Never." The Reds were fifteen games out of first by then, and splitting the series with the Phillies that weekend wouldn't be enough to appease anyone.

That Monday morning, members of the Reds' ownership group sided with Marge. She might have been crass and unpredictable, a liability with the press and an embarrassment with her big Saint Bernard, Schottzie, urinating on the floor and on the field. But even the most conservative members of the Reds' ownership group had to concede that Marge was on to something.

They fired Dick Wagner and decided to replace him with someone they could trust.

It was time to bring back Bob Howsam.

Howsam was in his mid-sixties now, five years older than he had been when he retired in 1978, and his first order of business as interim general manager was to survive the season. Bench was retiring in 1983; Howsam needed to make sure the great catcher got a proper send-off. Then that winter, he set his mind on rebuilding.

He traded for Tony Pérez, a sentimental move. He signed Dave Parker, the former MVP whom Pete had disparaged in his 1979 *Playboy* interview when talking about Black athletes and corporate sponsors. He launched a search for a new manager, and he knew exactly what he was seeking in a candidate. Howsam wanted the next Sparky Anderson, someone who could bring discipline and order to the clubhouse. He wanted Vern Rapp.

Everyone was shocked—even Rapp himself. He was a baseball lifer in his mid-fifties, who had spent most of his career managing in the minors and the 1983 season on the coaching staff in Montreal.

Rapp had intended to retire at the end of the year, and his only previous stint as a major-league manager didn't impress anyone. The St. Louis Cardinals had fired Rapp in 1978 after just 180 games for clashing with players, for suspending a relief pitcher who refused to shave his mustache, for banning music in the clubhouse after losses, for disapproving of alcohol on road trips, and for calling Ted Simmons, a future Hall of Famer and St. Louis icon, "a loser." Rapp wasn't a modern manager. He was barely a coach anymore, barely hanging on—and then an elaborate joke at the end of the 1983 season changed the course of Rapp's career, Pete's life, and arguably baseball history.

In Boston that fall, Carl Yastrzemski was retiring, and the local tributes to him were so over-the-top that the producers of a Boston radio show, *The Sports Huddle,* decided to satirize the situation by honoring the most obscure person who was also retiring from baseball. They settled on Vern Rapp and dedicated an entire show to him, interviewing Rapp and others who knew him, including the Reds' vice president, Chief Bender, another baseball lifer, who had worked with Rapp many times over the years. Howsam maintained later that he had always been considering Rapp for the job. He had known Rapp since the 1950s. He knew he was retiring and said he thought he'd be a good fit in Cincinnati. But Bender said it happened right then—right after the radio satire aired. Unaware the entire thing had been a joke, Bender finished his interview, warm with thoughts of Rapp, and mentioned his name to Howsam, who offered Rapp the job. Rapp couldn't wait to get started.

He posted corny taglines all over the walls of the clubhouse—like "When in Doubt, Slide"—while Howsam's son Robert Jr., an advertising executive, crafted a new slogan for the franchise. Robert Jr. finally settled on "Getting back to fun again." In 1984, he said, fans could expect to come to Riverfront Stadium and have fun. They could test their arms with a new radar gun to see how fast they could throw the ball. They could hang out in the new beer garden in the bleachers, complete with a German polka band. They could enjoy fireworks after every Reds home run, and they could watch the Reds win. Rapp predicted they'd be at least .500.

Instead, with Rapp in the dugout, the team was even worse than before. Rapp failed to earn the respect of the players or the reporters. Most treated him like a joke, just like the radio producers in Boston, and sometime in late June 1984, while Pete was fighting the radio broadcaster in the Expos' clubhouse and visiting Francona in the hospital, Howsam found himself considering a radical notion to undo his hiring mistake. It came to him while he was watching a game in San Diego, and it rattled around in his mind all the way home on the plane.

What if he fired Rapp, Howsam thought, and traded for Pete Rose?

"What if I brought Rose back," he said, "as manager?"

It was a problematic idea for many reasons. Pete had never managed a team at any level, and Howsam learned right away that Pete had no interest in *just* managing. In exploratory phone calls that summer, first with Reuven Katz and then with Pete himself, Pete explained to Howsam that if the Reds traded for him, he would need to be a player-manager. He had to stay on the field and keep chasing Ty Cobb's record.

"Bob," Pete asked Howsam at one point that summer, "do you think I can hit?"

"Yes," Howsam replied.

"Then why should I retire as a player?" Pete said.

Howsam had to decide if he wanted that distraction, and he had to weigh other concerns, too—namely, Pete's off-field problems, his affairs and his gambling. Howsam needed to know that Pete could settle down. He wanted assurances that Pete could be a role model for the players, and after speaking with Pete and others that summer, Howsam thought that the signs pointed to yes. That April, in a private ceremony at Reuven's house in Cincinnati, Pete had married his girlfriend, Carol. The couple was expecting a child around October—Carol's first and Pete's fourth—and in preparation for the baby Pete was moving out of the West Side condo he had shared with Tommy Gioiosa and into a large house on the East Side in a neighborhood that was dotted with trees and seeded with money: Indian Hill.

Carol was thrilled. Their new home was situated on five acres, with a horse barn, a garage filled with BMWs and Porsches, multiple televisions in the living room, a satellite dish beaming in games from across the country, and a Jacuzzi bath. For the first time in her life, she felt as if things were coming together for her, and Howsam convinced himself that things were coming together for Pete, too. If he offered Pete the job as player-manager, Howsam knew Pete would want to keep it. He would want to succeed, and to do that, Pete would know that he couldn't mess around off the field. He would have to stay, Howsam explained, "on the straight and narrow."

It was a rational way of thinking, classic Howsam thinking. He believed he could help both the Reds and Pete at the same time. But Howsam's calculations didn't account for Pete's proclivity for recklessness, his enduring belief that his choices wouldn't hurt him, and his inability to stop gambling—a reality that Pete refused to acknowledge, but that others around him were beginning to see.

By 1984, Pete had graduated from placing bets with friendly West Side bookies like Al Esselman to hanging around shady, small-time mobsters and established East Coast criminals. Pete had reportedly started placing bets with a syndicate run out of Dayton by Dick Skinner, an old-school bookie and convicted felon known to authorities as "the Skin Man." Skinner was believed to be the largest bookmaker in southwest Ohio, and to Skinner's dismay Pete fell thousands of dollars behind on his payments. Skinner was soon complaining about Pete all over Dayton and Cincinnati. Then, in early 1984, Pete made a new gambling connection: Joe Cambra, a man on the fringes of the Rhode Island mob with dark eyes, dark hair, a home in southern Massachusetts just across the Rhode Island border, and a winter retreat in West Palm Beach not far from the Expos' spring training facility.

Pete knew Cambra would take his money if he lost, but he thought Cambra was different than other bookies. In Pete's mind, Cambra *wanted* him to win. If it was true, it might have been because Cambra wasn't going to lose his house in Massachusetts or Florida if Pete had a good weekend. Cambra had backup. He was part of a spiderweb of bookies stretching across New England—the kind of men who kept guns and drew attention.

In February 1984—right around the time when Pete met Cambra in West Palm Beach—two Massachusetts State Police officers went undercover to infiltrate his sprawling bookmaking ring. The officers spent time in smoky barrooms in Fall River near Cambra's home in Somerset, watched suspects from unmarked cars, jotted down license plate numbers, flipped insiders to use as informants, and tapped phone lines. They were building a case—Operation Moby Dick, they called it. Because just like the white whale at the heart of Herman Melville's literary drama, the officers' prey was elusive and large. According to one estimate, Cambra and his fellow bookies generated half a million dollars in revenue every weekend.

Unaware that anyone was watching, Pete paid off his debts to Cambra on July 5, 1984, with two checks—one from his personal account in Ohio for just over $10,000 and a second from the Royal Bank of Canada for $9,000. Pete then had a great week at the plate. He batted .333 in the days before and after he signed the checks. But he might have had a secret connection to help him with that, too. According to three different sources, Pete acquired corked bats during his time in Montreal. Bryan Greenberg, a clubhouse manager and a carpenter by trade, said he didn't know if Pete used the corked bats in a game—a charge that Pete has denied and that his teammates on the Expos have denied as well. All Greenberg knew was that he made them for Pete—in violation of league rules—and he made them well. Greenberg knew what he was doing.

Even decades later, Greenberg could recall in detail how he corked Pete's Mizuno bats in his home workshop: how he drilled a hole in the top, how he hollowed out a column inside the barrel, how he placed circular rounds of cork into the empty space to give the bat more pop, how he glued the cork together with dots of adhesive to prevent the contraband from spraying everywhere if the bat shattered against a fastball, how he marked the bat with a dot so that Pete knew what he had in his hands, and how he refinished the top of the bat to conceal the hole so that no one could see it—not the umpires, not the opponents, and definitely not Bob Howsam.

In mid-August 1984, despite all the warning signs and everything he knew to be true, Howsam finalized a trade for Pete Rose at the summer meetings in Philadelphia, appointed him player-manager, and prepared to welcome him home a hero.

46

VERN RAPP LEARNED that he was fired in the worst possible way: a reporter gave him the news.

It was a Wednesday night, about an hour before game time. The Reds were on the road in St. Louis, getting ready to play the Cardinals. They were twenty games under .500 and twenty and a half games out of first place. And in his excitement about bringing Pete back to Cincinnati, Howsam made a mistake. He called ownership from the summer meetings in Philadelphia to let them know he had closed the deal, but he failed to contact Rapp in the visitors' clubhouse in St. Louis, and in the intervening time, one of the Reds' majority owners spilled the secret to Hal McCoy of the *Dayton Daily News*. McCoy asked Rapp about it on the field, and Rapp just looked at him, dumbfounded.

"*What?*" Rapp said.

Howsam had blundered the firing of a good baseball man, an error that he probably wouldn't have made a decade earlier. Players were laughing at Rapp's expense, and Rapp was so unsure about what he was supposed to do with himself that he stayed and managed the game against the Cardinals. But reporters didn't spend any time mourning Rapp. That night, Pete's old friend Scoops Lawson wrote a column for the *Post* under the headline "Reds' Savior." Scoops was thrilled to have Pete back in town, and Marge Schott was, too. "Pete Rose is Mister Cincinnati," she said, "and Mister Baseball." She predicted that he would bring fans back to the stadium in droves, and she was right.

Within hours of the announcement, the Reds sold $40,000 in tickets for their next game—Pete's homecoming on Friday night against the Cubs. Downtown merchants reported surging sales of hats and jerseys. Howsam's son Robert Jr. printed thirty-five thousand "I Was There" certificates to hand out at the gate at Pete's first game back as a Cincinnati Red, and baseball writers flew in from around the country to say that they were there, too. The press conference introducing Pete the following afternoon—on a makeshift stage near home plate—was the largest the team had seen in at least twenty-five years.

There were more than one hundred reporters assembled in the crowd and sixteen television cameras parked in front of the stage. Three local television stations interrupted regularly scheduled programming to carry the press conference live. New cable networks like ESPN and CNN beamed the event from coast to coast, and when Howsam finally introduced Pete, wearing a shiny Reds warm-up jacket over his shirt and tie, members of the media did things they knew they weren't supposed to do.

One television reporter asked for his autograph. A cameraman requested a photo with Pete. They broke their own rule, the sportswriter's credo. They almost cheered—from the de facto press box set up on the field.

Jerome Holtzman, the author of *No Cheering in the Press Box* and a longtime baseball writer with the *Chicago Tribune,* admitted that day that he was just as guilty as everyone else. Holtzman loved Pete because, for years, he said, Pete had answered all the questions. He was never guarded or scripted. This time, on the field, Pete spoke to reporters for more than an hour. Holtzman left with enough material for three columns, and the Cubs' broadcaster Harry Caray was almost emotional about the occasion. In bringing back Pete, Caray said that weekend, Howsam had pulled off the greatest move in Reds history. Pete was where he belonged: in Cincinnati, with Tony Pérez in the dugout and another old friend at his side. Tommy Helms was going to be Pete's first-base coach.

"Everybody," Helms said, "better get ready to hustle."

That Friday night, in his very first at bat, Pete gave the people what they wanted to see. He drove in a run to tie the game with a single to center field. He scampered all the way to third when the Cubs' outfielder misplayed the ball for an error, and he slid headfirst into the base even though it wasn't necessary. He went 2 for 4 on the night—his first multi-hit game in more than three weeks—and he continued hitting for what was left of the summer. In his twenty-six games in Cincinnati, Pete batted .365, an impressive and relatively rare burst of production for a man his age.

But on the last day of the 1984 season, Scoops Lawson failed to take note of Pete's statistical renaissance. Perhaps he was too busy with other matters. Scoops was retiring after thirty-four years as a baseball writer, and the Reds were honoring him on the field. They asked him to throw out the ceremonial first pitch. Howsam presented Scoops with his own Reds jersey, and Pete gave him a gold watch engraved with a message. "Scoops," it said. "Thanks for 34 years of baseball and friendship."

An era had ended in Cincinnati. It was over for Scoops—and somehow Pete was still going. He had outlasted everyone from the Reds teams of the 1960s, almost all the old beat writers, most of his former teammates, Dick Wagner and Johnny Bench. They had all drifted away or retired, and Pete was still there, the oldest player in baseball, hanging on. He had no interest in spending time at a cabin in the mountains of Tennessee, like Scoops, or taking a job with CBS radio, like Johnny. Pete couldn't walk away. Due to his inconsistency over the past two seasons, he had failed to reach Ty Cobb's hit record by August 1984, like he had once predicted he would do. He ended the season ninety-four hits behind him. He had to come back in the spring of 1985, even though he was about to turn forty-four years old—the age that Fred Hutchinson had been when Hutch learned that he was dying of cancer.

To make sure he was ready, Pete needed to work out that winter, he told the press. He planned to lift free weights, hit the Nautilus machines, get stronger, stay healthy—and he had a place in mind where he could get the help he needed. It was recommended by Tommy Gioiosa, frequented by Paul Janszen, and popular with other bodybuilders, juiced full of steroids.

Pete told the press he was headed to Gold's Gym.

The gym was a new and modern facility located off the circle freeway north of Cincinnati in a growing slice of suburbia called Forest Park—a concrete swath of neighborhoods, shopping centers, fast-food restaurants, racket clubs, strip malls, and office parks—and like every new gym in the mid-1980s Gold's Gym in Forest Park was trying to position itself as a healthy destination for beautiful people.

In addition to ten thousand pounds of weights and dumbbells, the gym had aerobics classes, exercise bikes, tanning beds, a juice bar, a child-care center for busy parents, a team of sculpted trainers ready to help clients, attractive women in spandex pants, muscular men in cutoff shirts, and two young entrepreneurs at the helm: Mike Fry and Don Stenger.

Fry ran the business side of the operation, while Stenger worked the room, putting in long hours to make the venture a success because he believed in the mission. Stenger wanted to help people get stronger and transform them, as he had been transformed. He was the son of a widowed carpenter from a big German family on the West Side, and until a few years earlier he had been just another guy working on the assembly line at the Ford factory in Cincinnati. Now, in his late twenties, Stenger flexed in front of mirrors and in front of others, glistening and strong, at three hundred pounds. He could bench-press the equivalent of a walk-in freezer, and he wasn't the only star at Gold's Gym in Forest Park.

Mr. Ohio 1984 became a gym member. A former runner-up Mr. USA did, too, and football players on the Cincinnati Bengals followed, until the parking lot outside was filled with Ferraris and Porsches and word got around. People wanted to be at Gold's—women, men, couples, Tommy, Paul, even cops. Fry and Stenger liked to say that they catered to everyone. But by the summer of 1984, the place had become popular for two reasons that didn't appear in the gym's advertisements and that people spoke about only in whispers: steroids and cocaine.

Patrons could easily find both drugs there in ample quantities—cash passing between hands at the juice bar—and Stenger was in the middle of that, too. He procured cocaine from Mike Fry to sell or to use for himself. He got high on the powder and stronger on steroids, and he helped feed the addictions of others. On occasion, at the gym, Stenger injected Tommy with steroids, plunging little syringes into Tommy's biceps, back, or hip. Then the two men hit the weights, grunting and sweating and bulging out of their shirts.

They were riding a roller coaster, and it seemed to be picking up speed. Tommy couldn't get off the steroids—the drug, once scary to him, was now an everyday essential, like water, like air—and Stenger was churning through so much cocaine that he decided to find his own supplier. Sometime in the late fall of 1984, just weeks after Bob

Howsam traded for Pete Rose, Stenger met with a man in South Florida who introduced him to Norman Janowitz, a drug dealer in his mid-fifties with a wife and a home on the edge of the Everglades.

Janowitz had tattoos on his arms, bushy brown hair, a long history of drug trafficking, and the connections to make big scores. Janowitz could get Stenger the cocaine he wanted at roughly $3,000 per kilo, and Stenger came up with a way to get the drugs home. He would fly down to Florida, conduct the deals, and then send the cocaine back to Cincinnati with a courier, a driver—a mule.

47

IT WAS THE last thing that Pete Rose and Tommy Gioiosa needed in their lives. They should have run from Gold's Gym—and from guys like Norman Janowitz. Law enforcement in South Florida called him "a danger to the community," and it wasn't just because Janowitz was a drug dealer. The man was known to carry a fully loaded handgun in his jacket pocket.

But trapped in a swirling pool of his own addictions—steroids, money, and the warmth of the spotlight that reflected off Pete—Tommy didn't see the danger. He was too big, too strong, and too important, at least in his own mind, inside the weight room at Gold's Gym. Tommy worked out with Stenger for up to six hours at a time. He walked around the place with a wad of cash in his tube sock. He convinced Mike Fry to give him a job at the gym as a manager in early 1985, and he made sure everyone knew that he and Pete Rose were friends, until it was almost a joke among the bodybuilders. Wherever Tommy was, there was Pete, or vice versa.

Pete would say later that he never went to the gym. But in the winter before the 1985 season, he bragged to reporters about going there and let Fry use him to attract customers. At first, it was just Pete's picture and name in newspaper advertisements. Then, as Tommy exerted more control as manager, Pete allowed the gym to put his name on sweatshirts and atop the marquee. He let them call the place "Pete Rose's Gold's Gym," and bragged some more. He said he was training with Stenger. He said he was there three days a week. He said he could work out at five o'clock in the morning if he wanted.

"I have a key," Pete said.

Fry loved it—Pete was good for business—and Stenger reaped his own rewards. Because he was close with Tommy, Stenger got access to Pete's inner circle, the secret world. He got invited to Pete's house in Indian Hill with Tommy. He watched games there in front of a rack of televisions with Pete and Tommy betting on seemingly everything. He went to the racetrack with Pete and watched Pete bet $1,000 per race. He gambled with Pete and began to think of it all as crazy. "Just crazy," Stenger said. "He couldn't help himself. The guy would bet that the sun wouldn't shine."

At the gym, Tommy didn't even try to hide it anymore. Paul Janszen would be pumping weights and could hear Tommy at the front desk, taking Pete's phone calls, logging his bets for the day, calling his bookies. To Paul, listening in, it seemed as if Pete always lost. Yet the next day, the phone was ringing again. Tommy was back on the horn, or the guys were running off to the track, with Paul Janszen on the outside—close enough to hear everything that was happening, the wild stories, the good times, but not close enough to come himself.

One day, coming home from the track, Stenger had to pull his car over because Pete was losing his mind in the passenger seat. A race was on the radio, and it was as if Pete were riding the horse himself, Stenger said, shaking the vehicle to the point that Stenger felt unsafe. But who was he to judge? By 1985, Stenger was sending as much as $100,000 to Florida to buy cocaine from Norman Janowitz and turning to the guys at the gym for assistance. Paul Janszen helped distribute Stenger's product for a spell, serving as a middleman, and Tommy Gioiosa agreed to be one of Stenger's mules—a driver bringing the cocaine home from Florida.

Why Tommy opted to do it remains a subject of contention four decades later. Tommy said he did it for Pete—or at Pete's urging—because Pete thought they could make money by helping Stenger, and the additional money could cover gambling debts. But Pete denied any involvement. Law enforcement found no links between

Pete and Stenger's cocaine distribution ring, and Stenger doesn't recall ever talking with Pete about it. What's clear is this: On two occasions in the summer of 1985, Pete Rose's first full season back in Cincinnati, Tommy agreed to ferry money to Florida for Stenger. He took his girlfriend, stayed at the Palm-Aire in Pompano Beach or the Holiday Inn in Fort Lauderdale—hotels less than ten miles from Janowitz's house—and lounged at the pool or in the room while Stenger conducted business. Then Tommy drove back to Cincinnati with their quarry: kilos of cocaine to be divided up and sold.

Tommy was making drug runs for Stenger at the exact moment that Pete was pushing toward 4,192 hits—one more hit than Ty Cobb.

Pete's quest was the talk of the baseball world that year—and the biggest story in Cincinnati. One of the local papers ran a contest awarding $4,192 to the person closest to guessing the day and time of Pete's record-breaking hit. Budweiser made a series of television commercials celebrating Pete's career. Bob Howsam's son Robert Jr. helped get General Mills to agree to put Pete on Wheaties boxes, and the Cincinnati city council started a movement to rename Second Street downtown in Pete's honor. The politicians wanted to call it "Pete Rose Way."

Kenneth Blackwell, a Republican originally from a small industrial town in northern Ohio, was aware that a municipal rule forbade the city to name public places after people until after they had been dead for a year, and he understood the reason for this rule. "The potential for community embarrassment is always present when living persons are involved," the chairman of the city's Committee on Names explained. Still, Blackwell and others pushed for "Pete Rose Way." The city shouldn't have to wait until Pete was dead to honor him, Blackwell argued, because Pete had embodied the spirit of Cincinnati his entire life: "Hard work, hustle, aggressiveness, and competitiveness."

Marge Schott, newly installed as majority owner of the team after making a play for control over the winter, agreed. She hoped that Pete would help the Reds draw two million fans in 1985—enough for her to at least break even—while others capitalized on Pete in their own way. Bob Howsam reminded people that he was the one who had traded for Pete Rose, calling it the greatest trade he'd ever made. Howsam's replacement in waiting in the front office, Bill Bergesch, told fans not to worry. Nothing would change after Howsam retired again that season. "Pete is my man," Bergesch said. *The Today Show* flew the co-anchors Bryant Gumbel and Jane Pauley to Cincinnati to interview Pete on a set near the river with Marge and her dog. The Cincinnati Art Museum commissioned Andy Warhol to paint a seven-foot portrait of Pete to be unveiled when Pete broke the record. Major League Baseball produced a television show on Pete called *Countdown to History* and sold it to more than a hundred stations across the country; any station that bought the show had the rights to interrupt regularly scheduled programming to carry Pete's record-breaking at bats live.

Pete also cashed in. He inked three book deals chronicling his life. He made an appearance out in Oregon for a questionable memorabilia dealer who had amassed a fortune through "time-share condominiums in the Caribbean" and international banking "in the Kingdom of Tonga." Pete agreed to sell this dubious dealer his beloved and de-jeweled Hickok belt—now worth roughly thirty thousand dollars—and he partnered with one other important man making a name for himself in the growing memorabilia industry: Mike Bertolini.

Berto, as Pete called him, was from Brooklyn. He was just nineteen, and he didn't look like the savvy businessman he was. He wore clunky, white tennis shoes and square glasses and weighed about three hundred pounds. But Bertolini had developed a revolutionary strategy to entice players like Pete to sign photos and baseball cards. He was willing to pay the players up front for their signatures knowing that he could turn around and sell the items for even more. He first got Pete's attention at spring training in 1985, when he offered him $10,000 to appear at a single show, and by May, Berto was living in Pete's house in Indian Hill, acting as Pete's private photographer and getting Pete's signature on the pictures he produced. He'd wake up in the morning to find that Carol had left him his favorite breakfast outside his bedroom door: chocolate-frosted Pop-Tarts.

Bertolini was going to be there to chronicle the moment that Pete finally passed Ty Cobb. Pete got him access to the clubhouse and the field, as if he were a member of the press, and then, with Berto taking his photos, Pete chipped away at Cobb's record all summer, a picture of steady confidence and calm in every instance, except perhaps one. Robert Howsam Jr. recalled a time when Pete couldn't find one of his bats in the dugout and went pale.

Later, Robert Jr. questioned why Pete was so upset over a misplaced bat. "One wonders if there was more to it," he said. But in the moment, he didn't pause to consider the reasons for Pete's outburst in the dugout, because they were living a dream—"a media dream," Robert Jr. called it. In July, *Sports Illustrated* sent one of its big-name writers to Cincinnati to do a cover story on Pete for the magazine. In August, the piece ran, glossing over all Pete's problems, and in September, with Pete just eight hits away from passing Cobb, the national press descended to write the fairy-tale story of Charlie Hustle setting the all-time hit record.

To Marge Schott's horror, he nearly did it on the road, in Chicago, on the second Sunday of September. Pete wasn't supposed to be playing that day, because the Cubs were starting a left-hander, and against lefties Pete always sat—a lineup reality that was so certain that the press, Carol, Marge, and Reuven Katz flew on to Cincinnati, the next stop on the schedule. But the evening before the game, the Cubs' left-hander fell off a bicycle and injured his shoulder. On Sunday morning, Chicago replaced him with a right-hander, and even though the Reds had a four-game home stand coming up that week against the Padres, Pete put himself into the lineup that day in Chicago, as if it were any other game, and got two singles right away. He had tied Cobb's record. Then he stayed in the game for his remaining at bats, stunning Marge in Cincinnati. She couldn't figure out what Pete was doing and felt lucky that evening when she learned that Pete went hitless the rest of the game and that rain washed out his final at bat.

This record needed to be broken at home; there was too much money at stake. But Marge wasn't splurging to fly the team back to Cincinnati that night on a private jet, even when the Reds' flight got delayed by three hours in Chicago. They would fly commercial as usual on United Flight 352, and when the plane finally landed in Cincinnati around midnight, Pete looked exhausted. He dodged reporters and refused to sign autographs for the fans who had crowded into the airport terminal to greet him, and for the next two days he disappointed people again. On Monday, he announced that he was keeping himself out of the lineup against the Padres, and on Tuesday he went hitless as flashbulbs fired every time he swung his bat.

Teammates had never seen anything like it, even Dave Parker, who had won a World Series with the Pirates in 1979. Parker wondered how Pete could play with the lights, fifty thousand fans cheering his name, and three hundred reporters crammed into the press box—and maybe just this once, Pete *couldn't* focus. He swung at pitches out of the zone all night and failed with his one good swing of the evening. In the bottom of the eighth, with a man on second and a chance to tie the game, he hit a line drive directly at the left fielder for an easy out.

Pete went home to Indian Hill after the game that night thinking about that last at bat. Forget about Ty Cobb and the reporters in the press box; the Reds were eight games out of first place and fighting to catch the Dodgers. He couldn't come up short with a runner in scoring position. But Pete felt good about his chances the next day. The Padres were starting Eric Show, a middling pitcher who had a 9-9 record in 1985. Show was going to throw strikes, pitch to contact, and Pete knew that he could hit whatever Show threw.

He had a lifetime batting average of .370 against the Padres' starter.

It was a perfect late summer night in Cincinnati the following evening, warm and clear. Pink clouds drifted across the sky. The Goodyear blimp buzzed through the gloaming, and it felt as if the entire city were packed into a few square blocks downtown. No one wanted to miss the first inning. They had waited too long for this, driven too far for this, paid too much for this, skipped work or night school for this, kept the kids up late for this, and would never see something like this again. Even Karolyn Rose had to be there.

Unlike Marge Schott, Karolyn had hoped that Pete would break the record on the road; she didn't want to be part of it. It hurt too much to see Pete, Carol, and their baby boy at the stadium, to think about what might have been, to ponder what she had lost. But now that it was happening only a few miles from her new home on the West Side, Karolyn decided to go. Everyone else was. Fawn, now twenty years old, had a seat in the stands. Petey, now fifteen, had a spot in the dugout. Pete's mother bounced and cheered behind home plate. Marge Schott smoked her cigarettes and shouted just a few rows away. Tony Pérez lingered on the sidelines. Tommy Helms stood near first base, coaching. Joe Morgan sat in the broadcast booth, calling the game for NBC, and millions of people from coast to coast watched as Pete stepped to the plate at exactly eight o'clock.

Later, if you were alive and watching, you remembered exactly where you were in this moment: how your family gathered around, how the barroom went quiet, how the crowd stood up on its feet in the cheap seats or gathered in the department store in front of the rack of televisions, how Pete crouched over the plate, eyes on the ball, how he ran the count to two balls and one strike with the flashbulbs firing, how he swung at Eric Show's next pitch, his bat moving through the top of the zone, and how he hit it to shallow left-center field for a single—4,192.

The Goodyear blimp flashed the number. Fireworks exploded in the dark. People who had never met Pete broke down and cried for reasons they couldn't fully explain, and Pete was soon crying, too, as the crowd roared and the standing ovation continued. Three minutes, four minutes, five minutes, and beyond.

Helms finally tried to comfort his friend by telling him it was okay. They didn't need to play baseball right now; he could rest. He deserved it. But Pete only cried harder, and then, at the urging of a backup catcher in the dugout, young Petey appeared out of nowhere. The boy trotted onto the field to hug his father.

Petey wasn't sure if it was the right thing to do. He didn't want to upset his dad in front of everyone in the greatest moment of his life. But the crowd loved it, and Pete did, too. For the first time that Petey could ever remember, his father wrapped his arms around him, hugged him hard, and let himself go.

48

Pete met Carol, Reuven Katz, and a handful of other close friends later that night at the Precinct, a restaurant and bar on the East Side, seven minutes upriver from the stadium on the edge of an upper-class neighborhood called Hyde Park. The Precinct had beautiful young waitresses, a hopping dance floor, a clientele that included the city's biggest stars, and a menu featuring juicy steaks that typically weren't served after midnight but would be tonight. Even though it was almost two o'clock in the morning when Pete finally showed up at the Precinct, the owner had the kitchen open for him and a table waiting.

Pete finally got home to Indian Hill around four o'clock, yet there wasn't much time for sleep. Before breakfast, he had to be at a local television studio to appear, via satellite, on the national morning shows. He hit every one of them that day; did a taping for *The Phil Donahue Show* downtown in front of a live audience; listened to a starstruck Donahue, the biggest name in daytime television, introduce him as "the greatest player in the history of baseball"; made everyone laugh and smile during the program; managed the Reds to a 2–1 victory that night against the Padres from the bench; and woke up the next day to celebrate yet again. The city was throwing a "Pete Rose Rally" on Fountain Square downtown—with Pete, Carol, all three of his children, the marching band from West High, seven thousand fans packed onto the square, and the local networks set up to carry the festivities live on television.

In a career punctuated by amazing moments, Pete was having one of the greatest weeks of his life; Mike Bertolini had proof of it. Pete's young memorabilia dealer captured it all on film—in photos Pete would sign thousands of times in the years to come. But by Friday night, Pete was struggling to enjoy it all. The first-place Dodgers blew out the Reds, effectively ending Cincinnati's playoff hopes with twenty games still left to play. Pete almost said it out loud—the Reds were done in 1985. And he knew that managing the team would be harder in 1986. Now that his pursuit of Ty Cobb was over, fans would want results, actual wins, and for the first time local beat writers wrote columns asking whether the Reds were better off without Pete. These writers were new and young, closer to Fawn's age than they were to Pete's. They hadn't been there in the 1970s. They hadn't seen what he had done in the past, and Pete had to sit there and answer their questions late that month while he concealed his real problems just out of view.

For starters, Pete couldn't place bets anymore with Joe Cambra, the bookie he liked in New England, because Cambra had legal problems. Operation Moby Dick, the undercover sting arranged by the Massachusetts State Police, had busted him and forty other bookies in a raid that nearly ensnared Pete—twice. The first time was the night before the raid, when a wiretap captured Cambra talking to his crime boss about how Pete wanted to bet $6,000 on a single football game.

"That's good action," Cambra said on the call. But the boss disagreed. It was too much money, he told Cambra. Too high.

"The guy's gotta be nuts."

The next night, the State Police fanned out across the region, serving warrants at a coordinated time. They wanted to prevent the bookies from alerting one another to what was happening, and the trooper Dick Rand drew the assignment of visiting Joe Cambra's home on Captains Way in Somerset. Rand couldn't remember later if he knocked on the door—or just knocked it down—but Rand recalled distinctly what happened next. While he sorted through Cambra's betting slips and notes, evidence of gambling everywhere, the phone rang. Rand picked it up. The man on the line asked for Cambra, and when he was told that Cambra wasn't available, the man chose to leave a message: "Just tell him that Pete Rose called."

Somerset was eight hundred miles from Cincinnati. "So I figured it was somebody local," Rand said later. "I never assumed it was Pete Rose—*the* Pete Rose."

Cambra went down while Pete got away, but Pete wasn't exactly in the clear. In January 1986, four months after breaking Ty Cobb's record, Pete had to answer his own knock at the door in Indian Hill. Dick Skinner was outside—the Skin Man, one of the most notorious bookies in southwest Ohio.

Skinner had come with a friend, and he was there to collect a large gambling debt that Pete allegedly hadn't paid. "I ain't shitting you," Skinner told his friend as they pulled up outside the house that night. "It seems he's been dodging me and dodging me for three fucking years."

At the house, Skinner played it cool at first. He pretended he was there to pick up an item that Pete had autographed for his nephew, and Pete tried to make some small talk.

"Where you been?" Pete asked. "To the track?"

That's when Skinner pounced. He cursed. He told Pete that he was disappointed in him. He asked for his money, and he didn't accept Pete's excuses. When Pete said that he hadn't paid Skinner because he was just a little "short" right then, Skinner said Pete could pay his debt in small chunks, a couple thousand dollars at a time. And when Pete said that he had Skinner's phone number—and that he *was* going to call him—Skinner shot back: "*Was* you?"

They talked for a while about other matters: the upcoming Super Bowl between the Chicago Bears and the New England Patriots, the spread on the game, the over-under, and Pete's picks, which way he was leaning. Then, out of nowhere, Skinner brought up a long-ago bet that he had tried to make on the Reds in 1977, almost a decade earlier.

It was a strange story to be telling now. Maybe he just wanted to get it on the record for someone else. The whole time that night, unbeknownst to Pete, Skinner was recording the conversation on a hidden device. The Skin Man had Pete on tape promising to pay up by spring training.

"That's three weeks," Pete said. "I'll straighten it out. I'll straighten it out. I'm not going to stiff ya."

Skinner left Pete's house, but he didn't seem confident about ever getting his money. Skinner had learned that Pete had moved on from him. Tommy had found him a new bookie.

"Some Ron," Skinner complained that night.

Somebody named Ron in the suburbs north of Cincinnati.

49

Tommy found Ron Peters through his usual connections—the bodybuilders at Gold's Gym. Someone knew a guy who knew a guy who was a bookie, and it was Ron.

Tommy liked Ron immediately; most people did. He was twenty-eight years old, smooth and handsome, with a dark mustache and an all-American story. Ron's father had escaped the ragged coalfields of eastern Kentucky to become a postal worker in tiny Franklin, Ohio, off the interstate, fifty minutes north of Cincinnati. He had wanted to give his three children a better life, and without question Ron's father succeeded. Instead of living in a coal-mining camp, the three Peters kids grew up in a quiet subdivision in Franklin. And instead of shoveling coal like his grandfather, young Ron, the middle child, played golf. As a boy, Ron wore out a path between his house and the Franklin Golf Club, and unlike other kids he didn't need to ditch his bicycle in the bushes and sneak onto one of the fairways to play his round. He was a club member and could swing his driver on the first tee with everyone watching and whispering. Ron Peters was one of the best young golfers in town.

Girls in Franklin were impressed. Ron ran with cheerleaders in high school in the 1970s and married one of them a few years after graduation in 1978. Her name was Lori, and Ron planned to support her—through golf. He got a job working as an assistant pro at a club north of Cincinnati. It was right off the circle freeway, not far from the future location of Gold's Gym—an exclusive place called Beckett Ridge.

The members there were wealthier than Ron, but Ron was smarter. Sometimes, he'd invite old high school teammates to come play with him in off-the-books competitions at Beckett Ridge, and they'd always leave richer, hundreds of dollars in their pockets. In these games, they would bet on themselves to win, and Ron would usually find a way to make it happen. He could make all the shots and see all the angles, including the next one: around 1981, he began running a sportsbook out of a condo complex near the course. Ron Peters had become a bookie.

Predictably, for Ron, the new venture went well. Ron told friends that he could make $20,000 in a single night—more than he made in an entire year as a golf pro—and the money opened doors to a life of ease and excess. Ron vacationed in Hawaii, lent $40,000 to friends without hesitation, invested in a saloon, drove Corvettes, became a father in the summer of 1983, named the boy Jonathan, and planned to raise the boy in a brand-new house on a brand-new street called Cinnamon Woods, a place that didn't exist and then in 1984 suddenly did. It was a two-story brick colonial, and it was perfectly located—both for Ron's golf interests and his growing gambling enterprise. The house was just north of Beckett Ridge and less than twenty minutes from Gold's Gym.

There, sometime around the fall of 1984, Tommy arranged to meet Ron for the first time. Each man wanted to feel out the other and discuss the terms of a new, secretive, and possibly lucrative arrangement. Tommy said he wanted a bookie who could take bets ranging from $1,000 to $5,000 per game, and Ron informed Tommy that he was good with that kind of action. He'd put no limit on Tommy's wagers, because Ron knew the money was really coming from Pete Rose, and he figured a man like Pete would always be able to pay his debts.

For a while, everything worked as planned. Tommy would call Ron with Pete's wagers on basketball and football, and then he would meet Ron whenever they needed to settle up. Sometimes, that was at the gym. Other times, Tommy drove his Porsche to Ron's house, or they'd meet somewhere in between.

Once, in a snowstorm, Tommy pulled up next to Ron's car on a side street near a Bob Evans up by the interstate and tried to throw a paper bag full of money out his window and into Ron's front seat. There was a bundle of cash inside the bag, and Tommy missed his target. It hit the side of Ron's car, and dollar bills went fluttering away with the snow. Ron had to chase them down in the cold while Tommy drove off, hollering, "Count it! It's all there!"

Other times, Pete was slow to pay, and Ron couldn't find Tommy at all—a development that surprised no one who was working as a bookie in southwest Ohio at the time. Al Esselman told stories about Pete's debts on the West Side, and the Skin Man told his stories in Dayton, until everyone in this little world knew that Pete couldn't be trusted. He was like one of those elusive river eels, the unwanted fish that people sometimes hooked by accident in Cincinnati. Pete was slippery in the murk. But people sometimes said the same thing about Ron Peters. Keith Sexton, a fellow gambler who had once considered Ron a friend, stopped working with Ron after he said Ron lied over a matter of several thousand dollars and fleeced Sexton out of the money. With Ron, Sexton said, everyone was a mark, even his friends, and this side of Ron seemed to grow worse, Sexton thought, as Ron developed a new and troubling habit in the 1980s: cocaine.

It was just fun, at first. But by late 1985, Ron was snorting cocaine in a way that didn't feel recreational anymore, and he was talking too much for a man who was supposed to be keeping secrets. Ron bragged about his new client Pete Rose in ways that felt reckless, and on at least one occasion he put Pete on speakerphone while Keith Sexton was sitting there so that Sexton could hear the Reds' player-manager placing his daily wagers.

Sexton, a longtime Reds fan, recognized Pete's familiar voice on the line, and he remembered thinking two things as he listened to the call. Pete was placing too many bets, Sexton said. No one could ever make money the way he was gambling—one $2,000 bet after another. And, Sexton realized, Pete was doing it with the wrong guy. If Ron ever got in trouble, Sexton thought, he'd flip on Pete in an instant. He wouldn't keep his silence the way Al Esselman, Joe Cambra, or the Skin Man had in the past.

Ron Peters would do anything to save himself.

50

Reds fans had reasons for hope entering the 1986 season. Pete had a winning record as a player-manager, and three magazines predicted that the Reds would win their division for the first time in seven years. "Why not?" *The Sporting News* asked. The Reds had strong pitching, young talent, Dave Parker, and Pete Rose—a player-manager who had no intention of just sitting on the bench. If anything, Pete said, he might play himself even more in 1986.

But he was almost forty-five years old, and he showed up at spring training with a series of maladies that reflected his age. Pete had stomach problems, the flu, a hernia. For only the second time in his career, he was going on the disabled list. Pete was injured and ineligible to play to start the year, and for a while that winter in Florida, Dave Parker's status was also in question. In yet another sign of the changing times, Parker had recently been forced to testify against a drug dealer who had supplied him, and other ballplayers, with cocaine in an ever-widening scandal that implicated more than a dozen players. According to testimony at the trial, everyone was using: the former NL MVP Keith Hernandez; Yogi Berra's son Dale; one of Boston's heroes from the 1975 World Series, Bernie Carbo; and Pete's old teammate in Montreal Tim Raines, who admitted to playing at times in a drug-induced fog that made it hard to decipher if a pitch was a ball or a strike.

Parker was apologetic about his cocaine use, though a little surprised that it was coming out now. He hadn't used the drug, he said, since 1982, and he believed there should be a statute of limitations for this kind of mistake, especially when so many other players had made the same choice. As Parker said in court, "Everybody was doing it. . . . It was sort of the in thing." Keith Hernandez called it "a love affair" for players. He estimated that at one point in the early 1980s 40 percent of the league was doing cocaine.

But the commissioner of baseball was now Peter Ueberroth, a savvy executive in his late forties, with good hair, a Southern California tan, and no patience for excuses. Ueberroth had made his fortune buying travel agencies and hotels and had risen to fame by staging the first great modern Olympics: the 1984 summer games in Los Angeles. Ueberroth was not going to be undermined by players doing drugs of any sort. He was determined to root them out of the game through mandatory testing—"We'll be relentless," Ueberroth said, "until that is done"—and Ueberroth had a new colleague in the front office that summer who complemented his talents in almost every way. Everybody loved the soon-to-be-appointed National League president: Angelo Bartlett Giamatti.

Giamatti was the exact opposite of Ueberroth. He was forty-eight in the summer of 1986—a year younger than the commissioner—yet he looked like Ueberroth's wayward uncle, with a beard gone gray, extra pounds on his waist, and a cigarette almost always dangling between his fingers. Giamatti smoked at least two or three packs a day, maybe more, disregarding every health warning, and he was different from Ueberroth in one other significant way. He had never been a businessman or a sports executive. Giamatti was an academic who for most of the past thirty years had studied—and taught—Renaissance literature at Yale. He preferred books over boardrooms and seminars over spreadsheets. He knew more about the works of Dante than he did about almost anything else, and he made self-deprecating comments about the biggest achievement of his professional life. In 1977, Giamatti had been elected president of Yale—the youngest president in the history of the university—and he greeted the news by saying that he'd rather be president of the American League. "I don't want to make it sound as if this were my second choice," Giamatti said that day. "But you do what you have to do."

Giamatti rooted for the Red Sox, loved Bernie Carbo and Fred Lynn, and wrote about baseball and its heroes in ways that made sportswriters jealous and others intimidated. When it was announced that Giamatti was leaving Yale to be president of the National League in 1986, the business manager at the league office started studying a book of vocabulary. He wanted to be able to keep up with Giamatti, who saw baseball as a metaphor for life; everyone, Giamatti said, wanted "to leave and to return home." He wrote sentences like "The game begins in the spring, when everything else begins again, and it blossoms in the summer, filling the afternoons and evenings, and then as soon as the chill rains come, it stops and leaves you to face the fall alone." People didn't speak like this in baseball's front office or even sometimes at Yale. One colleague there called Giamatti "frightfully distinguished"—so distinguished, in fact, that he almost didn't take the job with baseball. The NL presidency felt like a figurehead position; Ueberroth would be running the show. What would he be doing?

Giamatti's friend Fay Vincent—a corporate lawyer, a top executive at Coca-Cola, and the former chairman at Columbia Pictures—urged Giamatti to think about it in a different way. Yes, Vincent said, he wouldn't have many duties as National League president. But he could take the time to recalibrate his life, work on his health, exercise at the Yale Club in New York City, give speeches, write more, and when the owners got tired of Ueberroth, as inevitably they would, there would be Giamatti, the new commissioner in waiting, sitting at his desk just down the hall at the league office on Park Avenue in New York.

"They're going to turn to you," Vincent said, "because you're going to be there."

It was compelling advice from a man who understood the business world and who could imagine how millionaire owners might think. Giamatti accepted the job in June 1986, and he soon made it clear to his new colleagues in New York that they didn't need to brush up on their vocabulary in order to earn his respect. He had a way of putting ordinary people at ease, and he did it right away at the league office. He asked people to call him Bart. He belittled himself all the time with his self-deprecating wit. He joked that he was "middle-class, middle-aged, and middle-of-the-road"—not remarkable—and he never forgot that he was the grandson of Italian immigrants whose names no one could pronounce and whose paths were not promised.

Giamatti's mother may have descended from old New England money, but his grandfather Angelo had immigrated to America as a boy and earned a pittance working at a clock factory in Connecticut.

Giamatti could relate to anyone. He could have lunch with the vice president of the United States and advise young students. He could earn praise from team owners in their private suites, and he could chat up ballplayers in the dugout, with tobacco juice and sunflower seeds on the floor. He could even relate to Pete Rose.

For all their obvious differences, Pete liked Bart. But Pete wouldn't get the chance to see the new NL president at the World Series that fall. Cincinnati finished second in their division for the second year in a row and missed the postseason, while Pete bottomed out as both a player and a man. He appeared in just seventy-two games in 1986. He batted .219, the worst average of his career. He rotted away on the bench, a forty-five-year-old man who couldn't hit anymore, and sometime that year—exactly when remains a subject of dispute—he crossed a line from which there was no coming back.

Pete wasn't just a gambler anymore. He was a gambler betting on his own games.

He was a gambler betting on baseball.

51

THE TIMING OF Pete's first wager on a baseball game isn't clear. Pete can't remember or won't say, and the people around him can't or won't, either. It's an odd hole in the story, especially for a man who can summon, with instant recall, how many triples he hit for the Macon Peaches in 1962 or how many doubles he had for the Philadelphia Phillies in 1979. Pete should remember the moment when he made the biggest gamble of his life, cast his lot with the likes of Ron Peters, and placed a bet that could cost him his career, his reputation, everything. What's known is this: the chain reaction that led to his ultimate implosion began with a quiet moment in early 1986. Sometime that January—right about the time that the Skin Man came to Pete's house asking for his money—Pete made a trip to Franklin, Ohio.

Ron Peters, at that point, had been dealing with Tommy Gioiosa for about a year, money exchanging hands in paper bags out near the circle freeway. Now Ron wanted to finally meet his star gambler, Pete Rose, and he had a location in mind. He asked Tommy to bring Pete to the new restaurant that Ron had just opened in Franklin, Jonathan's Café.

The café was located at the corner of Second and Main Streets downtown, and Ron swore that it was more than just a way to launder his gambling proceeds. The restaurant—named after his son—had stained glass windows out front, sports memorabilia on the walls, and a menu that included twenty different imported beers. It was going to be the new family business, Ron said. Lori would work there as a cook and hostess, thirty hours a week, and Ron would work the room. "What I've done with Jonathan's," he told people, "is something I've always wanted to do." He had created a community gathering spot, and he hoped that Pete's presence at the café would help attract customers. If the atmosphere at Jonathan's was good enough for Pete Rose, it was good enough for folks in Franklin.

On the day of the visit, Pete came bearing gifts. He brought a signed baseball bat that Ron could display at the café, and at some point, after they arrived, Ron gave Tommy what *he* wanted: the winnings from Pete's recent bets—winnings estimated on this day at more than $30,000. The three men sat for lunch at a table near the bar. Everyone was in good spirits. Pete signed autographs for midday customers. Tommy left with a bundle of cash, and Ron got the attention that he wanted. In the days after Pete left, the local newspaper, *The Franklin Chronicle,* ran a picture of Ron holding the bat that Pete had signed at the café. Ron promised locals that Pete would be back again soon—perhaps to act as a celebrity bartender for a night—and though that never happened, there was reason to believe that it could. The signed bat was proof that Ron knew Pete, and so were the tickets that Pete left for Ron at will call at Riverfront Stadium that spring when Ron wanted to attend Reds games. The seats were free and down low, not far from Marge Schott.

But between the money exchanging hands and the cocaine in Ron's office at the café—the winnings over here and the losses over there—things were getting confusing, even manic, especially, it seemed, on Ron's end. Sometimes that year, he sat at the front window of his house in the suburbs, fretting that someone was out to get him. He became so convinced that it was true that he soon sold the house—before Lori could stop him—and relocated the family to a different house in a small town east of Franklin, yet the change of scenery didn't seem to improve Ron's frame of mind. Shortly after moving into the new house, Lori recalled, Ron took over the living room, counting stacks of money on the floor—an estimated $110,000 that he thought needed to be hidden, right away if possible. According to Lori, Ron moved it no fewer than four times.

All of it was cause for concern. Tommy began to worry about Ron and, around this time, Pete began funneling at least some of his gambling action to someone else. By March 1986, just two months after the lunch meeting at Jonathan's Café, Pete was calling in his bets to Mike Bertolini, who then placed the action with a pair of bookies he had found in New York, two brothers. According to a notebook that Bertolini kept at the time in his desk drawer, Pete's bets started on March 10 while the Reds were at spring training, and Pete was wagering a lot—sometimes placing as many as fifteen bets in a single day. On college basketball. On the NBA. On big games. On obscure games. It was a hard way to win and, according to the notebook, Pete didn't.

In the first week alone, according to Bertolini's notes, Pete lost $1,900 on Monday, $2,800 on Tuesday, $15,400 on Wednesday, $5,800 on Thursday, and $600 on Friday—a weekly loss of more than $26,000 and even more when accounting for the money that Bertolini lost piggybacking on Pete's bets.

"Total for the week!" Berto wrote in the notebook. "Bookie gets $31,610."

Pete said later—and maintains to this day—that he didn't start placing bets on baseball until the Mets-Astros playoff series that October, weeks after the Reds had been eliminated and weeks after Pete's final at bat as a player. "Betting on the playoffs," Pete remembers telling Tommy and others that day, "makes the games more exciting to watch!" But according to Bertolini's notebook, Pete was gambling on baseball by at least April and May 1986—with a handful of bets on the Yankees, Mets, Phillies, Braves, and his own team, the Reds. To crawl out of the hole he had dug for himself that March, Pete had apparently started wagering on the thing he knew best: baseball.

According to the notebook, Pete always bet on the Reds to win; it was messier for Bertolini. He liked to cheer for his hometown Mets, and, according to the notebook, Berto regularly bet on them to win, even when New York was playing Cincinnati, a decision that pitted Pete against Berto on at least four occasions that year. Pete was a rostered player in the game, batting second, and Berto was effectively cheering for the Mets' pitchers—Ron Darling, Bobby Ojeda, or Sid Fernandez—to strike out his friend so that Berto could win money.

One time, Bertolini remembered feeling stressed late in a Reds-Mets game when it looked like Pete might get a chance to knock in the winning run for the Reds—and lose the wager for Bertolini. Another time, according to the notebook, Bertolini bet on the Astros to beat the Reds because he loved Houston's starting pitcher, Mike Scott. And even though Pete was now gambling on pitchers he knew well, players he knew personally, he still didn't win all the time. One day, according to the notebook, he cleared more than $6,000, and another day he won more than $5,000. But on a single day that April, betting on both basketball and baseball, Pete frittered away any winnings he might have accrued. He placed eight bets and lost seven of them, according to Bertolini's notes, burning nearly $18,000 in cash within a matter of hours.

"Pete owes me," Bertolini's notebook says in multiple places.

"Pete owes me $14,300."

"Pete owes me $29,400."

"Call him."

Whenever it started, Pete knew it was wrong. "Absolutely wrong," he said later. "Let's get that on the record right now." A manager betting on his own team could harm the game—even if he was betting on the team to win. He could overuse a pitcher or refuse to rest a starter in pursuit of his own financial gain, and what he wagered—or didn't wager—could move markets in the underworld. Bertolini's bookies in New York surely noticed when Berto was betting against Pete. Any bookie in that situation would have been justified to wonder if Berto had inside information that would make it worthwhile to go against the Reds that night. The bookies also surely noticed when Pete didn't bet on the Reds at all. He wasn't betting against his team; he just wasn't betting *on* them. On multiple days, according the notebook, Pete sat it out, not wagering on the Reds after having done it the day before or earlier that week. It was another thing that could move markets in the underworld. And his debts—his mounting debts recorded in the notebook—were especially troubling. An athlete in arrears to a bookie is an athlete in danger of being owned by that bookie, a kept man, beholden. It was the reason why baseball had its rule against gambling in the first place and the reason why that rule—Rule 21(d)—was posted in every clubhouse, including the Reds' clubhouse at Riverfront Stadium.

But Pete couldn't stop himself. He was already betting on football and basketball—with Ron Peters in Franklin and the two brothers in New York. Why not baseball games, too? He knew every major-league roster. He believed in his players—"I thought they'd win every fucking night," Pete said—and it was his job, as manager, to watch. He *had* to sit there in the dugout for two or three hours every day. And if he had to do that, Pete reasoned, then he might as well bet on the games. "It'd be like going to the racetrack," he told himself. "I'm rooting for somebody. I'm taking sides."

In his mind, there was no way he was going to get caught. Pete knew he could trust Tommy and Berto; he'd known both of them since they were teenagers. But Bertolini said he began to feel pressure as Pete's losses mounted in New York: $50,000 . . . $100,000 . . . $250,000. "It was a huge number," Bertolini recalled, "a bookie's dream." Pete just kept losing. "Looking back on it now," Bertolini said, "Pete was just free money to them."

Bertolini was never worried for his safety or for Pete's, but it got to a point, he said, when he had to arrange a meeting between Pete and the New York bookies. In Bertolini's memory, the meeting happened in the basement of an old gymnasium, with the two brothers asking Pete to at least make an effort. He had to pay something, and not long after that, Pete started sending money to New York. He was never going to get clear of what he owed the two brothers—"The debt," Bertolini said, "never got satisfied"—but Berto felt better than Tommy did in the fall of 1986. Between the steroids, the women, the cocaine, and his own bookie problems, Tommy couldn't sleep. He was often agitated. He drove his Porsche around Cincinnati with a fury that worried his new girlfriend, a blond waitress named Kim. He was quick to anger, and he felt as if he were always chasing—

chasing Pete's losses. Sometimes, Tommy had to pay Pete's debts with his own money. Twice, he borrowed cash from Mike Fry at Gold's Gym in order to pay Ron Peters, and then in the fall of 1986 he turned to another friend at the gym for help: Paul Janszen.

Tommy said that Pete owed him $10,000 for money he had paid Ron, and he wanted Paul to meet Pete and pretend that he had been the one who paid it. Tommy figured that Pete would cough up the money to Paul Janszen—a much bigger man—and Paul agreed to play along with Tommy's ruse, tantalized by the thought of meeting Pete up close and in person. He'd do what Tommy asked. They arranged to gather at a family restaurant near the interstate on the West Side. Pete paid Paul the $10,000—just as Tommy predicted—and Paul could almost feel the ground shifting beneath his feet.

Long on the outside, circling this group at the gym in Forest Park, Paul was now inching into Pete's orbit—a West Side guy with full access to West Side royalty. He got invited to Pete's house in Indian Hill that fall; to small parties watching football games and the baseball playoffs; to gatherings where Pete was betting and Tommy was on the phone with Ron; to an autograph show that winter with Pete and Mickey Mantle up in New York; to an impromptu photo shoot at the event with Mickey, Pete, Tommy, and him; to a dinner on New Year's Eve 1986 at one of Cincinnati's nicest restaurants on the river; to rollicking nights at the racetrack in northern Kentucky; and to the precipice of an uncertain vista that Tommy never saw coming. After eight years of friendship, eight years of doing whatever Pete wanted, eight years of running his errands, hiding his girlfriends, and placing his bets, Tommy was being eclipsed by Paul Janszen.

Later, Pete would wonder why it happened. He would grab the memory of Paul Janszen in his mind, dust it off, turn it over, and come up with nothing. "I don't know why," Pete said. "I sit here and I think—I don't know why I ever befriended Paul Janszen. He didn't bring anything to the party." But that wasn't true. Paul could do all the things that Tommy did, and he could do them without embarrassing Pete.

On a rainy night that winter—in late February 1987, after Pete had already flown to Florida for spring training—Tommy and a group of buddies stirred up a ruckus inside Pete's private box at his favorite racetrack in Kentucky that incurred the wrath of the racetrack's owner, Jerry Carroll. The guys in the box were just having fun. In the seventh race of the night, one of them had put big money on a forty-to-one long shot to win, and this horse, Thanks Tom—a horse that had never won before and would never win again, a horse that had no chance—came galloping down the stretch in the slop in first place. A winner covered in mud. A miracle in the night. They had to celebrate, whooping and hollering, beer spilling on the floor.

But Carroll didn't like the sound of it—drunk guys, yelling and cursing. He had long been wary of Pete Rose's crew. He thought of them as trash—"just plain white trash," Carroll said—and he didn't like Tommy in particular because of his look, his attitude, even the way he walked. Whatever it was, Carroll thought it was no good for Pete, and he knew it was a problem for the track. Without hesitation that night, he instructed security to throw them all out—a choice that finally doomed Tommy in Pete's eyes.

Pete couldn't have Tommy acting crazy around important and established guys like Jerry Carroll, and Pete made up his mind. Paul Janszen was coming to spring training with him that year, not Tommy Gioiosa. Paul and his girlfriend, Danita, were flying down, bags packed and wheels up, not Tommy. Paul was in and Tommy was out. There was only one job left for Tommy to do.

In mid-March 1987, Pete's agent, Reuven Katz, wrote a check to Tommy for $34,000, and Tommy picked it up at Reuven's office in downtown Cincinnati. Tommy remembers telling Reuven that he was using the money to buy a car, and he also remembers how Reuven just stood there, his glasses perched at the end of his nose, eyeing him in withering silence.

The money was for Ron Peters, one final gambling debt, and Tommy said he paid it. He drove the money north to Jonathan's Café, split it with Ron, per an agreement they struck, and then kept going. Tommy was leaving Cincinnati. He was moving to California with his girlfriend. He was getting off steroids, and he was finished with Pete Rose.

Paul Janszen could have him.

52

BART GIAMATTI PUT the Cincinnati Reds front and center on his calendar in early 1987. A week before Tommy picked up the $34,000 check at Reuven's office, the new National League president made the Reds' camp in Tampa his first stop at spring training. He kibbitzed with the players, watched the team practice in the sun, and forgave Marge Schott for a cost-cutting measure that he noticed right away. The Reds were still using last year's baseballs, stamped with the signature of the previous National League president, not him.

"Does this mean your position isn't official yet?" Dave Parker joked.

Giamatti laughed. No, he replied.

"It means Mrs. Schott is a frugal businesswoman."

He planned to visit all twelve National League teams that winter in both Florida and Arizona. He wanted to meet as many people as he could. He did some writing, as his friend Fay Vincent had suggested. He published a piece in *Newsday.* He played catch with the commissioner Peter Ueberroth before a Red Sox game in St. Petersburg, and he enjoyed hanging out with ballplayers, especially Yogi Berra. Talking to Yogi about baseball, Giamatti said, was like talking to Homer about the gods.

But even that—a reference to Homer—painted Giamatti as an outsider. The only homer that most players knew was the kind they hit over a wall, and at times, among them, Giamatti felt out of place that winter. "I'm kind of like a Martian to them," he told one reporter in West Palm Beach in late March 1987. It was as if he were constantly answering the question that *The Philadelphia Inquirer* had once published in bold type: "How can an ex–university president and a Renaissance scholar be qualified to become president of baseball's National League?" Worst of all, Giamatti was every bit the figurehead that he feared he might be. He complained to Fay Vincent that he spent most of his time sitting around and wondering why he had taken the job in the first place.

"You gotta get me out of here," he told Vincent. "There's nothing to do."

But Vincent assured Giamatti that he was wrong.

"Just be patient," he told his friend.

Paul Janszen and his girlfriend, Danita, couldn't believe the size—or the style—of Pete and Carol's rental house in Florida when their taxi pulled up outside of it that winter on a quiet street north of Tampa.

It had a racquetball court, a weight room, an arcade filled with *Pac-Man* video games and pinball machines, a five-car garage with three bays large enough for stretch limousines, a chartreuse-and-gold kitchen, drapes the color of orange sherbet, pink carpeting in the dining room, mocha walls in the master bedroom, a circular bar carved out of rosewood, a greenhouse filled with orchids, and a balcony on the back of the house overlooking a heated indoor swimming pool. From the balcony, guests had two ways to get to the water. They could take the stairs to the patio below, or they could hop on one of two ten-foot slides connected to the balcony and go flying into the deep end. Or, if they weren't in the mood for swimming, they could skip the pool altogether and watch television in the den sitting on velour furniture that was best described as frat-house chic.

Pete loved it. He bragged about the house at training camp and greeted Paul and Danita at the door, smiling and excited to show them around. The place even had a name: the Hasslefree Ranch. WELCOME TO HASSLEFREE, read a sign outside. Paul and Danita settled into one of the guest bedrooms—as if they were on a honeymoon, only with Pete Rose—and Paul couldn't wait to go fishing in the lake behind the house, yet another amenity on the property.

But what Paul remembered most about his time at Hasslefree was how quickly things escalated. With Tommy out of the picture and Berto busy falling in love with a blond dancer he met in a nightclub in Tampa, Paul became Pete's new sidekick by the end of the first week. The Roses invited him and Danita to stay for the whole month, if possible, and Paul picked up Tommy's old duties. Paul hit the horse track with Pete and his friend the Cuban. He met a man there named Stevie who connected him with a new bookie willing to take Pete's action—someone on Staten Island in New York who went by the nickname Val. And before spring training was even over, Paul was Pete's new middleman, waiting at the Hasslefree Ranch for Pete to call with his picks so Paul could then relay them to Stevie, who passed them along to Val.

Paul had heard these phone conversations countless times before at Gold's Gym, with Tommy on the line, cash in his tube sock, and Pete on the other end, picking favorites and underdogs. He knew how it was supposed to work. But Paul wasn't a gambler. He had never bet on sports until the previous fall when he started hanging around Pete's house in Indian Hill, and he didn't glorify what he was doing now. He was a gofer, and he knew it. A gofer helping Pete lose money. Before they even left spring training, Pete and Paul had to cobble together thousands of dollars to cover losses with Stevie and Val.

In that moment, Paul and Danita knew they were running with the wrong crowd. They were out of place here. Yet because it was Pete Rose's crowd—and because Paul was starting to believe that Pete was his friend—it was impossible to walk away. Paul was at Pete's table at the track, everyone stopping by to say hello and shake Paul's hand. Danita and Carol were growing close. Players were getting to know Paul—some would even work out with him that year—and he was traveling in a way that he had never imagined was possible for a kid like him from the West Side. When spring training ended in early April, Paul flew north on a private jet with Pete, Tommy Helms, and Carl Yastrzemski to attend one of those lucrative autograph shows in Nashville, with all the typical perks. There would be cash at the door and cash under the table, everyone making money and the fans leaving happy. People lined up that weekend to pay $3 for Helms's autograph, $7 for Pete's, and $10 for the signature belonging to perhaps the greatest of the living legends—Joe DiMaggio, now seventy-two years old and gray, with a newly installed pacemaker clicking inside his chest.

DiMaggio signed for one session in Nashville; that was enough for most guys. But Pete worked two, signing in prime time on both

Friday and Saturday nights that weekend. Then he hopped back on the plane, flew the rest of the way home to Cincinnati, and reported to his office at Riverfront Stadium to prepare for the season. Opening day 1987 was upon him.

53

The Reds got off to a hot start that April. They won eight of their first ten games, scored runs in bunches, beat great pitching, and found themselves all alone in first place after two weeks—reason for excitement in Cincinnati.

After the Reds beat the Astros 8–0 in mid-April, driving Nolan Ryan from the mound in the fifth inning, reporters started comparing the 1987 Reds to the Big Red Machine of the 1970s. They looked like a juggernaut, and that was great for Pete in lots of ways. In addition to winning on the field, he was winning with Val in New York every time the Reds won, because Pete was betting that spring on the Reds to win.

But Pete wasn't just betting on the Reds. He bet on other games, too. Lots of games, too many games. Paul wasn't even sure that Pete understood the betting lines sometimes—it was confusing with baseball—and Paul began to worry as the losses mounted over the course of late April and early May. Over that stretch, the Reds cooled off, going 14-14. If Pete was betting on his team every night, he was now losing money because of the percentage that Val skimmed off the top either way. And between that and his other losses, Pete was soon in debt. Again.

The size of the debt that Pete accrued remains under dispute decades later. Pete believes he was down just $31,000; Paul said it was more like $67,000. And Paul and Pete would never agree on many other details from the spring of 1987. What's clear is this: others were also concerned about Pete's gambling that year. "Everybody worried about it," said Arnie Metz, Pete's friend, the groundskeeper who did the triple-headers with him down at spring training. "But there was nothing we could do. Nothing, you know? Because he was spiraling like a 747 coming down out of the sky."

In the frantic chaos, it was Paul Janszen who was screaming at the back of the plane. To appease Val in New York, Paul said he dipped into his own personal savings to pay off a significant portion of Pete's debt. He cleaned out a safety-deposit box, borrowed money from family, and cobbled together $44,000 to send to Val in New York. Then, because they were still short, Val cut off ties with Pete, and Paul found himself in his car on the road to Franklin, Ohio. He was going back to Ron Peters so that Pete could keep betting.

This should have been the easy part. By May 1987, Pete had been placing bets with Ron for about two and a half years. But Ron only added to the chaos. Two months earlier, his wife, Lori, had left him, filing for divorce just a few days before Tommy picked up the check in Reuven Katz's office to pay Pete's outstanding debts, and the couple was already fighting over money. Ron said that Lori took $30,000 that he had stashed in the house, and he also claimed that Tommy had never paid him. And so, when Pete went on a hot streak that spring and summer, winning and winning—maybe $40,000 by the All-Star break in July—it was now Ron who wouldn't pay. Pete felt stiffed and Paul did, too. Paul complained all over town—to anyone who would listen—that Pete owed him $44,000.

Chuck Zimmerman, a Cincinnati police officer, was at the racetrack one day when he first heard the story from Paul, and nothing about it surprised him. He had known both Tommy and Paul for years, going back to their barroom days at Sleep Out Louie's in the early 1980s. He was close enough with Tommy that he had watched him leave the bar with duffel bags full of cash to pay off Pete's bookies. He had worked security detail for Pete at signing shows, and he had watched Pete gamble enough that Zimmerman knew how it usually ended: Pete lost. Zimmerman considered him one of the worst gamblers he had ever met.

But a criminal? A man who required police attention? It seemed unlikely. Zimmerman stood along the rail that day and listened to Paul's story about how Pete wouldn't pay up. He remembered Paul saying that he was going to get even—that he was going to get his money from Pete, one way or the other—and Zimmerman also remembered feeling bad for Paul. Zimmerman just couldn't get involved. This wasn't a police matter. This wasn't his problem. Like a lot of people in Cincinnati, Zimmerman didn't want to know what he didn't know about Pete Rose. He wished Paul the best and turned back to his race card, trying not to think about it again.

The situation, by that point, was much worse than anyone could have imagined. The man who had purchased Pete's Hickok belt—and dozens of other pieces of sports memorabilia from prominent athletes in the 1980s, including bats, World Series rings, and autographed baseball cards—had been missing for months. He was on the run from authorities who had charged him in Oregon with fraud and racketeering. The man had allegedly swindled athletes and collectors by paying them for their memorabilia with shares in businesses that did not exist and he was seemingly good at hiding. The man stashed his $5 million collection in a storage unit in Southern California and then holed up for a while in a Las Vegas motel under an assumed name.

Now, in the summer of 1987, authorities had finally located the man: he was dead, in that motel. Police found his decomposed body in his room—the cause of death was unknown—but they still couldn't find his collection. His storage unit had been cleaned out. FBI agents out west had questions for anyone who might know the whereabouts of the contents while agents in Ohio were closing in on a different target, a target unrelated to the dead memorabilia dealer in every way except one: this man knew Pete Rose, too.

On a Monday in late June 1987—an off day for the Reds—federal agents showed up on a quiet street in suburban Cincinnati, less than five miles from Gold's Gym, and produced a warrant to search the home of Mike Fry, the gym's owner. Inside, they found cocaine, marijuana, and steroids; scales for weighing the drugs; records documenting drug deals going back to 1985; almost $10,000 in cash; and two weapons, including a semiautomatic pistol equipped with a silencer.

Together, it was enough to put Fry in prison for more than forty years—a sentence that Fry wished to avoid, if possible. In addition to his gym and his house in the suburbs, he had a young daughter whom he hoped to raise and a fresh understanding of the mistakes he had made. As he said around this time, "I will never be involved with drugs again." In mid-October—less than two weeks after the Reds collapsed, finished second in the division for the third year in a row, and missed the playoffs yet again—Fry pleaded guilty to a set of reduced charges and agreed to assist federal agents with their investigation into others. He said he would tell the agents everything he knew about cocaine and his former partner at the gym, Don Stenger.

Stenger, by then, had moved on. He was off drugs, clean. He was no longer buying cocaine and distributing it at Gold's Gym. He wasn't even living in Cincinnati anymore. Stenger was running a new fitness center in New Jersey and winning over customers there with his attention to detail and his ability to relate to people trying to shed a few extra pounds. Stenger seemed to genuinely care that his clients were getting stronger and healthier, and they loved him for it. Some clients—including top lawmakers in the New Jersey state legislature—came to the gym just to work out with Don.

Federal agents didn't care. With Fry's guilty plea and assistance, they were coming after Stenger, too. They wanted to talk with him—and his former girlfriend—about their past. Stenger was headed back to Cincinnati. He and his former girlfriend were meeting with the FBI, the DEA, and the IRS, and by the end of December 1987 both agreed to reveal everything they knew and to help implicate other guilty parties. Stenger was going to set up a drug deal with his old cocaine supplier in Florida, Norman Janowitz, and Stenger's former girlfriend agreed to wear a wire to incriminate others, including potentially Paul Janszen.

It was New Year's Eve 1987 when Stenger finalized his plan with authorities and early January 1988 when Stenger's old girlfriend finalized hers. Paul didn't know it, but Pete's gambling debts were the least of his troubles.

The FBI was closing in.

54

Marge Schott couldn't wait for the 1988 season to begin. It was going to be Pete's fourth year as manager in Cincinnati, and Marge predicted that it would be his best. "The fourth time is a charm," she joked.

Pete had a talented roster, featuring young stars about to be big names—Barry Larkin at shortstop, Chris Sabo at third base, Eric Davis in center field, Paul O'Neill in right, and one of the best closers in baseball in the bullpen, John Franco. Pete also had a new general manager. In the offseason, Marge had fired Bill Bergesch and replaced him with Murray Cook, a confident Canadian and former minor-league infielder, seasoned by recent front-office stints in New York and Montreal. Cook's first order of business was trading away bats to shore up the Reds' pitching rotation. He shipped a young backup shortstop to Kansas City for a starting pitcher. He sent the aging Dave Parker to Oakland for two more pitchers, and then Cook turned his focus to clearing the locker room of lackeys and gofers—Pete Rose's friends.

Cook didn't know who the men were or what they did for Pete. He just knew that some players were concerned. Shortly after Cook was hired, players told him that there were too many people coming and going. Too many folks with no reason to be inside a major-league locker room. Too many outsiders with access—a concern shared by baseball's newly hired director of security, Kevin Hallinan. A longtime cop, Hallinan had a thick accent left over from his childhood in the South Bronx and a specific way of seeing the world after twenty-five years with New York Police Department. He briefed Ueberroth that he was worried that Pete Rose was running with an unsavory crowd, and baseball executives seemed to take the information seriously. Before the 1988 season started, Giamatti arranged to sit down with Pete at baseball's winter meetings in Dallas to stress the importance of keeping "unauthorized guests" out of the clubhouse going forward.

The meeting was significant enough in Giamatti's mind that he documented it on paper and told Hallinan to keep his summary of the meeting in a safe place—just in case. But when the press learned about the meeting with Giamatti, Pete acted like it was no big deal. He said he was amenable to keeping guests out of the clubhouse, even his own guests, and he assured everyone that it wouldn't be a problem in 1988 because Murray Cook had traded away the real violator: Dave Parker. In front of a crowd of reporters and fans gathered in Dayton a few weeks before spring training started that season, Pete claimed that Parker always had too many associates hanging around, people taking his mind off baseball. "That was one of Dave Parker's problems," Pete said.

Parker was furious about how his time had ended in Cincinnati. He thought that Bergesch had been fired to take the heat off Marge and that he had been traded to take the pressure off Pete. Now Pete was accusing him of inviting people into the clubhouse, when everyone knew that Pete was the biggest offender, with Tommy Gioiosa, Mike Bertolini, or Paul Janszen always there in recent years. Parker didn't know who these guys were; no one did. Yet Parker was gone, banished to Oakland, and Paul was still there at Pete's side, heading into spring training in 1988. On the Friday night of Valentine's Day weekend that February, Paul accompanied Pete to an autograph show at a Holiday Inn in suburban Cleveland, like usual.

"PETE ROSE!!!" advertisements screamed. "Get there early!"

By then, Paul was staying close to Pete only to collect his money; he wanted his $44,000, and once he got it, he swore he would be out. But what happened that night would almost ensure that Paul would never see it. Pete brought a woman with him to the show, a young aerobics instructor almost half his age. Carol and Danita got suspicious and followed them to the hotel, and when they caught Pete there with his mistress, the aerobics instructor, Paul agreed to lie to Carol and tell her she was his girlfriend, not Pete's. Arguments and crying ensued, chaos at the Holiday Inn, until finally a shaky détente took hold. Pete could stay and do the autograph show the next day, signing baseballs and cards for $8 apiece, but Paul was out. Carol demanded it. He wasn't going back to spring training with

Pete the following week. He wasn't going anywhere. From then on, Paul usually couldn't even get ahold of Pete anymore.

He tried calling for his money. No answer.

He tried reaching Pete at spring training. Nothing.

At one point, Paul even started calling players he knew on the team, anyone who might be able to get a message to Pete. Still, he got nowhere. Paul had been cut loose. He was floating away, and he might have drifted off forever, lost and anonymous, were it not for the federal agents secretly working with Stenger that winter.

On a Wednesday in early March 1988, Stenger led the DEA to Norman Janowitz in Florida. Authorities watched while Janowitz climbed into a gold Chevy Caprice, drove to a storage unit three miles outside Fort Lauderdale, opened it to retrieve what he needed, and rode off to deliver seven kilos of cocaine to Stenger. Then, as the sun began to set in Florida, agents raided Janowitz's storage unit and his house. They took everything: his cars, his scales for weighing cocaine, and a stunning amount of money. Inside Janowitz's home, agents found a locked safe containing nearly $1 million in cash and sixty-five silver bars.

Norman Janowitz was arrested, and Paul Janszen was next. The day after the bust in Florida, and less than a month after the blowup at the Holiday Inn near Cleveland, Paul heard a knock at the door of his modest condo on the West Side of Cincinnati.

The FBI was outside.

Special Agent Jayme Gentile had just two years of experience on the job with the FBI, and she hardly looked imposing on Paul Janszen's doorstep. Gentile was just a little over five feet tall. But she was also ex-military. Her superiors at the FBI considered her one of the smartest agents in the Cincinnati office, and in her short time there, she had used her intelligence to bring down drug dealers, would-be killers, sex traffickers, and kidnappers—bad actors, bad guys. Right away, Gentile got the sense that Paul Janszen wasn't one of them.

At the door of his condo, he was nervous but polite. A big man, but not intimidating. He invited Gentile and her partner into his kitchen and then steeled himself for what they had come to discuss: Don Stenger, the activities at Gold's Gym, Pete Rose, Ron Peters, gambling, and the missing memorabilia in Las Vegas, including Pete's Hickok belt. The FBI had heard that Pete was making his own efforts to track down the belt and that Paul was helping Pete with that, just like Paul helped with everything else.

Paul didn't know anything about where to find the missing memorabilia. About everything else, he preferred not to talk. He had no intention of saying anything, especially about Pete. His instinct was to protect the Reds' manager at all costs. Even if he knew something about Pete and gambling, he told the agents that day, he'd never say. Gentile's partner asked if he had a good lawyer, and when Paul said no, the agent advised him that it might be time to get one. Gentile and her partner got up and left, and Danita just looked at Paul. She knew they were in trouble.

Shaken by the meeting, Paul retreated to the bathroom to be alone. He got into the shower, ran the water cold, and as it washed over him, he came up with a plan. They were leaving the condo immediately and moving into a hotel off the interstate in the suburbs. If two FBI agents could show up unannounced at his condo, maybe they were watching him there. Maybe they were watching him *now.* He wanted to get away. He needed time to think and a safe place to make his next move. Paul was calling Reuven Katz for help.

At a meeting in Reuven's office a few days later, Paul sat with Danita and told Reuven everything: how he had legal problems, how he needed an attorney, how he was hoping Reuven might recommend one, and how he needed the money that Pete owed him in order to defend himself from whatever charges the FBI was sure to bring against him any day now. Then, for the first time, Paul Janszen told the truth.

"Did you tell Mr. Katz that you had bet on baseball for Pete Rose?" an investigator would ask Paul later.

"Yes, sir. I did," Paul answered.

"Did you tell him that you had bet on the Cincinnati Reds?"

"Yes, sir. I did," Paul said again.

"And what did Mr. Katz say?"

"Reuven put his head down," Paul replied, "and he made a gesture with his hands, and he said, 'That's it; it's over.'"

"Did he call you a liar?"

"No, sir," Paul said.

If it happened like this, it must have been a low point for Reuven. Exactly one year earlier, Reuven had given Tommy Gioiosa that check for $34,000 so that Tommy could pay Ron Peters. Now Paul Janszen was in his office asking for even more money, and if he was telling the truth, it seemed possible that Paul's legal problems could soon be Pete's, too. Reuven picked up the phone and did the only thing he could do: he called Pete at spring training to discuss the situation.

In hindsight, it might have been Pete's last chance to save himself, the ultimate payoff pitch. The breaking ball was coming on the outside corner, and Pete needed to decide if he was swinging or not—if he was paying Paul Janszen or not. A lifetime in baseball had come down to this: one final gamble, on the phone with Reuven, talking about Paul. Pete didn't take long to make up his mind. He knew what he was doing. He refused. He wasn't swinging at this pitch. He didn't think he owed $44,000 to Paul Janszen. He never agreed on that number. He authorized Reuven to pay Paul a much smaller amount—$10,000—and Reuven alerted Paul that he could come pick up his check, without telling him that the dollar figure on the check was much lower than Paul wanted.

It was a Friday in mid-March, two weeks until opening day. The Reds were playing the Blue Jays that afternoon in their new spring training complex in Plant City, Florida. Fans were flocking to the stadium there, clogging the roads, and Pete was making preparations for the season. On the day that Reuven's office issued the check to Paul Janszen, Pete made roster moves. He demoted ten players to the minor leagues, met with many of them to deliver the news face-to-face, spoke with reporters, and did something he hadn't done in six months. He got into the batting cage that morning and swung—just to see if he still had it—and he did. While reporters watched, Pete hit ten line drives in a row. Base hits every time. He was forever young in the Florida sunshine.

"Hit pretty good," Pete said afterward. "Didn't I?"

But back in Cincinnati, it hardly felt like spring. It was spitting snow, cold and gray, and Paul Janszen couldn't believe what Pete Rose had done when he arrived at Reuven's office to collect his money. Paul had expected to pick up a check for $40,000. Instead, it was a fraction of that. An insult. It was nothing. Paul stormed outside and went straight to a phone booth on the street to call his newly acquired attorney.

"Set it up," Paul told him on the phone. Set up a meeting with the FBI. Paul was ready to tell Jayme Gentile and her partner anything they wanted to know.

55

MORE THAN FIFTY-FIVE thousand fans—a regular-season record—came out to see the Reds play on opening day that April in Cincinnati. They watched Johnny Bench settle into his seat in the broadcast booth to call the game for local television. They showered Bart Giamatti with polite applause as the NL president threw out the ceremonial first pitch in a dark suit and tie, and they cheered for Marge Schott, who came prepared for the occasion. She presented Pete Rose with a bridal veil before the game.

"You know what this means, right?" she asked him.

Pete nodded. He knew. No more second-place finishes.

"I don't want to be a bridesmaid this year," Marge said.

The Reds beat the Cardinals that day and won four out of their next six games—the start that Pete wanted and needed. But they played average baseball for the rest of the month, couldn't string together more than two wins in a row, and struggled at the plate. Despite all their talent, the Reds had only one player batting over .300 by the last week of April, and when the New York Mets came to town for a three-game series that weekend, the club hit a new low. That Friday night, the Reds spotted the Mets four runs on walks and errors. Then they clawed back to tie the game—only to blow that, too. With two outs in the ninth, the Reds gave up a double to one of the Mets' weakest hitters—the second baseman Tim Teufel—and New York's star first baseman Keith Hernandez did the rest. Hernandez drove in Teufel a moment later to win the game 5–4 and drop the Reds' record to 11-10 on the year.

Pete was angry after the loss—and, he admitted, a little confused. Baseball had always been his escape during hard times. Gambling concerns? No problem. He started his forty-four-game hitting streak in 1978 around the exact moment when teammates remember league officials meeting with Pete to discuss his relationships with bookies. Divorce? Not an issue. He batted .468 from the moment Karolyn filed her papers in court in 1979. It was as if he could convert off-field angst into on-field heroics, channeling personal failure into professional greatness in a way that had often surprised others. But as a manager this trick eluded him. He couldn't stop his defense from misplaying ground balls or prevent his pitchers from conceding doubles to the likes of Tim Teufel. He couldn't do anything but watch. As his life was coming unglued off the field—with the FBI circling and Reuven writing checks—the same thing was happening at the ballpark, and it all came to a head in the second game of the Mets series that weekend.

In the seventh inning that Saturday night—with Cincinnati trailing 4–2—the Reds' pitcher uncoiled a fastball that hit Tim Teufel square in the back. Convinced that it was intentional, that Pete had called for it, Teufel's teammate Darryl Strawberry jumped out of the dugout and ran straight at the Reds' pitcher. If he wanted to hurt Teufel, one of the nicest men in baseball, Strawberry thought the Reds should have to deal with him: one of the baddest men in New York.

Both benches cleared, and Pete ran straight into the fray, right at Strawberry himself. It was like Shea Stadium 1973. Darryl Strawberry was the new Bud Harrelson. Pete had found his spark and the Reds responded after the melee on the field. In the eighth, they came back to tie the game 5–5.

But the umpires weren't going to tolerate this sort of behavior the way they had in 1973. They ejected Strawberry from the game. They ejected the Reds' pitcher, too. And when Pete ran out of the dugout to start yet another fight in the ninth inning—over a call that Pete didn't like at first base that allowed the Mets to score the go-ahead run—umpire Dave Pallone was ready and waiting for him. When

Pete got in Pallone's face, poking his finger and shouting, Pallone happily did the same. Then Pete bumped Pallone—twice—driving his shoulder into Pallone's chest, and Pallone had no choice. He ejected Pete from the game.

In baseball, Pallone didn't have many friends. His colleagues called him a scab—"a goddamn scab" and an "incompetent scab asshole"—for crossing the picket line as a minor-league ump during the umpire strike of 1979. And behind his back, lots of people in the game whispered about Pallone for reasons that had nothing to do with umpiring. Pallone was gay and still trying to hide that fact in 1988. Now, by arguing with Pete and then ejecting him, Pallone incited the wrath of an entire stadium. For the next ten minutes, fans in Cincinnati pelted the field with trash—an outburst that baseball hadn't seen in years. Cups, coins, rolls of toilet paper, and handheld radios fell from the sky like rain. People were throwing anything they had.

Owner Marge Schott and general manager Murray Cook immediately tried to get ahold of Bart Giamatti in New York. They wanted to run interference for Pete, plead his case to the National League president, argue that Pallone had instigated the altercation by poking Pete in the face—a charge that Pallone denied—and get out in front of whatever punishment might be coming. But they couldn't reach Giamatti that night, and Giamatti wasn't likely to be swayed, even if he had picked up the phone. In his opinion, nothing justified unprofessional behavior, and what he had seen in Cincinnati wasn't just unprofessional. It was ugly. "Such disgraceful episodes are not business as usual," he said, "nor can they be allowed to become so."

On Sunday, less than twelve hours after Pete's argument with Pallone, Giamatti dispatched the league's director of security, Kevin Hallinan, to Cincinnati to conduct interviews on the ground and then got to work in New York. Giamatti reviewed the videotape of the incident, spoke with the league's supervisor of umpires, summoned the Reds' broadcasters to meet with him for stirring unrest on the airwaves, spoke with Hallinan about what he had found in Cincinnati, and came down hard on the man in the center of it all: Pete Rose. Giamatti was fining him $10,000 and suspending him for thirty days—the harshest punishment any manager had faced since Leo Durocher had been suspended for the 1947 season for consorting with bookies and gamblers.

"The National League," Giamatti said in issuing his decision, "will not tolerate the degeneration of baseball games into dangerous displays of public disorder."

Pete was out until June.

Baseball's old-timers shook their heads at Giamatti's stern ruling and his fancy wording. The Yankees' manager, Billy Martin, famous for feuding with umpires, bug-eyed and crazy, thought thirty days was too long of a suspension even if Pete had punched Pallone in the face. "If I'm going to get thirty days," Martin said, "I'll go for the jugular vein." Reds fans and Reds players agreed. The closer John Franco wondered if Pete had stabbed someone. "Did he?" Franco asked. Johnny Bench came to Pete's defense, and the local press did, too. A columnist for *The Cincinnati Post* criticized Giamatti for being too smart for his own good. "Take him out to the Shakespeare festival," he wrote.

Others took Giamatti's side. If a manager was allowed to bump an umpire, the Mets' pitcher Ron Darling argued, fistfights would come next, and soon they wouldn't be playing baseball anymore. They would be fighting every night instead. Pete didn't disagree with that assessment; he knew he never should have touched Pallone. But he felt that Giamatti had overdone it by suspending him for a month, and he made an official appeal, with the help of Murray Cook, Reuven Katz, and some evidence.

At a hearing in New York a few days later, Pete pointed out to Giamatti that the great Frank Robinson had once been suspended for just three days for bumping an umpire back in 1976. But Giamatti countered with his own historical case: a little-known 1943 incident when a long-forgotten New York Yankees pitcher had earned a thirty-day suspension for making contact with an ump. In that argument, the pitcher, angry about a questionable call, grabbed the home plate umpire by the lapels of his coat, shook him so hard that his cap fell off his head, and seemed intent on throwing him to the ground before worried teammates intervened.

The ruling was final. Giamatti was standing by his decision to suspend Pete for thirty days, and he had nothing more to say about it. At the end of the day in New York, Giamatti slipped away, leaving Pete to face the media alone. And still, Pete didn't apologize. He couldn't take responsibility for pushing Pallone, for fighting, for anything.

"I hate to say it," Pete admitted, as he stood before about fifty reporters, "but I would probably do it again, if the situation came up. It's just the way I am."

56

PETE FLEW HOME to Cincinnati to find his world eroding at the edges. It wasn't just that the Reds were losing while he was suspended, going 12-16 and falling into fourth place. It wasn't just that the team didn't seem to care. It was that Paul Janszen was gaining ground, working with Special Agent Jayme Gentile and others at the FBI in Cincinnati.

Paul met with agents twice in late March 1988, and on opening day, at their direction, he began recording conversations with the FBI's next target: Ron Peters. At first, Paul and Ron talked only about gambling. They discussed the significant debt that Ron still owed Pete and Paul, and about new bets that Paul began placing on the Reds every day—a standing wager of $200 on the Reds to win. It was like old times again. Paul was placing bets and Ron was taking the action—only this time the FBI was listening in. Then, during a conversation on a Thursday in mid-May, right in the middle of Pete's suspension, Paul brought up a different topic while the tape recorder rolled. He wondered if Ron might be able to supply him with a little cocaine.

Paul had no use for the drugs—or for the gambling. The conversations were a sort of performance art, a show for Jayme Gentile and the other FBI agents listening in on the line. He was just cooperating, like Fry and Stenger before him. He was giving authorities

According to one of his longtime mistresses, Pete—pictured at spring training in 1978 with his teammates Joe Morgan and Mario Soto—could do whatever he wanted. *(Courtesy of Tom Rogowski)*

The sportswriters ignored Pete's off-field problems. They liked him. In early 1978, Pete notched his 3,000th hit, and reporters wrote glowing pieces about his legacy. His son, Petey, watches as he is interviewed after the game. *(Courtesy of Getty Images)*

At the end of September 1978, President Jimmy Carter invited Pete to the White House for Pete Rose Day in Washington. Pete brought his agent and his kids—Fawn (*far left*), almost fourteen, and Petey, almost nine. (*Courtesy of Getty Images*)

Back home in Cincinnati, the new management seemed tired of Pete. At the end of the 1978 season, team president Dick Wagner declined to offer Pete a lucrative multiyear contract that matched what he could get elsewhere and let him leave town. (*Courtesy of Getty Images*)

In December 1978, Pete signed a four-year contract with the Philadelphia Phillies worth $3.2 million and joined his new teammates: (*from left to right*) Mike Schmidt, Larry Bowa, and Manny Trillo. (*Courtesy of Getty Images*)

Pete's marriage to Karolyn didn't survive his first season in Philadelphia, and he moved on. He was dating another woman, Carol Woliung. She was younger than Karolyn, blond, and about to become a cheerleader for the Philadelphia Eagles. (*Courtesy of PARS International*)

Around this time, Pete befriended a young baseball player from New Bedford, Massachusetts, Tommy Gioiosa. Tommy wanted to be just like Pete and was soon doing all of Pete's dirty work: paying his bookies, placing his bets, and hiding his women. (*Courtesy of Tommy Gioiosa*)

The Philadelphia Phillies had underperformed for decades. The owners hoped Pete would change that by giving the Phillies swagger and showing them how to prepare. No one loved swinging in the batting cage more than Pete. (*Courtesy of Associated Press*)

In 1980, Philadelphia's investment paid off. At age thirty-nine, Pete helped lead the Phillies to their first-ever World Series title. (*Courtesy of Getty Images*)

In August 1981, Pete reached a milestone that had seemed impossible twenty years earlier. He passed Hall of Famer Stan Musial for most hits in the National League: 3,631. President Ronald Reagan called to congratulate Pete while Musial (*left*) and Commissioner Bowie Kuhn (*right*) enjoyed the moment with him. (*Courtesy of Associated Press*)

In 1984, Pete recorded his 4,000th hit while playing for his third team, the Montreal Expos. He was forty-three and seemed to be barely hanging on. *(Courtesy of Associated Press)*

In August 1984, the Reds made a trade to bring Pete back to Cincinnati, and an old friend welcomed him on the field: the architect of the Big Red Machine, General Manager Bob Howsam. Howsam announced that Pete would be both a player and a manager while he pursued Ty Cobb's all-time hit record: 4,191. *(Courtesy of Associated Press)*

The Reds' owner, Marge Schott, was thrilled to have Pete back home. "Pete Rose is Mister Cincinnati," she said, "and Mister Baseball." Within hours, the team sold $40,000 in tickets for their next game. (© The Enquirer–*USA TODAY NETWORK*)

In September 1985, Pete hit a single to left-center field at Riverfront Stadium to pass Ty Cobb and become baseball's all-time hit leader, a record that most people thought would never fall. (*Courtesy of Associated Press*)

At the time of the historic hit, Ron Peters, a bookie near Dayton, was already taking Pete's bets on football and basketball. Within the year, things escalated: Pete began using Ron to bet on his own games, violating a rule of baseball that every player knew and thrusting Ron into the middle of the scandal still to come. Ron stands with his lawyer outside a Cincinnati courthouse in 1989. (*Courtesy of Associated Press*)

Paul Janszen, a West Side guy and a friend of Tommy Gioiosa, began running Pete's bets to Ron Peters and other bookies in early 1987—an arrangement that worked for a while and then didn't. Paul and Pete soon had a falling-out. (*Courtesy of Associated Press*)

The incoming commissioner of baseball Bart Giamatti—pictured here with future president George W. Bush and his wife, Laura—learned in early 1989 that *Sports Illustrated* was investigating allegations that Pete was betting on baseball. Giamatti loved the game and took the allegations seriously. (*Courtesy of Getty Images*)

Tommy Gioiosa refused to cooperate with baseball's investigation, but he was increasingly alone in protecting Pete. (*Courtesy of Associated Press*)

John Dowd, an attorney formerly with the U.S. Department of Justice, was hired by Giamatti to investigate Pete's gambling. Within weeks, Dowd had credible sources on the record, including Paul Janszen and Ron Peters. (*Courtesy of Associated Press*)

Backed into a corner, Pete accepted a lifetime banishment from baseball in August 1989—"a sad end of a sorry episode," Giamatti said that day. But it wasn't really the end. It would be fifteen years before Pete could even start to admit the truth. (*Courtesy of Associated Press*)

everything they wanted so that he could start over. Paul had begun to think of his time with Pete Rose, Tommy Gioiosa, Ron Peters, and everyone at Gold's Gym as a dark period in his life. The decisions he had made in that little window of time sat on his chest like a sack of rocks. He couldn't breathe. And there was only one way for Paul to get clear of it. Only one way for Paul to live going forward.

Go clean, he thought. Be clean.

"Wipe the slate clean," he said.

On the Friday before Fourth of July weekend, with the Reds seven games under .500 and ten games out of first place, Paul drove to Jonathan's Café in Franklin to meet Ron Peters there one last time. It was a beautiful summer day, warm and sunny, and Ron invited Paul to go for a ride. Despite his divorce—and the missing $30,000 that Ron said his wife had taken—Ron had a new maroon Corvette, license plate CAFE, that he liked to show off, and he preferred doing business in the Corvette rather than inside the restaurant.

The FBI had been watching Ron at Jonathan's Café for months now, building a dossier that was growing thicker by the day. Agents knew that drug deals typically happened in the bathroom, that Ron sometimes stored cocaine in soap dispensers for easy access, that shady visitors sometimes arrived with briefcases handcuffed to their wrists, and that local police couldn't be trusted to go after him. They were too close with Ron, laughing with Ron over beers at the café in downtown Franklin.

The FBI knew even more after Paul's car ride with Ron in his Corvette. Special Agent Gentile watched and listened that day as Ron sold Paul an ounce of cocaine and then agreed to do Paul one more favor. Ron said he'd introduce Paul to his cocaine supplier. The meeting happened a few weeks later at a Chinese restaurant in a little town north of Cincinnati, and Gentile didn't waste any time afterward. She obtained warrants to search Ron's home, his Corvette, his restaurant, his office, everything, and walked out with boxes of evidence that included betting slips, tally sheets, notes, and phone records. Ron was going down just like everybody else who had been targeted in the Gold's Gym sting, and there was reason for Ron to be afraid. On the cocaine charge alone, the young father and popular bar owner faced twenty years in prison and a $1 million fine.

"Do you understand that?" a judge asked him.

"Yes, sir," Ron said, nodding.

If possible, he needed to cut a deal.

Late that summer—shortly after FBI agents raided Ron's house and cleaned out his desk at Jonathan's Café, a desk where Ron had once snorted cocaine through a straw—Kevin Hallinan got a phone call in New York. The man on the line was a retired FBI agent in Cincinnati, now working as a private investigator, and he had a tip from a street-level source that he thought would interest the league's director of security. The retired agent told Hallinan that, according to the tipster, Pete was gambling with bookies—and possibly on baseball.

There were no names attached to the tip. No specifics, no mention of Ron Peters, and there was one other challenge to investigating it fully: Hallinan said the FBI in Cincinnati wanted him to stand down for now. Gentile and others were still working the Gold's Gym case and potentially pursuing criminal charges against Pete Rose himself. By launching his own investigation, Hallinan could gum it up and get in the way. The former New York cop reluctantly had to spend the fall and early winter biding his time while Bart Giamatti waited around for a different reason, a reason that he shared, in confidence, with his friend Fay Vincent one night late that summer. Peter Ueberroth was stepping down after four years as commissioner. The owners were going to be appointing a new leader, and a few owners had approached Giamatti to tell him to be ready. Giamatti informed Vincent that he was next in line.

It was the prophecy that Vincent had written two years earlier, and it was coming easy. The owners' vote in Montreal, just after Labor Day 1988, would be unanimous. All twenty-six owners supported Giamatti, and it wasn't just because he could dazzle them with his words. During his time as president at Yale, Giamatti had stared down a long and disruptive strike of secretarial, maintenance, and dining hall workers, refusing to buckle to their demands even after angry students occupied his office and staged a sit-in. Owners hoped Giamatti might be similarly stubborn with players whose union contract was set to expire at the end of 1989. Maybe Giamatti could play tough with them, too—a possibility that the head of the players' union found discouraging when he learned that Giamatti had won the owners' approval. "Obviously," the union chief said, "we don't want what happened at Yale to happen here."

Over dinner at his favorite Italian restaurant in New York, Bart Giamatti quietly celebrated with Vincent and then made two requests in the days to come: he wanted Vincent to negotiate his contract, and he asked him to be his deputy commissioner, his trusted partner in this impossible baseball dream. Giamatti could be the front man—charming and intelligent, the enlightened king of America's pastime—and Vincent could be the crown prince, minding the store. As a longtime corporate executive and lawyer, Vincent could help Giamatti run the business side of things. Vincent accepted. He loved baseball, too, and Vincent soon began commuting into the city from his home in Connecticut to help Giamatti get ready for the official transition at the end of March 1989.

It was an exciting time for baseball. Despite the looming possibility of a strike and Ueberroth's inability to institute any sort of serious drug policy for players—problems that presented existential threats to the game—owners were making money like never before. The Mariners—a losing team that had sold for $13 million in 1981—were now valued at five times that figure, and the Phillies, which sold for $30 million the same year, were one of a few teams estimated to be worth more than $100 million. Ruly Carpenter never should have walked away. Between aggressive licensing deals, increased souvenir sales, and rising attendance, almost every team was turning a profit by the end of 1988, and new television contracts negotiated that winter ensured more riches. In one of his last acts as commissioner, Ueberroth finalized a four-year, $1.1 billion television deal with CBS in December and announced an additional $400 million deal with ESPN right after the new year. For the first time, fans would be able to watch nationally televised baseball games at least four nights a week, and owners would have another $1.5 billion to split among themselves. *Billions,* Ueberroth said. "That's with a 'b.'"

But away from the spotlight that winter—far from the Madison Avenue hotel in New York where Ueberroth announced the ESPN deal and nowhere close to the gala that Ted Turner threw at the winter meetings in Atlanta, complete with half a dozen open bars and a healthy contingent of Atlanta Braves' cheerleaders wearing next to nothing—Giamatti had a problem he should have seen coming, but didn't: the *United States of America v. Paul Janszen.*

In January 1989, just a week after baseball released the details of its lucrative ESPN contract, federal authorities offered Paul a deal to reward him for his help, and Paul reported to the courthouse in downtown Cincinnati to stand next to his lawyer and plead guilty to a single charge: filing a false tax return. He was apologetic that day. "I'm very sorry," he told the judge. "It'll never happen again." And the judge, looking down on him from his lofty perch in the room, took pity on Paul. Instead of going to prison, he was headed for a six-month stay in a local halfway house—the best deal that any of Pete's former associates would receive. His slate was clean, just as he wanted, and his future was laid out before him. Paul and Danita could get married and live the life of their choosing. There was just one matter left to settle. On January 20, less than a week after his guilty plea, Paul wrote Reuven Katz a letter asking one last time for the money that Pete owed him.

"Last year, Danita and myself met with you at your office and discussed a certain situation involving Pete Rose," Paul wrote to start the letter. "I have a feeling that you and Mr. Rose discussed our meeting and concluded that a non-committal stance by yourself might discourage me and I'd dry up and blow away."

"Well," Paul continued, "I haven't and don't intend to."

Paul proceeded to recap everything that had happened between them, including Pete's affairs with women, the blowup at the Holiday Inn the year before, Carol's fury, Paul's banishment, and his repeated attempts to recover his money. If the letter ever came out, it could serve as a timeline, a historical document, at least from Paul's perspective. Then, after insulting Pete—saying he was too ignorant to recognize the damage that Paul could do if he went public with these claims—Paul got to the point.

"Reuven," he wrote, "I've waited for over a year now, and enough is enough. I don't care what story Mr. Rose tells you. I know and he knows the truth and I'm prepared and anxious to prove this in court if necessary. I wasn't put on this earth to be Pete Rose's doormat. It's time for him to take responsibility for his actions and if need be get some professional help along the way before he has nothing left."

Paul sent the letter off to Reuven and waited.

"P.S.," Paul added, "a meeting with my lawyer can be arranged at your request."

In the halfway house, nights were hardest for Paul. In the dark of his room, he lay in bed thinking of all the ways he had failed and all the people he had disappointed, including himself. If things had gone differently, maybe he never would have met Pete Rose. Or maybe they'd still be friends. Paul would be getting ready to go to spring training. He'd be out there with Pete spending his days on the banquet circuit and his nights at the racetrack in Kentucky, laughing and winning big. Pete had a great month at the track that January.

Just a few nights after Paul fired off his letter, Pete lounged in a private box there with the man who had once banished Tommy Gioiosa from the grandstand, track owner Jerry Carroll, and Pete and Jerry hit it big. They accurately predicted the winners of six different races that night, including two long shots, and, in doing so, split a pot of money that had been growing for weeks: $265,000. They had won the Pik-Six jackpot, and in this moment Pete could have done almost anything with his half of the winnings, including pay off Paul.

But on the day of the Pik-Six, Reuven Katz and his law partner Robert Pitcairn Jr. made it clear to Paul's lawyer that Pete had no intention of buying Paul's silence. "Pete will not pay any money to Paul to avoid negative publicity," Pitcairn informed Paul's lawyer. "I hope that's not what Paul has in mind." The best Pitcairn could offer at this point was their cautious consideration. He asked Paul's lawyer to render in detail the exact specifics of the alleged debt. "We will then analyze it and respond to you promptly," he wrote.

Jerry Carroll wanted to wait a few months before claiming the Pik-Six ticket. A jackpot this big would attract media attention, and though he had done nothing wrong, it wouldn't look great that the track's owner had shared in the winnings. The most prudent path forward was to cash the ticket long after most people had forgotten it had happened. But Pete was impatient. It was cold in Cincinnati. The money was just sitting there, and he cracked within a couple of days. Pete had his friend the longtime groundskeeper Arnie Metz claim his half of the winnings, and together Pete and Arnie flew to Florida—with Pete in first class, Arnie in coach, and a duffel bag full of cash between them.

It was, as Pete would say, a gambler's delight. They had two weeks until spring training with nothing to do, money in their pockets, and ready access to the old triple-header circuit in Tampa. They could pick up the Cuban and hit the horse track, the dog track, jai alai. Or they could just relax at the Reds' training complex in Plant City. Some days, Pete brought his younger son, Tyler, now four, to the ballpark to watch fantasy camp games played between old Cincinnati players and Reds fans who were wealthy enough to afford the experience. On other days, Pete hit in the cage while Tyler sat behind a protective screen.

But something felt off. Beat writers were hearing rumors that Pete was being investigated for tax problems, and a court reporter for the *Dayton Daily News* was chasing down a different and more troubling news tip: he heard that Dick Skinner, the Skin Man, Dayton's most notorious bookie, had a tape recording of Pete talking about gambling debts. People were asking questions. The IRS was digging in, and for the first time since the Dick Wagner era executives in Cincinnati's front office were openly grumbling about Pete. Marge Schott, upset that the Reds had finished second again in 1988, told reporters that Pete had one last chance with her, maybe just one more year. As it turned out, Pete had less time than anyone knew.

The FBI had decided not to file charges against Pete—at least for now. Special Agent Gentile learned that her superiors in Washington didn't want "another John DeLorean case," a reference to the famous car builder who had been arrested for cocaine trafficking in 1982, only to be acquitted at trial later. Pete's alleged misdeeds with gamblers were now Kevin Hallinan's to pursue, if he wanted, but by mid-February 1989, Hallinan wasn't the only one interested in discovering the details of that story. Anxious for results, needing to be heard, and apparently not interested in waiting around anymore for Reuven Katz, Paul Janszen had notified someone else about Pete Rose and his bets on baseball. Paul picked up the phone and called the switchboard of Time Inc. in midtown Manhattan. He wanted to talk to someone at *Sports Illustrated.*

The call came in on a Tuesday or a Wednesday that winter, the magazine's off days. Most staffers took Tuesday and Wednesday as a weekend, after putting the latest issue to bed on Monday night. Almost no one was in the office; it was a miracle that Paul's phone call reached anyone. But his message about Pete Rose and gambling made it to the letters desk, where someone funneled it to an editor who then called the first reporter who came to mind on an off day in the middle of the winter: Robert Sullivan.

Sullivan was in his mid-thirties and nowhere close to the most famous writer at *Sports Illustrated.* On a staff that included Frank Deford, Peter Gammons, Rick Reilly, and Rick Telander, Sullivan was decidedly second team—a "staff writer" on the masthead, not a "senior writer." Yet he had a history of reporting on gamblers and mobsters. Sullivan once broke a story about the murder of a jai alai kingpin who had crossed Whitey Bulger's Winter Hill Gang, and he had written about college athletes who were intentionally losing games in exchange for cash payouts. He was perfect for the Paul Janszen tip, whatever this was. Also, he was free. When the editor called him that day, Sullivan was in his apartment in Greenwich Village working out.

Sullivan spoke on the phone to Janszen and became convinced that at the very least Paul knew Pete. The two men seemed to be friends. Sullivan thought he needed to fly to Cincinnati. Top editors agreed, and the issue was deemed important enough that senior editor Sandy Padwe was immediately informed about the Janszen conversation. Padwe got a call about it that day at his weekend house in Connecticut, two hours north of the city.

Padwe was almost fifty years old, but he was part of a new guard at the magazine: a stable of editors and writers focused on breaking news and doing investigations. He demanded precision from his writers. He had a detective's ear for things that didn't sound right, and he brought to the magazine real newsroom experience. In his previous post, Padwe had served as deputy sports editor at *The New York Times.*

He wanted Sullivan on a plane to Cincinnati as soon as possible. Sullivan met with Paul there. And even when negotiations broke down—Paul wanted financial compensation for talking and the magazine wasn't inclined to pay—*Sports Illustrated* stayed on the story. Padwe wanted to approach it in the way *The New York Times* might have.

Put a handful of writers on it, Padwe said. Send them to Cincinnati and beyond. Find as many sources as possible who had firsthand knowledge of Pete's gambling and do it quickly. If Paul Janszen could call *Sports Illustrated,* he could call another magazine.

There was no time to waste.

It was supposed to be a secret; *Sports Illustrated* didn't want anyone to know that it was investigating Pete Rose for betting on baseball. But by February 17—a Friday—Ueberroth learned what the magazine was doing through a tipster of his own. He shared the information with Giamatti and Vincent, and the two men decided they couldn't sit back and wait for *Sports Illustrated* to write something. They needed to be proactive. They needed to act now.

On the first day of spring training that Sunday, Pete ran wind sprints with his players, teased them for being out of shape, and gave interviews—the usual fare—and then at some point late in the day he drifted off to a practice field and stood in the middle of it all alone. It was a strange place for reporters to find Pete. Perhaps he just needed to collect his thoughts.

Pete had been summoned to New York. He was leaving in the morning, and in his gut, he knew why.

Bart Giamatti wanted to talk to him about gambling.

57

THE MEETING AT the commissioner's office with Giamatti, Ueberroth, and Vincent that Monday was casual to start, even friendly. Pete knew Ueberroth and Giamatti well from their dealings over the years, including from the suspension they had doled out after his fight with Dave Pallone the year before, and the three men bantered in the way that old colleagues do, smiling and laughing.

With Fay Vincent, it was different. Pete and Vincent had never met, and Vincent's first impression of Pete wasn't flattering. In an attempt to fit in with the executives and his own lawyers, Reuven Katz and Robert Pitcairn, flying in from Ohio, Pete had worn a suit to New York. But the one he picked was all wrong for the occasion. It was dark and shiny, like sharkskin. Instead of looking as if he belonged in a Park Avenue boardroom—what Pete had intended—he looked like a mobster, Vincent thought, and it didn't help that the suit was a touch too small for him. Pete seemed to be bursting out of a shell of slick polyester as he sat there, laughing and chatting with the other men.

Vincent quickly tired of the conversation. They were wasting time, and Vincent decided to put an end to it. He interrupted everyone to inform Pete that they had called him to New York to ask him a question, a serious question, and Vincent explained they were looking for an honest answer.

Everyone fell silent.

"Have you bet on baseball?" Fay Vincent asked. "On Major League Baseball?"

As everyone waited for Pete's answer, Pete seemed to have at least one sympathetic listener at the table. Ueberroth was leaving his post as commissioner in just a few weeks; he didn't want to have an epic gambling scandal, involving one of the game's biggest stars, hanging over the end of his tenure, and he didn't relish the idea of passing it on to Giamatti. Ueberroth wanted the case settled, and according to one source who worked in baseball's front office at the time, he was open to letting Pete off with some sort of light punishment—if Pete admitted to what he had done and if he agreed to seek treatment. It could have been like the cocaine scandal that Ueberroth had navigated three years earlier where Dave Parker, Keith Hernandez, and every other player avoided suspensions by donating a small portion of their salaries to drug abuse programs and doing community service. Baseball didn't necessarily need to enforce the strict wording written into Rule 21(d) and ban Pete from the game for life, if he had indeed wagered on his own games. All Pete had to do to save himself was stop, spin on his axis differently, and, for once, admit he had made a mistake.

But Pete couldn't do it. He wouldn't do it. The same qualities that made him a successful baseball player—and one of the greatest hitters of all time—ensured his failure now. Pete wasn't going to let Paul Janszen win, if that's what this was about. He wasn't going to admit to anything in that room on Park Avenue filled with polished men wearing the right kinds of suits. He was going to fight his fight, as he was taught to do on the West Side of Cincinnati in Jimmy Schlank's abandoned swimming pool. He was going to refuse to go down, as he did that night in the boxing ring long ago. He was going to listen to his late father. "Hustle, Pete. . . . Keep up the hustle." He was going to foul off the fastball on the outside corner to see another pitch. He was going to bunt the ball down the line to win the batting title, and he was going to take out the catcher at home plate in a meaningless game, breaking his shoulder at the joint.

Pete Rose was going to lie.

Sure, Pete admitted in the room in New York, he was a gambler and he bet on lots of things: the horses, the dogs, even football games. But no, he said that day. He did not bet on baseball.

"I'm not that stupid," Vincent recalled him saying.

It was convincing; they believed him. Even Vincent, who didn't know Pete, was swayed. As Pete left the commissioner's office that day, handshakes all around, Vincent told Giamatti that it seemed as if Pete were telling the truth, and Giamatti agreed. It didn't make sense that a man of Pete's stature would bet on baseball. He *couldn't* be that stupid. When news of the meeting leaked to *The New York Times* the following day, Ueberroth chose to downplay the significance of it. He acted as if they just wanted to talk to Pete in general. "There's nothing ominous," Ueberroth told *The New York Times,* "and there won't be any follow-through."

But inside the commissioner's office, the men who had attended the meeting with Pete were already discussing several possible "follow-throughs." And Fay Vincent knew his preference. With *Sports Illustrated* circling, Vincent believed they had to check it out. They had to know if Pete was telling the truth. They needed to launch their own investigation, and Vincent had a man in mind for the job: a towering Irishman, a former Marine Corps judge advocate, and longtime attorney with the U.S. Department of Justice who liked to work, who liked to grind.

It was time to call John Dowd.

By any measure, Dowd was overqualified to investigate Pete Rose. In the 1960s, Dowd served in the Marines and attained the rank of captain. At the peak of the Vietnam War, he prosecuted and defended fellow Marines facing court-martial proceedings. Then, in the 1970s, he got hired at the Department of Justice and led an elite team of DOJ lawyers, colloquially called Strike Force Eighteen, who were intent on rooting out corrupt politicians and business leaders with Mafia connections. As a result of their work, prominent men faced criminal charges, including at least two U.S. congressmen, and *The New York Times* dispatched a reporter to Washington to write a story that described Dowd as "an authentic Good Guy," striving for what was right in a small office across the street from FBI headquarters that Dowd had barely taken the time to decorate. He had only two items of note on the wall in those years: a picture of his wife and kids and a printed list of Abraham Lincoln's many failures that his father had given him, to remind him that with hard work anything was possible.

In the 1980s, this work paid off for Dowd. He left his government post for a series of private practice jobs at top Washington law firms. He represented, among other clients, the governor of Kentucky and a U.S. Air Force colonel who had secretly provided arms to Nicaraguan rebels. He earned himself a corner office at Heron, Burchette, Ruckert & Rothwell. Located on Thomas Jefferson Street in Washington, about half a mile from the Watergate Hotel, this office had a fireplace, a sitting room, and a beautiful view of the Potomac River. And though Dowd could hardly believe the size of his office, the room seemed to match the stature of the man, as a lawyer. Dowd's reputation—as a courtroom litigator and a white-collar-crime expert—was impeccable. Vincent thought Dowd the perfect lawyer for the Pete Rose case, and he figured that Giamatti would like him. The Dowds were New Englanders by birth, just like the Giamattis, and they were patriots by nature. Dowd's family had a long history of serving in the military.

Fay Vincent called Dowd at his home in Northern Virginia within a day or two of the meeting with Pete in New York, and Giamatti got on the phone with him that night. It was late, after ten o'clock. Dowd was in his kitchen, and it took a moment for him to understand the stakes of the conversation or even the identity of the man on the other end of the line.

Giamatti, Dowd had to remind himself . . . *English professor* . . . *Yale.*

He had just returned home from working a criminal tax case in Georgia. He was exhausted, his tie unknotted and his dress shirt wrinkled, and since he'd been in court all week, Dowd had missed the stories in the papers reporting that Pete Rose had flown to New York for undisclosed reasons. Dowd didn't know that the news of the secret meeting in the commissioner's office had leaked to *The New York Times*—or that the *Dayton Daily News* was now reporting that the meeting seemed to be about gambling. He didn't know anything. Giamatti had to start at the beginning. The conversation lasted about an hour.

But by the time they got off the phone that night after eleven o'clock, the two men had come to terms on an agreement. In the investigation of Pete Rose, Dowd would have the full authority of the commissioner; the Reds would have to give him anything he wanted. In turn, Dowd had to be perfect—whatever he did, Giamatti said, the world would see it—and he had to start now. Giamatti wanted his new special counsel on a plane to Cincinnati the next morning, because the FBI had already found baseball its first witness, and he was a good one: Paul Janszen.

Dowd had no subpoena power. Paul didn't have to talk to him, and there was a strong argument to be made that he shouldn't. Since Paul had already pleaded guilty and was already serving his time in the halfway house, he had nothing to gain from the meeting and a lot to lose. As Paul told Dowd, "I was born in Cincinnati, Ohio. I am a Cincinnatian." Did he really want to be the guy who turned on Pete Rose? At best, if he did, Paul would sink his chances of ever getting his money from Pete, and at worst he would become an outcast in his own city, a local pariah. He'd be Cain, condemned to wander the earth alone.

But it had been a full year since the incident at the Holiday Inn near Cleveland, eleven months since the insulting check for $10,000, four weeks since Pete's lawyers sent Paul's lawyer a letter essentially saying they didn't believe Paul, and maybe just days since Paul called *Sports Illustrated.* The money was never coming. Paul could see that now, and he remained committed to starting over, to wiping the slate clean. In fact, if anything, agreeing to talk to Dowd was an easy decision for Paul to make. "A breeze," Paul told the FBI. On the last Friday of February 1989—just four days after Pete's meeting at the commissioner's office in New York and one day after baseball retained Dowd as special counsel—Paul went to a hotel in downtown Cincinnati to sit next to Danita and meet with three investigators: Kevin Hallinan; a former FBI agent who often did work for Major League Baseball; and Giamatti's man, John Dowd.

Paul was wound tight as they got started. With a tape recorder rolling in a room that was way too cold for the winter day outside, he spoke for minutes at a time without stopping. It was as if he couldn't tell his story fast enough. He talked about how he'd befriended Tommy Gioiosa, and how he'd met Pete Rose, and how he'd gotten invited to go with Pete to spring training in 1987, and how he couldn't believe it. "I said, 'Damn, Danita, he wants me to come down.'" So they did, he told the investigators. They went to Florida, and everything was great, at first. Paul told them how Pete had met him and Danita at the door of his big rental house near Tampa and how they all had fun together in Florida—before Paul started placing Pete's bets on baseball games with strangers in New York.

At this point, Dowd didn't know if Paul was telling the truth. He saw this case as a typical investigation into organized crime, where the subjects involved were criminals and, therefore, accomplished liars, possibly looking out for their own self-interest. Dowd wasn't going to believe anyone unless he could corroborate their statements. But it was clear from the start that Paul was a great witness. He was a storyteller, spinning his tale in chronological order, with time stamps, dates, names, and spellings, and he had evidence to support what he was saying. Paul brought photocopies of notes showing, he said, what Pete bet on certain days. He produced betting records he said he'd taken from Pete's house, allegedly written in Pete's hand, listing games, teams, and point spreads from April 1987. He showed Dowd a photo of him standing with Tommy, Pete, and Mickey Mantle in New York before everything went bad, proving that at the very least they knew each other, and Paul also had tapes. In recent months, he hadn't just recorded those telephone conversations with Ron Peters at the request of the FBI. He had recorded conversations with others, including Mike Bertolini, Pete's young memorabilia dealer in New York, and Stevie, the guy from the track in Tampa who had introduced Paul to Val, the bookie. And in these conversations Paul baited the other men into discussing Pete's gambling, his debts, and the possibility that Pete should seek help to overcome what had obviously become an addiction.

"Don't you think he should?" Paul asked Berto at one point on the tapes.

"Are you crazy?" Berto replied. It would be a scandal. "You know what kind of fucking scandal, man." Pete couldn't do it. "I don't think he can get help, Paulie," he said.

Then Bertolini paused.

"Are your phones clear?" he asked Paul. "Is this a cool phone?"

In the weeks ahead, investigators would sometimes play these tapes just to hear the incessant cursing, Bertolini's Brooklyn accent, and the screaming void of madness on the edge of Pete's universe. But for now inside the hotel, Dowd stayed out of the way as much as possible, an expert lawyer plying his trade. He let Paul talk and got him on the record while Paul sought Dowd's approval. Paul hoped he was giving Dowd what he wanted.

"Let me ask you this," Paul said, stopping himself several minutes into the interview. "Do you want me to go through all of this . . . like this . . . or . . . ?"

Dowd assured him that he was doing fine. Just fine.

"Don't worry about us at all," Dowd said. "Just tell it the way you remember."

"Okay," Paul replied, and he kept going, feeling better. "I'm on a roll now."

Over the course of that day and the next, Paul filled tape after tape, until Dowd had a typed transcript that stretched on for 160 pages and contained enough evidence to break the case wide open. Between Paul's testimony and phone records that investigators acquired in the weeks ahead, Dowd accumulated a mountain of facts that showed, at a minimum, a curious pattern of phone conversations just before Reds games in the spring of 1987. Paul would call Stevie, Val, or Ron Peters. Then he'd call Pete in the Reds' clubhouse. Then he'd call the bookies again. And there was usually a similar volume of calls *after* the games. Paul phoned the clubhouse, or Pete's house, or placed additional calls—five, or twelve, or nineteen calls—to hotlines providing up-to-the-minute game scores for a fee. It was a manic rush of calls, and the Reds' off days could be even worse. On one off day that spring, Paul called Pete's house five times, the clubhouse once, Ron Peters once, and then, that night—presumably while Paul and Pete were watching games together at Pete's house in Indian Hill—four calls went out from the house to Ron and five more went to the hotline.

Dowd knew, however, that Pete's lawyers could easily argue that it was Paul Janszen who had the problem, that it was Paul Janszen who was betting on baseball. He was the one calling the hotline nineteen times a day. He was the one sending threatening letters to Reuven Katz. He was the one with the criminal record. Dowd needed to confirm that the handwriting on the betting records that Paul had provided belonged to Pete, and he also needed a second source with intimate, firsthand knowledge of Pete's gambling.

Dowd wanted to talk to Tommy Gioiosa.

58

TOMMY HAD TRIED to bury his mistakes in Cincinnati and leave them in the ground.

With his girlfriend, Kim, he left town as he had promised, after everything fell apart with Pete in the spring of 1987. Tommy went to Southern California for a while, lived in an apartment near the beach in San Diego, helped a friend open a gym there, and stopped using steroids for the first time in years—a change that made Tommy feel almost human again. But things didn't work out on the West Coast.

By late February 1989, when Dowd was recording Paul Janszen inside the hotel in Cincinnati, Tommy and Kim had bottomed out, abandoned their brief and glorious life in San Diego, and moved back across the country to live with Tommy's parents in his childhood house on Covell Street in New Bedford, Massachusetts. Kim had a job waiting tables at a TGI Fridays across the border in Rhode Island, and Tommy spent his days lifting weights, gambling at a dog track in a nearby town, and thinking about the past. Sometimes, he couldn't avoid it.

Twice in recent months, including once after moving home to New Bedford, FBI agents and IRS investigators had shown up at Tommy's door—just as they had outside Paul's condo in Cincinnati. They wanted to discuss Gold's Gym, gambling, big-cash winnings at the track, and Pete Rose, and on their second visit, the one in New Bedford, Tommy agreed to meet with the agents at a motel near the public golf course in town. Yellow legal pads were on the bed, and their offer was on the table. In exchange for Tommy's cooperation—and any information he had about Pete's gambling—the agents would be willing to help Tommy, as they had helped Paul. They just wanted to know what he knew.

Tommy had no reason to protect Pete at this point. It had been two years since he had been excommunicated from Pete's inner circle and two years since he had been replaced by Paul Janszen. He could have told the agents everything, and deep down he knew that he should have. It was the right thing to do. His old friends from Gold's Gym were getting arrested one by one; he could be next. Kim didn't understand why Tommy wouldn't want to reveal every last secret of his dark days in Cincinnati.

But Tommy refused to turn on Pete—even when agents informed him that Pete wouldn't be loyal to him if the roles were reversed; even when reporters started calling him on Covell Street after they learned about Pete's meeting at the commissioner's office in New York in late February 1989; and even when Dowd invited Tommy to come to New York in March to sit down and talk. "Please call me," Dowd said, "as soon as possible."

Tommy just couldn't do it. He still loved Pete too much: for befriending him in the first place, for saving him when he was lost, for inviting him to stay in his house in Cincinnati, for letting him live in the West Side condo, for getting him tryouts with the Phillies, Orioles, and Blue Jays, and for introducing him to a million-dollar world of red Porsches, gold jewelry, beautiful women, late nights at the track, and sunny days at the ballpark.

It didn't matter what federal agents told him or how much Kim didn't understand.

"I'm with Pete," Tommy said that March.

Dowd would have to find his answers somewhere else. The problem for Tommy was that it was easy for Dowd, the easiest case he had ever prosecuted.

All Dowd had to do was drive to Franklin, Ohio.

Ron Peters called his lawyer the moment Dowd's investigators showed up at Jonathan's Café around mid-March. It was a weeknight around closing time at the law practice in downtown Franklin. Most people had gone home for the day. But Alan Statman didn't keep the usual hours. He was young, about thirty years old. He was still at his desk when Ron called, and Statman hustled over to Jonathan's to intercede on behalf of his client.

Ron would be happy to talk to the investigators about what he knew about Pete Rose, Statman said that night, and he made it clear that his client could give them everything they wanted. Ron could provide detailed information that Pete bet on baseball and on the Reds. Ron just wasn't going to have that conversation here, at the bar. They'd need to arrange to meet on a different day, with some clear terms of engagement. In the meantime, Ron had some important business to conduct. Like Paul, he wanted to sell his story to the media—for the highest price possible—and he instructed Statman to set up meetings with *Sports Illustrated* at his law office.

By then, senior editor Sandy Padwe had at least five writers on the story, including three of his best investigative reporters, who had joined the staff in recent years and had experience, outside of journalism, working as a police chief and a U.S. Senate investigator.

They weren't there to buy anything from Ron; they were there to take it. And they already had most of the story, anyway. One of the reporters had done a jailhouse interview with Mike Fry, the former owner of Gold's Gym, now serving an eight-year prison sentence in Indiana and looking for any way to curry favor with authorities and gain early release. Ron had seriously misjudged the situation. He didn't have leverage over anyone here—except for perhaps Pete—and the meeting with *Sports Illustrated* did not go as he hoped.

Instead of paying him, the two *SI* reporters who came to Statman's office managed to eke out enough on-the-record details to confirm that Ron Peters was Pete's "principal bookmaker" and that Pete's dealings with Ron were enough to get Pete "banned from baseball"—a suggestion that Pete bet on the Reds. With these details in hand, *Sports Illustrated* then circled back to Ueberroth and Giamatti, who were forced to break their silence on the matter in New York.

On Monday, March 20, the outgoing commissioner and the incoming commissioner issued a joint statement announcing that Dowd was investigating Pete for unspecified allegations of a serious nature. The magazine had backed baseball into a corner with its reporting; Ueberroth and Giamatti had to say something now. But more interesting was what Ueberroth said behind closed doors. On the same day of the prepared statement, he asked to meet in secret with the top editors at *Sports Illustrated*—not just Sandy Padwe, but Sandy's bosses. They gathered in a suite at the Dorset Hotel on West Fifty-Fourth Street, and Padwe seethed with anger as Ueberroth proceeded to plant subtle seeds of doubt in the room. Did they really have the story? Were they really sure Pete Rose bet on baseball?

It was, in Padwe's opinion, a textbook power play by one of the decade's biggest power brokers. Ueberroth seemed to be trying to get *Sports Illustrated* to flinch in order to buy more time for baseball's own investigation—and Ueberroth succeeded on that front, to a point. Back at the magazine offices later that day, Padwe was told to shelve the long, multipage Pete Rose gambling story that he and others had planned for that week's issue. They would have to scramble on deadline and replace it with a much smaller article on Pete's gambling. It was to be just one page, shoehorned into the "Scorecard" section at the front of the magazine.

Padwe was crushed. They had spent weeks chasing this story—the story of a lifetime, one of the biggest sports scandals of the century, involving one of the most celebrated players in baseball history. Padwe knew that they had it. He knew his writers had gathered the goods on Pete Rose, and he couldn't believe that they were burying it. They were burying their own story. He went home to his apartment that night on West Seventy-Ninth Street frustrated and angry, as angry as he had ever been. And somehow, it didn't matter. When the story came out—just hours later—people couldn't believe what they were reading about Pete Rose.

The magazine reported that Pete was under investigation for betting on baseball, that Pete was allegedly gambling on his own games, that Ron was his bookie, that Tommy and Paul ran his bets out of Gold's Gym, that lots of people at the gym knew it, and that on at least one occasion Pete had gone to Franklin to visit Ron at Jonathan's Café—an allegation that Pete denied to *Sports Illustrated.* He claimed he didn't know Ron and refused to admit to anything else. "I did not bet on baseball," Pete told the magazine.

That morning, a Tuesday, Pete drove to the Cardinals' facility in nearby St. Petersburg to manage a Reds spring training game and stepped out of his car into the teeth of a media scrum that he hadn't seen since 1985. Dozens of reporters hounded him outside the visitors' clubhouse, and dozens more descended upon Franklin in search of Ron Peters. Amid the chaos that morning, Ron tried to sell his story again—this time to *The Cincinnati Enquirer*—and once again, he failed. Reporters weren't going to pay for anything when they could follow Ron to Jonathan's Café, grab tables there for lunch, and pepper Ron with questions while he darted about the room. He needed a shave and a place to hide. At least Pete had help.

That day, the Reds barred the press from entering the visitors' clubhouse in St. Petersburg before the game, and Pete granted just one interview under controlled circumstances. He spoke to his old friend, the Reds' radio broadcaster Marty Brennaman, for Marty's usual pregame show. Marty had known Pete for fifteen years and expected to find him in a shattered state inside the clubhouse, given the commissioner's investigation, the *Sports Illustrated* article, and the allegations it contained. Instead, with Marty in the clubhouse, Pete was his normal self. He told Marty during their interview that he was cooperating with the commissioner's office and looking forward to opening day—both true. But just how Pete was cooperating would have stunned Marty, if Marty had known the details.

A few days earlier, at the request of John Dowd, Pete picked up a pen in Florida and submitted a lengthy handwriting sample, following prompts to make sure Dowd had every letter and every number Pete could ever write in multiple variations.

"Warren Bud Smith," Pete wrote.

"Cook F. Young, Jr."

"1 2 3 4 5 6 7 8 9 0."

On and on it went for several pages. Dowd then sent off the sample to a forensics expert to compare against the betting records that Paul Janszen had turned over back in February. Dowd wanted to know if Pete had written the betting sheets, but he wasn't waiting around to get his answer. While the forensics expert got to work studying Pete's handwriting down in Florida, Dowd drove north from Cincinnati to Franklin.

He was ready to interview his next witness: Ron Peters.

It was Thursday when Dowd arrived in town, just forty-eight hours after the *Sports Illustrated* story broke, though for Ron it had to feel like much longer. The presence of the media at the café was hurting business, killing the waitresses' tips, making them angry, and forcing Ron to stay hidden inside the kitchen during peak hours. He couldn't work the room, couldn't bus tables, couldn't do anything he used to do, and he had failed in his attempts to do the one thing he really wanted: to sell his story.

But Alan Statman wasn't worried about his client when Ron appeared at the law office that day for his interview with Dowd. Statman was thinking, once again, about opportunities. If Dowd wanted Ron on the record, Statman wanted something in return. He wanted Major League Baseball and Bart Giamatti to vouch for his client in his pending criminal case in federal court. He wanted Giamatti to write, in effect, a nice letter to the federal judge about Ron.

Dowd agreed; this was standard operating procedure. In exchange for Ron's full and honest testimony, Dowd would draft something for Giamatti to sign, and they'd get it to the federal judge before any sentencing procedures. They'd take care of Ron, if Ron took care of them, and Ron nodded. He was ready to go, cool and confident. He sat before Dowd like a golfer who had just come in off the eighteenth green and calmly told him everything he knew: how Pete bet on baseball through Tommy and Paul; how Pete bet on the Reds to win; how Pete had probably gambled $1 million with him over the years; and how on several occasions Pete had called in the bets himself, including once about five minutes before the first pitch, as Ron watched the Reds game on television. Pete was on the phone, Ron said, and then there he was in the dugout. In Ron's opinion, Pete had a problem—a big gambling problem.

"At a later time," Dowd asked when they were done, "would you be willing to give this information under oath to us?"

"Sure," Ron replied.

"Taking your deposition?"

"Sure," Ron said again.

"It would be a lot shorter," Dowd said, but it might involve a polygraph test.

Ron didn't mind. He would do whatever Dowd wanted. Then, while Dowd walked out the front door into a crowd of reporters and tangle of television cameras, Statman slipped Ron out a back window and into a waiting car.

Ron had wiped the slate clean, just like Paul Janszen, and he got what he wanted as a result, per his agreement with Dowd. A few weeks later, shortly after Ron pleaded guilty to distributing cocaine and making a false statement on his tax return, Dowd wrote a letter to the judge, praising Ron for his "candid, forthright, and truthful" cooperation in the Pete Rose investigation, and Giamatti signed it without a second thought.

"Sincerely yours, A. Bartlett Giamatti."

Ron was sentenced to just two years in prison—and Dowd now had enough evidence that he didn't even need Tommy Gioiosa anymore. In early April, just a few days after Ron pleaded guilty, Tommy stepped out of his house on Covell Street in New Bedford to go to the gym and federal agents swooped in to arrest him before he even made it to his car. The charges were tax evasion and cocaine trafficking.

Tommy didn't understand what was happening; neither did his girlfriend, Kim. She had been inside the house getting ready for her shift at the TGI Fridays. Now she was trying to get to her own car to follow the agents. She didn't even know where they were taking Tommy. All she knew was that Tommy was scared and poorly dressed for the occasion. Unaware that the federal agents were outside, he had walked out the front door of the house that day wearing an old blue sweatshirt emblazoned with a yellow logo.

"Gold's Gym," the logo said. "Cincinnati, Ohio—Home of Pete Rose."

It was an embarrassment for Pete, but it wasn't even the worst thing that happened to him that week. The forensics expert had completed his microscopic review of Pete's writing samples and had come to a conclusion: The handwriting on the betting records that Paul Janszen had produced seemed to belong to Pete. In his expert opinion, Pete Rose was the author.

59

Almost every day that spring, Dowd spoke by phone with either Vincent or Giamatti in New York, keeping them informed of what he was finding and adjusting his own schedule to fit Giamatti's. It wasn't unusual for the two men to talk well after eleven o'clock at night. It felt to Dowd like Giamatti never slept. Now Dowd called Giamatti to give him the news: he had it, they had it. Between Paul Janszen's testimony and Ron Peters's deposition, the phone records and bank receipts, the handwriting analysis and a hundred other interviews, Dowd felt the evidence was clear that Pete had gambled on baseball and wagered on his own team.

The only thing left to do now was to interview Pete himself. A date was set for the third week of April, an off day for the Reds. A site was chosen to throw off the press, a Catholic school in Dayton. Pete's lawyers instructed Dowd to meet them in the basement of the school after hours, and both sides showed up with a strategy in mind.

At Giamatti's direction, Dowd planned to show Pete everything. Let him see the preponderance of the evidence: the phone records; the bank deposits; the checks Pete had written in his own hand to pay off his many debts; and the courtesy tickets he had left for Ron Peters. Let him hear what Ron Peters, Paul Janszen, and others had to say. Let him listen to the tape recording that Paul had made of his phone conversation with Mike Bertolini almost two years earlier, and let Pete react to it all. Let him come to the realization that there was no way out.

Pete, on the other hand, planned to give Dowd nothing. He wasn't just fighting for his life in the game at that point; he was fighting to salvage his livelihood. Carol was pregnant again and due to give birth to their second child, and Pete's fifth, late that summer. Pete needed to keep his job with the Reds to support his family, to pay the mortgages on his houses in Indian Hill and Florida, to cover his mounting legal bills, and to finance the lifestyle that he and Carol had come to expect, including presumably his gambling. He had no other craft, he reminded himself going into the meeting with Dowd. No other marketable skills. What would he do without baseball? How would he survive? Or, as Pete put it, "How the fuck am I going to eat?"

It was its own sort of collision at home plate; someone was going to end up on his back in the dirt. And Pete walked into the Catholic school in Dayton projecting confidence that it wouldn't be him. Dowd was surprised by how big Pete appeared in the doorway. Everything about him was solid, thick. Dowd instantly understood why infielders had feared Pete whenever he came barreling toward second base. Dowd was six feet four, and he didn't want to tangle with him. Pete looked to Dowd like a fullback, and Pete subtly let Dowd know right away that no one was tough enough to take him down. To get to the deposition, Pete had flown all night from Los Angeles, where the Reds had just wrapped up a six-day road trip. He had hardly slept, and it didn't matter. Pete was ready to go.

"You understand that you're under oath?" Dowd said.

Pete nodded.

"Can I have your answer for the record, please?"

"Yes."

"Thank you," Dowd said.

It was a little after four o'clock in the afternoon, the basement was quiet, the press was nowhere to be found, and the deposition had begun. Over the course of the next seven hours with Dowd, both that evening and the next morning, Pete admitted to betting on football with bookies going back to the 1970s. "Give me a thousand to win on the Bengals," he told Dowd, showing him how he might place a wager, "plus three." He conceded that at times he lost money with these bookies—which explained the checks that Dowd had in his possession. He confessed to inviting Paul Janszen to spend spring training with him in 1987. He was willing to say that he had flown to spring training in 1989 with the money from his big Pik-Six victory with Jerry Carroll at the track—more than $100,000, he said, packed inside a satchel—and he was also willing to tell Dowd that he'd met Ron Peters, once.

But Pete maintained that Ron wasn't his friend. He couldn't explain why there were phone calls from his house or his hotel rooms to Ron in Franklin. He blamed these calls, and other things he couldn't explain, on his associates, especially Paul. He suggested that Paul was the one with the gambling problem, that Paul was the one who was unhinged. Then he said he didn't want to talk about Paul at all. "Are we through with Paul Janszen?" Pete asked Dowd on the second day. "Are we through talking about Paul Janszen?" Pete was pretty sure that all his problems could be traced back to Paul. "If I was a betting man," Pete told Dowd, "I would bet my life that this whole thing started with Paul Janszen." It was Paul who deserved scrutiny, not him. In Pete's mind, he was guilty of only one thing. "John," Pete said at one point, "I was a horse shit selector of friends."

It was the kind of story that had worked with Ueberroth, Giamatti, and Vincent in the commissioner's office in New York two months earlier and that in some ways had worked for Pete his entire life. But Dowd didn't believe it. As he played the Bertolini tape inside the Catholic school near the end of day two, Dowd thought he saw physical changes in Pete, as if the man were crumbling on the inside, the blood draining from his face, his skin turning gray, and Dowd knew why. In just eight weeks, he and his team had unraveled years of Pete's lies, and they were about to put everything they had learned on paper. Their report, the *Dowd Report*—filed to Giamatti a few weeks later, after an all-night editing session at Dowd's law office in Washington—would be long enough to fill an entire book, even when boiled down into a summary. It was 225 pages long, and it included nine volumes of exhibits, stretching on for almost 3,000 pages more.

At this point, Dowd said later, a good lawyer would have grabbed Pete around the collar and shaken him until he realized that his best option, maybe his only option, was to admit what he had done and broker a deal with Giamatti and Vincent in New York. Both men seemed open to the possibility. Vincent discussed potential deals with Reuven Katz three times that spring and summer, including once on a Saturday morning in Dayton, just eight days after Dowd finished taking Pete's deposition. And Dowd wanted to help, too. He said he wanted Pete to visit him at his house on Cape Cod, where they could walk on the beach, with no court reporters present and no tape recorders running, and discuss how they could break him down and build him back up again. "Every day, people who are addicted come to Jesus and get well," Dowd said. Why couldn't Pete?

But in his meetings with Reuven, Vincent made it clear that he and Giamatti were unwavering on two points. First, there could be no easy out for Pete. Rule 21(d) stated that a player who bet on his team had to be declared permanently ineligible and barred from participating in baseball; therefore, Pete would have to be declared permanently ineligible and would have to apply for reinstatement at a future date. Second, baseball would not accept an agreement in which Pete denied the facts of the case. He had to admit that he bet on baseball.

Still, Pete couldn't do it. He didn't want to be dismantled, broken down, and rebuilt, and his lawyers apparently couldn't persuade him to change his mind. Instead of settling, they asked Giamatti for thirty days to run their own investigation. Then they sued Giamatti in Cincinnati's Common Pleas Court, asking a local judge, who was up for reelection the following year, to block the commissioner from ruling on Pete's case. They argued that the forensics expert had made a mistake. They claimed that the handwriting on the betting records wasn't Pete's, but a forgery, possibly drafted by Paul Janszen to frame Pete. They demanded that Giamatti be removed because he had prejudged Pete months earlier, and they cited as evidence of his bias a one-page document that had leaked in recent weeks: the April letter, written by Dowd and signed by Giamatti, praising Ron Peters for his honesty. Instead of coming to Jesus, they were going to war.

Giamatti, Vincent, and Dowd saw it for what it was: the legal equivalent of a stall tactic. Even if Pete prevailed in local court—"the traffic court," Vincent called it derisively—baseball's lawyers believed they could get the case moved to a federal judge, and then Dowd and Vincent knew that Pete wouldn't be able to stop Giamatti. But for now the legal move worked. In late June—in front of a packed courtroom in Cincinnati and a national television audience watching live coverage at home on ESPN—the local judge sided with Pete, granting him a temporary restraining order and forcing Giamatti into a protracted legal battle that seemed likely to last all summer. Eight weeks in court. Eight weeks in the news. Eight weeks of people asking questions about Bart Giamatti, Pete Rose, the truth, and baseball.

Dowd remembers Giamatti being a steadfast presence throughout this summer of doubt. In Dowd's memory, Giamatti never wavered and always believed that in the end baseball would prevail in its fight against Pete Rose. But Vincent recalled one night that summer when Giamatti seemed less sure.

"It was the low point for John and me and Bart," Vincent said decades later. Giamatti had asked them to be perfect. He felt they had failed on that count by vouching for Ron Peters in the middle of their pursuit of Pete Rose, and Giamatti was so angry about that failure, Vincent said, that he turned his frustrations on Dowd and Vincent after the restraining order was handed down.

"I can see the room we were in," Vincent said, trying to conjure the memory of the day. "It was a hotel or a restaurant in New York City." The exact location isn't clear in his mind. All Vincent remembers for sure is that Giamatti was furious. "He took John and me and yelled at us and screamed at us. 'I'm screwed, you guys.' I mean, Bart went bananas over the proceeding in Cincinnati, because it made him look stupid. . . . 'Like I'm biased—I'm the one that loses the case.' . . . He went crazy." It was the first time Vincent had ever seen Giamatti like that, and he left the meeting that day distraught, because Giamatti was right: they had made a mistake, and there was nothing they could do to change it now. "There was no ending that was upbeat," Vincent said. No way to ease the disappointment. "We all went our separate ways," he said.

The summer felt as if it might last forever.

Pete seemed to relax the day he won his restraining order, regaling reporters the way he once had. He was fun and light and witty. He spoke about the judge's ruling with Marty Brennaman on the Reds' pregame radio show. He told the press afterward that he talked to Marty only because he was paid a standing fee to do the show. And he joked with the sportswriters that he would do the same with them, except they couldn't pay him enough. "From what I know," he said, "there's not enough to collect here." Everyone laughed and the jokes kept coming. That night, on local television, Pete said he couldn't be as bad as everyone had been saying. "I go to the racetrack to enjoy myself," he said, "and I end up being Al Capone."

His friends and loved ones agreed. They believed Pete was telling the truth when he said he didn't bet on baseball, and they were relieved that someone—the local judge—was finally listening. In recent weeks, Pete's mother, Laverne, now remarried and seventy-four years old, hadn't left her new apartment on the West Side, due to the shame she felt. Now, for at least one day, Laverne walked free, basking in her son's legal victory.

At Riverfront Stadium that afternoon, Reds fans did the same. They showered Pete with love as the Reds took on the Dodgers. People hung banners in the upper deck that read, PETE 1, BART 0, and players rushed to Pete's defense by attacking Giamatti. "What do you expect when you're dealing with a Yale yuppie?" said the Reds' reliever Rob Dibble, who could throw a fastball a hundred miles per hour, had grown up in Bridgeport, Connecticut, and thought of Yalies and other East Coast elites as *those people.* "You can't trust those guys," he said.

The moment was short-lived. Security moved through the stadium that day like the thought police, confiscating any signs that referenced Giamatti. The Reds lost to the Dodgers 7–0 and kept losing—both on and off the field that summer. Over the next month, they went 6-21. Got swept by Philadelphia. Got swept in Montreal. Lost ten in a row. Lost fifteen out of sixteen and lost most of their opening day starters to injuries. Players collided in the field, chasing down pop flies, took line drives in the face, pulled themselves out of the game with elbow soreness, injured themselves running out ground balls, and rotted away on the disabled list. Those still playing at the end of July looked around the field realizing they weren't even the Reds anymore. "Who *are* these guys?" the Phillies' star Lenny Dykstra asked the Reds' first baseman Todd Benzinger after reaching first in one game late that month. Benzinger had to admit he didn't know, and the injuries and the losses were the least of Pete's problems.

Just one day after the local judge ruled in Pete's favor, the Cleveland *Plain Dealer* prevailed in a legal challenge, forcing the judge to release Dowd's report, unredacted and in its entirety. Pete's secrets and the secrets of almost everyone who had ever gambled with him—Paul Janszen, Tommy Gioiosa, Ron Peters, Mike Bertolini, and the rest—were now printed in newspapers across the country for people to dissect and debate. Every average fan now knew almost everything there was to know about Pete Rose, and most agreed that it wasn't pretty. At an autograph show that weekend in Atlantic City, people still lined up to meet Pete—hundreds and hundreds of people—but he was treated more like a circus freak than a hero. While Joe DiMaggio and Ted Williams signed autographs out in the open, Pete was forced to work at a table surrounded by temporary walls to keep the reporters at bay and the gawkers from watching.

"Get those cameras out of here!" a police officer shouted. "No cameras allowed! Stand back! Move aside!"

It was a moment when most managers would have gotten fired. The team wasn't performing, and Pete had become a distraction. Television crews followed him everywhere, even into the bathroom. Reporters asked questions while he shaved. Boom mics lurked around every corner. Players pushed through them just to reach the field or their lockers, and Pete did everything he could to disappear. Some days, on the road, before games, he sat in the visitors' bullpen in the outfield, just to dodge ESPN, CNN, the national networks, everyone. But Marge Schott was reluctant to dismiss Pete while his lawsuit against Giamatti was still pending, just in case Pete was telling the truth, just in case Pete prevailed. The Reds were stuck with him as the case moved from the local court in Cincinnati to a federal court in Columbus; as lawyers met in the judge's chambers there, trying to elude reporters; as Xerox machines churned in the night inside law firms across Ohio, pumping out legal briefs; as the judge sorted through the arguments and ruled to keep the case in the federal court; and as Pete's lawyers exhausted every avenue, until finally they had nowhere left to turn. When the Sixth Circuit of the U.S. Court of Appeals ruled against returning the case to Cincinnati in late August, Pete had two choices: challenge Giamatti's authority in federal court in a historic hearing and probably lose or negotiate an endgame.

On Monday, August 21, four days after the appellate court ruling, Pete managed the Reds to a 6–5 victory in Chicago over the Cubs. A few hours later, Carol went into labor back in Cincinnati, and by the time his players woke up on Tuesday morning, Pete was gone. He had flown to Cincinnati and had informed the Reds' traveling secretary that he had no plans to rejoin the team. He needed to stay with Carol and their new baby, a girl. He had documents to sign with Reuven Katz—secret documents that Pete spoke about with almost no one, including his bosses in the Reds' front office—and he had a previously scheduled engagement that he intended to keep. That Wednesday night, one day after the birth of his daughter, he was set to make an appearance on the Cable Value home shopping network, selling his memorabilia and chatting with interested buyers calling in from their living rooms across the country on a toll-free 800 number.

Pete flew to Minneapolis on a private jet with his friend Arnie Metz. He sat in a soulless studio in the suburbs designed to look like a baseball clubhouse, and he bantered with a well-trained Cable Value Network host named Alan, pretending as if he were still a baseball player, still a manager, still someone who mattered. At one point in the studio that night, Pete picked up a ball and said, "Boy, I can't wait to get ahold of them Cardinals next week."

Alan, the host, got the hint. They were not to talk about Giamatti. They were not to discuss gambling. Pete was there to sell, and that's what they did. For two hours, between ten o'clock and midnight central time that night, they peddled autographed Pete Rose baseballs for $39.94, autographed Pete Rose photos from the night he broke Ty Cobb's record for $79.92, autographed Pete Rose bats for $229.92, and autographed Pete Rose jerseys for $399.92—or, as Alan the host said, "four payments of $99.98."

"Here's a piece of history."

Alan didn't know it, but everything was already slipping away by the moment.

For days, Fay Vincent and Reuven Katz had been hashing out the legal terms of Pete's surrender. In just the past several hours, somewhere between Cincinnati and Minneapolis, Pete had finally signed off on a five-page agreement that ended his life in baseball. He scrawled his signature next to Giamatti's, accepting permanent banishment, accepting permanent ineligibility, and off the set that night, far from the little building in the suburbs of Minneapolis, the news had started to break. Giamatti was making a major announcement in the morning.

Baseball sent out a press release, inviting reporters to a nine o'clock event in the Sutton Parlor at the New York Hilton, four blocks from the league office. Reporters soon learned that Pete was to hold his own press conference an hour later in Cincinnati, and then they learned why. Giamatti was going to announce some sort of banishment for Pete Rose—a conclusion that felt inevitable and abrupt at the same time, especially for Pete himself. On his last night as a ballplayer, he wasn't sliding headfirst into third base. He wasn't barreling into home. He wasn't sitting in the dugout, writing his lineup card. He wasn't even doting on his new daughter, born the day before. He was in that television studio, dead inside and smiling into the cameras broadcasting over Channel 30 while the baseball world, his world, moved on without him.

Journalists worked late into the night, hustling on deadline to learn the details of Giamatti's ban. One of the *Sports Illustrated* writers who had met with Ron Peters appeared on ABC's *Nightline.* Copy editors around the country scrambled the next day's front pages, making room to strip massive three-inch headlines above the fold, announcing Pete's banishment or suspension—they weren't sure which word to use. Reporters gathered in the parking lot outside the Cable Value Network to ask Pete himself, and when Pete finally emerged through a back door after midnight with Arnie Metz at his side, the press shouted questions at him.

Pete had no comment at the studio and no comment a short time later at the small airport where his plane was waiting. He relented to only one request: Pete agreed to give a spot on the plane to a friendly reporter he had known for more than fifteen years. The three men settled into their seats—with Arnie and the reporter sitting close together near the front of the plane and Pete in the back on his own—and shortly before one o'clock local time the plane took off flying east, wheels up in the night. They were going home, racing home to Cincinnati, and although Pete was tired—he looked tired—he didn't sleep in the back of the plane.

He turned on a light to stave off the darkness.

ACT V
WRECKAGE

60

ON THE MORNING of Pete's banishment, Bart Giamatti awoke in New York City feeling the weight of the moment.

He devoured *The New York Times* in the dark. He read every word of the front-page story that accurately reported what was about to happen that morning—that Pete Rose was going to accept a lifetime ban, ending his fight with Giamatti—and then Giamatti headed down to the lobby to wait for his car. Kevin Hallinan was supposed to collect Giamatti at seven o'clock that morning, two hours before the press conference, but Giamatti was in the lobby about half an hour early—a development that Hallinan had expected and planned for. He was waiting for his boss and drove him across town to the offices of Major League Baseball.

At the front doors, on Park Avenue, Giamatti managed to slip past the line of television trucks parked on the curb without notice. Due to the early hour, the camera crews inside the trucks were all asleep at the wheel; no one expected to see the commissioner just after sunrise. But as Giamatti entered the building, he felt bad about it, hesitated, and told Hallinan to go wake everyone up. He'd give the crews a couple of minutes. He'd say something for their cameras—an act of kindness that Hallinan would never forget. In the defining moment of his career, Giamatti was thinking about the low-level network staffers who had stayed up all night. He didn't want them to get yelled at for missing their shot.

At the press conference two hours later, however, Giamatti was all business. He stood on a stage at the New York Hilton, with Vincent and Dowd to his left, a teeming crowd of reporters in front of him, and the logo of Major League Baseball behind him, and delivered the news that everyone had come to hear with his opening line.

"The banishment for life of Pete Rose from baseball is a sad end of a sorry episode," Giamatti said. "One of the game's greatest players has engaged in a variety of acts which have stained the game, and he must now live with the consequences of those acts."

Across the country, business ground to a halt, and life stopped in Cincinnati. Phones at some police stations on the West Side didn't ring for the next ninety minutes as people watched Giamatti and then Pete. The Cincinnati Bengals delayed morning meetings so that players could watch the news. Bank tellers huddled around small, handheld televisions. Office workers packed into boardrooms to watch together. The hallways at Procter & Gamble echoed with the sounds of the press conferences, playing as if in stereo—in every office, on every floor. People sat in their cars, stunned. Fans cursed, angry. Pete's mother, Laverne, watched from her new apartment on the West Side, wishing she were dead, and Bart Giamatti became a star.

Some reporters thought Giamatti's press conference in New York too theatrical and his demeanor at the Hilton too imperious. He seemed to enjoy the moment a little too much, they said, throwing around big words to bury Pete Rose and making Pete look foolish in the process. Pete had insisted on wording in his signed agreement that the document was neither an admission nor a denial of guilt on his part. Pete seemed to think that this wording would help get him reinstated some day, and he seemed to genuinely believe that it would prevent Giamatti, Vincent, and Dowd from ever giving their opinion on the matter—as if the evidence they had compiled didn't exist, as if Dowd hadn't written his report documenting Pete's gambling, as if Pete could say, "I made some mistakes," and leave it at that.

But by the time Pete uttered those very words at Riverfront Stadium that morning, quivering and for once afraid in a small room filled with too many reporters and not enough air-conditioning, he realized he had miscalculated yet again. Giamatti had already told reporters at the Hilton, and millions of people watching at home on television, that he thought Pete bet on baseball—and the Reds.

The legal language in the agreement had applied only to what Pete chose to say about his guilt or innocence. It didn't apply to Giamatti or anyone else.

In his effort not to appear weak, Pete had ended up looking stupid, doomed by his own choices, failed by his advisors in Cincinnati, and outwitted by smarter men in New York—a stark reality that was almost sad to watch for the reporters who knew Pete best. They couldn't explain why Pete, the ultimate fighter, would have ever signed a document, ensuring his permanent banishment, if he didn't bet on baseball and the Reds, and Pete couldn't fully explain it, either. In the steamy room at Riverfront Stadium, he just continued to say that he hadn't bet on baseball, Giamatti was wrong, and he looked to Reuven Katz for help. Reuven stepped forward and quickly shut down the press conference, blaming it on the heat inside the room. "It's just so beastly hot in here," he said.

While Pete ducked outside into the tunnels of the stadium and climbed into his gold Mercedes, eager to leave as soon as he could, Giamatti held court in New York, comfortable and relaxed on the stage at the Hilton, a professor again, teaching. He opined about the dangers of gambling and sports. He said that a competitor placing bets on his own games—"covert" and "conspiratorial" bets—was a player with a conflict of interest, more invested in himself than he was in the team, and more beholden to outside forces than any commissioner could tolerate. He defended his decision to remove Pete Rose from the game, with facts, with details, and he almost begged people to criticize him.

"I will be told that I am an idealist," Giamatti said. "I hope so."

He thought it important to find ideals in baseball—"the national game," he called it—and to protect these ideals at all costs. And he believed that, in time, the sport would grow stronger as a result of his investigation into Pete Rose. The glory of the game would reassert itself, he said. Then he told the reporters that he, Vincent, and Dowd would be happy to answer any questions that they might have, and everyone began to shout over one another.

"Wait a minute, wait a minute," Giamatti said, holding up his hands to hush the crowd. "Don't scream." He'd stay there all day if they wanted. But they had to be civilized. This was going to be a conversation. "Just take it easy," Giamatti said.

For the next forty minutes, he answered everything, deferring to Vincent or Dowd when he thought they were better suited to respond and cupping his hand over his ear so that he could better hear each question. Giamatti remained calm even when one reporter suggested that he was responsible for the controversy.

"Have you read the *Dowd Report,* sir?" Giamatti asked, smiling.

If the previous six months had been marked at times by missteps, the press conference was a master class in crisis management. *The Sporting News* called Giamatti brilliant afterward. *The New York Times* credited him for handling the situation with resolve. Even the Cincinnati newspapers had to praise his eloquence, and by the time Giamatti walked off the stage at the Hilton in New York that morning, he was ready to move on.

He wasn't going to spend the rest of his life, he said, discussing Pete Rose or chasing down new allegations about him. He wanted to talk instead about the possibility of adding new expansion teams. He was thrilled about the recent sale of the Seattle Mariners for $76 million—almost six times what the Mariners had sold for eight years earlier—and he was eager to discuss the playoff races in both leagues. Giamatti's beloved Boston Red Sox had a chance to win their division, and the defending AL champs, the Oakland A's, were trying to hold off the Angels and Royals out west. The A's owned the best record in baseball and had two of the most exciting young power hitters in the league in José Canseco and Mark McGwire. "The Bash Brothers," the press called them, because they hit towering home runs and then slammed their thick forearms together at home plate to celebrate.

"I'm looking forward to the World Series," Giamatti said.

But the A's were keeping their own secrets that summer, and in his pursuit of Pete Rose, Giamatti failed to notice the threat that these secrets posed to the game, to him, and to everyone else. While Dowd was investigating the gambling allegations around Pete, José Canseco was injecting himself with steroids in Oakland, and his teammate Mark McGwire had joined him—or was about to start—powering the A's to three consecutive AL pennants and changing baseball forever. The Pete Rose investigation was over and the steroid era had begun, with needles and juice, players using syringes inside clubhouse bathrooms, and shady doctors building perfect hitters in hidden labs.

Every important home-run record would soon fall, until even casual fans began to suspect that something was wrong and until every great player lived under a cloud of suspicion. Were they hitting home runs because they were talented or because they were taking steroids? Were they breaking records because they were good or because they were cheating? Fans often didn't know the difference, and baseball officials didn't know either. For years, no special counsel was hired to dig up the truth. Instead, baseball looked the other way in the 1980s and 1990s, refusing to take on the players' union to fight for the one policy that could have prevented widespread steroid use, the policy that the former commissioner Peter Ueberroth had briefly pushed for in 1985 and then dropped: mandatory drug testing.

This new era brought excitement at first, and baseball needed it. By the mid-1990s, years of players' strikes and owners' lockouts had finally led to a labor stoppage that shut down the 1994 season in the middle of August, canceled the World Series that October, and infuriated fans like never before. When play finally resumed in late April 1995, a sign at Riverfront Stadium in Cincinnati best captured the fans' sentiments. OWNERS & PLAYERS, the sign said. TO HELL WITH ALL OF YOU. Muscle-bound sluggers hitting impossible home runs helped people forget about the strike and brought fans back to the ballpark for a while.

But the statistics amassed in this little window of time—between 1995 and the adoption of a stringent drug testing policy a decade later—ultimately hurt the game more than anything Pete Rose ever did. As juiced-up hitters claimed iconic records held by baseball legends, fans turned on them, booing and jeering men whom they now considered false idols. The low point came in 2005, when several star players were called to testify before Congress and lied about their steroid use—or, as Mark McGwire did that day, declined to discuss "the past." Meanwhile, on the field, players continued to swing for the fences, whether they were using steroids or not, enamored with the long ball and with the lucrative contracts that home-run hitters like McGwire demanded.

The result was a decline in play that made the game boring to many fans by the 2020s. Strikeout rates soared to record highs. Batting averages plummeted to levels not seen in more than fifty years. Baseball fans tuned out. Television ratings for the World Series hit historic lows, and no one even argued anymore that baseball was America's pastime—a troubling set of circumstances that finally pushed Major League Baseball to introduce sweeping changes in 2023 in an effort to revitalize interest in the game. The league increased the size of the bases, to encourage stolen bases and movement. Officials banned the shift—making it illegal for defenses to stack extra infielders on one side of the diamond—to generate more hits. The commissioner instituted a pitch clock to speed up the game, and the league continued to invest in partnerships with legalized gambling platforms—partnerships that started in 2018 in order to give baseball a slice of America's new, fast-growing sports gambling industry.

In this new landscape, players still can't bet on the game—Rule 21(d) remains in effect—and league officials argue that they have more protection against wrongdoing, not less. Legalized gambling platforms can track down to the minute what's being wagered, where, and on whom. Security consultants can flag any curious activity and then they can trace it all the way back to the source—usually, someone's phone—in ways that weren't possible in the 1980s when John Dowd was chasing Pete Rose. Still, it worries some people, especially those who were there in the 1980s. A player interested in gambling back then, Fay Vincent said, used to have to go out of his way to do it, finding a bookie like Ron Peters to take the action and recruiting runners like Tommy Gioiosa and Paul Janszen to secretly place the bets. Now a player can do it from his couch or have a friend do it for him—easy access that, Vincent predicts, will lead to another massive sports gambling scandal at some point. There's simply too much money at stake, he said, with more than a hundred billion dollars being legally wagered on sports every year. "I think there's a very high probability of more Pete Roses," Vincent said in 2023, "and there's going to be more corruption."

At a minimum, it casts Pete Rose in a slightly different light. Under today's rules, a legalized gambling platform could have sponsored him. Pete could have played for the Reds and shilled for Fan-

Duel or DraftKings on the side—a reality that would have shocked Bart Giamatti. He just didn't live long enough to see it.

On the Friday before Labor Day weekend 1989—just eight days after Pete's banishment and about a month before the postseason began—Giamatti and Vincent chartered a plane to escape the city, as they often did in the summer, flying north to their vacation homes in New England. Giamatti had a little cottage on Martha's Vineyard, an unpretentious home with weathered shingles off Beach Road on the northeast shores of the island, and Vincent had a house on Cape Cod.

The two men were happy that morning as they took off in New York, and Vincent thought Giamatti looked like his usual self when he got off the plane on the Vineyard around midday. But at least one of Giamatti's friends, a doctor in Connecticut, had been concerned about his health of late and had told Giamatti as much. He was worried about his weight and his cigarette smoking, and shortly after lunch that Friday, Giamatti felt ill, lay down in his bedroom inside his cottage, and suffered a heart attack.

The call for help went out around three o'clock as a Priority 1 alert, and emergency vehicles came racing down Beach Road. Police officers showed up first and administered CPR on the floor of Giamatti's bedroom, and a volunteer EMT soon arrived to relieve them. The medic had no idea who the patient was at first. He just knew that he was fifty-one—too young to die—and, together with the police officers, he went to work on Giamatti, pumping on his chest and trying to reestablish a pulse for an hour and a half. They worked inside the house, then inside the ambulance while one of the police officers drove, sirens wailing, and then inside a bay in the emergency room at the island's small hospital six miles away. Doctors and nurses were on the case now. Everyone wanted to save this man.

It was no use. At 4:32 that afternoon, doctors at the hospital called it.

Bart Giamatti was gone.

61

Fay Vincent got the news of Giamatti's death late that afternoon at his home on the Cape, and he was careful not to blame Pete Rose for it. Like others, Vincent thought Giamatti had been in poor health for years, and an autopsy that weekend confirmed it. The medical examiner found evidence of constrictive coronary artery disease and signs of at least one previous heart attack that Giamatti had suffered, maybe without even realizing it.

But it was impossible for people to just forget the events of the summer, or disentangle Pete and Bart, now that Giamatti was gone. His old driver at Yale suggested that the stress of the Rose inquiry had hastened his early death. Grieving fans went on sports talk radio to blame Pete, and one of the nation's most prominent sports broadcasters seemed inclined to agree. On the night Giamatti died, Howard Cosell told a reporter that Pete was a "two-bit thug" who at the very least had ruined Giamatti's brief tenure as commissioner. "And now he is gone," Cosell said, mourning Giamatti, "and there are sportswriters out there saying this thug named Rose should be admitted into the Hall of Fame."

It wasn't a hypothetical conversation at the time. Under the existing rules of the National Baseball Hall of Fame in Cooperstown, Pete's name would appear on every ballot sent out to the Baseball Writers' Association of America in December 1991, five years after his last at bat with the Reds. The writers could choose to enshrine Pete in Cooperstown like any other player, and many of the 450 writers tasked with the job said that they would indeed support him. The Hall of Fame already included a long list of miscreants: gamblers, alcoholics, drug users, adulterers, cheaters, spitballers, ball scuffers, liars, deadbeats, racists, and at least two great hitters once accused of conspiring to throw games so that they could place money with bookies and win—Ty Cobb and Tris Speaker.

Pete could join them there—or not. It was up to the voters, a point that Giamatti made clear during his press conference in New York shortly before his death. "You have the authority," he told the reporters gathered at the Hilton that morning, "and you have the responsibility, and you will make your own individual judgments." Frankly, Giamatti said, he was looking forward to seeing how they sorted through what he called "the relationship of life to art—which you will all have to work out for yourselves."

But by early 1991, opinion had begun to shift on this matter due to Giamatti's death and a series of other events. Less than two weeks after Giamatti's heart attack on the Vineyard, a jury at the federal courthouse in Cincinnati convicted Tommy Gioiosa of conspiracy to distribute cocaine and conspiracy to defraud the IRS by claiming winnings at the racetrack that really belonged to Pete. Tommy kept waiting for Pete to show up at his trial and support him, or to call with a few words of encouragement. Facing the possibility of almost forty years in prison, Tommy just wanted to know that Pete still cared about him, or appreciated him for never talking to Dowd. But Pete couldn't sit in the gallery inside the federal courthouse or consort with Tommy anymore; the IRS was coming after him, too. When the judge sentenced Tommy to five years in prison in February 1990, and authorities perp walked him, handcuffed, in front of the media on his way to a holding cell in Kentucky, Tommy finally told ESPN what he refused to tell Dowd a year earlier. Of course Pete had bet on baseball and the Reds.

"It's time I take care of Tommy Gioiosa," Tommy said, as if he were finally coming to his senses, "and let Pete Rose take care of Pete Rose."

Certainly, Pete had the wherewithal and the tools to do it. He hired a new publicist, from a prominent marketing firm in Cincinnati, wrote a new book, penned by the respected writer Roger Kahn, and he had the chance to recast his story on *The Phil Donahue Show*, *Primetime Live*, *20/20*, and *60 Minutes*. But he lied to Kahn for the book. He lied to his publicist, too. He continued to deny that he had bet on baseball in every interview he did. And while his publicist was out there working for Pete—not trying to change Pete's image, she said, but hoping to change the communication of that image—Pete followed Tommy to prison.

In late April 1990, Pete pleaded guilty to filing a false tax return, a confession that seemed inevitable after Tommy's conviction. In July, a judge sentenced Pete to five months in a federal prison camp in Illinois, and in October, Pete watched the Cincinnati Reds win the World Series from inside that prison—cheering with other inmates in front of a small television in a communal room while his team swept the Oakland A's and celebrated on the field without him. It was the first World Series that Cincinnati had won since 1976, and it was impossible for the Reds' players not to think about their old manager that night. While they sprayed champagne on each other in the locker room—the way Pete always loved to do after winning—Pete drifted back to his prison bunk to go to sleep in a dormitory filled with criminals. He said he was happy for his players, but it was odd. "It was strange," he admitted. And it wasn't the only thing that slipped away from him that year. Three months later, in January 1991, a committee at the National Baseball Hall of Fame voted to change the rules about who could and could not be enshrined in bronze at Cooperstown.

Going forward, the committee said, candidates who were on baseball's ineligible list could not appear on any ballot. Players had to be in good standing, a suggestion that the board at the Hall of Fame accepted a few weeks later with little discussion or debate. Pete Rose could no longer receive votes of any kind, and many baseball writers understood why, at least in theory. Bob Broeg, who had covered the St. Louis Cardinals for the *Post-Dispatch* since 1946, explained to his colleagues that if Pete were elected, the new commissioner, Fay Vincent, wouldn't come to the ceremony. The two league presidents wouldn't come, either. People would lose faith in the Hall of Fame, and everything baseball had built in Cooperstown could collapse into dust. "If Pete's elected while under suspension," Broeg said, "he would take down the whole Hall."

Still, many writers were upset about the rule change—not because they planned to vote for Pete, but because they would never get the chance to cast judgment either way, to vote yes *or* no, to consider the relationship of life to art, as Giamatti had suggested, and work it out for themselves. For the first time in more than five decades, the Hall had prescreened a player out of the pool of possible candidates and revoked the writers' privilege to decide.

"Give me the opportunity *not* to vote for him," said Jack O'Connell, a baseball writer with the *Hartford Courant.*

"It's crazy," agreed Phil Pepe, a veteran sportswriter at the New York *Daily News.* But what were they going to do? Refuse to vote? Shred their ballots?

The committee had spoken. "The Committee to Make Sure Pete Rose Doesn't Get into the Hall of Fame Next Year," said Frank Dolson, the sports editor of *The Philadelphia Inquirer.*

The baseball writers couldn't do a thing.

62

WILLIE STARGELL—THE LOVABLE Pittsburgh Pirates star and one of Pete Rose's contemporaries, who'd been elected to the Hall of Fame in 1988—saw only one road to redemption for Pete.

"Pete should apologize," Stargell said in 1991. "Everybody, including me, wants Pete to say he's sorry. I believe, if he does, then he has the chance to have the ban lifted. Then things would fall into place for him."

Many of Pete's friends agreed, even those he had hurt. Tommy Gioiosa said Pete should have gone on tour, visited college campuses, spoken to athletes and kids for free about the dangers of gambling, confessed to everything, begged for forgiveness, *wiped the slate clean.* "It would've made him a better person," Tommy said. "But that didn't take place."

Pete couldn't even seem to decide if he had a gambling problem or not. Prior to sentencing in his federal court case, he told the judge that he was suffering from a sickness, and he briefly sought group counseling for it. "I went to two or three meetings," he said years later, "and I'm sitting there, and this guy's saying what he did, and this guy's saying what he did, and this guy's stealing money from his grandma to gamble. And I just said to myself, 'I don't have anything in common with these fucking people. Why am I here? Why am I here?' These people were stealing to make bets and stuff like that. All I did was bet on baseball games, and I just quit going because it made me feel real funny."

Pete couldn't share his feelings or cry with a bunch of strangers, and he didn't understand the gravity of what he had done. Or, if he did understand it, he couldn't admit it. He couldn't even say that he bet on baseball out loud. For fifteen years, Pete continued to lie, hurting Paul Janszen, Ron Peters, and Tommy Gioiosa, misleading his closest friends and loved ones, and winning converts to his cause.

One national poll, conducted in 1999, a decade after his banishment, found that 36 percent of people believed that Pete didn't bet on baseball—he had said it so much that he had willed the belief into existence—and these feelings were especially prevalent among white working-class midwestern men. They gave him standing ovations at public events, paid money for his autograph, told him to stay strong, wept in his presence, feeling blessed to stand next to the great Pete Rose, and supported him in 2004 when he finally published a book admitting what most reasonable people already knew: Yes, he had bet on baseball and the Reds, he finally said. And yes, he should have said it sooner.

"I'm human," Pete said during his book tour that winter. "I made a mistake. I'm sorry I made that mistake. I'm looking for a second chance. I won't need a third."

The book became a *New York Times* bestseller, and for a moment Pete thought it might help him get reinstated. But sales stalled, and what had once been a sensation quickly became yet another public relations crisis for Pete Rose. Somehow, his book managed to upset almost everyone.

Friends and loved ones, who had believed him all these years, were blindsided by the new and sudden revelations in the book about his gambling, while critics panned the book for not going far enough. Pete seemed to be cashing in, they wrote, not coming clean. He refused to admit that he bet on baseball in 1986 while he was still a player, despite evidence showing otherwise. At times, he painted himself as the victim. Even the book title—*My Prison Without Bars*—sounded whiny, as if he hadn't helped build the prison walls with his own choices. Perhaps worst of all, he lashed out at Paul Janszen and John Dowd. He picked fights over little pieces of evidence instead of taking full responsibility for his mistakes. He didn't sound very sorry, critics said, and reinstatement eluded him every time he asked for it: in 2004, in 2015, in 2020, and in 2022. Nothing changed. If anything, his situation only grew worse.

In the years after his book came out, Pete divorced his second wife, Carol. He moved to Las Vegas, where he got a standing gig signing autographs at Caesars Palace and Mandalay Bay. He lost his job as a postseason commentator at Fox Sports after reporters learned about his relationship with a teenage girl in the 1970s from legal briefs filed in an unnecessary lawsuit he brought against his old nemesis Dowd. Then, with the pandemic shutdown, he lost his gig in Las Vegas and every other signing show. For a while, with the shows not convening, he struggled to make a living in his usual way, like lots of people at the time. He was forced to supplement his income by recording short birthday greetings for people on a newfangled app that a young assistant helped him navigate on his phone, and he was relieved when the autograph shows reopened in 2021 and he could start signing again, though he realized that he couldn't travel across the country as he once had. He couldn't do red-eye flights anymore and didn't like to be gone for days at a time. He was old—old and tired and sitting at a diner in Las Vegas, asking himself questions.

Why am I here? Why am I here?

"I'm fucking eighty," Pete said. "Where'd the time go?"

It's a question that many people who knew Pete in the 1970s or 1980s ask themselves today. Or it's the question that they avoid asking because they feel as if no time has passed at all. They can reach out and touch a moment from forty or fifty years ago, and the memory comes rushing back in like a column of water, flooding them with happiness or anger, nostalgia or regret. With Pete, people usually gravitate to extremes.

Paul Janszen, for starters, would like his fifteen years back. Fifteen years of Pete's fans calling him a liar. Fifteen years of feeling ostracized and criticized in Cincinnati. Fifteen years of being whispered about in the dining rooms of local restaurants while he tried to enjoy quiet meals with Danita. Fifteen years of being blamed for bringing down Pete Rose. "Every night because of Pete's unyielding, narcissistic behavior, I'd hear stories about me on the radio," Paul said. "I was the bad guy because Pete said he didn't do it. I was the blackmailer, the liar."

It left Paul guarded, wary of reporters, and disappointed with humanity in general at times. But he refused to leave Cincinnati, his home. "He didn't run," Dowd said years later with admiration. Paul persevered and came out stronger on the other side, still married to Danita and living in the suburbs of Cincinnati in a house off the circle freeway not far from the old Gold's Gym location. "I weathered the storm," Paul said. "I can survive anything." The same can't be said of Ron Peters.

Alan Statman took his old client golfing shortly after Ron was released from prison in 1991, and Statman thought Ron looked good. He was still young and confident, still handsome, and still one of the best golfers in the tiny town of Franklin. But his job prospects were meager. Ron sold kitchen supplies for a while and hated it. His annual salary, he told Statman, was less than the gambling action he used to have riding on a single game, and it was hard to adjust to the humdrum rhythms of ordinary, everyday life. Depressed and unsatisfied, Ron started using drugs again. He began living beyond his means. He got arrested for stealing from a local Sears, and he traced all his problems back to Pete Rose—"the Pete Rose incident," he called it.

Ron was convinced that if he had never met Pete, he wouldn't have gotten caught for running his sportsbook out of Jonathan's Café. He wouldn't have lost everything. In 1999, he set out to recapture what he once had. Ron said he was moving to Florida, where he hoped to join a country club and start a new bookmaking operation, just as he had done twenty years earlier, and he brazenly announced this plan in an interview with *The Cincinnati Enquirer.*

Ron felt there was no point in trying to hide it. According to him, local and state governments had blurred the line between legal and illegal gambling by running lotteries, selling scratch-off tickets, and building new casinos that were starting to pop up all over the country. Why was the gambling that went on in those casinos legal and his bookmaking not? Why was he the criminal? And who was going to stop him, anyway? He moved to Florida as he promised. But a few years later, authorities picked him up there for failing to pay child support. According to police, he was $45,000 behind in his payments. He was coming back to Ohio, and he was never leaving again. He died there alone in 2016 at the age of fifty-nine. Authorities found his body in his apartment in Warren County after neighbors complained of strange odors. No one had seen Ron in nine days.

"There's going to be illegal gambling from now until the end of time," Ron had said in his final interview with the *Enquirer.* "And I'm going to be part of it," he predicted. Because he was good at it, he said. A smart and dedicated bookie.

"It was everything to me. It was my life."

During this time, Pete met twice with two different baseball commissioners to discuss reinstatement—once in 2002 and again in 2015. But both meetings ended the same way: with no change to Pete's status. He remained exiled from the game and ineligible for the Hall of Fame, and many former players believed it to be the right decision.

Gene Garber, who struck out Pete to end his hitting streak in 1978, said that without the gambling scandal Pete would have been one of the top five players ever admitted into the Hall. But Garber felt he couldn't support Pete's candidacy because Pete knew the rules. They all knew the rules. "Pete played how many years in the big leagues?" Garber asked. "And how many times did he go past a poster in the clubhouse, in the walkways, out to the stadium, that said you cannot bet on your games?" Pete must have seen it thousands of times, Garber said, "time after time after time." It was the wallpaper of their lives and one of the few certainties in the game. Garber knew what would have happened to him, anyway, had he been the one to break the rule: "I would've been suspended from baseball forever."

Fred Lynn, who played against Pete in the epic 1975 World Series, agreed. He remembered not only the signs on the clubhouse doors but the speeches from baseball officials and law enforcement officers every year at spring training about gambling and the dangers it presented to the game. "You could probably commit a lot of other crimes," Lynn said, "but don't bet—that was number one. They didn't want another Black Sox Scandal. They didn't want anybody being able to say, 'This guy fixed a game.' They didn't want organized crime getting in there. So it was very, very specific. Don't do it. We're watching. I got the message right away."

In time, even some of Pete's former teammates turned against him, but there was no consensus. Some fought for Pete. At the Hall of Fame induction ceremony in July 1995, both of the men being honored that day—the former Phillies center fielder Richie Ashburn and third baseman Mike Schmidt—advocated that Pete deserved to stand with them in Cooperstown. "If Rose had been a druggie, he would have been in here," Ashburn told reporters that day. "If he was a drunkard, he would have been in here." And Schmidt, Pete's former teammate in Philadelphia, went even further. He wore a small No. 14 pin in the lapel of his suit coat and argued during his induction speech that Pete belonged in the Hall—a position that played well with the crowd. Officials estimated that twenty-five thousand people were there that day—the largest crowd to ever attend a Hall of Fame induction ceremony at the time—and when Schmidt mentioned Rose's name, many fans stood up and cheered.

"Peeeeete," they chanted. *"We want Pete."*

Schmidt smiled and said nothing for a long beat. A pro, he let the moment breathe, the roar of the crowd filling the warm summer afternoon in the hills of central New York. "Pete stood for winning," Schmidt said finally. "We all know that."

But to his left and to his right in that moment, more than thirty living Hall of Famers didn't cheer. This elite group of men who knew Pete—including Whitey Ford, Stan Musial, Tom Seaver, Reggie Jackson, Steve Carlton, Yogi Berra, Warren Spahn, Bob Feller, and two of Pete's former teammates from the Big Red Machine, Joe Morgan and Johnny Bench—didn't clap at all.

"We want Pete. We want Pete."

"You can have him," Bench muttered under his breath.

63

The problem for Bench—and for baseball—was that there was no outrunning Pete. Somehow, even though he was banned from the game, he still loomed over the sport—never there and always around. "Pete loves two things, wholeheartedly. Two things," said Terry Rubio, his former mistress, who's still alive today in Tampa. "Pete and baseball." He could go away for a while, but Pete always came back, dredging up questions that baseball didn't want to answer and banging on the door to the Hall of Fame—a building that contains his memorabilia but not his plaque. In this way, Pete became like the other stars whom baseball doesn't like to discuss: the steroid users from the 1990s and those linked to performance-enhancing drugs in the early twenty-first century. Most of them can't get into the Hall of Fame, either.

Terry Francona—Pete's former teammate who spent more than forty years in the game as a player and a manager and may one day find himself enshrined in Cooperstown—has reached a point where he believes there should be a compromise. He'd like to see some kind of historical reckoning for Pete and the stars who played during the steroid era. Writers, Francona said, should vote them into the Hall if they believe they are worthy of the honor for their accomplishments on the field, and then the Hall, Francona said, should put the details of the players' choices on their plaques at Cooperstown.

"I know what happened," Francona said in recent years, thinking it over, "and it has certainly cost Pete dearly." But he also knows what he saw in the 1980s playing with and against Pete in his final years. "If Pete's not a Hall of Famer as a player, there isn't one," Francona said. And he believes that when the best players aren't in Cooperstown, it's the fans who lose. Put him in, Francona said, and let the fans debate him until the end of time. Put him in, he said, and let people learn from his mistakes. "Let the fans come to their own conclusions."

In a little house on the West Side of Cincinnati, a house far smaller than the one she lived in decades ago, Karolyn Rose isn't sure if that will ever happen. She's seen Pete in person only a couple times since their divorce in 1980, and she hasn't talked to him in more than forty years. But she sees him on television in her living room every now and then, and she worries about him. "I know that he must be hurting," she says. "Sometimes, he don't look good."

She has told her children, Fawn and Petey, that when he's dying, they are to go to him. She doesn't want him to be alone, she says, and she jokes that maybe she'll go, too. She'll let everyone say their goodbyes. Then she'll throw them all out of the room and tell Pete that he's not getting out of this world until she tells him how she really feels.

"Yeah," Karolyn says again, "I worry about him."

Tommy Gioiosa worries about Pete these days, too. For a long time, he didn't want to think about him, and he definitely didn't want to talk to him. He was angry about how things had ended in Cincinnati, and Tommy's first few months in prison in 1990 didn't make him feel any better. He bounced around to three different facilities, got in a fight behind bars in Oklahoma, and ended up getting shipped across the country to a medium-security federal prison in the woods of northern Pennsylvania. The place was called McKean, and it could easily have fallen apart for Tommy there in the way that things can for young, angry men in prison.

But Tommy decided to focus on himself. He volunteered to work seven days a week in the forestry and landscaping departments at McKean, and he took his own advice. He agreed to tell his personal story—the story of his addictions, addictions to steroids, to fame, and to Pete Rose—to a collection of drug counselor trainees at the prison. The warden, a slender man with warm eyes and an enduring belief that people could change, was impressed by Tommy's talk that day. He thanked him for sharing, and within a few weeks Tommy was receiving passes out of the facility to speak at nearby high schools, colleges, rotary clubs, YMCAs, and chambers of commerce. The rooms at times were small, but the crowds were huge—200 students, 500 students, 750 teachers and students—and people were moved by what Tommy had to say. They wrote to him in prison afterward to tell him that he was saving lives. "I want you to know that you certainly touched at least two unsuspecting worthwhile teenage boys with your openness," one mother wrote to Tommy in 1990. "I thank God for men like you. You are truly one of the TOUGH GUYS!"

With letters like these—and others from associate wardens and correctional counselors praising him—Tommy won early release in late 1992, after just two and a half years behind bars. He resettled in Florida, got a job as a distributor at Herbalife, opened his own smoothie and nutrition bar near the beach, earned enough money to buy a beautiful house on the water, forgave everyone who testified against him during his trial in Cincinnati, and finally reconnected with Pete in a chance meeting at the Mandalay Bay casino in Las Vegas. Pete was signing autographs that day roped off from a crowd and Tommy was walking by when suddenly the two old friends were face-to-face.

For a moment, Tommy felt the anger rise up inside him again. He was going to punch Pete Rose. He was going back to prison. He was going to make a mistake in front of the crowd inside the casino that would cost him everything. But then Tommy felt the anger wash away. Pete smiled, put his hand out, and invited him to sit down, and Tommy recognized that times had changed, that *he* had changed. "I used to want to be Pete," he said. Now he realized he was good just being Tommy.

He sat there for a while as Pete signed, and signed, and signed.

64

IN LATE 2021, with COVID deaths declining, the vaccination rate rising, and pandemic restrictions lifted in most places, Pete got back out on the road again for autograph shows and signed as much as he ever had before—in Nashville, Chicago, Jacksonville, Philadelphia, and Cincinnati. He returned to his hometown for multiple events, trying to make up for the year he had lost and working with a new sense of urgency because time was running short.

He thought a lot about dying—every day, Pete told friends—and he wanted to make sure he had enough money to leave to his children and their children, his grandkids, after he was gone. Over lunch one day in Las Vegas, at a restaurant where he knows everyone and has nicknames for his favorite servers, Pete calculated that his banishment had cost him roughly $100 million since 1990, between lost earnings as a manager and lost sponsorship deals.

He wasn't looking for sympathy; Pete knew it was his fault. But it did seem to him like a big price to pay, too much, and the more he thought about it sitting at his table in the restaurant, the more frustrated he got, gesturing at people around the dining room as he talked. "I didn't hurt you," Pete said over a glass of orange juice. "I didn't hurt her. I didn't hurt him. I hurt me. I hurt my family. And for guys to say, 'He hasn't been punished enough'—well, what's enough? Thirty-one years and $100 million? That's not enough? Come on. The guy who shot the pope got out."

Why hadn't he been forgiven? he wondered. Why couldn't he get a second chance? "I fucked up—I know," Pete said. "But enough is enough. . . . What do they want? To cut my fucking arms off?" In his mind, baseball had already cut off everything else: his access to the game, his contact with players, his ability to earn a living, and his connection to one of the only things he ever truly loved. "I don't know if anybody knows more about baseball than me," he said, "yet I can't be a part of it. I can't help somebody become a better player. . . . And 99 percent of people have no idea how being suspended for thirty-one years has affected me mentally.

"Drives me crazy," he said. "Drives me crazy."

He was pretty sure that in the end he wouldn't even be able to have the funeral that he wanted, the wake that he sometimes imagined. He liked to picture himself being laid out in a casket at home plate in the Reds' new stadium in Cincinnati, with thousands of people paying a small fee to file past his body and all the money going to Knothole baseball, the youth baseball league where Pete got his start on the West Side decades ago.

"I think that would be interesting," Pete said, "and I think a lot of people would show up. You'd have to think that a full house would show up. That's thirty-seven thousand people. That's almost a million bucks to Knothole baseball. Just for me laying out there in a casket." It probably wasn't possible—he knew that. By late 2021, the Reds, like Major League Baseball, kept their distance from Pete Rose, due to all the public relations problems that he caused. But if Pete had to think about dying, he liked to think about it this way, and he was convinced that the money—the mourners' donations—had to go to his old youth baseball league. "Who else would I give it to?" he said. "Gambling Anonymous? I mean, what the fuck?"

It was no longer lunchtime at the restaurant by then. Pete had sat at the table for so long that he was on his second or third glass of orange juice, and it was almost dinner. The crowd in the once-busy dining room had thinned out to a few customers sitting at a handful of lonely tables scattered around the room, and at this point the people who were still there couldn't resist the urge anymore: they started to approach Pete. They didn't want his autograph. They just wanted him to know that they recognized him, that they knew him, that they had seen him play once decades ago, that they had cheered for him then with their children, or their fathers, or their first husbands, and that they still cheered for him now.

One customer wept as he spoke to Pete, overcome with emotion, and another customer lingered. She was a redheaded woman in her sixties, and she seemed to be flirting with Pete. She said she knew he liked to gamble, but she preferred to remember him from something else. "From what your profession used to be," she said.

"Well, what did my profession used to be?" Pete asked.

"You used your hands," the woman said, "used your arms."

"Used my feet?" Pete asked.

"Sometimes, if you had to."

"Used my elbows when I slid?"

"Could've done that, too."

This went on for a couple of minutes until Pete and the woman finally downshifted into small talk. They discussed what it was like to live in Las Vegas, and how it was better than living in Los Angeles, and how he had fared against her team, the Dodgers, and Sandy Koufax, a baseball Immortal whom the woman had watched play when she was a child.

"Koufax," Pete muttered. "Don't mention him. He was tough."

Pete had struggled against Koufax. But the woman didn't mind.

"You were good," she assured him. "You still are."

"Well," Pete said, after a while, "you have a good day."

"You, too," the woman said, smiling.

She walked away. Pete sighed, and then he called out for his favorite server, a young woman. "Pee-wee!" he shouted, using his nickname for her. He wanted more orange juice.

"That fucking orange juice is good today," Pete said.

At his autograph shows across the country late that year, Pete replayed a version of that restaurant conversation with fans who had driven hundreds of miles to see him, people from three states away, or admirers who had waited their whole lives for this moment. In October 2021, fans took pictures with Pete at a new casino that he helped christen in downtown Cincinnati, and two months later, in December, a huge crowd lined up to get his autograph at a memorabilia store in a strip mall in the suburbs, not far from the old Gold's Gym location where it all unraveled on Pete decades ago.

Pete took a seat in the back of the room that night, and for the next few hours people gave him things to sign: baseball cards, bats, jerseys, hats, treasured photos, cereal boxes, action figures, street signs, childhood lamps, and even body parts. A young woman from Detroit in cat-eye glasses and a green cardigan leaned over Pete's table, rolled up her sleeve, presented him with the inside of her left forearm, and mustered up the courage to make her request. "I'm so nervous," she said, "my mouth is so dry." She asked Pete to sign his name carefully and slowly just beneath the crook of her elbow. Her father, she said, had been Pete's biggest fan. He had died a few years earlier, and this was a gift in his honor. She was leaving the store, she said, and heading straight for a tattoo parlor to get Pete Rose's signature etched on her arm forever.

Pete smiled at the woman and did as he was told, signing and signing to keep the line moving and the people happy. They had paid $59 to get in the door and claim a signature—more if they wanted special inscriptions—and Pete wanted to be perfect for them. He selected the right pen for each item. He urged people to be careful with his freshly inked signatures—"Don't smear it," he said, "don't smear it"—and he told stories to fill the silence while he signed photos of himself as a young man standing next to Johnny Bench or playing at Crosley Field.

"I loved Crosley Field," he said. "I was at the last game at Crosley."

Among professional collectors there's an inside joke. Pete has signed so much over the years, they say, that if an item has been signed by him, it's worth less than it would be without his signature. It's not true, of course. "I hate to even say it," one collector said. He knew he could take anything that Pete signed for $59 that night and sell it for even more. It's just that Pete is so prolific, and unlike other players, who set limitations on what they'll do, Pete will sign anything, anytime, at any show: World Series flags, bottles of wine, bleacher seats, posters.

"You know, when I was a senior in high school," he told one man that night while he signed, "I played in the Dayton amateur league. Every Tuesday and every Thursday."

"You made lots of errors," the man recalled.

"No, I didn't," Pete said, laughing. "My errors were off the field."

Outside, in the parking lot, it was dark and cold, and there was evidence that the little strip mall in the suburbs had seen better days. The *A* in the green illuminated sign for the Dollar Tree next door had blinked out. But fans kept coming to the memorabilia store, five hundred people before the night was through, and none of them cared about what the mall looked like, what Pete had done in the past, or whether he had apologized the right way years ago. They knew how he felt because he signed it that night. He put it on their baseballs and on their photographs. Again and again, he picked up one of his pens, and he wrote six simple words.

They were words that once upon a time could have changed his life; words that, if he had spoken them to Bart Giamatti in New York, could have earned him sympathy; words that, if he had uttered them sooner and with sincerity, could have gotten him into the Hall of Fame decades ago; words that could have put him back on the field; and words that by his own calculation could have saved him $100 million. Now, however, they were just that: words. And they came cheap. For an extra $35 fee that night, Pete wrote them as a special inscription right above his signature, and then he moved on to the next town to write them there, too. He signs the same inscription night after night and day after day, at show after show and in town after town. He signs it and he signs it until he cannot sign it anymore.

"I'm sorry I bet on baseball," he writes.

"I'm sorry I bet on baseball."

"I'm sorry . . ."

ACKNOWLEDGMENTS

Anyone who loves sports loves a sports argument. Pete Rose is the ultimate one, and I am grateful to all the people who discussed the details of his life with me—the wins, the losses, the man, the mistakes—starting with Pete Rose himself.

Pete had never spoken to an author writing a biography about him, unless he had some sort of editorial control over the project. That changed with this book. He began granting interviews to me in September 2021, first on the phone and then in person, and he gave generously of his time for a while—even though he knew this was a work of journalism and history that he could not bend to his liking. I spent three days with him in Las Vegas and one full day with him at an event in Cincinnati later that year. After that event, Pete stopped returning my calls, for reasons he never explained—though maybe, in hindsight, he did. "We're talking about the dark days of my life now," he said in one of our last interviews. Apparently, he didn't want to do that. I appreciate the time that we did have together.

I must also thank many former baseball officials and ballplayers, people who knew Pete well, including Larry Bowa, Bernie Carbo, Norm Charlton, Dave Collins, Rob Dibble, Dan Driessen, Doug Flynn, George Foster, John Franco, Terry Francona, Gene Garber, Tommy Helms, Keith Hernandez, Davey Johnson, Bill Lee, Mike Lum, Fred Lynn, Sam McDowell, Dave Parker, Tony Pérez, Mickey Rivers, Nolan Ryan, Art Shamsky, Tim Teufel, Luis Tiant, and Don Werner; the Reds' former longtime broadcaster, Marty Brennaman, who met with me inside his home; the Reds' former general manager Murray Cook, who spoke to me on multiple occasions; the

Reds' former traveling secretary, Dan Lunetta; Bob Howsam's son Robert Jr. and Robert's wife, Sara; two former Expos staffers, Ron McClain and Bryan Greenberg; the former umpire Dave Pallone; Ray Fosse's wife, Carol; the former spokesman for Major League Baseball in the 1980s, Rich Levin; multiple journalists who once covered Rose, including Peter Gammons, Wes Hills, Dennis Janson, Jerry Kirshenbaum, Hal McCoy, Craig Neff, Sandy Padwe, Dan Shaughnessy, Samantha Stevenson, Robert Sullivan, and Willie Weinbaum; and team officials across the league, including Rob Butcher and Phil Castellini of the Cincinnati Reds, Jay Horwitz and Harold Kaufman of the New York Mets, Bonnie Clark and Deborah Nocito of the Philadelphia Phillies, Pam Kenn of the Boston Red Sox, Bart Swain of the Cleveland Guardians, Jason Zillo of the New York Yankees, Gene Dias of the Houston Astros, and Matt Bourne in the league office. Finally, I was fortunate enough to interview two former commissioners of baseball who had to wrestle with the problem of Pete Rose. Bud Selig spoke to me in 2023, and Fay Vincent talked with me at length on several occasions. Without all their help, this book isn't possible.

But since much of this story happened off the field, I am also indebted to people who helped me re-create that world, too—through interviews and primary-source documents. I must thank for starters the man who investigated Pete Rose in the 1980s: John Dowd. His memories and his documents were critical to rebuilding what happened. I must also thank others who investigated Pete—Joe Daly, Kevin Hallinan, and Jayme Gentile; Pete's only surviving sibling, Dave Rose; Pete's oldest child, Fawn; and Pete's first wife, Karolyn, who invited me into her West Side home on two occasions; Pete's longtime mistress, Terry Rubio Fernandez, who spoke to me multiple times from her home in Florida; Pete's friends Mike Bertolini, Jerry Carroll, Bob Czerwinski, Walt Harmon, Jimmy Jones, Arnie Metz, Harry Panaro, Jeff Ruby, Carl Witsken, and Chuck Zimmerman; the family of Art Luebbe, including his sister Jan Wiethorn and his son Tom; the longtime Cincinnatians Pat Donovan, John McMichen, Jinny Sander, and Ed Thompson; the oldest child of Al Esselman, Jackie Esselman Frey; Ron Peters's lawyers, Alan Statman and Dave Chicarelli; Peters's former friends Randy Bluhm, Keith Sexton, and Jeff Woodward; the former Massachusetts State Police troopers Jim Murray and Dick Rand, who busted Pete's bookie Joe Cambra in the 1980s; Mickey DeVise, the reference librarian at the Cincinnati Museum Center's Library and Archives; Ed Rivera, in the clerk's office at the federal courthouse in Columbus, Ohio, who ordered case files for me and allowed me to spend days in his office reviewing them; Daniel Neeley, the librarian at Western Hills High School, who shared school archives with me; the research assistants Joe Capozzi, Patrick Geshan, and Melinda Miller, who helped me gather material along the way in Florida, New York, and Ohio; and three of the men who placed Pete Rose's bets on baseball: Mike Bertolini, Paul Janszen, and Tommy Gioiosa.

During research for this book, I interviewed Bertolini by phone for hours and had the chance to meet both Paul and Tommy in person, talking with them at length about their time with Pete in the 1970s and 1980s. All three confirmed certain things for me, especially Tommy, who answered every question I had, anytime I called, and shared personal scrapbooks with me from his many years with Pete.

Lastly, I am grateful as always to my own team: my wife, Eva; my boys, Mac and Cal; my parents, Keith and Terry; my agent, Richard Abate; my editor, Maria Goldverg, who brought this book to life; my publisher, Lisa Lucas, who saw the value in this story from the start; everyone at Pantheon, including Michiko Clark, Lisa Kwan, Nora Reichard, and Amelia Zalcman; the people who read over my shoulder along the way, Jeff Goldscher, Tom Haines, and James O'Byrne; Jim Tobin, for his unflinching feedback and advice; and Andrew Bauer, who read early drafts of this book in the way they were meant to be read. He read them as a baseball fan.

It's the way I always saw this book and the way I hope you see it, too, because there's nothing quite like a baseball story. Like Bart Giamatti once said, we all want the chance to leave and to return home.

NOTES

Abbreviations Used in Notes

Newspapers

AC	*Atlanta Constitution*
BG	*Boston Globe*
CE	*Cincinnati Enquirer*
CP	*Cincinnati Post*
DDN	*Dayton Daily News*
DJH	*Dayton Journal Herald*
GT	*Geneva (N.Y.) Times*
LAT	*Los Angeles Times*
NYDN	*New York Daily News*
NYT	*New York Times*
PDN	*Philadelphia Daily News*
PI	*Philadelphia Inquirer*
RDC	*Rochester (N.Y.) Democrat and Chronicle*
SI	*Sports Illustrated*
SN	*Sporting News*
TT	*Tampa Tribune*

Books

MP	*My Prison Without Bars,* by Pete Rose with Rick Hill
PRMS	*Pete Rose: My Story,* by Pete Rose and Roger Kahn
PRS	*The Pete Rose Story: An Autobiography,* by Pete Rose

Epigraph

vii "Anyone who would": "Numbers Don't Tell Full Story," *CE,* Sept. 12, 1985.

vii "He can't run": "Pete's Passage," *PI,* Dec. 5, 1978.

vii "But this is a Pete Rose story": Gioiosa, interviews with author, Oct. 28 and Nov. 4 and 15, 2021.

Introduction

4 twenty-five million children: "Put Me In, Coach: Youth Baseball Participation on the Rise," *USA Today,* Aug. 23, 2019.

4 sixteen thousand men: Frank Labombarda, the head of research at the Elias Sports Bureau, was incredibly helpful to the author for the book. This stat and others listed below come from him and the Elias Sports Bureau.

4 "And again the flashbulbs go off": WLW radio broadcast, Sept. 11, 1985.

4 "It's a slider inside": WLWT television broadcast with announcers Ken Wilson and Joe Morgan, Sept. 11, 1985.

4 "This is his game": Ibid.

7 fans in America wagered: In 2022, according to the American Gaming Association, legal sports betting brought in $93 billion—a figure that was briefly a record until 2023's totals surpassed it. In the first quarter of 2023 alone, Americans legally wagered more than $31 billion on sports. "Commercial Gaming Revenue Tracker," American Gaming Association, May 16, 2023.

7 could have pooled: In March 2023, *Forbes* published a story with the valuations for each team, which, when combined, would be worth about $70 billion dollars. "Baseball's Most Valuable Teams 2023," *Forbes,* March 23, 2023.

8 "I don't know": "4,192: Pete Singles Past Ty Cobb," *CE,* Sept. 12, 1985.

1

11 Pete was about twelve: Rose, interview with author, Sept. 20, 2021.

11 thirty-five cents for automobiles: "Ferryboats," *CE,* July 20, 1952.

11 Mr. Kottmyer knew what he was doing: "Circle Bridges Doom Ferries, but Owners Are Philosophical," *CE,* Sept. 3, 1962.

11 Pete liked riding: Rose, interview with author, Sept. 20, 2021.

11 The two-story clapboard house: According to the Hamilton County Auditor, Rose's childhood home was built in 1886 and had just six rooms.

11 Pete shared a bedroom: Rose, interview with author, Sept. 20, 2021.

12 Sometimes, outside Schulte's, Pete gambled: Walt Harmon (Pete Rose's childhood friend), interview with author, Dec. 13, 2021.

12 a singular intensity: Ibid.

13 "99 and 44/100 percent pure": P&G made this claim in advertisements for the soap.

13 neighborhood of machinists: Details about the residents of the neighborhood, where they worked, and what they did come from U.S. Census records for Anderson Ferry during Rose's childhood years, 1940 and 1950.

2

13 According to the story: Both Harry and Pete Rose told this story over the years to explain why the father went as Pete.

13 Big Pete's parents had divorced: Sometime between 1910 and 1913, Harry's mother, Eva, Pete's paternal grandmother, divorced her first husband, Otto Rose, who himself was a railroad man. Then, on July 9, 1913, she got remarried to Harry Sams. In the 1913 marriage record for Harry Sams and Eva Rose, Eva lists herself as being "a divorced woman." Hamilton County marriage license No. 273.

13 a railroad worker: U.S. Census records for Harry Sams, 1920.

13 competing under the name Pete Sams: Details of Harry Rose's brief fighting career come from multiple sources, including "Benzinger on Rainbow Card," *CP,* May 28, 1929; "Cleveland Boys Win Four State Titles," *CP,* April 3, 1930; "Ring Comedian Wins Decision," *CP,* Feb. 13, 1930; "Huff and M'Murty Draw," *CP,* May 6, 1930; "Attractive Fistic Card," *CE,* May 30, 1930; and "Payne Wins Fight by Wide Margin," *CP,* July 10, 1930.

14 often placed side bets: Tom Zimmer, interview with author, May 17, 2022.

14 "Let's show them": Details from his television appearance come from a retrospective story on Harry Rose's life that appeared in *The Cincinnati Post.* "Pete the First, a Man Called Smash," *CP,* Dec. 10, 1970.

15 married a young German girl: Dearborn County (Ind.) Clerk of Courts, marriage license for Harry Rose and Laverne Bloebaum, Feb. 24, 1934.

15 Tareyton cigarettes: Rose, interview with author, Sept. 24, 2021.

15 a whole mess of Bloebaums: U.S. Census records for Laverne's father, Edward H. Bloebaum, 1930.

15 $1,400 a year: U.S. Census records for Harry Rose, 1940.

15 eyeglasses: Rose, interview with author, Sept. 20, 2021.

16 Laverne had to take work: Ibid.

16 Big Pete was obsessed: Details about Harry Rose's obsession with Pete's greatness come from multiple sources, including *PRS,* 40; *MP,* 17; *PRMS,* 70; Rose, interview with author, Sept. 20, 2021; "One Rose as Good as the Next One," *CP,* April 5, 1963; and "The Mom at Home Base," *CE,* May 12, 1985.

16 another boy, Dave: Dave Rose was bigger and stronger than Pete and a promising baseball prospect, too. But their father sometimes went out of his way to denigrate Dave and diminish his potential. "One Rose as Good as the Next One," *CP,* April 5, 1963, and "Charlie Hustle Gives Twelve Dimes on the Dollar," *SI,* May, 27, 1968.

16 always one of the smallest: Team photos and home video from this time show that Pete barely reached the shoulders of some of his teammates during his childhood. Additional details come from interviews the author conducted with people who knew Rose when he was a boy, including Carl Witsken, Walt Harmon, Harry Panaro, and Bob Czerwinski.

16 Pete's teammates remembered seeing him: Harmon, interview with author, Dec. 13, 2021; Witsken, interview with author, May 23, 2022; and Tom Luebbe, interview with author, May 27, 2022.

17 afternoons at the track: Pete Rose, interview with author, Oct. 18, 2021; Dave Rose, interview with author, Feb. 4, 2022; Tom Zimmer (son of childhood friend and future major-league player and manager Don Zimmer), interview with author, May 17, 2022; *MP,* 28.

3

17 always asking for money: Rose, interview with author, Oct. 20, 2021.

17 almost three thousand: "Senior High Leads Enrollment," *Western Breeze,* Oct. 8, 1958.

17 The kids descended: These surnames come straight out of the *Western Hills Annual* yearbooks during the time that Rose attended school there.

18 "Pow Wow": These events were regularly featured in both the city and the school newspapers including "Pow Wow Today," *CE,* Nov. 21, 1956; and "Annual Pow Wow Heightens Spirit," *Western Breeze,* Nov. 26, 1958.

18 tailback, punt returner, and placekicker: Rose, interview with author, Sept. 20, 2021.

18 didn't even want to be seen: Harry Panaro (Pete's former classmate), interviews with author, Oct. 21, 2021, and May 23, 2022.

18 He enjoyed geography: Rose, interview with author, Sept. 20, 2021.

19 "I don't think so": Ibid.

19 A regional manager for a coupon company: "Knot Hole Baseball," *CP,* May 10, 1956.

19 bound for a baseball scholarship: "Local Athletes Return," *CE,* March 30, 1963.

19 a future electrician: "Marriage Licenses," *CE,* Nov. 25, 1970.

19 Art Luebbe: Details about Art Luebbe come from the St. Xavier High School yearbook, 1959, and interviews the author conducted with two of his surviving relatives—Art's sister, Jan Wiethorn, June 7, 2022, and Art's son, Tom Luebbe, May 20, 2022, who provided not only memories of Art playing with Pete but photos and old videos of the boys when they were young.

19 The Witsken twins: Witsken, interview with author, May 28, 2022.

19 the Stamps were a juggernaut: Details of the Green Stamps epic summer come from interviews with former players and their family members, including Witsken, Luebbe, and Wiethorn, as well as the following newspaper stories about the team: "Knot Hole Baseball," *CP,* June 13, 1956; "Knot Hole Baseball," *CP,* July 11, 1956; "Knot Hole Baseball," *CP,* Aug. 1, 1956; "Finals Are Gained by S&H, Solomons in Class A Series," *CE,* Aug. 12, 1956; "Triple Header Set at Deer Creek Park," *CE,* Aug. 17, 1956; "Pitching Is Big Factor," *CE,* Aug. 19, 1956; "Cincinnati Captures Three Titles in National Knot Hole Tourney," *CE,* Aug. 27, 1956; "Knot Hole Titles Go to Locals," *CP,* Aug. 27, 1956.

20 big, goofy grin: Green Stamps team video, shot by Art's father in the summer of 1956, courtesy of Jan Wiethorn and Tom Luebbe.

20 The Green Stamps named Pete: "They're Captains," *CP,* Oct. 19, 1956.

20 especially, it seemed, with each other: Rose, interview with author, Sept. 21, 2021.

20 He had been cut: Ibid.; *PRMS,* 48; *PRS,* 47.

4

21 Both the father and the son: Rose, interviews with author, Sept. 20 and 21, 2021.

21 one of the greatest seasons: Details about the 1957 West High football season come from multiple sources, including the *Western Hills Annual,* 1958; *The Western Breeze,* the West High student newspaper; *The Cincinnati Enquirer; The Cincinnati Post;* and Panaro, interview with author, May 23, 2022.

21 "The winner of": "Elder–Western Hills Play for City Title Today," *CE,* Nov. 22, 1956.

22 Victory Dance: "Wonderful West Hi . . . ," *CP,* Nov. 10, 1956.

22 "Pow Wow": "Pow Wow Today," *CE,* Nov. 21, 1956.

22 *"This is my school!": CP,* Nov. 10, 1956.

22 eleven thousand people: "Western Hills Decisions Elder, 20–13," *CE,* Nov. 23, 1960.

22 Harry Panaro smuggled him: Panaro, interviews with author, Oct. 21, 2021, and May 23, 2022.

22 like a screwdriver: Rose, interview with author, Sept. 20, 2021.

22 "Fuck school": Ibid.

22 Without football: Rose has talked extensively over the decades about what happened to him during his sophomore year, including with the author in 2021. Rose, interviews with author, Sept. 20 and 21, 2021. Additional details can be found in *PRS,* 47; *MP,* 20; and Pete Rose, *Play Hungry: The Making of a Baseball Player* (New York: Penguin Press, 2019), 39.

22 among the first to notice: Panaro, interviews with author, Oct. 21, 2021, and May 23, 2022.

23 to talk about their wayward son: *PRS,* 49.

23 might just drop out: *PRMS,* 79.

23 stopped listening to his father: Rose, interview with author, Sept. 21, 2021.

23 Jimmy Schlank: Details about Rose's boxing trainer come from multiple sources, including—Pete Rose, interview with author, Sept. 21, 2021; Harmon, interview with author, Dec. 13, 2021; Dave Rose, interview with author, Feb. 4, 2022; "Twenty-Four Bouts Staged in Golden Gloves Finals," *CE,* Feb. 20, 1936; "Ohio's Joe Louis Chaser," *CP,* Feb. 26, 1936; "Disputed Decision Eliminates Schlank," *CP,* Feb. 27, 1936; "Post Glove King Makes Debut in Pro Division," *CP,* June 2, 1936; and "Feud Flares Again," *CE,* July 12, 1937.

24 didn't care much: Rose, interview with author, Sept. 20, 2021.

24 "A swimming pool": Rose, interview with author, Sept. 21, 2021.

24 "fight your fight": Ibid.

24 Virgil Cole: Details about Cole, his life, and his fight against Rose come from multiple sources including Pete Rose, interview with author, Sept. 21, 2021; Harmon, interview with author, Dec. 13, 2021; Dave Rose, interview with author, Feb. 4, 2022; Eugene Cole (Virgil Cole's younger brother), interview with author, June 2, 2022; Virginia Cole (Virgil Cole's wife), interview with author, June 2, 2022; "Amateur Boxing," *CE,* April 11, 1957; "Virgil Cole

Made His Name as a Young Boxer," *CE,* Dec. 25, 2003; "Rose a Proud Papa?," *DDN,* May 21, 1977; "Rose the Boxer? It's an Old Story, Really," *CP,* May 23, 1977; and Rose's autobiographies, namely *PRMS* and *MP.*

25 "They're killing him": *PRMS,* 72.

25 "He's not getting hurt": Ibid.

25 "He Once Bested Pete Rose": "Virgil Cole made his name as a young boxer," *CE,* Dec. 25, 2003.

25 "Champ": Virginia Cole, interview with author, June 2, 2022.

26 "He couldn't knock me out": Different versions of this quotation have appeared over the years, but the general gist of the story has remained the same. *PRMS,* 73; *MP,* 15.

5

26 batting leadoff: "Mustangs Stopped in First Round," *Western Breeze,* May 15, 1958.

26 around the Fourth of July: "No-Hitter Fired by Postal Hurler," *CE,* July 3, 1958.

26 wearing No. 55: *Western Hills Annual,* 1959.

26 Pete scored touchdowns: Details about Rose's feats on the football field in the fall of 1958 come from four sources: *Western Hills Annual,* 1959; *The Western Breeze,* the West High student newspaper; *The Cincinnati Enquirer;* and *The Cincinnati Post.*

27 starting second baseman: *Western Hills Annual,* 1959.

27 Griesser got the credit: "Griesser Leads Western over Elder, 31–14," *CE,* Nov. 28, 1958.

27 Charlie Schott was voted: "Schott Takes Honors at Banquet," *Western Breeze,* June 11, 1959.

27 would soon sign Brinkman: News accounts varied on the exact amount of his contract, but details can be found in multiple sources, including "Sport Sparks," *CE,* Jan. 24, 1961; "$65,000 Offered for Eddie Brinkman," *CP,* May 19, 1961; and "Brinkman Inks Senators' Pact," *CE,* May 24, 1961.

27 "Watch Brinkman go": "Baseball and Butterflies Mix Well for Brinkman, Pro," *Okmulgee (Okla.) Daily Times,* April 10, 1964.

28 "Too small": "Glory Days: Pete Rose's Competitive Drive Always There," *CE,* June 25, 2016.

28 He suited up: "Feldhaus Football League Champions," *CE,* Dec. 5, 1959.

6

28 Buddy was a full decade older: Details about Bloebaum's age and jobs come from U.S. Census records for Bloebaum between 1920 and 1950; news stories of his career, including "Cue Champion Booked," *CE,* Feb. 28, 1932, and "Scouts' Shouts Bring Kids Out," *DDN,* May 15, 1957; and Rose, interview with author, Sept. 21, 2021.

28 Duckworth Democrats: "Harmony Lines Up Talent," *CP,* April 18, 1931.
29 "making plays of the sensational variety": "Another Win," *CE,* Aug. 3, 1931.
29 the Bunnies struggled to compete: "Cedar Rapids Fans Get Final Warning," *Akron Beacon Journal,* June 18, 1932.
29 injured his leg: The details about Bloebaum's leg injury differ depending on the newspaper. But the general account can be found in multiple sources, including "Islanders Beat Peoria, 5–0, Before 1,600 in Opening Game," *Rock Island (Ill.) Argus,* May 15, 1933; "Baseball Chatter About Islanders," *Rock Island (Ill.) Argus,* May 16, 1933; "Sport Trail," *Rock Island (Ill.) Argus,* May 27, 1933.
29 The next time: "Solway Team Strengthened," *CP,* July 7, 1933; "Third Game Carded," *CE,* July 30, 1933.
29 "seventy-five times as brilliant": "Equipment at Bunny Park Is Very Latest," *Cedar Rapids Gazette,* June 8, 1931.
29 He batted .285: "Averages for Valley League Ballplayers," *Davenport (Iowa) Quad-City Times,* Sept. 4, 1932.
29 thirty points lower: Ibid.
30 To find young talent: "Reds Set Clinic, Tryout Camp," *DDN,* June 24, 1952.
30 the Reds appointed Seghi: "Phil Seghi to Redlegs' Front Office," *Green Bay (Wis.) Press-Gazette,* April 7, 1958.
30 Uncle Buddy directed him: Rose, interview with author, Sept. 21, 2021.
31 starting to develop a philosophy: The best summary of Rose's hitting philosophy can be found in his 1985 book with Peter Golenbock, *Pete Rose on Hitting.* The book is hard to find these days, and the copy the author obtained was the version on tape, courtesy of the son of the former Reds general manager Bob Howsam, Robert Jr., and his wife, Sara.
31 "See the ball": Rose, interview with author, Oct. 20, 2021.
31 "Punch-and-Judy hitter": Two other baseball prospects in the Reds' system were familiar with how Seghi felt about Rose at that time: Panaro, interview with author, and Czerwinski, interview with author, Oct. 21, 2021.
31 In recent months, Seghi had signed: "$100,000 Bonus Given Youth, 18," *CE,* April 2, 1959; *Fresno Bee,* April 3, 1959; "Brosnan Added, Jeffcoat Departs," *CE,* June 9, 1959; "Redlegs Aiming High with Bonus Players," *Ithaca (N.Y.) Journal,* Jan. 4, 1960.
31 $15,000 contract: "8 Geneva Players Invited to Workouts for Early Training," *RDC,* Jan. 29, 1960.
32 "Ron has the equipment": "Flender in First Minor Test," *CE,* July 8, 1959.
32 twenty-nine points higher: "AA Star Rose in Finale Tomorrow," *DDN,* June 21, 1960.
32 June 16, 1960: "Rose, Moore Had Big Hitting Week," *DDN,* June 19, 1960.
32 shirked his scouting duties: In his son's 1970 memoir, *PRS,* Pete Rose Sr. recounts that it was a Friday night, and Uncle Buddy was supposed to be in Piqua, Ohio. This is consistent with a news account from that time. "Reds Slate 4 Tryout Camps," *CE,* May 29, 1960.
32 Crosley Field: *PRS,* 64; Czerwinski, interview with author, Oct. 21, 2021.
32 $7,000: *PRS,* 65.

33 began to negotiate: Ibid.
33 Several scouts were attending: "'59 Bat Leaders Lagging Behind in Amateur Play," *DJH,* June 21, 1960.
33 there was a rumor: *PRS,* 65.
33 "Goodbye, seven thousand dollars": Ibid., 66.
33 "I'd like to sign": Ibid., 66.
33 "I want to go right now": Ibid., 67.
33 considered playing another game: *DDN,* June 21, 1960.
33 On the flight to New York: Over the course of decades, this memory remains consistent for Rose. The details about Rose's flight come from two places: *PRS,* 67; and Rose, interviews with author, Sept. 20 and 21, 2021.

7

37 shedding minor-league teams: "NY-P May Have Only 6 Teams in 1960," *GT,* Jan. 25, 1960.
37 didn't even have a real stadium: Details about Shuron Park come from multiple places: Minor Myers Jr. and Dorothy Ebersole, "Baseball in Geneva," Geneva Historical Society, 1988; "Showers May Mar Redlegs' Opener with Auburn Tonight," *GT,* April 30, 1960; "Baseball Continues to Strike Out in New York," *GT,* March 14, 1960; and interviews with three former Redlegs players who played there at the time, Harry Panaro, Art Shamsky, and Pete Rose.
37 "We want baseball": "Geneva Track Coach Envisions Good Year," *RDC,* April 13, 1958.
37 ended with a fire: "Fire Strikes Shuron Park," *RDC,* Aug. 31, 1959; "Ball Club Makes Request for City Help at Shuron," *GT,* Jan. 29, 1960.
37 edge of bankruptcy: "Ex–Redleg Owner Files Bankruptcy," *GT,* April 14, 1960.
38 a car broke down: "Several Redlegs Stranded; Most of Club Has Arrived," *GT,* April 22, 1960.
38 wasn't anywhere near ready: "Work Begins on Shuron Park," *GT,* April 8, 1960; "Shuron Not Ready—Redlegs Are Homeless," *GT,* April 23, 1960.
38 On the cusp of opening day: *GT,* April 23, 1960.
38 "It's Fun to Be a Fan!": Advertisement, *GT,* April 8, 1960.
38 Paid attendance: "Redleg Fans Get Money's Worth in High Scoring Opener," *GT,* May 3, 1960.
38 sportswriters joked: "Bad Weather, Lack of Fans Threatens Salvation of NY-P," *GT,* May 23, 1960.
38 nearly $10,000 in debt: "Cincinnati Reds Send Funds, Redlegs Continue," *GT,* June 30, 1960.
38 The average home attendance: *GT,* May 23, 1960.
38 might have to disband: Ibid.
38 Players booted: Details about the lackluster performance of the Geneva Redlegs come from multiple stories in *The Geneva Times* in the spring of 1960, including May 4, 6, 8, 13, 19, and 23, and June 4, 7, 17, and 20.

39 He sent a check: *GT,* June 30, 1960.
39 "We are doing all we can": "Redlegs Help Geneva with Money, Players," *RDC,* July 1, 1960.
39 Seghi had run the math: "In the Press Box," *State* (Columbia, S.C.), May 13, 1960.

8

39 the stewardess on the plane: *PRS,* 67.
39 The plane landed in Rochester: According to *The Geneva Times,* Rose arrived in town on Friday, June 24. "Redlegs Take Fourth Place as Paul Wins 2–1 Squeaker," *GT,* June 25, 1960.
40 "I'm your new second baseman": "The Rose Legend Began Quietly in Geneva, N.Y.," Associated Press, Sept. 10, 1985.
40 Lefty Venuti had other plans: Ibid.
40 dispatched him to a hotel: Ibid.; *PRS,* 70.
40 lots of reinforcements coming: *GT,* June 25, 1960.
40 didn't speak English: Rose, interview with author, Sept. 22, 2021; Pérez, interview with author, Nov. 29, 2021.
40 a town called Violeta: Pérez, interview with author, Nov. 29, 2021; "A Look at the Real 'Pearl of the Antilles,'" *CE,* Sept. 21, 1986.
41 For $2.50: *CE,* Sept. 21, 1986.
41 life was hard: Pérez, interview with author, Nov. 29, 2021; *CE,* Sept. 21, 1986.
41 started the season: Details of Pérez's performance in the field come from newspaper coverage that spring, including "Redlegs Impress Except in Baserunning in 13 Inning Loss," *GT,* May 2, 1960; "Perez Single Saves Redlegs from Going Hitless," *GT,* May 4, 1960; "Redlegs Host Leading Erie," *RDC,* May 22, 1960; "More or Less About Sports," *Wellsville (N.Y.) Daily Reporter,* May 24, 1960; and "Morera's First Hit of Series a Grand Slam in Redleg Win," *GT,* May 31, 1960.
41 fell into a slump: "Only Two Redlegs Hitting Better Than .300 Now," *GT,* June 24, 1960.
41 dipped below .300: "Redlegs Averages," Ibid., June 24, 1960.
42 At the plate: "Redlegs, Doval Face NY-P's Top Winning Hurler Tonight," Ibid., June 27, 1960.
42 .234: "Redlegs Averages," Ibid., July 14, 1960.
42 Big Pete watched: *PRS,* 74.
43 rented a room: *PRS,* 71; Associated Press, Sept. 10, 1985; Rose, interview with author, Sept. 22, 1960.
43 Sherman McGuire: In interviews with the author and his 1970 autobiography, Rose said he knew the man only as Mr. McGuire. But his full name appeared in an Associated Press story on Sept. 10, 1985. Further details come from the 1960 Geneva City Directory and the 1950 U.S. Census records for T. Sherman McGuire, 15 Copeland Avenue, Geneva.
43 Cubans on the team yelling: *PRS,* 71.
43 going to be famous: Associated Press, Sept. 10, 1985.

43 "Rose is an aggressive": *GT,* June 27, 1960.
43 last place: "NY-P League Standings," Ibid., July 30, 1960.
44 "we'll die by the wayside": *GT,* June 30, 1960.
44 traveled all the way: "Seghi Coming to Watch Redlegs Who Bow to Braves, 4–2," *GT,* July 16, 1960.
44 The visit was well timed: "Redlegs Lose Twice Before Largest Crowd of Season," *GT,* July 19, 1960.
44 He publicly called out: "Discouraged Farm Director Speaks—DeBenedetti to Play but No Other Help Seen for Redlegs," *GT,* July 19, 1960.
44 just .207: Ibid.
44 "It's hard to believe": Ibid.
44 Seghi picked up the phone: "Reno DeBenedetti Fired at Geneva," *RDC,* Aug. 20, 1960.
44 In the Reds' estimation: *PRS,* 78.
44 a respectable finish: "Unofficial Redleg Averages," *GT,* Sept. 8, 1960.
45 "a fiery youngster": "Pete Rose Most Popular," *GT,* Sept. 6, 1960.
45 one play in particular: "Redlegs Win First Twin Bill Since June 5," *GT,* Aug. 1, 1960.
45 most popular player: *GT,* Sept. 6, 1960.

9

46 The Redlegs players scattered: "Redlegs Head for College, Jobs After Finishing with 6–5 Win in 11 Innings," *GT,* Sept. 7, 1960.
46 sporting goods: Ibid.
46 hired to work in the rail yards: "Red Rookie Rose Highly Touted," *CP,* Nov. 29, 1961; Rose, interview with author, Sept. 22, 2022.
46 It didn't pay much: Ibid.
46 difficult work, even dangerous: "Suits Filed," *CE,* March 6, 1960; "Tractor Rolls from Loading Dock, Kills Man," *CE,* April 24, 1960.
46 had a clear view: Rose, interview with author, Sept. 22, 2022.
47 training bat: Dave Rose, interview with author, Feb. 4, 2022.
47 "I'm swinging": Ibid.
47 wasn't clear that the Tarpons: "The Tarpons and Tampa," *Tampa Times,* March 22, 1961.
47 the warmer weather: *PRS,* 80.
48 Flender barely recognized: "Only 25 Years Ago, Rookie Named Rose Reported to Minors," *CE,* June 22, 1985.
48 Pete was now listed: "Roster of the 1961 Tampa Tarpons," *Tampa Times,* April 18, 1961.
48 less enthused: "'New' Tarpons Set for Game Tonight," *Tampa Times,* April 17, 1961; "Optimism Rules as Tarps Ready for FSL Opener," *Tampa Times,* April 18, 1961.
49 "Sure, I could use": *Tampa Times,* April 18, 1961.
49 a cavernous ballpark: "City Has Al Lopez Field Ready for Chicago Team," *TT,* Feb. 5, 1954; *Tampa Times,* April 18, 1961.

49 "We will be hustling": *Tampa Times,* April 18, 1961.

49 lonely, lost: *PRS,* 79; *PRMS,* 96; and *Play Hungry,* 73.

49 on opening night: "Tarps Serve FSL Notice They Should Be Tough," *Tampa Times,* April 20, 1961.

50 "the Toast of the Tarpons": "Slugger Pete Rose Is Toast of Tarpons," *Tampa Times,* May 2, 1961.

50 two would-be triples: "Tarps Belt Saints Twice 5–1, 7–3 on Rose's Power," *TT,* June 11, 1961.

50 crowds exceeding: Box score, *TT,* Aug. 28, 1961.

50 broke even: "Mac Loses Money but Not Here," *TT,* Sept. 9, 1963.

50 Zippo lighters: Rose, interview with author, Sept. 23, 2021.

51 thought him a "hot dog": *CE,* June 22, 1985; *PRS,* 85.

51 swinging in his underwear: "From Minors to Majors, Rose Still Goes at It Head First," *DDN,* Sept. 12, 1985.

51 "Excellent habits": "Pete Rose Looks Good," *CE,* Nov. 28, 1961.

10

52 a comfortable routine: *Play Hungry,* 85.

52 frequented a tavern: The establishment, called Jimmy White's La Concha Bar, had a long history of narcotics, underaged drinking, and even murder. The owner, Jimmy White, shot and killed his girlfriend just a few years before Pete came to Tampa.

52 They could trade: "Pete Rose Looks Good," *CE,* Nov. 28, 1961.

52 risen to prominence: "'Dreams Come True' for Luther Williams in Bank," *Macon News,* Oct. 31, 1928.

52 complained about the smell: "Eliminate Smell of the Pulp Mill," *Macon News,* Oct. 18, 1962.

52 dreaded the haze: Art Shamsky, interview with author, June 27, 2022.

52 YMCA: Rose, interview with author, Sept. 23, 2021; Shamsky, interview with author, June 27, 2022.

52 The son of a cotton mill worker: Clyde Helms, U.S. Census records, 1950; Clyde Helms obituary, *Charlotte News,* March 3, 1965.

52 he thought he was good enough: "Helms on Slow Boat to Majors, but Redlegs Want It That Way," *Charlotte Observer,* May 22, 1962.

53 "I don't know about that": "A Rose Grew in Macon," *Macon Telegraph,* April 7, 1963.

53 Sometimes, in the dugout: *PRS,* 85.

53 barroom brawl: "Bristol Lists Batting Order for Peaches," *Macon Telegraph,* April 11, 1962.

53 induce pain: "Training the Bristol Way," *Macon News,* March 21, 1963.

53 He timed Pete running: *Macon Telegraph,* April 11, 1962.

53 32–5: "Peaches Humiliate Dodgers, 32–5," Ibid., April 25, 1962.

53 He liked Pete: Tommy Helms, interview with author, Oct. 21, 2021.

53 "Makin' Out": *MP,* 44.

53 once to break the monotony: *CE,* June 22, 1985; *PRMS,* 100; *PRS,* 91; Shamsky, interview with author, June 27, 2022; and Rose, interview with author, Sept. 23, 2021.
54 broke curfew: Rose, interview with author, Sept. 23, 2021.
53 "prettiest girls": *MP,* 44.
53 persuaded a teammate: Ibid.
54 a new Corvette: Rose, Helms, and others have recounted this story in multiple places over the years, including "Only 25 Years Ago, Rookie Named Rose Reported to Minors," *CE,* June 22, 1985; *PRMS,* 99; *PRS,* 91; Dave Rose, interview with author, Feb. 4, 2022; and Pete Rose, interview with author, Sept. 23, 2021.
54 Helms held out: "Ex-Peaches Going Strong," *Macon Telegraph,* March 8, 1963.
54 "Friendship League": "Warm Farewell for the Blazer from Ex-mates, Friends," *St. Louis Post-Dispatch,* Feb. 9, 1960.
55 The Blazer was in trouble: "Reds Plug Pete Rose," *DDN,* Oct. 12, 1961.
55 Beat writers loved Hutchinson: Details about Fred Hutchinson come from multiple sources, including "Hutch on Rookies, Kids, Rummy," *St. Louis Post-Dispatch,* Jan. 8, 1964; "Baseball Mourns Fred Hutchinson" and "Hutch Was a Great One," *Des Moines Register,* Nov. 13, 1964; "Fiery Hutchinson Loses Fight Against Cancer" and "You Think of Hutch—and Dam Breaks with Flood of Memories," *SN,* Nov. 28, 1964; and Pete Rose, interview with author, Sept. 23, 2021.
55 "If I had any guts": "Hustle Puts Rose on Second," *CP,* April 8, 1963.

11

56 Hutch hesitated: "Chisox Ruin Reds' Debut, 1–0," *CE,* March 10, 1963.
56 On the bench: Details about this game against the White Sox come from multiple sources, including "Reds Go 14 Innings to Nip Chisox, 1–0," *CE,* March 11, 1963; "Reds Nip White Sox to End Famine, 1–0," *TT,* March 11, 1963; "Rookies, Old Vets Star in Reds' Win," *Tampa Times,* March 11, 1963; "Rose Starts Reds' Winning Rally," *CP,* March 11, 1963; "White Sox Lose in 14th, 1–0," *Chicago Tribune,* March 11, 1963; and *PRMS,* 106.
56 first chance at the plate: "Harper Gets Extra Batting," *CP,* March 12, 1963.
57 "How 'bout that?": "Brash Kid Rose Can Use Needle Along with Bat," *SN,* March 23, 1963.
57 his old nickname: *TT,* March 11, 1963.
57 Earl Lawson sat up: Details about Earl Lawson come from multiple sources, including World War II draft card for Earl Mountjoy Lawson, No. 1247; World War II Army Enlistment Records, enlistment date of Jan. 18, 1943; retirement coverage for Lawson in 1984 including "The Dream Finally Ends," *CP,* Sept. 29, 1984; "After 34 Years of Writing Reds, Lawson's Advice Still Good," *CE,* Oct. 1, 1984; his obituary, "Lawson Was Hall of Fame Writer," *Sacramento Bee,* Jan. 16, 2003; and Lawson's memoir, *Cincinnati Seasons.*

58 Scoops didn't think: "Lawson Says Reds Are Not Hustling," *CP,* June 18, 1962.
58 "I'm sick and tired": "Pinson Pokes Post Sportswriter," *CE,* June 21, 1962.
58 "Hustle is young Pete's middle name": *CP,* March 12, 1963.
58 "the kid is a real hustler": *Macon Telegraph,* April 7, 1963.
58 He was brash and young: "Brash Kid Rose Can Use Needle Along with Bat," *SN,* March 23, 1963.
58 "I'm going to take a real good look": "Rose Slated for Thorough Trial," *SN,* March 15, 1963.
59 flocked to see: In 1962, the Yankees drew about 1.4 million fans at home, second highest in the majors, and a record 2.2 million fans on the road.
58 fans began buying: "Yanks vs. Reds Here," *TT,* March 17, 1963.
58 Eight thousand people: "Largest Lopez Field Crowd Views Reds," *TT,* March 18, 1963.
58 Pete's father: "Reds' Clutch Hitting Subdues Yanks," *CE,* March 18, 1963.
59 scaled light posts: *TT,* March 18, 1963.
59 wasted no time: Accounts of this game can be found in multiple sources on March 18, 1963, including "Reds' Clutch Hitting Subdues Yanks," *CE;* "Heavier Post Is Hitting," *CP;* "Reds Use Power to Top Champs," *TT;* and "Yanks Suffer Gloomy St. Pat's Day; Lose," *Fort Lauderdale News.*
60 "is the type of player": *CP,* March 18, 1963.
60 worn a sundress: Mantle, *Mick,* 93; "Just Kidding, Pete," *NYT,* July 12, 1985.
60 Henry Hustle: *DDN,* April 8, 1963.
60 Charlie Hustler: *Macon News,* March 21, 1963.
60 Mantle and Ford: The story of the nickname's origin was reported in multiple newspapers at the time and again many times over the years, including *Macon News,* March 21, 1963; "Charlie Hustle Still Around," *DDN,* March 31, 1963; "Rose Getting Through Test," *CP,* April 1, 1963; "Dayton's Bloebaum Bird-Dogged Nephew Pete Rose for Cincinnati," *DDN,* April 8, 1963; "Ruby's Report," *Louisville Courier-Journal,* April 9, 1963; "Rookie Rose Silenced Cincy's Skeptics," *SN,* Oct. 26, 1963; "As He Looks to Record, Rose Looks Back at Cobb," *NYT,* July 22, 1985; and "Rose Plays the Odds for Admission to Hall of Fame," *NYT,* Jan. 6, 2004.
60 "The Mick gave it to me": "A Rose Called Scooter Is Now 'Charley Hustle,'" *TT,* Aug. 18, 1963.

12

61 "Peanut Jim" Shelton: "Enquirer Throwback: Peanut Jim," *CE,* May 19, 2016.
61 this parade included: "We'll Win 1963 Flag, Reds Declare," *CP,* April 8, 1963, and other local coverage.
61 57-0: Including exhibition games, the Red Stockings won sixty-four games in 1869. They also recorded one tie, though it was a disputed game. The Troy Haymakers walked away from the field in the middle of the game, angry over an umpire call.

61 They defeated: Scores of these blowouts come from local coverage in the various towns, including *Wisconsin State Journal,* July 31, 1869; *New Orleans Times-Picayune,* Aug. 27, 1869; *CE,* Sept. 1, 1869; and *Harrisburg (Pa.) Telegraph,* Sept. 16, 1889.

61 he'd rather run: Lee Allen, *The Cincinnati Reds* (New York: Putnam, 1948), 5.

62 overnight train: "Hutch Says Reds NL Team to Beat," *TT,* April 4, 1963; "Reds Tip Mets, 5–0; Begin Journey North," *CE,* April 4, 1963.

62 "I deserve this chance": *Macon Telegraph,* April 7, 1963.

62 Hutch still wasn't sure: "Psychologist Hutch Has Rose Sleep in Hotel Opener Eve," *DDN,* April 9, 1963.

62 a circus that was already starting: "For Rose It's All a Dream," *CE,* April 9, 1963.

62 Before the train: "Reds Nip Chicago, 3–2; Pitching Good," *CE,* April 6, 1963.

62 knocking on the door: *CP,* April 5, 1963.

63 Hutch gave Pete the news: "Reds Keep Rose, Dayton Sandlotter in '60," *DDN,* April 7, 1963.

63 "Go home and see your folks": *DDN,* April 9, 1963.

13

63 Blasingame had seen it coming: Interviews with Don Blasingame and Gordy Coleman, "Reds Official History," MI-97-102, Moving Image Index, Cincinnati History Library and Archives, Cincinnati Museum Center.

63 "You've got a chance": *DDN,* April 9, 1963.

63 less gracious: The details about how Rose was received by his teammates appear in multiple places over the years, including "Reds Official History," MI-97-102; "ESPN SportsCentury—Pete Rose," MI-12-14, Moving Image Index, Cincinnati History Library and Archives; "Living Life by the Numbers," *Time,* July 10, 1989; and *PRMS,* 108.

64 reframe this moment: *PRMS,* 108; *Play Hungry,* 112; and Rose, interview with author, Sept. 20, 2021.

64 performed in blackface: Evidence of the school plays performed in blackface can be found in the *Western Hills High School Annual* yearbooks during the years that Rose attended school there, 1956–1960. Kids wore blackface in the productions of *You Can't Take It with You* and the *Dixieland Drag* show, among others.

64 "The Negro players": "Young Ideas," *NYDN,* Sept. 8, 1963.

64 Robinson was furious: Frank Robinson, *My Life Is Baseball* (New York: Doubleday, 1968), 153.

64 "just nonsense": Ibid., 154.

65 Black players spoke warmly: Some of Rose's biggest defenders over the years were his Black teammates in Cincinnati, including Joe Morgan, Ken Griffey, and George Foster.

65 watermelons and short ribs: "Did you hear the one about the . . . ?," *PI,* July 31, 1978.

65 Pete was different: George Foster, interview with author, March 13, 2023.

65 The day dawned cool: Details of opening day 1963 come from multiple sources, including "Cloudy and Mild," *CE,* April 8, 1963; "We'll Win 1963 Flag, Reds Declare," *CP,* April 8, 1963; "Rhodes, Rose, Billboards New to Fans," *CE,* April 9, 1963; "O'Toole Hurls Reds Past Pittsburgh, 5–2," *CE,* April 9, 1963; "Cloudy, Cooler," *CE,* April 9, 1963; "Psychologist Hutch Has Rose Sleep In Hotel Opener Eve," *DDN,* April 9, 1963; "'Off to Good Start,' O'Toole Says, After He Realizes A Goal," *DJH,* April 9, 1963; Dave Rose, interview with author. Feb. 4, 2022; and Pete Rose, interview with author, Sept. 23, 2021.

65 Laverne made sure: A photograph, staged by the Reds, captured the Rose family that day. "Rose Through the Years," *CE,* April 15, 2015.

66 weep for the memory: Dave Rose, interview with author, Feb. 4, 2022.

66 a single twinge of anxiety: "Reds' Rookies Not Nervous," *CP,* April 9, 1963.

66 "I'm starting": Pete Rose, interview with author, Sept. 23, 2021.

66 "I saw the pitch": *CP,* April 9, 1963.

67 2 for 23: "Three's a Crowd on Bench—Freese, Harper, and Rose," *DDN,* April 17, 1963.

67 reporters speculated: "Reds Leave on Road Trip; California via Pittsburgh," *DJH,* April 19, 1963.

67 the Blazer did no better: In the starting lineup during this stretch, Blasingame was 4 for 23.

67 "Trot 'em on out": "Hutch Starts Over with Freese, Rose, and Harper," *DDN,* April 27, 1963.

67 "Rose will replace": Ibid.

67 he hadn't sulked: "Hutch Hitches Wagon to Reds' DP Duo as Stars of Tomorrow," *SN,* May 25, 1963.

67 Pete batted .338: "Robinson Wants More Maloney," *DDN,* May 16, 1963.

67 Then .403: "Tsitouris' 3rd Victorious Route Job Lands Reds in 3rd Place Tie," *CE,* June 23, 1963.

68 "The kid": "Luck Finally with Reds? Winning Despite 'Leaks,'" *CE,* May 21, 1963.

68 the Reds sold Don Blasingame: "Reds Get Neal, Taylor from Mets," *CE,* July 2, 1963.

68 Nankai Hawks: "Don Blasingame, Veteran Infielder, Dies at 73," *NYT,* April 16, 2005.

68 Pete was just getting started: *SN,* May 25, 1963.

68 Rookie of the Year: *TT,* Aug. 18, 1963.

68 Jaguar E-Type: "They Helped," *CE,* May 9, 1963.

68 Pontiac Grand Prix: "Those Buses Cost," *CE,* May 13, 1963.

68 Sometimes that summer: Karolyn Rose, interview with author, Dec. 2, 2021; Pete Rose, interview with author, Sept. 23, 2021; "Pete's a Rose in Wife's Book," *Fort Worth Star-Telegram,* Aug. 3, 1978.

14

69 Karolyn Ann Engelhardt: Over the years, Karolyn Rose gave almost as many interviews as her husband. Details in this section come from the author's interviews with her in her home on Dec. 2 and 3, 2021, as well as the following sources: "Crazy Whirlwind? It's Krazy Karolyn," *Miami Herald,* Feb. 25, 1976; Parr, *Superwives,* 89; "Superwives: 'Big Momma' Makes Charlie Hustle," *CP,* June 14, 1976; archival television news footage featuring Karolyn and held at the Cincinnati History Library and Archives; and a series of first-person stories written by Karolyn, with help from the *Indianapolis Star* reporter Fred D. Cavinder, titled "Bed of Roses" and published in *The Cincinnati Post* in February 1979. Karolyn said at the time that these stories were excerpts from her forthcoming memoir. The book was never published.

69 Her father, Fritz: Details about Karolyn's heritage come from multiple primary source documents, including U.S. citizenship application for Fred Engelhardt, Jan. 2, 1940, and the ship manifest for the SS *Columbus,* arriving in New York City on April 17, 1926. It lists Fritz Engelhardt as having $25.

70 Miss Extrovert: Our Lady of Angels school yearbook, *Amaranth,* 1960.

70 her three dream jobs: Karolyn Rose, interview with author, Dec. 2, 2021; "The Not-So-Private Life of Pro Baseball's 'Supercouple,'" *Miami Herald,* Dec. 17, 1978.

70 The airlines refused to hire: Karolyn Rose, interview with author, Dec. 2, 2021.

70 one quality: Ibid.; *PRMS,* 114.

70 He was in the lobby: Karolyn Rose, "Bed of Roses."

71 Karolyn remembered: Karolyn Rose, interview with author, Dec. 2, 2021.

71 She didn't worry: *Miami Herald,* Feb. 25, 1976.

71 always punctual: Anyone who has ever spent any time with Pete Rose knows that he is dedicated to two things: working hard and showing up on time. "My dad," he told the author, "was the most punctual guy I've ever seen."

71 Once, on a date: Karolyn Rose, interview with author, Dec. 2, 2021.

71 report to basic training: Details come from multiple sources, including "Pete Rose on K.P. When He Gets Good News," *CE,* Nov. 27, 1963; "Pete Rose at Fort Knox Throws Hand Grenades," *CP,* Dec. 26, 1963; and *PRS,* 117.

71 Some teammates were shocked: "ESPN SportsCentury—Pete Rose," interview with former Reds pitcher Jim O'Toole, MI-12-14, Moving Image Index, Cincinnati History Library and Archives.

72 "Because nobody else": *A.M. Cincinnati,* interview with Karolyn Rose and her mother, Bena, April 9, 1976, MI-97-102, Moving Image Index, Cincinnati History Library and Archives.

72 "You're supposed to be": *CP,* Dec. 26, 1963.

72 "Are we married yet?": *Superwives,* 94.

72 "I'm not a singles man": "McKechnie Draws Cheers at Baseball Dinner Here," *CE,* Jan. 26, 1964.

72 his own wedding reception: *CP,* June 14, 1976.

15

73 Karolyn had to return: Karolyn Rose, interview with author, Dec. 2, 2021.
73 "bat girls": "Goodbye to the Reds," *TT,* April 10, 1963.
73 they were moving up: Details about the International Inn come from coverage in the *Tampa Tribune,* including "Tampa Inn on Schedule," May 28, 1961; "Fernand Lacoste New Head Chef International Inn," Dec. 13, 1964; "Tallest in Town," Dec. 24, 1963; and advertisement, Feb. 24, 1964.
73 beautiful hostesses: "International," *TT,* Dec. 3, 1963; "Three More," *TT,* Dec. 6, 1963.
73 She sat by herself: "Spouses Behind Baseball Scene," *Tampa Times,* April 8, 1964.
74 Phil Seghi lowballed him: "Rose, 2 Others Come to Terms," *CE,* Feb. 29, 1964; *CE,* Oct. 1, 1984.
74 "good money": "Rose Wants to Be Best," *CE,* Aug. 24, 1963.
74 sophomore jinx: "No 'Sophomore Jinx' for Cincinnati's Rose," *TT,* March 17, 1963; "Pete Laughs Off 'Jinx,'" *CE,* March 22, 1964.
74 a terrible April: "Reds Help Johnson Make History by Taking No-Hitter," *DDN,* April 24, 1964; "Finger Pad Keeps Robby in Game," *DDN,* April 26, 1964; "Rose's Fielding Damaging," *DDN,* April 20, 1964; "Rose Fades; Klaus Makes Most of It," *DDN,* June 15, 1964.
74 He batted .183: "Lou Smith's Notes," *CE,* July 29, 1964.
74 Coaches fought: "Otero, Temple Tangle in Clubhouse Fight," *CE,* Aug. 29, 1964.
74 2-for-28 tailspin: "Rose Is Benched Again," *CE,* Aug. 16, 1964.
75 They needed six outs: Details of this game, and the aftermath, come from the news coverage of the game in both Cincinnati and Philadelphia as well as other sources, including "Did Cardenas Put a Match to Phils' Gas Tank?," *DDN,* Oct. 3, 1964; "Reds Blow 3-Run Lead, Lose to Phils," *CE,* Oct. 3, 1964; "Reds Muff Chance to Regain First Place," *CP,* Oct. 3, 1964; "It's Not Over Yet—Phils Rally, Nip Reds, 4–3," *PI,* Oct. 3, 1964; "Weird Is the Word: But There's Still Some Life in Phillies," *PDN,* Oct. 3, 1964; "Cardenas Mastered Baseball; Now, Life Is a Different Story," *CE,* Oct. 27, 2002; and Frank Robinson's memoir, *My Life Is Baseball,* 161.
75 "Cárdenas learned fifty more words": "Waite Hoyt Interviews, 1964," MI-96-159, Moving Image Index, Cincinnati History Library and Archives.
75 like a weapon: "O'Toole Tabs Red Pilot Sisler as 20-Victory Omen," *SN,* Nov. 21, 1964.
75 "You say I miss the ball": Robinson, *My Life Is Baseball,* 161.
76 Lots of guys: "Venezuela Rosters," *SN,* Oct. 31, 1964.
76 The baby, a girl: "Reds' Rose Papa for First Time," *CE,* Dec. 30, 1964.
76 attic space: Karolyn Rose, interview with author, Dec. 2, 2021.
77 Caracas fans turned on Pete: "Sparky Given Gate; Steered Navigators into Fog of Defeats," *SN,* Dec. 5, 1964; "Pete Rose Fined," *CP,* Nov. 30, 1964.
77 "Those people": "Latins Carry Guns at Ball Games," *CP,* Dec. 22, 1964.

77 didn't even mention: "A Rose Is a Rose, but Pete's Grown Up Now," *TT,* March 10, 1965.

77 He ended up batting .351: "Venezuelan Vanguard (Final Averages)," *SN,* Feb. 20, 1965.

77 "I know I'm a better ballplayer": *TT,* March 10, 1965.

77 when he was arrested: Details of Robinson's arrest in 1961, and the fallout from it, come from multiple news accounts and personal remembrances, including Robinson, *My Life Is Baseball,* 114–17; Lawson, *Cincinnati Seasons,* 153–54; Lawson's jailhouse interview, written on deadline in 1961, "Robinson Arrested on Weapons Charge," *CP,* Feb. 9, 1961; "Frank Robinson Is Bound to Jury on Gun Charge," *CP,* Feb. 17, 1961; and "Reds' Robinson Stands Mute, Waives Gun Case to Grand Jury," *CE,* Feb. 18, 1971.

78 "That's an awfully big bat": "Rose Calls Robby Reds' Best Ever," *DJH,* Dec. 10, 1965.

78 part Choctaw: Bench declined to be interviewed for this book. Details about his indigenous roots come from genealogical research conducted by the author on Bench's grandfather Clay Bench. Choctaw Nation, Choctaw Roll, Field No. 274, Dawe's Roll No. 585, Clay Bench. Other details about Bench's life, his career, and his relationship with Pete Rose come from interviews the author conducted with reporters and broadcasters who covered Bench; memoirs written by Joe Morgan and Bob Howsam; Bench's own words in interviews he gave in the 1970s and 1980s; an oral history with Johnny Bench, conducted by the Oklahoma Historical Society, Voices of Oklahoma project, in 2012; and Bench's memoir, *From Behind the Plate.*

79 Howsam loved Pete Rose: Bob Howsam, the longtime executive for the Cincinnati Reds, died in 2008. To understand how he felt about Pete, the author relied on three sources: voluminous press accounts over the years in which Howsam spoke about Rose; an interview with Bob's son Robert Jr. and his wife, Sara, in 2022; and Bob Howsam's unpublished memoir, *My Life in Sports,* written with Bob Jones in 1999 and shared with the author by Robert Jr. and Sara. This work was an invaluable resource.

16

79 pan for gold: Details about Howsam's childhood and early life come from Howsam's *My Life in Sports,* 19; U.S. Census records for his father, Lee Wilfred Howsam, 1920 and 1930; and Lee Howsam's petition for U.S. citizenship, filed Nov. 29, 1922.

80 "the wholesome theatrical aspect": Howsam, *My Life in Sports,* 119.

80 "Attention Baseball Fans": Advertisement, *CE,* Oct. 22, 1965.

80 never be able to shake: Details about the night of the plane crash come from Rose, interview with author, Oct. 1, 2021, and the voluminous press accounts of the accident.

81 "I could see it": Rose, interview with author, Sept. 28, 2021.

81 moved out: To describe the apartment and the move, the author relied on the following: Karolyn Rose, interview with author, Dec. 2, 2021; Pete Rose,

interview with author, Sept. 24, 2021; Cincinnati City Directories from the late 1960s; and a visit to the Hilltop Garden apartment complex in June 2022, where the author received a tour of an apartment that was identical to Pete and Karolyn's from a current resident.

81 It stood like a towering lamp: There aren't many pictures of Rose's life inside this apartment, but one appeared in *The Cincinnati Enquirer* on March 2, 1968. In it, the trophy is standing in the corner of the little room.

82 could carpool: Shamsky, interview with author, June 27, 2022.

82 "Get me straight": "100 Grand Pete's Goal," *TT,* May 17, 1968.

82 Willie Mays money: According to UPI, in the spring of 1968 only eight players in the majors earned more than $100,000: Hank Aaron, Roberto Clemente, Don Drysdale, Juan Marichal, Mickey Mantle, Willie Mays, Frank Robinson, and Carl Yastrzemski.

82 one of the two most exciting: According to Bill Ford, a columnist for *The Cincinnati Enquirer,* Rose made this comment during contract negotiations before the 1968 season. But Ford didn't write about it until almost seven months later, and Rose denied the comment. "All-American Rose," *TT,* Aug. 26, 1968; "'Pete Rose Day' Proposed," *CE,* Aug. 29, 1968.

83 "He *is* the most exciting": These positive quotations come from multiple columns in 1968, including "Reds Conspiring Against Rose by Eliminating Moon People," *DDN,* Feb. 14; "Big Men Raise Pay Level," *DDN,* March 7; "100 Grand Pete's Goal," *Tampa Times,* May 17; "McCool Sent Home, Nolan's Arm Hurting," *DDN,* July 30; and *CE,* Aug. 29.

84 "We can't get him out": "Bench's One-Handed Tag Dazzles Leo Durocher," *DDN,* July 13, 1968.

17

84 cover of *Sports Illustrated:* "Charlie Hustle Gives Twelve Dimes on the Dollar," *SI,* May 27, 1968.

85 Ford cried: "Ford Puts Away Yank Pinstripes," *NYDN,* May 31, 1968.

85 A local clothier: "Pinson Ailing, Lineup Changed," *DDN,* June 29, 1968.

85 A hairline fracture: "Pete's Thumb Broken," *CE,* July 7, 1968.

86 took no joy: Fawn Rose, interview with author, Feb. 2, 2002.

86 "go-go spirit": *SI,* May 27, 1968. It wasn't the first time that Big Pete complained about his son Dave to the press. In an interview with a *Cincinnati Post* reporter in 1963, he called Dave lazy.

86 he had to win: "Pressurized Pete Gets His Title," *DDN,* Sept. 30, 1968.

86 For the next two games: "What Rose Needs Is Mays; Elixir," *DDN,* Sept. 28, 1968; *DDN,* Sept. 30, 1968; Lawson, *Cincinnati Seasons,* 186.

87 Pete stayed up late: Details of Rose winning the batting title come from multiple sources, including "Rose Batting Champ (.335)," *CE,* Sept. 30, 1968; "Rose Beats Out Alou for Title," *CP,* Sept. 30, 1968; "Rose Wins Batting Championship" and "He Survived the Strain," *DJH,* Sept. 30, 1968; *DDN,* Sept. 30, 1968; and "Swat King Rose Handled Pressure Like a Champion," *SN,* Oct. 12, 1968.

88 Pete Rose was everywhere: Details of Rose's whirlwind life after the 1968 season come from multiple sources, including "The Wrong Move," *Tampa Times,* Nov. 6, 1968; "Rose Is All Hustle, Even as Spectator," *TT,* Nov. 6, 1968; "Pete's Busy on Banquet Trail," *CP,* Jan. 3, 1969; MacGregor advertisement, *CE,* March 2, 1969; Gatorade advertisement, *CE,* Aug. 13, 1969; and Hyde Park Clothes advertisement, *CE,* Oct. 9, 1970.

88 Karolyn was pregnant again: "Six Extra Incentives," *DDN,* April 3, 1969.

88 The one they ultimately chose: Hamilton County Auditor, property record, 6142 Oakhaven Drive, Cincinnati.

88 28 percent: "Baseball Falls Behind Football in Fan Appeal," *Miami Herald,* April 14, 1969, and "Baseball Yields To Football," *SN,* May 3, 1969.

89 were alarmed: "Kuhn's Wit Sharp, Newsmen Discover in a Frisco Interview," *SN,* May 3, 1969.

89 more people had watched: "Football's Second Century Hits High Gear Tomorrow," *Chicago Tribune,* Sept. 19, 1969.

89 $10 million for the privilege: "Up, Up, and Away Goes N.L. Entry Fee," *SN,* May 25, 1968.

89 a record $37 million: "The Diamond Sparkles with Dollars, Divisions, and Drum-Beating," *Television Age,* Feb. 10, 1969.

90 unconstitutional and un-American: "Reserve Clause Next Target, Says Players' Lawyer," *DDN,* Feb. 22, 1969.

90 on the last day of the season: Details of the final day, Rose's fear of losing to Clemente, and his decision to bunt can be found in the game coverage, including "Reds, Rose Win in Finale," *CE,* Oct. 3, 1969.

90 The governor of Ohio: "Pete Rose Day to Be Nov. 1," *CP,* Oct. 7, 1969.

90 Karolyn gave birth to a son: "Pete Rose's Wife Has a Son," *CE,* Nov. 18, 1969.

90 Pete struggled to win over: "Thieves Steal Bags of Garbage," *CE,* Jan. 26, 1970.

18

91 triple-headers: The term comes from Pete's longtime friend and gambling partner Arnie Metz, interview with author, Oct. 22, 2021. The process was also described in detail by the longtime broadcaster Al Michaels, who was with the Reds in the early 1970s, before becoming a national broadcasting voice. See Michaels, *You Can't Make This Up,* 52–53.

91 Cancha Club: "Jai Alai Fans Praise Cancha Club Dinners," *TT,* Jan. 6, 1973.

91 "a citadel of conservatism": Howsam, *My Life in Sports,* 119.

92 workers at the betting windows: The author interviewed two people who worked at the racetrack during this time, the betting window worker Pat Donovan and the usher John McMichen, who would later coach Pete Jr. when he was in high school. Both recounted Rose's activities at the track.

92 official complaints: "The Private Life of Pete Rose," *DJH,* June 17, 1970.

92 "Stay home": Ibid.

92 good at playing down: In almost every feature that was ever written about her, Karolyn downplayed her disappointment or made light of it with self-

deprecating humor, including the first story that was ever written about her. "Pete Rose? Well, Who's He?," *DDN,* April 11, 1968.

92 on the road: Karolyn spoke about her jealousy and her concerns about what Pete was doing on the road in multiple places over the years, including her unpublished memoir, excerpted by *The Cincinnati Post,* "Bed of Roses," Feb. 12, 1979; a lengthy interview on *A.M. Cincinnati* in April 1976, MI-94-14, Moving Image Index, Cincinnati History Library and Archives; and Karolyn Rose, interview with author, Dec. 2, 2021.

93 "like it was on fire": Karolyn Rose, "Bed of Roses."

93 he forgot that he had sent: "Sorry About That, Honey," *DDN,* March 29, 1968.

93 his shortcomings: Howsam, *My Life in Sports,* 176.

93 "Our biggest concern": Jim Bouton with Leonard Shecter, *Ball Four: My Life and Hard Times Throwing the Knuckleball in the Big Leagues* (New York: World Publishing Company, 1970), 446.

94 hated the decision: Details about the hiring of Sparky Anderson and his personal biography come from multiple sources, including "Sparky Given Gate; Steered Navigators into Fog of Defeats," *SN,* Dec. 5, 1964; "Sparky's Bringing Seasonin' to Season," *CE,* Oct. 10, 1969; "'My Conscience Is Clear'—Bob Howsam," *CP,* Oct. 10, 1969; and Sparky Anderson, *They Call Me Sparky,* with Dan Ewald (Chelsea, Minn.: Sleeping Bear Press, 1998), 85. In the book, Sparky writes about the time he grabbed an umpire around his throat, an incident confirmed by the author in one of the local newspapers at the time. "Today, No Joy in Mudville: Lusty Sparky Is Thrown Out," *Rock Hill (S.C.) Evening Herald,* May 12, 1965.

94 up to $105,000: "Rose's $100,000-Plus Salary Vindicates a Team and a City," *DDN,* March 1, 1970.

95 "99 percent Black": Curt Flood oral history, Black Champions collection, University Libraries, Washington University in St. Louis.

95 "Really powerful men": Ibid.

95 "I don't understand": Dick Young column, *NYDN,* March 14, 1970.

95 the foundation of the sport: "MONEY—Sums Up Ballplayers' Demands," *CP,* Dec. 17, 1969.

95 "Curt Flood should get down": "Give Thanks Curt—Howsam," *CP,* Jan. 24, 1970.

95 angry letters: A sampling of these letters can be found in *The Sporting News* in 1970. "Curt Flooded with Letters, Many Critical," *PI,* Jan. 25, 1970.

95 Willie Mays snorted: "Full Support of Players Not Behind Curt Flood," *DDN,* Jan. 25, 1970.

96 publicly announced his opposition: "Yaz to Challenge Association's Approval in Flood Case," *BG,* Jan. 18, 1970.

96 "I think Curt's a helluva outfielder": "Rose to Get over $100,000," *CP,* Jan. 13, 1970.

96 support tweaking: "Smoking the Hot Stove," *CE,* Feb. 18, 1970.

96 figured there were three: "Seaver Makes Mets History: 80G," *NYDN,* Feb. 14, 1970.

96 "Like when is his birthday?": "Catcher's Single, So Make Your Pitch," *CE,* Aug. 3, 1968.

96 staying in shape: "Sports Notes," *CE,* Feb. 23, 1970.

96 dating airline stewardesses: At the time, Bench embraced the idea that he was popular with young women, including stewardesses. He spoke openly about his life as a bachelor both in interviews and in his 1972 memoir, in which he titled one chapter "Bachelorhood: The Good Life." "'I'm Not Ready for a Wife,' He Says," *DDN,* March 23, 1970; Bench, *From Behind the Plate,* 116.

96 "Everything about him": "Rosy Reds Outlook Shared by Wives, Girlfriends," *DDN,* Oct. 12, 1970.

97 a car dealership: Rose and Bench held the grand opening for the dealership right before spring training, Feb. 17–19, 1970.

97 Mercury Cougar hardtop: "Enter (Running) Pete," *TT,* March 3, 1970.

97 "the most important guy": *PRS,* 32.

97 "Don't forget to hustle": Ibid., 77.

97 "My dad never believed that": Ibid., 202.

97 she loved her daddy: Fawn Rose, interview with author, Feb. 2, 2022, and "Pete Rose Jr. Wants to Play Outfield," *DDN,* March 22, 1970.

98 Pete seemed distracted: "Sound Off," *CE,* Dec. 3, 1969.

98 At the end of the last game: "Assorted Cincinnati Reds Footage," MI-12-19, Moving Image Index, Cincinnati History Library and Archives.

98 a city impound lot: "Cincinnati Reds/Crosley Field Film Footage," MI-99-61, Moving Image Index, Cincinnati History Library and Archives; "It's Pay or There Goes Car," *CE,* Aug. 11, 1971.

19

99 its share of issues: Details about the problems at Crosley Field come from multiple sources, including Crosley Field Clip File, Cincinnati History Library and Archives; "DeWitt: Park, Roads Old," *CE,* May 22, 1962; "Crosley Field Problems Aired at DeWitt's Personal Session," *CE,* June 24, 1964; "Police Try to Prevent Fans' Lament: 'They Took Me Out at the Ballgame,'" *CE,* June 21, 1964; "If You Want to Go to the Ballpark and Not Get There, Here's How," *CE,* April 10, 1964; and finally the details about the traffic that delayed the start of the game come from "Sisler Calls Drill on Reds' Off Day," *CE,* Oct. 3, 1964.

99 The new stadium downtown: "Underway on the Riverfront," *Cincinnati Magazine,* Nov. 1967; Riverfront Stadium Clip File, vol. 2, 1967–1970, including, most important, "Cincinnati Riverfront Stadium," *CE,* Dec. 27, 1970, Cincinnati History Library and Archives.

100 "They got fifty-two thousand seats": Pete Rose interview, MI-96-158, Crosley Field final game footage, Moving Image Index, Cincinnati History Library and Archives.

100 ten to thirty points: "Rose Says Astroturf Will Yield .400 Hitter," *DDN,* Jan. 6, 1970.

100 But he was also sad: "Young Reds Live up to Clippings on an Old Ballpark's Final Day," *DDN,* July 25, 1970.
101 "We want Johnny": "Reds Bid Victorious Farewell to Crosley," *CP,* June 25, 1970.
101 he found the chants embarrassing: "Helms Theft of Second Base Not in the Box Score," *DDN,* July 25, 1970.
101 "I just think about winning": "Perez Isn't Thinking of Triple Crown, Yet," *CP,* June 29, 1970.
101 "Everything is beautiful": "Pete, Bowie Get First 'Ejection,'" *DJH,* July 1, 1970.
102 fuses blew: "Fans Blow Fuses over All-Star Game," *DDN,* June 2, 1970.
102 there were no more tickets: "All-Star Tickets Devoured," *CE,* June 28, 1970.

20

102 McDowell was the opposite of Rose: Details about McDowell come from multiple sources, including Sam McDowell, interview with author, July 26, 2022; "Sam of 1,000 Ways," *SI,* Aug. 17, 1970; and McDowell's revealing personal memoir, *The Saga of Sudden Sam.*
103 "This is *not* an exhibition": "From Giles to Howsam—Four Rickey Men," *CP,* Feb. 7, 1979.
103 "the biggest, most hopeless": "'Sudden Sam' Struck Out His Demons: Lefty's Fall and Rise a Motivating Story," *New York Post,* June 17, 2001.
103 he liked Sam: Rose, interview with author, Sept. 24, 2021.
103 Pete invited Sam and his wife: Details about the night before the 1970 All-Star Game come from the author's interviews with four people who were there: Carol Fosse (Ray's wife), interview with author, Oct. 28, 2022; Sam McDowell, interview with author, July 26, 2022; Karolyn Rose, interview with author, Dec. 2, 2021; and Pete Rose, interview with author, Sept. 24, 2021. Fosse, who died in 2021, also recorded his own memories for posterity on his website, www.rayfosse.com. Fosse, "1970 All-Star Game: The Way It Was."
104 Fosse was the best catcher: McDowell, interview with author, July 26, 2022.
104 Ray had once refused: "Memo to Sims from Fosse—'Having Wonderful Time, Don't Miss You,'" Cleveland *Plain Dealer,* Feb. 27, 1969.
104 He went to bed first: Karolyn Rose, interview with author, Dec. 2, 2021.
104 fifty million viewers: "What's On? An All-Star TV Night Topped by Two Winners," *NYDN,* July 16, 1970.
105 the highest-paid exotic dancer: "The Wild One," *CE,* July 14, 1970.
105 "He cussed a lot": "Watch Out for Morgana," *Lancaster (Pa.) New Era,* July 14, 1970.
105 Her employer in Newport: Advertisement, *CP,* July 13, 1970.
105 they detained Karolyn Rose: Karolyn Rose, "Bed of Roses."
105 made it onto the field: "Morganna Boots Play; Misses Bench Kisses," *CE,* July 15, 1970.
106 showered: McDowell, interview with author, July 26, 2022.
106 a terrible night: Details about the game, the collision at home plate, and its

aftermath come from the author's interviews with several players and family members who were there that night, including Ray's wife, Carol Fosse; the Orioles' All-Star second baseman Davey Johnson; NBC's color commentator, Tony Kubek; Sam McDowell; Pete's teammate Tony Pérez; Karolyn Rose; and Pete Rose himself. Additional details come from press accounts in *The Cincinnati Enquirer, The Cincinnati Post,* the Cleveland *Plain Dealer,* the *Dayton Daily News,* the New York *Daily News,* the *Philadelphia Daily News,* and *The Sporting News;* NBC footage from the game and the collision; and several retrospective news accounts, including ESPN's 1970 All-Star Game feature, July 13, 1987; "And Then Came . . . the Crash!," *DDN,* July 11, 1988; and "All-Star Legacy Endures with Help from the Play," *TT,* July 10, 1988.

107 growing soybeans: "Back Home—Cards Release Hickman," *Memphis Commercial Appeal,* July 17, 1974.

21

108 what McDowell would remember most: McDowell, interview with author, July 26, 2022.

109 Karolyn couldn't believe it: Karolyn Rose, interview with author, Dec. 2, 2021.

109 Fosse's wife hurried down: Carol Fosse, interview with author, Oct. 28, 2022.

109 "Could he have gotten around you?": "Robby Raps Pete," *CP,* July 15, 1970.

109 "I don't know if it was necessary": "Fosse Escapes with a Bruise," *San Francisco Examiner,* July 15, 1970.

109 "I was right there": "Rose Proves Real Homer as All-Star," *PDN,* July 15, 1970.

109 "That dirty S.O.B.": *San Francisco Examiner,* July 15, 1970.

109 "bulldog play": "'Tremendous Collision'—Hodges," *DJH,* July 15, 1970.

109 "If Pete slides": *PDN,* July 15, 1970.

109 "The catcher is vulnerable": Ibid.

110 "This left Rose with little alternative": "Our All-Stars," Cleveland *Plain Dealer,* July 16, 1970.

110 "If he had tried to slide": *San Francisco Examiner,* July 15, 1970.

110 Posey's agent: "Buster Posey's Agent: Eliminate Collisions," ESPN.com, May 26, 2011.

111 "politely slide": "Bruising Collisions Jar the Playoffs," Associated Press, Oct. 6, 2011.

111 "A star is born": "Isn't Fosse Now a Star?," Cleveland *Plain Dealer,* July 16, 1970.

111 because his manager: Carol Fosse, interview with author, Oct. 28, 2022; Ray Fosse, "1970 All-Star Game: The Way It Was," www.rayfosse.com.

112 "girls' softball": "Rose Faces a Whole New Ballgame," *CP,* Aug. 24, 1989.

112 "uncalled for": "The Grandest Game of All-Stars," *Odessa (Tex.) American,* July 6, 1995.

112 "I did not have the ball": *CP,* July 12, 2005.

112 "Could I have hit thirty?": "Rose's Hit & Run," *Pittsburgh Post-Gazette,* July 12, 2015.

113 single moment that December: Rose has written about his father's death over the years in both *PRMS,* 139–40, and *MP,* 72. The details here also come from Rose's interview with the author on Sept. 24, 2021, and newspaper stories about his father's death that ran in both *The Cincinnati Enquirer* and *The Cincinnati Post.*

22

117 a tiny battleship: Jackie Esselman Frey (Al Esselman's daughter), interview with author, May 11, 2022.

117 the son of German immigrants: After coming to the U.S. in 1911, Al Esselman's father, Johann Franz Heinrich Esselman, changed his name to the more Americanized John Frank. He died in September 1922, just before Alphonse was born.

117 dropped out: Alphonse Esselman, U.S. Census records, 1940.

117 affinity for numbers: Jackie Esselman Frey, interview with author, May 11, 2022.

118 nothing good ever happened: Details of the incidents at Nick Grippo's pool hall can be found in newspaper accounts, including "Judge Flays Offenders," *CE,* Aug. 26, 1934; "Fights at 68 Pounds and Draws 30 Days," *CE,* May 25, 1935; "Two Café Owners Fined," *CE,* June 30, 1936; "City in Brief," *CE,* June 4, 1941; and "City in Brief," *CE,* May 8, 1944.

118 stabbed a man: "Stomach Contents Made an Issue," *CE,* Jan. 18, 1929.

118 he had style: These details come from four people who knew Esselman: Jackie Esselman Frey, interview with author, May 11, 2022; Panaro and Czerwinski, interviews with author, Oct. 21, 2021; and Jimmy Jones (his West Side friend), interview with author, Oct. 22, 2021.

118 it was confusing: Jackie Esselman Frey, interview with author, May 11, 2022.

118 raided his house: "Café Man Held After Raid," *CE,* July 9, 1953.

118 pleaded guilty: "Gaming Fines Lightened as Trio Pleads Guilty," *CE,* Jan. 30, 1954.

118 this time it was undercover FBI agents: Details about the case the federal government built against Esselman in the early 1960s can be found in his federal criminal court file held at the National Archives in Chicago, criminal case No. 10446—a fifty-page file that the author retrieved in 2022.

119 Esselman's wife: Jackie Esselman Frey, interview with author, May 11, 2022; Jimmy Jones, interview with author, Oct. 22, 2021; Western Hills golf notes, published in the local papers in the 1970s.

119 spring of her senior year: Jackie Esselman Frey, interview with author, May 11, 2022.

119 Right around the time: Rose can't remember the exact time he started placing bets with Esselman. But based on his memory, and the memory of his West Side friend Jimmy Jones, it was no later than the early 1970s, and he began consorting with Esselman far earlier than that. In his memoir *My Prison Without Bars,* Rose writes that he was going to the racetrack with Esselman as early as 1963.

119 sit with Esselman at his office: Rose, interview with author, Oct. 21, 2021.
119 bet with Esselman almost every night: Ibid.
119 Pete disappeared: Karolyn Rose, interview with author, Dec. 2, 2021.
120 The first of these allegations: Detailed accounts of the allegations involving Tris Speaker and Ty Cobb, including lengthy transcripts from witnesses, can be found in "Charges Cobb-Speaker Bet on a 'Fixed' Game," *BG,* Dec. 22, 1926; "Famous Players at Hearing; Cobb Has Inning on the Stand," *Pittsburgh Post,* Jan. 6, 1927; and "American League Door Shut on Cobb, Speaker," *Chicago Tribune,* Jan. 13, 1927.
121 a new gambling rule: "Landis Banishes Cox for Gambling," *NYDN,* Nov. 24, 1943.
121 "small, sentimental bets": "Bets 'Sentimental,' Says Bill Cox," *NYDN,* Nov. 24, 1943.
121 "from hoodlums and hoodlumism": "Chandler Here, Says He'll Use 'Big Stick' on Baseball," *St. Louis Star and Times,* April 15, 1947.
121 Every spring, baseball officials: Ibid.
121 Denny McLain: "Baseball Suspends McLain for Ties to Gambling," *NYT,* Feb. 20, 1970.
122 Pete had to look at it: Hal McCoy (longtime *Dayton Daily News* sports reporter), interview with author, Jan. 6, 2022.
122 "everybody bet on that": *MP,* 81.
122 In the early 1970s: Details about the case the federal government built against Esselman and seventeen other men in the early 1970s can be found in his federal criminal court file at the National Archives in Chicago, criminal case No. 11995—a 289-page file that the author retrieved in 2022.

23

123 "You make $100,000": "Rose Will Sign for Token Raise," *DJH,* March 11, 1971.
123 If Yaz was worth: "Yaz Signs Three-Year Contract, Estimated over $500,000," *BG,* Feb. 18, 1971.
123 wanted Yaz money: "Bench Asking $500 G's," *CE,* Feb. 10, 1971.
123 Pérez was asking for $110,000: "Pact OKd by Perez," *DJH,* March 11, 1971.
124 "plateaued": "Rose Miffed—No Raise," *DJH,* Jan. 27, 1971.
124 already in decline: "Pete Rose's .316 'Off Year,' Reds Official Says," *Miami Herald,* Feb. 26, 1971.
124 Karolyn joked: "What It's Like Down South," *CP,* April 8, 1971.
124 genuinely hurt: "Bob Hertzel," *CE,* March 14, 1971.
124 "You figure that out": "Itchy Rose Will Settle for $5,000 Pay Hike," *DJH,* March 11, 1971.
124 "Sure, my batting average": "Blow to Rose's Pride," *DJH,* March 15, 1971.
124 "I'll sit here": "Rose Says He'll 'Sit,'" *CE,* March 5, 1971.
125 least of all Karolyn: Karolyn Rose, interview with author, Dec. 2, 2021.

125 "Big Momma": *Superwives,* 89.
125 Pete crumbled: "Pete's First Day Pleasant, Takes Half-Hour Workout," *DDN,* March 14, 1971.
125 a token raise: "Salary Stinko but Pete Still Smells Like a Rose," *PDN,* March 23, 1971.
125 a friendly wager: The details about the wager appear in "'Animal Pete' Nips Sparky," *CP,* March 20, 1971; and "Pete's Repeater Pistol Off to Red-Hot Start," *SN,* April 3, 1971.
126 "I've got to get": "What Have You Done for Me Lately?," *TT,* March 28, 1971.
126 baseball writers had picked: Associated Press, April 3, 1971.
126 the team struggled: Details of their struggles come from press accounts, including "Even Unneeded Run Savored by Sparky," *DDN,* April 28, 1971; "Reds Rarity: Perez Sidelined," *CE,* April 28, 1971; "Bench Is Perplexed as Reds Bow, 2-1," *CE,* May 31, 1971; "Johnny Bench Will Keep Hat on Head," *DDN,* March 16, 1972; and "Tolan Reinjures Achilles Tendon," *CE,* May 7, 1971.
126 tipping his cap sarcastically: "Johnny Bench Will Keep Hat on Head," *DDN,* March 16, 1972.
126 now Tolan was out: "Tolan Reinjures Achilles Tendon," *CE,* May 7, 1971.
126 George Foster: "Reds Get Outfielder for Geishert, Duffy," *CE,* May 30, 1971.
126 "I can feel my stroke": "Nolan Stifles LA, 6–2," *CE,* July 22, 1971.
127 "TV, glamour": "Gomez Remains Bench's Top Fan," *CP,* Sept. 8, 1971.
127 stop playing basketball: "Hoping for Fast Start, Rose Signs Pact Early," *CE,* Nov. 19, 1971.
127 only coach the team: "3 Reds to Play Basketball," *CP,* Nov. 11, 1971.
127 emergency meeting: Howsam, *My Life in Sports,* 113.

24

128 had come to loathe: Details about the Morgan trade come from multiple sources, including author interviews with Pete Rose and Tommy Helms; news coverage from *The Cincinnati Enquirer, The Cincinnati Post,* the *Dayton Daily News,* and the Dayton *Journal Herald;* Sparky Anderson's three memoirs, *Sparky!, They Call Me Sparky,* and *The Main Spark;* Joe Morgan's memoir with David Falkner, *Joe Morgan: A Life in Baseball;* and Howsam's unpublished memoir, *My Life in Sports.*
128 hated the fact: Morgan and Falkner, *Joe Morgan,* 103.
128 hated his manager: Ibid., 112.
128 "a troublemaker": The term appeared in multiple places both at the time and in the years to come: "Morgan No Troublemaker," *CE,* Dec. 1, 1970; Hertzel, *Big Red Machine,* 45; and Anderson and Burick, *Main Spark,* 117.
128 too radical: "The Tragic Story Behind Tolan," *CE,* Sept. 28, 1973. Later, Anderson would concede that his handling of the Tolan situation was "the biggest mistake I ever made." Hertzel, *Big Red Machine,* 43.

128 a walk-off home run: "Morgan Mashes Reds, 5–4," *CE,* Sept. 20, 1971.
129 at a Holiday Inn: "Dobson to Start World Series Fourth Game," *DJH,* Oct. 11, 1971.
129 a resort in Scottsdale: "New Hotel Has Old Idea," *Arizona Republic,* Nov. 8, 1961; "Building on the Past 1961: Scottsdale's Executive House Hotel," *Arizona Contractor & Community,* Nov./Dec. 2019.
129 everyone had heard the rumors: "Reds Deny Trade Talk," *CE,* Oct. 11, 1971.
129 over a cup of coffee: "Sam McDowell Coveted," *CP,* Nov. 29, 1971.
129 needed to tell: "Sparky's News Jolts Pete Rose," *DJH,* Dec. 1, 1971.
129 "This is Tommy Helms": "Basketball Leads to Trade?," *DDN,* Nov. 30, 1971.
129 Almost everyone else took: "'Trade Howsam for Seal,' Baseball Fans React to Swap," *CE,* Nov. 30, 1971; "Cincy Fans Oppose Deal," *DJH,* Nov. 30, 1971.
129 "Smilin' Bob": "Baseball Chatter," *CE,* Dec. 9, 1971.
129 best defensive second baseman: Helms won the National League Gold Glove award at second base in both 1970 and 1971 with a fielding percentage of .983 in 1970 and league-leading .990 in 1971.
129 most consistent slugger: Over his final three seasons in Cincinnati—1969, 1970, and 1971—Lee May hit thirty-eight, thirty-four, and thirty-nine home runs, respectively.
130 "Do you realize": *DJH,* Dec. 1, 1971.
129 hard for Howsam: Howsam, *My Life in Sports,* 113.
130 "Joe stole forty bases": "Morgan Surprised Reds Dealt May," *CP,* Nov. 30, 1971.
130 Morgan wasn't sure: Morgan and Falkner, *Joe Morgan,* 123.
130 heard from a Black teammate: This guidance came from a reliable source—Jimmy Wynn, a Black player who had grown up in Cincinnati and graduated from Taft High School there. Ibid., 139.
130 "I was sorry to hear": "Reds Lost Valuable Trio," *CP,* Nov. 30, 1971.
130 worried enough: Morgan didn't think Anderson prejudiced; he thought the opposite, in fact. In his memoir, Morgan wrote that he knew Anderson would "see me as a person, not a color." However, Anderson was worried about Morgan's attitude—a fact Anderson admitted on multiple occasions and that Morgan learned about shortly after arriving in Cincinnati. Anderson and Burick, *Main Spark,* 117; Hertzel, *Big Red Machine,* 45; Morgan and Falkner, *Joe Morgan,* 140.
131 "I'm not a troublemaker": "Morgan No Troublemaker," *CE,* Dec. 1, 1970.

25

131 Pete hated not playing: "Once-Happy Champs Show Signs of Stress," *CE,* Dec. 12, 1971.
131 took to the floor: "One Last Shot?," *DJH,* Dec. 1, 1971.

131 continued playing: "Pete Rose Back in Hoop Action," *DDN,* Jan. 27, 1972.
131 a rare Italian sports car: Details about the car come from "That's a Mangusta Way Down There," *CE,* Dec. 9, 1971, and interviews the author conducted on Sept. 6, 2022, with four people familiar with the car or the man who sold it to Rose—Stephanie Eckert; Frank Zappasodi; Gina Grawe; and Rose's former friend and associate Paul Janszen.
131 slicing it wide open: "Pete Rose: Young at Heart," *TT,* March 2, 1972.
131 at a party: "Howie Cosell Is a Jerk, Says This Feller," *CP,* Feb. 4, 1972; "Laughs Roll at Western Hills Sports Stag," *CE,* Feb. 4, 1972; "Humor Hits Some Tender Nerves at Cincy Clambake," *SN,* Feb. 26, 1972.
132 "I knew there was a way": "Anderson Wants to Get a Fat (Big) Early-Season Lead," *DDN,* Jan. 26, 1972.
132 thought it ridiculous: "Bench to Lose Weight but Not Willingly, He Says," *CP,* Dec. 9, 1971.
132 appear like one: "Bench Admits to Play Slice," *DJH,* Jan. 15, 1972.
132 celebrity events: "On the Road with Johnny," *CP,* Jan. 31, 1972.
132 "Live hard": Ibid.
132 the Cloisters: Bench wasn't shy about showing off his condo to reporters in the 1970s. The details about the place come from multiple news stories and property records, including "Bench's Bachelor Pad the Most; Once Couldn't Afford Alligators," *DDN,* April 21, 1971; "Bench Refuge from Hits, Kids," *DJH,* May 28, 1971; "Johnny Bench's Mount Adams Retreat," *CP,* Sept. 9, 1972; and the Hamilton County Auditor, property record, 1026 Hatch Street, Cincinnati.
133 "Conceited? No, I'm not": *CP,* Sept. 9, 1972.
133 just proud: *DJH,* May 28, 1971.
133 opted to keep: *CE,* June 5, 1971.
133 it was all gone: According to news accounts, Bench began divesting himself of the car dealership in April 1971, the dealership was officially renamed that fall, and the bowling alley was sold around that time, too. "Bench Sells His Interest, Keeps Name on Agency," *DJH,* April 14, 1971; "Bench Going 'Back to School,'" *CE,* Sept. 4, 1971; "Lincoln-Mercury Agency Under New Ownership," *DDN,* Oct. 7, 1972.
133 "like icy rain": Details about the banquet at which Rose made this joke come from three contemporary accounts written at the time: "Reds' Hall Is Small, but He Fires a Blazer," *SN,* Feb. 19, 1972; "Past Haunts Reds' Speakers," *CE,* Jan. 31, 1972; and *CP,* Jan. 31, 1972.
133 the divide between the two: Three different sources confirmed this divide: Morgan and Falkner, *Joe Morgan,* 142; Marty Brennaman (longtime Reds broadcaster), interview with author, Aug. 1, 2021; and Hal McCoy (longtime *Dayton Daily News* reporter), interview with author, Jan. 4, 2022. McCoy put it bluntly: "Rose and Bench did not like each other."
133 talking about retiring: "The Comeback of John Bench Begins," *TT,* Feb. 26, 1972.
134 couldn't be friends with both: Morgan and Falkner, *Joe Morgan,* 142.

26

134 glass door: "Rose Arrives Minus Beard," *CE,* March 1, 1972.

134 "It's okay": "'. . . And in Left Field for Cincinnati, Pete Rose . . . ,'" *CE,* March 1, 1972.

134 "There's no problem": "Sparky Shifts Rose to Left," *DJH,* March 1, 1972.

134 batting .170: "Phillie Rookie Decked by Carroll," *CP,* March 30, 1972.

134 "You just get": "Bench Attacks the Ball—Klu," *CP,* March 1, 1972.

135 would have to make concessions: "Kuhn Happy but Anticipates Changes in Rules," *NYDN,* June 20, 1972.

135 47–0: "Players Vote Immediate Strike," *Tampa Bay Times,* April 1, 1972.

135 Howsam was furious: "Howsam Bites Back at Miller," *DDN,* April 6, 1972.

135 buy a new Pontiac: "Aaron Recalls Bad Old Days," *CP,* March 1, 1972.

135 With the clubhouses locked: "Reds' Players Don't Want Strike," *CE,* March 31, 1972; "The Morning After," *TT,* March 30, 1972; and "Both Sides Refuse to Budge as Clubhouses Are Padlocked," *DDN,* April 2, 1972.

135 to the betting windows: "Tee Shirts Boost Bunker Candidacy," *CE,* April 10, 1972.

135 about $5,000: "Pete Rose Loses $5,310 in Pay," *DDN,* April 14, 1972.

135 let the players know it: Details about opening day 1972 come from the game coverage in four local papers: *The Cincinnati Enquirer, The Cincinnati Post,* the *Dayton Daily News,* and the Dayton *Journal Herald.*

136 locker room was quiet: "Sounds from the Cellar," *CE,* April 27, 1972.

136 *"Home run for Lee May": CE,* April 27, 1972.

136 "a massive malfunction": "Stadium Scoreboard Not Yet Operable for Game Tonight," *CE,* May 5, 1972.

136 "Give me two weeks": "Sharp-Tongued Sons, Wives Make Baseball a Family Affair," *DDN,* May 7, 1972.

27

136 The comeback began: Details of Rose's workout after the loss to the Cubs in mid-May 1972 come from three sources: "Postgame Workout for Frustrated Rose," *DJH,* May 11, 1972; "Man in a Cage," *CE,* May 12, 1972; and George Foster's memories of the day, shared with the author. Foster, interview with author, March 13, 2023.

138 close game in San Francisco: "Giants Drop 6th Straight," *San Francisco Examiner,* May 17, 1972.

138 "I think we can beat them": "Sparky Sees Success in Big Houston Series," *CP,* May 29, 1972.

138 Over the next four nights: Details of the Reds' four-game series against the Astros come from game coverage in *The Cincinnati Enquirer, The Cincinnati Post,* the *Dayton Daily News,* the Dayton *Journal Herald,* and the *Houston Chronicle* between May 30 and June 3, 1972.

139 claim the NL pennant: Details of game five of the 1972 NLCS come from multiple sources, including the WLW Radio game call and postgame club-

house interviews with Rose, Bench, and Howsam, Oct. 11, 1972; "Reds Capture Pennant," "Foster, Who Scored 'the' Run, Enjoys Quiet," and "Reds Agree Pirates Should Share No. 1," *CE,* Oct. 12, 1972; "It Was a Night to Remember," "One Hell of a Good Time Was Had by All," "Mrs. Bench Gave an Order and Johnny Obeyed," "Bench's Home Run Put It Back to Normal," and "What can You Say?," *CP,* Oct. 12, 1972; "Johnny Be Good," "Bizarre Finish Makes Reds N.L. Champions," and "One Errant Slider and Bucs Plodded into Death Chamber," *DDN,* Oct. 12, 192; "Reds Earn Series Berth 4-3" and "Sparky: Reds, Bucs Even," *DJH,* Oct. 12, 1972; and "Reds Win Flag on Moose Wild Pitch, 4-3," "Reds' Bench Erupts with Johnny," and "The Strike That Bounced," *Pittsburgh Post-Gazette,* Oct. 12, 1972.

139 When it emerged: Authorities raided the home of the alleged bookie Albert C. Isella on Sept. 25. But the story of his connection with the umpires didn't make it into the press until almost a month later, and baseball officials quickly dismissed it, without naming any of the umpires. "Gambling Raid Uncovers Book Listing Major League Umpires," *Baltimore Sun,* Oct. 20, 1975; "Umpire, Gaming Study Set," *Baltimore Sun,* Oct. 21, 1972; "Umpires Face No Charges," *Baltimore Sun,* Oct. 25, 1972.

28

139 Nearly a quarter of a million: "Who's Gonna Win? The Baddest 25," *DDN,* Oct. 11, 1972.

139 They gathered on Fountain Square: *CP,* Oct. 12, 1972.

140 Pete Rose agreed: "Are Bad-Enough A's Mad Enough to Make a Series of It?," *PDN,* Oct. 14, 1972.

140 "We want people": *PDN,* Oct. 14, 1972.

140 To Howsam's horror: Howsam, *My Life in Sports,* 119.

140 "Mustache Day": For the promotional event, held June 18, 1972, the entire Oakland roster did as Finley wanted. Twenty-five players, the manager, the coaches, the announcers, and even the opposing team, the Cleveland Indians, grew mustaches for the game.

140 much smarter: The scout's name was Al Hollingsworth, and the details about what he compiled, and how the A's used it, can be found in "The Oakland Scouting Report," *CP,* Oct. 23, 1972; "Cincinnati Comes Up Loser Again," *Oakland Tribune,* Oct. 23, 1972; and Turbow, *Dynastic, Bombastic, Fantastic,* 83.

141 Karolyn and the kids: "Fans Came Out for Reds," *DDN,* Oct. 10, 1972.

141 "How's your daddy doing?": "The Wrong Catcher," *NYDN,* Oct. 15, 1972.

141 "super fastball": "Rose Smells a Catfish," *DDN,* Oct. 16, 1972.

141 "nothing fastball": "Reds Down 2–0, Search for Answers," *NYDN,* Oct. 16, 1972.

141 pronounced the field there awful: "Another Furor Blooming?," *DJH,* Oct. 18, 1972.

142 Heavy rains: "Coast Deluge Postpones Game No. 3," *NYDN,* Oct. 18, 1972.

142 "Don't you people know": "Karolyn Rose Goes to Bat," *CE,* Oct. 20, 1972.

142 how Pete could talk like that: "'Rose Pops Off Too Much'—Hunter," *CE,* Oct. 21, 1972.
143 "*Jim* Hunter": "'We'll Win It All Because of Morgan—Tolan,'" *CP,* Oct. 21, 1972.
143 "Call them what you want": NBC telecast of game five, Oct. 20, 1972.
143 "About this big": "A Win Does Wonders for Sparky's Heartburn," *NYDN,* Oct. 21, 1972.
144 once again favorites: "Reds Go Limit in Series," *TT,* Oct. 22, 1972.
144 "Hey, hey, hey": "Kuhn Says Williams Hit by $500 Fine," *NYDN,* Oct. 22, 1972.
144 It was a line drive: The clip of the final out of the 1972 World Series on YouTube, courtesy of Major League Baseball. www.youtube.com/watch?v=-1bf7iVm73s.

29

144 sat in the locker room: "IF . . . but Fate Smiled on A's," *CP,* Oct. 23, 1972.
144 batting just .214: World Series seven-game box score, *Miami Herald,* Oct. 23, 1972.
144 postgame victory party: "Fonseca Lauds Reds' Character," *DJH,* Oct. 24, 1972.
145 "I want to say": Ibid.
145 He was dating: "'Who'd Want to Be Engaged to You?,'" *CE,* Jan. 29, 1973.
145 He wanted the freedom: "A Busy End to Johnny Bench's Busy Day," *CE,* Feb. 1, 1973.
145 national syndication: "'Devil' Tops 'Nun' in Humor with Hellishly Comic Davis," *DDN,* Feb. 15, 1973.
145 *"A bachelor swinger":* Advertisement, *CE,* Oct. 20, 1972.
145 rumors circulated: "Rose, Perez on Block," *CE,* Nov. 26, 1972.
145 "This year:" "Rose (Money) Howsam," *CE,* March 3, 1973.
146 asked for a short reprieve: "Rose Arrival in Camp Reunites Big 5 Agitators," *DDN,* March 8, 1973.
146 six and a half hours: "White Sox Subs Cuff Reds 11–3," *DJH,* March 16, 1973.
146 "a little earthy": "A Girl Finds Savoir Faire in Dolphins Locker Room," *Miami News,* June 25, 1973.
146 "Come on, girls": "A Strange Way to Peddle Hair Spray," *Newsday,* May 2, 1973.
146 "Every summer": "Pete Rose = Hustler," *CP,* April 17, 1973.
146 angry about it: "Playoff Hero Foster Departs," *CE,* April 1, 1973.
147 getting more letters: "No, Girls, He Isn't Engaged—Yet," *CE,* July 29, 1973.
147 "This isn't over yet": "Hal King, Then Tony Jolt L.A.," *CP,* July 2, 1973.
147 That night in Houston: Details of the games in Houston and San Francisco come from multiple accounts, including "Giants: A Comeback Classic!," *San Francisco Examiner,* Sept. 4, 1973; "Reds Acted Like Crazy Fans Watching Dodgers Lose on T.V.," *DDN,* Sept. 4, 1973; "Reds Watch Dodgers Fold

and Celebrate First Place Tie," *CP,* Sept. 4, 1973; and KSFO radio broadcast, Sept. 3, 1973.

30

148 "I don't think of the Mets": "Yanks 6 Ways Better; Staub Key to Mets," *NYDN,* April 1, 1973.

148 Seaver probably wouldn't start: "Mets Concerned over Seaver's Arm," *NYDN,* Oct. 3, 1973.

148 Berra changed course: "Reason to Smile: Tom's Arm Terrific," *NYDN,* Oct. 4, 1973.

149 "Tom Seaver, Tom Seaver": "Will Seaver Make the Reds Believe?," *NYDN,* Oct. 3, 1973.

149 a terrible time: "Reds, Mets in Shadows; Accent to Be on Pitching," *DJH,* Oct. 6, 1973.

149 For seven innings: Details of Seaver's pitching in game one—and Rose's late-inning heroics—come from multiple accounts published on Oct. 7, 1973, including "Seaver's Best Not Enough," "For 7½ Innings It's Quiet—Then BOOM," and "Billingham Thought 'Blue' Day Was in Offing," *CE;* "Non-smoker Billingham Said He Needed Cigaret" and "Rose, Bench HRs Splatter Mets, 2–1," *DDN;* "Seaver's RBI and 13 Ks Not Enough" and "Billingham's Heat Pack Chills Met Hot Hitters," *NYDN;* "The Reds Were Dead Until Pete Rose" and "Bench's Homer Beats Mets, 2–1," *PI;* "Bench and Rose Provide a Rx for a Sick Billingham" and "Seaver Says Bench Hit Nothing Ball," *NYT;* plus the NBC television broadcast from Oct. 6, 1973.

149 "Rose remembers things": "Tom Seaver's Arm Is Tired," *NYT,* Oct. 6, 1973.

150 never seen fans react: Tony Kubek, NBC broadcast of game one, Oct. 6, 1973, and Tony Kubek, interview with author, Oct. 14, 2022.

151 a good relationship: Details of Rose's relationship with Bud Harrelson come from multiple sources, including Pete Rose, interview with author, Sept. 28, 2021; Karolyn Rose, interview with local television host Bill Brown, 1974, MI-04-32, Moving Image Index, Cincinnati History Library and Archives; "Harrelson Remembers, with Respect. Rose's Help as a Rookie," *NYT,* Oct. 9, 1973; "A Rose Is Not a Rose Unless He's Battling," UPI, Oct. 9, 1973.

151 "What the hell": "Mets' 5–0 Win Evens Series," *CE,* Oct. 8, 1973; "Rusty Was Best Swinger in the Game," *NYDN,* Oct. 9, 1973.

151 Pete couldn't let him talk: Morgan and Falkner, *Joe Morgan,* 187.

152 pelted him with garbage: Details about Rose's fight with Bud Harrelson and its aftermath come from multiple sources, including Pete Rose, interview with author, Sept. 28, 2021; *PRMS,* 155; Morgan and Falkner, *Joe Morgan,* 187; "Bud Harrelson Remembers NLCS Brawl with Pete Rose," Fox Sports, Oct. 8, 2013; *NYT,* Oct. 9, 1973; UPI, Oct. 9, 1973; "Met Fans See Red Over Rose," *DDN,* Oct. 9, 1973; "I Play Hard and Clean, I'd Do It Again—Rose" and the Pat Harmon sports column, *CP,* Oct. 9, 1973; "'He Called

Me a Name,' Rose Claims," "Got Me Late—Harrelson," and "Shea's Near Tragedy," *DJH,* Oct. 9, 1973; "Brawl Mars Mets' 9-2 Win" and "Fans Don't Have License to Kill," *PI,* Oct. 9, 1973; "Slide by Rose Sparks a Free-for-All," *NYDN,* Oct. 9, 1973; "Pete Rose: 'I'm No Little Girl Out There'" and "'Twas an Ugly, Angry Scene in the Fifth at Shea," *CE,* Oct. 9, 1973.

152 "It could have killed him": *PI,* Oct. 9, 1973.

31

153 After the game: Details about the aftermath of the fight between Rose and Harrelson come from several sources, including Pete Rose, interview with author, Sept. 28, 2021; Karolyn Rose, interview with author, Dec. 2, 2021; Howsam, *My Life in Sports,* 123; *NYT,* Oct. 9, 1973; UPI, Oct. 9, 1973; *DDN,* Oct. 9, 1973; *CP,* Oct. 9, 1973; *DJH,* Oct. 9, 1973; *PI,* Oct. 9, 1973; *NYDN,* Oct. 9, 1973; and *CE,* Oct. 9, 1978.

153 "A Rose Is Not a Rose": UPI, Oct. 9, 1973.

153 hated confrontation: Fawn Rose, interview with author, Feb. 2, 2022; Terry Rubio Fernandez, interview with author, Feb. 12, 2023; and Hal McCoy, interview with author, Jan. 6, 2022.

153 "like a person on the run": Morgan and Falkner, *Joe Morgan,* 188.

154 She called Sparky: "Pete Left Room for Game Only," *DDN,* Oct. 10, 1973.

154 awoke with an idea: Details about the plan to have Harrelson and Rose shake hands come from multiple sources, including Pat Harmon column, *CP,* Oct. 10, 1973; "What Else to Say of Rose? He's Reason for Game 5," *DDN,* Oct. 10, 1973; "Inspiration Aids Perez," *DJH,* Oct. 10, 1973; "Peace Feelers Fail," *NYDN,* Oct. 10, 1973; and "Met Fans Silenced by Pete's Bat," *PI,* Oct. 10, 1973.

154 "That's not the way": *NYDN,* Oct. 10, 1973.

154 The abuse that afternoon: Details about game four come from multiple sources including Rose, interview with author, Sept. 28, 2021; Morgan and Falkner, *Joe Morgan,* 187; Howsam, *My Life in Sports,* 123; *CP,* Oct. 10, 1973; *DDN,* Oct. 10, 1973; *DJH,* Oct. 10, 1973; *NYDN,* Oct. 10, 1973; and *PI,* Oct. 10, 1973.

155 "I don't have": *PI,* Oct. 10, 1973.

155 "If they ever cut Rose open": "Sparky Looks Older, but Mantle Will Catch Up," *DDN,* Nov. 18, 1976.

156 The Mets won: Details about game five come from multiple sources, including "Fans Antics Make Sparky 'Ashamed,'" "Mets' Fans Run Amok," and "Pete Rose: A Pro," *CE,* Oct. 11, 1973; Pat Harmon column and "If We'd Just Scored in the First Inning—Rose," "Metsomaniacs Ruin Otherwise Splendid Memory," *DDN,* Oct. 11, 1973; "Miracles Still Happening for Mets!," "Rose: Mets' Fans 'Don't Deserve Championship,'" and "'Nightmare' Stuns Reds," *DJH,* Oct. 11, 1973; "Mob Scene Frightens Players, Fans, Officials; 5 Go to Hospital" and "Pete Rose: A Professional Player All the Way," *NYDN,* Oct. 11, 1973; "Day to Recall—and Forget" and "Mets Beat Reds, 7–2; Win Flag," *PI,* Oct. 11, 1973; and Howsam, *My Life in Sports,* 124.

156 Ozark Airlines DC-9: "Pete Showers Roses on Reds Fans," *CE,* Oct. 11, 1973; "Mrs. Rose: I Can't Believe It's Over," *CP,* Oct. 11, 1973; "Reds Welcomed Home in Winning Style," *DDN,* Oct. 11, 1973.

156 "Daddy fights just like Joe Frazier": "Karolyn's Fears, Fawn's Tears," *CE,* Oct. 12, 1973.

157 A few weeks later: "The MVP Is the Biggest Honor I've Gotten—Pete Rose," *CP,* Nov. 21, 1973.

157 larger house: The house, located at 5946 Countryhills Drive, had four bedrooms and three baths, according to the Hamilton County Auditor records.

157 open a new restaurant: "Pancakes to Parmigiana, Pete Rose's New Place Has It All," *CP,* Jan 17, 1975.

157 "I think it's hard for a wife": Karolyn Rose interview, MI-04-32, Moving Image Index, Cincinnati History Library and Archives.

157 "I have the shit detail": "The Real Mrs. Pete Rose," *CE,* March 31, 1974.

158 "You gonna tell me": This exchange comes from Karolyn Rose's lengthy interview on *A.M. Cincinnati* in April 1976, MI-94-14, Moving Image Index, Cincinnati History Library and Archives.

158 having an affair: In 2015, John Dowd, Major League Baseball's special counsel who investigated Rose in 1989, made allegations on a radio show that Rose had committed statutory rape in the 1970s by having sex with underage girls. Rose denied the charges and, in 2016, filed a defamation suit against Dowd in federal district court, case number 2:16-cv-03681-PBT. The author reviewed this voluminous file in its entirety. In it, the unnamed woman alleges that Rose first called her in 1973, when she was "fourteen or fifteen years old." Sometime after that, but before her sixteenth birthday, they began having a sexual relationship that lasted for "several years." In the legal filings, Rose says that it was his "information and belief" that she was sixteen. The case was ultimately dismissed in 2017, with the consent of both Dowd and Rose. "The strangest twist in this story: If Rose had just let John Dowd's comments from two years ago slide, nobody would have been the wiser," *The Cincinnati Enquirer* wrote in 2017. "Filing a lawsuit against a high-powered attorney has proved to be another bad gamble by Rose."

158 the girl remembered it differently: In 2023, the author spoke to the young woman, now in her mid-sixties. To protect herself and her family, she declined to be interviewed.

32

159 social event of the year: Details about Johnny Bench and Vickie Chesser's brief courtship and opulent wedding come from multiple sources, including WKRC-TV nightly news report, Feb. 21, 1975, MI-93-10L, Misc. Cavanaugh Footage, Moving Image Index, Cincinnati History Library and Archives; "Reds Spotlight: Vickie Bench—exclusive interview," *Reds Alert,* May 1, 1975, Ohio History Center Archives & Library; "Miss S.C. USA Queen," *State* (Columbia, S.C.), March 23, 1970; "Bachelor Bench Abdicates," *CE,* Jan. 21, 1975; "The Wedding," "'Maybe He'll Play Better Now,'" and "Johnny

and Vickie Swing to Same Pitch," *CE,* Jan. 30, 1975; "Reds Toss Quips at BOY Dinner," *CP,* Jan. 27, 1975; "'This Is Bananas,' She Said," *DJH,* Feb. 19, 1975; "Johnny Bench, Vickie Exchange Vows," *CE,* Feb. 22, 1975; "Cincinnati Event: A Star Is Wed," *CP,* Feb. 22, 1975; "Johnny Catches a Bride," *DJH,* Feb. 22, 1975; and "Johnny, Vickie Team Up," *DDN,* Feb. 22, 1975.

160 "We need to win": "Johnny Reflects on His New Life with Vickie Bench," *CE,* Feb. 24, 1975.

160 didn't want it to dip: "Woes for Rose," *CE,* March 2, 1975.

160 Mario Núñez: Details about Rose's relationship with Mario Núñez come from multiple sources, including Metz, interview with author, Oct. 22, 2021; Terry Rubio Fernandez, interview with author, Feb. 12, 2023; *Dowd Report,* Exhibit 2b, deposition of Pete Rose, April 21, 1989, 85; "Tampa Maître d' Can't Believe He Got to Meet the President," *Tampa Times,* April 16, 1980; "Fight Game to Survive Without USA Cable," *TT,* Dec. 2, 1983; "'Charlie Hustle' and 'The Cuban' Just Seemed to Hit It Off," *TT,* Sept. 9, 1985.

160 staying at Pete's house: "Nothing Can Match Pitching in Series," *TT,* Oct. 15, 1975; and "Superstitious? No," *CE,* Oct. 7, 1975.

160 On the day that the Reds lost: Details about Anderson's request that Rose move to third base come from multiple sources, including raw television interview footage from May 1975 with Rose and Anderson for the local show *Big Red Machine,* Bill Brown #13, MI-04-43, Moving Image Index, Cincinnati History Library and Archives; *PRMS,* 169; "Sparky Plucks Rose for Still-Thorny Third," *CE,* May 3, 1975; "Rose Moves to Third," *CP,* May 3, 1975; and "Rose to Be Next at 3d Base Spot," *DJH,* May 3, 1975.

161 "They cannot lose": *CE,* Oct. 7, 1975.

33

162 "We won 111": "The Wall: The Losers Will Feel Like Climbing It," *PI,* Oct. 11, 1975.

162 "I know what they throw": "Yesterday a Day of Rest, Except for Rambling Rose," *DJH,* Oct. 9, 1975.

162 "I lead the league": "A Look at Those Awesome Reds, from the Mound to the Bench," *BG,* Oct. 10, 1975.

163 "Boston should be": "Rose Can't See Anybody Beating Reds," *NYDN,* Oct. 9, 1975.

163 Tiant dominated game one: To write about the 1975 World Series, the author interviewed multiple players who were in it, including Pete Rose, Tony Pérez, Dan Driessen, Doug Flynn, Bill Lee, Fred Lynn, Luis Tiant, and Bernie Carbo and four reporters and broadcasters who covered it: Marty Brennaman, of WLW Radio in Cincinnati; Peter Gammons, of *The Boston Globe;* Tony Kubek, of NBC; and Hal McCoy, of the *Dayton Daily News.* Their memories were crucial to rebuilding these scenes, along with NBC television footage; press coverage from primarily *The Boston Globe, The Cincinnati Enquirer, The Cincinnati Post,* the *Dayton Daily News,* the Dayton *Journal Herald,* and *The Sporting News;* Johnny Bench, oral history, Voices of Oklahoma project, 2012;

Karolyn Rose, interview with author, Dec. 2, 2021; and several memoirs, listed in the bibliography, including Howsam's *My Life in Sports.*

163 "the weakest five-hitter": "Lose His Cool? Not Anderson," *BG,* Oct. 12, 1975.

163 in game two: In addition to the author's aforementioned interviews with the players who participated in this World Series and the reporters who covered it, details about game two of the 1975 World Series come from the following sources: the NBC broadcast of game two, Oct. 12, 1975; "'No Reason to Hang Our Heads'—Lynn," "Reds Find the Starter Button . . . and Run Over Sox in Ninth, 3–2," and "He Takes a Bit of Lee-way," *BG,* Oct. 13, 1975; "It Takes 18 Innings, but Wall Breached" and "'Sometimes You Do . . . ,'" *CE,* Oct. 13, 1975; "Reds Give Bosox 'Blues in Ninth,'" *CP,* Oct. 13, 1975; "Reds Tie Series with 9th Inning Rally," *DDN,* Oct. 13, 1975; "Reds Wait Till 9th to Beat Sox, 3–2," *NYDN,* Oct. 13, 1975; and "Reds' Last-out Rally Evens Series," *PI,* Oct. 13, 1975;

164 "It's like I've been injected": "Billingham Stays Cool," *DJH,* Oct. 13, 1975.

164 "It opens the pores": "He Takes a Bit of Lee-Way," *BG,* Oct. 13, 1975.

164 "We can come back": "'Sometimes You Do . . . ,'" *CE,* Oct. 13, 1975.

34

164 he announced that his West Side restautant: "Pete Rose's Restaurant," advertisement, *CE,* Oct. 14, 1975.

164 "to see if he is going to make a mistake": "Rose's Favorite Television Series Is the Series," *BG,* Oct. 14, 1975.

164 he predicted: *DDN,* Oct. 13, 1975.

165 "the Reds Badge of Courage": "Open City, Ohio-Style," *BG,* Oct. 18, 1975.

165 "Just a raw kid": "No Ticket, Tie, Coat—Just Rose," *CE,* Oct. 18, 1975.

165 "I'm mad": "Pity Poor Pete—It's Almost Over," *CE,* Oct. 17, 1975.

165 "kind of pressure I like": "Story of Homemade Bat," *CE,* Oct. 18, 1975.

165 It rained for the next three days: National Oceanic and Atmospheric Administration, local climatological data reports, Oct. 18–22, 1975; Northeast Regional Climate Center; regional news coverage of the storm including "2.5-In. Rain Soaks N.E.," *BG,* Oct. 19, 1975.

165 to assemble in the lobby: "Rained Out Reds Off to College," *DDN,* Oct. 20, 1975; "Reds Lose Way to Practice Site," *CP,* Oct. 20, 1975; "Motel Turmoil," *DJH,* Oct. 20, 1975.

165 Sparky didn't mind: *DDN,* Oct. 20, 1975.

166 Pete paced the room: *DJH,* Oct. 20, 1975.

166 under the covers: "Maybe There's a Leak in His Hotel Room," *CE,* Oct. 19, 1975.

166 appearing with Fred Lynn: Details about the press conference come from multiple news stories, including "World Series Like a Party to Rookie Lynn," *CE,* Oct. 19, 1975; *BG,* Oct. 19, 1975; and *NYDN,* Oct. 19, 1975.

166 anxious to play: Lynn, interview with author, Sept. 23, 2022.

166 "You know he won't be graceful": "Pete Rose . . . He's Easy to Hate," *BG,* Oct. 19, 1975.

167 speaking engagement: "Fenway's Real Pooh-Bah," *BG,* Oct. 21, 1975.
167 *Monday Night Football:* "Rain," *DDN,* Oct. 19, 1975.
167 sixty-six million fans: "7th-Game Audience Bigger Than Super," *BG,* Nov. 11, 1975.
168 a hot prospect: "Lawson's Notes," *CP,* June 25, 1965; Bernie Carbo, interview with author, Sept. 30, 1970.
168 a baserunning mistake: The disputed play came in the bottom of the sixth in game one of the 1970 World Series with the score tied 3–3, one out, Helms on first, and Carbo on third. The Reds' batter hit a high chopper that bounced straight up in front of the plate and was collected by the catcher. Carbo ran home and straight into chaos at home plate. The umpire was blocking his path, and the catcher tagged him out.
168 "It was a play that couldn't happen": "I Remember . . . ," *CE,* Oct. 13, 1972.
168 traded him away: "Carbo Gets News at Steak House," *CE,* May 20, 1972.
168 Lynn knew: Lynn, interview with author, Sept. 23, 2022.
168 "The worst swing": Rose, interview with author, Sept. 28, 2021; Lynn, interview with author, Sept. 23, 2022; Carbo, interview with author, Sept. 30, 2022.
168 Bernie was looking for it: Carbo and Hantzis, *Saving Bernie Carbo,* 15; Carbo, interview with author, Sept. 30, 2022.
168 It was 11:18 p.m.: NBC television broadcast, Oct. 22, 1975.

35

169 "Don't you wish": This quotation comes from multiple sources, including Carbo, interview with author, Sept. 30, 2022; Carbo and Hantzis, *Saving Bernie Carbo,* 16; Bernie Carbo interview, WEEB radio, Southern Pines, N.C., April 8, 2022; and "Carbo Almost Regrets HR," *BG,* Oct. 22, 1975.
169 blacked out: Morgan and Falkner, *Joe Morgan,* 204.
169 "No, no, no": "Fisk Homer in 12th Edges Reds, 7–6," *NYDN,* Oct. 22, 1975.
170 Fisk turned to Lynn: Lynn, interview with author, Sept. 23, 2022; Wilson, *Pudge,* 138.
170 church bells: "Church Bells Ring for Fisk," *BG,* Oct. 22, 1975.
170 felt sick: In interviews with the author, both Rose and Pérez confirmed Anderson's state of mind after game six. Anderson himself also wrote or spoke about it in other places, including "SportsCentury Pete Rose," ESPN, MI-12-14, Moving Image Index, Cincinnati History Library and Archives; Anderson, *Sparky!;* and "Reds Make Anderson Forget 'If We Lose,'" *PI,* Oct. 23, 1975.
170 "This is some kind of game": *NYDN,* Oct. 22, 1975.
170 "We're going to win": Anderson, *Sparky!,* 120.
170 Seventy-five million people: *BG,* Nov. 11, 1975.
171 the Spaceman didn't spend a single moment: Bill Lee, interview with author, Oct. 7, 2022.
171 "Bill Lee loves it": NBC television broadcast, Oct. 22, 1975.
171 "They got *one*!": Ibid.
171 "Up, up, away": *PI,* Oct. 23, 1975.

171 fuming: Lee, interview with author, Oct. 7, 2022.
172 He was waiting on: Pérez, interview with author, Nov. 29, 2021.
172 "The Boston fans": NBC television broadcast, Oct. 22, 1975.
172 Fred Lynn was sure: Lynn, interview with author, Sept. 23, 2022.
173 "He got all the clutch hits": NBC broadcast, Oct. 22, 1975; *PI,* Oct. 23, 1975.
173 standing ovations: "No Sleep for Pete Rose as Series Hero Returns," *CP,* Oct. 23, 1975.
173 "Sportsman of the Year": *SI,* Dec. 22, 1975.
173 black-tie ceremony: "Diamond-Belted Rose Says Keep Clause," *NYDN,* Jan. 9, 1975.
173 new car: *DDN,* Oct. 23, 1975.
173 license plate PETE: "The King of Hustle," *Reds Alert,* March 13, 1976, Ohio History Center Archives & Library.
173 and he had a Porsche: "Rose Was . . . Rose: Battler and MVP," *BG,* Oct. 23, 1975.
173 thrilled to have the Hickok award: At the ceremony where he accepted the belt, Rose said it was the greatest award he had ever won. *NYDN,* Jan. 9, 1975.
173 "I wish opening day": *BG,* Oct. 23, 1975.
174 The two men had plans: "Pity Poor Pete—It's Almost Over," *CE,* Oct. 17, 1975.
174 As Gowdy recalled: "SportsCentury Pete Rose," ESPN, MI-12-14, Moving Image Index, Cincinnati History Library and Archives.

36

177 treated his wives: The author documented these marriages through Hillsborough County, Fla., marriage and divorce records.
177 eighth wife: Hillsborough High School yearbook, 1967.
177 Crime ran in the family: Details about Ralph Rubio's background and family come from multiple sources, including "'Tito,' Tampa Gambler, Murdered," *Tampa Times,* March 9, 1938; "Bar Operators' Cases Continued," *Tampa Times,* April 30, 1952; "Vice Raiders Arrest 8," *Tampa Times,* June 14, 1968; "Officials Accused of Protecting Prostitution," *TT,* June 28, 1968; and Terry Rubio Fernandez, interviews with author, Feb. 12–13 and 15, 2023.
177 Terry could get into any club: The author recorded multiple interviews with Terry Rubio Fernandez in February 2023. This detail, and others here, come from these interviews.
178 an arbitrator ruled: Details about the reserve clause ruling and its fallout come from press coverage, including "Arbitrator Frees 2 Baseball Stars," *NYT,* Dec. 24, 1975; "Wanted: New Ghostwriters," *NYT,* Dec. 28, 1975; "The Scene," *PI,* Jan. 11, 1976; and "If There's No Spring Training It'll Be Owners' Fault—Miller," *CP,* Jan. 30, 1976.
178 he attended a ceremony: "'Pete Rose Dr.,'" *DJH,* Feb. 28, 1976.
179 a young Cincinnati police cadet: "Rolls-Royce blues," *CP,* April 20, 1976.
179 floated around: "Reds Take 'Shots,'" *DJH,* March 8, 1976.

179 The first day: In interviews with the author, both Pete Rose and Terry Rubio Fernandez confirmed that they met during spring training in 1976 at an informal workout away from Al Lopez Field. Rose, interview with author, Oct. 18, 2021; Rubio, interview with author, Feb. 12, 2023.
179 the Cuban finally approached her: In Rose's memory, he sent a batboy to talk to Rubio. Rubio distinctly remembers that it was Mario Núñez who approached her.
180 Terry remembered: Terry Rubio Fernandez, interviews with author, Feb. 12–13 and 15, 2023.
181 The night before: "WS Oddsmakers? All Greek to Billy," *NYDN,* Oct. 17. 1976.
181 "I ain't moving": Mickey Rivers, interview with author, Feb. 17, 2023; "Rivers Unwilling to Accept Blame," *DJH,* Oct. 20, 1976; "Yankees Lacked a Vital Quality—Class," *CE,* Oct. 23, 1976.
181 totally crazy: Rivers, interview with author, Feb. 17, 2023.
181 almost subdued: "Reds Take Series in Stride, Clubhouse Celebration Is Subdued," *CP,* Oct. 22, 1976.
181 "I just couldn't get": "'Professional' Crowd Greets Returning World Champs," *Lexington Herald and Leader,* Oct. 23, 1976.
181 Karolyn flew home: The *Cincinnati Enquirer* photographer Mark Treitel documented Karolyn's presence on the plane in a photo shot on Oct. 23, 1976.
181 "togetherness": "A Reds-Hot Celebration Draws Thousands," *CP,* Oct. 22, 1976.
182 "They used Tony Perez": "Reds 'Used' Perez, Charges Morgan," *CE,* Dec. 18, 1976; Morgan and Falkner, *Joe Morgan,* 218.
182 "My God": "Trade Can't Sever Bond Between Perezes and Roses," *CE,* Jan. 9, 1977.
182 never became a wife: Bench made this comment to the reporter Barbara Walder during a lengthy question-and-answer story with *Harper's Magazine* in 1976, which later got picked up by newspapers across the country, including *The Boston Globe, The Cincinnati Enquirer,* and *The San Francisco Examiner.* In the interview, Bench said he didn't mind if a woman wanted to have a job. "But what happens when you get home? A man still wants an economist in the kitchen, a lady in the parlor, and a whore in the bedroom. A man wants to be pampered."
182 "a true tragedy": "Johnny 'Broke Heart,' Vickie Says," *CE,* Feb. 1, 1977.
182 didn't try to hide: This detail is confirmed by multiple sources, including a *Lexington Herald and Leader* photograph of Rose and Rubio together, shot by David Perry in October 1976; Sokolove, *Hustle,* 183; and Terry Rubio Fernandez, interviews with author, Feb. 12–13 and 15, 2023.
182 her own room: Terry Rubio Fernandez, interview with author, Feb. 12, 2023.

37

183 Tommy Gioiosa always knew: The author interviewed Tommy Gioiosa on multiple occasions between 2021 and 2023 for more than ten hours. Details

of Gioiosa's childhood and his life in general come from these interviews; interviews with other people who knew him; personal scrapbooks that Gioiosa shared with the author in his home that included old court documents and prison records; news stories about Gioiosa both before and after he met Pete Rose; and Gioiosa's federal case file, *United States of America v. Thomas P. Gioiosa,* CR-1-89-038, which the author reviewed in its entirety, including roughly two thousand pages of courtroom transcripts from his trial in 1989.

183 In his sophomore year: News clippings from the *New Bedford (Mass.) Standard-Times,* 1975–1976, various dates, Gioiosa scrapbook.

183 lack of size: Ibid.

183 He batted .561: High School All Americans, Official Athletic Sketch, 1976, Gioiosa scrapbook.

183 looks from the Cleveland Indians: "Tony's Better as Netminder," *New Bedford Standard-Union,* n.d., Gioiosa scrapbook.

184 "I have a prize": Joseph Fournier to Bob Humphreys (Virginia Tech baseball coach), May 6, 1976, Gioiosa scrapbook.

184 Tommy befriended: Gioiosa, interview with author, Oct. 25, 2021; Pete Rose, interview with author, Oct. 1, 2021; Karolyn Rose, interview with author, Dec. 2, 2021.

184 back pain: Howsam, *My Life in Sports,* 147.

185 "our ability to keep": "Howsam Responds to Negotiations Charges," *CP,* March 2, 1977.

185 finally worked out: "Rose Signs Two-Year Contract," *CE,* April 6, 1977; "$700,000-Plus Deal for Rose," *CP,* April 6, 1977; "Reds to Sign Rose for $375,000," *DJH,* April 6, 1977.

185 she flew north: Terry Rubio Fernandez, interview with author, Feb. 12, 2023.

185 He had made arrangements: Rubio stayed in the home of Rose's friend Gordon Granick, a detail that the author confirmed not only with Terry Rubio Fernandez but with one of Granick's sons who was there at the time. Paul Granick, interview with author, Feb. 14, 2023.

185 Thirty-nine times: "There Were Good Points, Too, for Reds' Fans to Remember," *DDN,* Oct. 3, 1977.

186 "You're damn right": "Rose Blows Steam as 3 'Regulars' Rest," *DDN,* Sept. 14, 1977.

186 went to the racetrack: The author didn't need to rely simply on interviews with Terry Rubio Fernandez to confirm this fact. Rubio appears next to Rose in a photograph shot by the *Lexington Herald* on Oct. 14, 1976. The paper did not publish the picture in the next day's paper; it chose a different image instead that did not include Terry. But decades later, the paper, now renamed the *Lexington Herald-Leader,* posted the photo on its website, identifying Rubio as a friend of Rose's.

186 Terry was pregnant: Terry Rubio Fernandez, interviews with author, Feb. 12–13 and 15, 2023.

38

186 Terry knew the baby: Terry Rubio Fernandez, interviews with author, Feb. 12–13 and 15, 2023. Rose came to a settlement with Rubio in 1980, but did not publicly acknowledge the girl as his daughter until a second court case brought by the girl herself in 1996 once she was an adult. "Pete Rose Acknowledges Daughter, 18," *TT,* Nov. 22, 1996.

187 The Reds had a harder time: Terry Rubio Fernandez, interviews with author, Feb. 12–13 and 15, 2023.

187 the three men: Metz, interview with author, Oct. 22, 2021.

187 had been a cheerleader: Details about Woliung come from the news coverage in her hometown newspaper in Lawrenceburg, Indiana, including "Carol Woliung to Be Featured; LHS Band Boosters Plan Booth," *Dearborn County Register,* Sept. 9, 1971; "Woliung-Foerster Wedding Performed at St. John's," *Dearborn County Register,* May 24, 1973; and "Court House News," *Dearborn County Register,* March 31, 1977.

187 the "nicest ass": Rose, interview with author, Sept. 29, 2021.

187 being followed: Terry Rubio Fernandez spoke about Rose being followed in interviews with author, Feb. 12–13 and 15, 2023. The detail also appeared elsewhere. The private investigator himself, William Dantschisch, confirmed it for the press in 1989, and Dantschisch's daughter, Lee Tarbutton, also recalled her father speaking about it. Tarbutton, interview with author, Sept. 30, 2021.

188 "You might say": "Job Security," *PI,* March 1, 1978.

188 a different man: Details about Wagner's childhood, professional career, and how he handled himself in the front office come from multiple sources, including Brennaman, interview with author, Aug. 1, 2021; Rose, interview with author, Oct. 19, 2021; Howsam, *My Life in Sports,* 162; "Reds VP Wagner Pulls No Punches, Gets Job Done," *CE,* May 9, 1976; "Reds' New 'Mr. Big' Sees Himself as a Doer," *CE,* Feb. 26, 1978; "Reds' Wagner Wore Many Hats, Now He'll Don the BIG ONE," *DDN,* March 5, 1978; "Wagner's New Position Forces Him to Pay Attention to Games," *DDN,* March 6, 1978; and "Dick Wagner Opens Up," *Cincinnati Magazine,* April 1982.

189 In front of Fawn one day: The exact timing of this confrontation isn't clear. But both Karolyn Rose and Fawn Rose recounted it in separate interviews with the author.

189 Pete moved out: *The Cincinnati Post* was the first to break the news. "Pete Called Out at Home," *CP,* June 19, 1978.

189 started staying with his friend: Granick, interview with author, Feb. 14, 2023; Karolyn Rose, interview with author, Dec. 2, 2021.

190 dark and persistent rumors: Wagner died in 2006. But before his death he gave interviews indicating his knowledge of Rose's gambling. "ESPN SportsCentury—Pete Rose," MI-12-14, Moving Image Index, Cincinnati History Library and Archives. Additional accounts of Wagner's concerns were also published after the fact in several stories, including "Rose Inves-

tigation Widens," *CP,* July 28, 1989, and a *New York Post* report also from July 1989.

190 One day early in the 1978 season: Dave Collins, interview with author, Dec. 14, 2021.

190 Henry Fitzgibbon: Rose confirmed meeting with Fitzgibbon in an interview with author, Oct. 18, 2021, and in *MP,* 80. Fitzgibbon also confirmed meeting with Rose before his death in "Earlier Rose Probe Mostly Blank," *CE,* March 30, 1989, and Sokolove, *Hustle,* 200, 211. Additional details come from Barbara Karnes (Fitzgibbon's daughter), interview with author, Sept. 29, 2021.

191 Pete was fine: Rose, interview with author, Oct. 18, 2021; *MP,* 81.

191 "Pete played that night": Collins, interview with author, Dec. 14, 2021.

191 stop hanging out: Brennaman, interview with author, Aug. 1, 2021.

39

191 he logged his 3,000th hit: Details about Rose's 3,000th hit and his thoughts on reaching Cobb's record come from the news coverage of the game in the following stories: "Rose: Strongly Macho and Glad of It" and "Everyone Has a Memory of Pete Rose," *CE,* May 6, 1978; "3,000 Hits Behind Him Now, Rose Says 3,630 Is Next," *CP,* May 6, 1978; "A Hit to Remember," "Rose Still Good for a Few More," and "What Manner of a Man Is This One-of-a-Kind Rose?," *DDN,* May 6, 1978; and "Sparky Gave Rose the Incentive," "Select Company," and "Rose a Walking Bubble Gum Card," *DJH,* May 6, 1978.

192 chocolate-flavored beverage: At local grocery stores in Cincinnati, a six-pack of Pete sold for $1.89.

192 4,191: In recent years, baseball researchers and historians studied Ty Cobb's statistics and adjusted his hit total to two fewer hits than previously believed: 4,189. But these changes did not happen until much later. "How Many Hits Did Ty Cobb Make in His Major League Career? What Is His Lifetime Batting Average?," *Baseball Research Journal,* Spring 2019, and "Sept. 8, 1985, the Day Pete Rose Really Broke Ty Cobb's Record," *CE,* Sept. 8, 2015.

192 .274: "Major Leaders—Individual Batting," *CE,* June 18, 1978.

192 broke the news: *CP,* June 19, 1978.

192 cherry bombs: "Giants Get Crowds, Problems," *CE,* June 22, 1978; "Giants Glad to Get 3–0 Gift," *DDN,* June 22, 1978; "Ugly Signs Mar Rebirth in Frisco," *DJH,* June 22, 1978.

193 The press first mentioned: "Sparky's Faith in Hume Backfires When Dodgers Load Bases," *CE,* June 25, 1978.

193 "Nothing, kid": "Rose Erupts in Anger, but Doesn't Faze the Reds," *DDN,* July 1, 1978.

193 reunited with Karolyn: "Martin Bemoans Injuries; Rose, Zimmer Reunited," *CP,* July 11, 1978; "The Roses May Bloom Once More," *CP,* July 13, 1978.

193 "Thanks," he told Pete: Details of Rose tying Holmes's record at thirty-seven games in New York come from multiple news accounts, including "Rose Fever

Overwhelms Nation's Sporting Press," *CE,* July 25, 1978; "Hits and Ovations Rolling In for Rose" and "Adversity, Thy Name Is Rose," *CP,* July 25, 1978; "A (Pete) Rose by Any Other Name" and "Rose Beats 'the Book,'" *DDN,* July 25, 1978; "Rose Ties Records as Reds Win, 5–3" and "Holmes Proud of Rose," *DJH,* July 25, 1978; "Mets Unable to Stem Rose, See Victory Plucked Away," "Mets Want Rose to Peter Out," "Rose Hits 37, Ties Holmes," *NYDN,* July 25, 1978; and "Rose Hits in 37th Game in Row, Tying Mark, as Reds Beat Mets," *NYT,* July 25, 1978.

195 "I might go forever": "Torrid Rose Spurs Reds into Break High if Not Mighty," *CE,* July 10, 1978.

40

195 "Congratulations": "Will DiMaggio's Mark Fall? He's Sure It Will Some Day," *PI,* July 31, 1978.

196 Many people thought: *NYDN,* July 25, 1978.

196 batting cage that Friday: "Off Day at Riverfront Busy Tuneup Time for Reds," *CE,* July 28, 1978; "What's a Guy on a Tear Do on a Day Off?," *CP,* July 28, 1978.

196 an extra $215,000: "Reds' Blunder May Make Rose a Free Agent," *NYDN,* July 27, 1978.

196 "And have you checked": *CP,* July 28, 1978.

196 an hour-long interview: "Talk Show Draws 6,000 to See Rose," *CE,* July 28, 1978; "Rose Ducks Wild Pitch at Talk Show," *CP,* July 31, 1978; "Tube Test," *PI,* Aug. 1, 1978.

196 "You're going to love me": "Rose Marches on Atlanta," *CP,* Aug. 1, 1978.

197 "We're Pulling for You Pete!": Ibid.

197 The Braves had to push: Details about the night when Rose tried to run his hit streak to forty-four consecutive games come from multiple sources, including "Rose Hits Niekro to Make It 44," "This Rose Can't Be Called by Another Name," and "Braves Defeated by Reds in Ninth, 3–2," *AC,* Aug. 1, 1978; "Rose Gets 44th, Reds Win," *CE,* Aug. 1, 1978; "Niekro's Visit Pleases Rose" and "Before Game Niekro Said He Felt Like the Villain," *CP,* Aug. 1, 1978; "The Last Ghost Is Caught," *DDN,* Aug. 1, 1978; and "Rose Bangs 44th Hit to Tie Keeler" and "Villain—That's Role Niekro Faced," *DJH,* Aug. 1, 1978.

197 Pete had more hits off Niekro: According to Frank Labombarda, the head of research at the Elias Sports Bureau, Rose had sixty-four hits off Niekro over the course of his career, four more than Rose got off any other individual pitcher.

199 The jitters: Details about the night when Rose went for his forty-fifth consecutive game with a hit come from multiple sources, including Rose, interview with author, Oct. 18, 2021; Gene Garber, interviews with author, Jan. 19–20, 2022; Dave Collins, interview with author, Dec. 14, 2021; "Rose Streak Ends," "Money Trail," and "Rose Fills the Pockets of Turner," *AC,* Aug. 2, 1978; "Braves Stop Rose's Streak at 44 Games," *CE,* Aug. 2, 1978;

"Pete Boiling at Way Garber Pitched Him," "Meet Larry McWilliams, Pete," and "Rose Knows How DiMag Felt—Empty," *CP,* Aug. 2, 1978; "Rose Acts Bitterly as 'the Streak' Ends" and "Rose: Hope I Face Garber Again," *DDN,* Aug. 2, 1978; "Rose Streak Ends" and "Older, Wiser Rose Becomes Prototype of '70s Hitter," *DJH,* Aug. 2, 1978; "Offstage . . . Rose Week One to Remember" and "Pete Rose Bleeps Part of the Game," *AC,* Aug. 3, 1978; "Back in the Swing," "Rose Says . . . 'I'll Get Garber, I Didn't Know I Was on T.V.,'" and "The Thrill Still There for Pete Rose," *CE,* Aug. 3, 1978; "Rose May Be the Best Baseball Has to Offer," *Washington Post,* Aug. 3, 1978; and archival television footage of Rose's final at bat against Garber.

199 Gene Garber: The author interviewed Garber over two nights in Jan. 2022. Additional details about Garber's life in the summer of 1978 come from news coverage in *The Philadelphia Inquirer,* the *Philadelphia Daily News,* and *The Atlanta Constitution* at the time of the trade.

199 "morning and evening": "G-e-n-o Spells Relief for Braves' Bullpen," *Atlanta Journal and Constitution,* Aug. 13, 1978.

200 Pete batted just .229: Frank Labombarda, head of research, Elias Sports Bureau.

200 "I'll never live it down": Garber, interview with author, Jan. 20, 2022.

41

201 touched by Tommy Holmes's warmth: *DJH,* July 25, 1978.

201 He was angry: Details about Rose's anger come from multiple sources listed previously, including news coverage on Aug. 2–3, 1978, in the following papers: *The Atlanta Constitution, The Cincinnati Enquirer, The Cincinnati Post,* the *Dayton Daily News,* the Dayton *Journal Herald,* the New York *Daily News,* and *The Philadelphia Inquirer.*

201 "Garber pitched me": "Pete Rose 'Empty' as Streak Ends," *DDN,* Aug. 2, 1978.

202 "Did you see him jump": *AC,* Aug. 3, 1978.

202 "One question, Pete": *DDN,* Aug. 2, 1978.

202 helped tell the story that Pete wanted: In recent years, Rose still felt Garber had wronged him. In an interview with the author in Oct. 2021, Rose said, "I know he is not supposed to throw it right down Broadway, in the express lane, but he didn't really come at me. . . . You could at least throw me a fucking strike."

202 "People don't let me forget": Garber, interview with author, Jan. 20, 2022.

202 "Pete Rose Day in Washington": Details about Rose's visit to Washington come from several sources, including *Congressional Record,* Sept. 25, 1978; Presidential Daily Diary, Sept. 25, 1978, Jimmy Carter Presidential Library and Museum; "Rose a Hit with Congress During His Day in D.C.," *CE,* Sept. 26, 1978; and "Rose Stands Capitol on Dome," *CP,* Sept. 26, 1978.

202 passed a resolution: All the quotations and comments made about Rose on the floor of Congress come straight from the *Congressional Record,* Sept. 25, 1978.

203 "Who's in there?": *CP,* Sept. 26, 1978.

203 Karolyn brushed tears: Karolyn kept a low profile on the visit to Washington. While the White House's daily log records that she visited the Oval Office along with Pete and the kids, she did not stand in the photo with the president. It was only after they returned from Washington that she began making public appearances at Pete's side again. "Reconciliation for the Roses?," *CP,* Sept. 27, 1978.

203 "Thank the good Lord": "The other Rose: Flash and sass, spirit to match," *PI,* Dec. 10, 1978.

203 getting frustrated about sending Terry money: In interviews with the author, both Pete Rose and Terry Rubio Fernandez said that Pete sent her money for a while and then stopped out of frustration. Rose, interview with author, Oct. 18, 2021; Terry Rubio Fernandez, interviews with author, Feb. 12–13 and 15, 2023.

204 Players complained: "Bench Says Sparky Too Nice, Reds Need a 'Get Tough' Policy," *DDN,* Aug. 28, 1978.

204 lost control of the locker room: "Backlash," *DDN,* Aug. 29, 1978.

204 Howsam jetted in: "Howsam Tells Reds How, Pirates Show 'Em," *CE,* Aug. 30, 1978; "Howsam Talks with Reds," *CP,* Aug. 30, 1978; "Howsam's Clubhouse Chat a Clear-the-Air Seminar," *DDN,* Aug. 30 1978; "Howsam's Talk No Help," *DJH,* Aug. 30, 1978.

204 blue-tinted glasses: "Miffed Rose Gets Record Salary Offer," *DDN,* Oct. 2, 1978.

204 Reuven Katz: "Katz Could Play on Any All-Star Law Team," *CE,* June 24, 1979; "Lawyer Reuven Katz Strikes with Win-Win Style of Negotiating," *CE,* May 8, 1984.

204 Wagner made Pete an offer: Wagner and Rose tried to blame each other for why negotiations fell apart and Rose signed elsewhere. Wagner didn't want to be known as the man who ran Rose out of town, and Rose didn't want to look as though he abandoned Cincinnati. Given what is now known about Wagner's feelings on Rose during the 1978 season, Wagner clearly didn't seem to be interested in re-signing Rose.

204 somewhere around half a million dollars: The terms of the offer were never officially disclosed or confirmed.

204 Pete called Wagner a liar: Rose called a press conference in Reuven Katz's office on Oct. 12, 1978, to complain about Wagner to the local press contingent.

204 getting creative: Details of the offers that other teams made to Rose come from multiple sources, including Pete Rose, interview with author, Oct. 18, 2021; *PRMS,* 203; "Million-a-Year Bids Stall Rose's Decision," *CE,* Nov. 30, 1978; "Money War: Phils Out, Four Still Seek Rose," *DDN,* Dec. 1, 1978; "The Plot Thickens: Rose Rejects Phils," *AC,* Dec. 1, 1978; "Pete on Phils' Royal-Ties: Not Enough Bucs," *CE,* Dec. 1, 1978; and "These Offers Failed," *CP,* Dec. 5, 1978.

205 "Horses," Turner muttered: *AC,* Dec. 1, 1978.

205 a show dog: Rose made this statement in front of a horde of baseball writers

when he was introduced as the newest Phillie at baseball's winter meetings in Orlando, Florida, on Dec. 5, 1978.

205 detested the Reds' president: "Ban the Club," *CP,* Dec. 5, 1978.

205 Wagner delivered to Sparky: Anderson, *Sparky!,* 129.

205 "The Big Dead Machine": "Requiem for Big Dead Machine," *CE,* Aug. 30, 1978.

205 "Does Phildelphia Have a Kmart?": *PI,* Dec. 10, 1978.

206 Gioiosa was coming: Details about Gioiosa's stay with the Roses come from multiple people, including Gioiosa, interview with author, Oct. 26, 2021; Karolyn Rose, interview with author, Dec. 2, 2021; and Fawn Rose, interview with author, Feb. 2, 2022.

206 didn't understand: Fawn Rose, interview with author, Feb. 2, 2022.

206 "When you hold a strong hand": "No Rose Garden," *TT,* Feb. 21, 1979.

206 one morning that winter: Gioiosa, interview with author, Oct. 26, 2021.

206 front-page news: This story ran on the front page of *The Cincinnati Enquirer* on Feb. 17, 1979, which fits with the story that Gioiosa told to the author decades later. Gioiosa arrived in Cincinnati sometime in Jan. 1979.

206 Terry decided to confront Karolyn: In interviews with the author, both women confirmed this fact.

207 a black-tie roast: All the quotations from the roast come directly from the event itself, which was filmed for the local NBC affiliate and is archived today in the television footage holdings at the Cincinnati History Library and Archives, under the title "Pete Rose Roast," MI-97-98. Additional details and context were supplied by George Foster. Foster, interview with author, March 13, 2023.

42

209 "I really want to prove": "Virtually Born a Phillie, Ruly Is Ready to Win," *PI,* Dec. 5, 1978.

209 a $600,000 boost: "Pete Switches Stance on Phillies' 2d Pitch," *PI,* Dec. 19, 1978.

209 ticket sales and merchandise sales: "The Selling of Pete Rose," *PDN,* April 5, 1979.

209 "Don't get upset": "Van Buren Gave Fans a Run for Their Money," *PDN,* Dec. 6, 1978.

210 Pete welcomed the pressure: Details of Rose's first spring training with Philadelphia come from multiple sources, including "Rose Starts Race Against Time Carrying the Phils on His Back," *PI,* March 1, 1979; "Campy Stories from Training Camp," *PI,* March 18, 1979; and "Concepcion: Socks and Shrimp, Pickoffs and Chicken Pox," *CE,* March 25, 1979.

210 let himself believe: Gioiosa, interview with author, Oct. 25, 2021.

211 "So the interview's over?": In 2022, the author tracked down Stevenson. Details about the interview—and its aftermath—draw on the author's interview with her, Oct. 27, 2022; news coverage of her *Playboy* interview after it came out; and the 1979 interview itself, *Playboy,* Sept. 1979.

211 Pete didn't like: "Rose Playboy Interview Heats Up Again," *CE,* Aug. 28, 1979.
211 probably didn't help: Stevenson, interview with author, Oct. 27, 2022.
211 "He wanted so badly": *CE,* Aug. 28, 1979, and Stevenson, interview with author, Oct.27, 2022.
211 In the *Playboy* interview: *Playboy,* Sept. 1979.
212 It was going to be hard: Stevenson, interview with author, Oct. 27, 2022.
212 Pete denied the comment: "Rose Denies He Took Drug; *Playboy* Stands By Its Charge," *PI,* Aug. 5, 1979.
212 traveling light: "Karolyn Rose: 'Just a Plain and Simple Girl,'" *PI,* Aug. 12, 1979.
213 driving Karolyn's Porsche: In a *Sports Illustrated* cover story that ran on Aug. 19, 1985, Carol Rose admitted that Karolyn once punched her. "She split my lip," Carol told *Sports Illustrated.* Details of this incident also come from Karolyn Rose, interview with author, Dec. 2, 2021; Fawn Rose, interview with author, Feb. 2, 2022; and Stevenson, interview with author, Oct. 27, 2022. Stevenson said she was there at the stadium the night that Karolyn chased Carol down on the street.
213 $14,000 a month in alimony: It's unclear how much Pete ultimately ended up paying Karolyn during the year they were officially separated. But this figure appears in the divorce records at the Hamilton County Common Pleas Court in Cincinnati. *Karolyn Rose v. Peter Edward Rose,* A7907917. Karolyn made the request for $14,000 a month on Sept. 11, 1979.
213 more money than some people made: According to the U.S. Census Bureau, the median income in the United States in 1979 was $16,530.
213 $37,000 in jewelry: *Karolyn Rose v. Peter Edward Rose,* A7907917.
214 finished second in a popularity poll: "Choose a Phillies Manager" contest, *PI,* Sept. 20, 1978.
214 analyzing the baseball playoffs: *The NFL Today,* CBS archival footage, Oct. 7, 1979.
214 "A gambler's delight": Rose, interview with author, Oct. 19, 2021.

43

215 wasn't sure the best team had prevailed: "The Happy End to a Long Ordeal," *PI,* Oct. 13, 1980.
215 He and catcher Bob Boone: "Rose Was Johnny on the Spot," *PDN,* Oct. 22, 1980; "Final Outs of 1980 World Series, Through Bob Boone's Eyes," *Beyond the Bell* (MLB blog), Oct. 21, 2020.
215 flashing a victory sign: "By Dawn's Early Light, Vet Is Still There," *PI,* Oct. 22, 1980.
215 "It's the greatest thing": Carpenter, postgame interview, NBC television, Oct. 21, 1980.
216 "gross neglect of duty": "Karolyn Divorces Pete Rose," *CE,* Aug. 1, 1980.
216 Pete hadn't seen his children: "Rose's Son Gets Court OK," *PDN,* Oct. 22, 1980.
216 didn't want to prevent: Karolyn Rose, interview with author, Dec. 2, 2021.

216 Karolyn got full custody: *Karolyn Rose v. Peter Edward Rose,* A7907917.
216 "Might you retire?": *PDN,* Oct. 22, 1980.
217 Under oath at a hearing: "Charges Against 3 Dropped in Phillies Drug Case," *PI,* Feb. 5, 1981.
217 illegally prescribing and delivering amphetamines: In the summer of 1981, months after the charges were dropped, *The Philadelphia Inquirer* did a multi-part series on the amphetamine scandal that is a good source of information on the investigation—"The Pill Probe," July 1981.
217 "What's a greenie?": "Doc Phill-ing Orders? Players, Wives Say No," *PDN,* Jan. 8, 1981.
217 The doctor was stunned: "The Doctor Says of the Phillies: 'These Guys Lied,'" *PI,* Feb. 7, 1981.
217 overwhelming power: Randy Lerch, *God in the Bullpen: The Randy Lerch Story,* 5.
217 *Encyclopaedia Britannica:* At the time of publication, these old *Britannica* ads featuring Rose could be found on YouTube. Rose also mentioned them during his testimony about amphetamines.
217 bought a condo: According to the Hamilton County Auditor, Rose purchased the condo at 5209 Clear Lake Drive on Feb. 27, 1981.
217 Tommy could run errands: Gioiosa, interview with author, Oct. 26, 2021. Gioiosa also testified in federal court about all the different things he did for Rose. CR-1-89-038, Aug. 1989.
218 Sometimes, Tommy thought: Gioiosa, interview with author, Nov. 4, 2021.
218 a glowing feature: "Charlie Hustle Is Back in Town," *CE,* April 3, 1980.
218 tryout with the Toronto Blue Jays: Bob Engle (scouting supervisor of the Toronto Blue Jays) to Pete Rose, July 23, 1981, Gioiosa scrapbooks; Gioiosa, interview with author, Oct. 24, 2022.
219 He drove Pete and little Petey: Gioiosa, interview with author, Nov. 15, 2021.
219 open-mic comedy hour: "Reagan Connects," *DDN,* Aug. 11, 1981; "New Hotline: Reagan to Rose," *PDN,* Aug. 11. 1981.
219 Reagan's voice: Ronald Reagan, Presidential Daily Diary, Aug. 10, 1981, Ronald Reagan Presidential Library.

44

220 "Congratulations on being an Oriole": Jack Baker to Gioiosa, handwritten on Orioles stationery and undated, Gioiosa personal collection, and "Orioles Sign Gioiosa," *CE,* Dec. 1, 1981.
220 seventy-five times: "Ruly Carpenter, 81, Dies; Owned the Phillies' First Championship Team," *NYT,* Sept. 16, 2021.
220 "All I need to pass Cobb": "Rose Eyes Titles, Not Rocking Chairs," *Tampa Bay Times,* March 7, 1982.
220 "an awful lot of residual money": "Rose a Budding Millionaire," *PI,* Feb. 23, 1982.
220 "I'm going to catch him": "Rose's Eternal Youth for All Fans to Savor," *PI,* June 23, 1982.

220 Tommy hit well: Gioiosa, interview with author, Oct. 24, 2022.
221 He had tweaked his back: "Rose Injures Back Playing Tennis," *CP,* Feb. 26, 1982.
221 "Rest in peace": Gioiosa, interview with author, Oct. 24, 2022.
221 "Anybody'd be concerned": "Sore Back Puts Rose in Unusual Spot—off the Field," *PI,* March 2, 1982.
221 "I used to use three uniforms": "Rose Dives into Foster Deal," *DJH,* Feb. 9, 1982.
221 It seemed unnecessary: "Baseball Notes," *CE,* March 2, 1982; "Million Dollar Man," *DDN,* March 2, 1982.
221 doubled down: "Rose Has Aug. '84 on His Mind," *CP,* March 1, 1982.
221 He predicted he'd pass Cobb: "Rose Has Aug. '84 on His Mind," *CP,* March 1, 1982.
221 "Tommy G is sure a great guy": Baker to Rose, n.d., Gioiosa personal collection.
222 helping Pete with his girlfriends: In interviews with the author, both Gioiosa and Rose acknowledged that Gioiosa would help get Rose's girlfriends where Rose wanted them to be.
222 Pete's treasured Hickok belt: Gioiosa, interview with author, Nov. 15, 2022, and Janszen, press conference, Sept. 8, 1989.
222 "You guys are crazy": Gioiosa, interview with author, May 18, 2023.
222 ground balls: Gioiosa, interview with author, Oct. 24, 2022.
222 "*Cold* cash": Rose, interview with author, Oct. 20, 2021.
222 Or he didn't have to patch: Gioiosa, interview with author, Nov. 15, 2021.
222 didn't seem to think twice about ignoring him: Ibid.
222 Tommy wrote home: Gioiosa to his parents, n.d., Gioiosa scrapbooks.
223 He felt as if he had let everyone down: Gioiosa, interview with author, Oct. 26, 2021; Gioiosa, testimony at federal trial, CR-1-89-038, Aug. 1989.
223 Tommy leaned against the kitchen counter: Gioiosa, interview with author, Oct. 26, 2021.
223 a cheaper source: Details about Janszen selling steroids to local bodybuilders in the 1980s were confirmed in three places: Gioiosa, interview with author, Oct. 28, 2021; "Say It Ain't So, Pete!," *Penthouse*, Sept. 1989; and Janszen's own testimony at Gioiosa's federal trial, CR-1-89-038. Janszen testimony, Aug. 30, 1989, 74–75.
223 Paul was about the same age: Details about Janszen's background come from multiple sources, including Janszen, interview with author, April 15, 2022, and July 2, 2022; Chuck Zimmerman, interview with author, Nov. 11, 2021; Gioiosa, interviews with author, Oct. 26, 2021, and May 18, 2023; "Friends Paint Complex Portrait of Rose Accuser," *CP,* July 7, 1989; *Penthouse,* Sept. 1989; and Janszen's interviews with MLB's special counsel, John Dowd, in the *Dowd Report,* Exhibit 26, Janszen interview, Feb. 24–25, 1989.
224 Pete was killing them at first: "At Last, Matuszek Gets First Crack," *PDN,* Feb. 17, 1984.
224 Francona listened to Pete's stories: Francona, interview with author, Nov. 18, 2022.

224 Pete grabbed an Expos broadcaster: "Rose Grabs Reporter over Remarks," *Ottawa Citizen,* June 17, 1984; "Media Softest on the Expos," *Montreal Gazette,* June 19, 1984.

224 nagging injuries: "The Final World," *CP,* April 21, 1984.

45

225 In Marge's parlance: Schott's racist remarks didn't come out until 1992 during depositions for a lawsuit filed against her by a former employee. She denied being a racist, but admitted to using some of the terms. Multiple parties confirmed hearing her speak in this way, including the former Reds general manager Murray Cook in an interview with the author. According to the former *Cincinnati Post* sportswriter Mike Bass, the *Post* also confirmed these comments with eight former Reds employees, but the newspaper declined to run the story. Bass, *Marge Schott Unleashed,* 199.

225 Marge tried to shame Wagner: "Air Mail," *DDN,* May 15, 1983.

226 "I Don't Like Dick Wagner": "Wagner's Firing Fuels Sale Rumors," *DJH,* July 12, 1983.

226 "Pete Rose Forever": "Fans Takes to Air with Wagner Jibe," *CP,* July 7, 1983.

226 had to concede: "Owners 'Agonized' over Wagner," *CP,* July 13, 1983.

226 set his mind on rebuilding: Details about Howsam's return to Cincinnati can be found in his unpublished memoir, *My Life in Sports,* and news coverage from the local papers in 1983.

226 Everyone was shocked: "Reds' Hiring of Vern Rapp Stirs Disbelief at Playoffs," *CP,* Oct. 5, 1983.

227 didn't impress anyone: Details about Rapp's turbulent tenure in St. Louis can be found in multiple sources, including "Rapp Feuded with Players as St. Louis Boss," *CE,* Oct. 5, 1983, and "It's Time for the Players to Look at Themselves and Say, 'Maybe We're the Guys Causing the Trouble,'" *St. Louis Post-Dispatch,* July 17, 1977.

227 an elaborate joke: *Sports Illustrated* first wrote about the joke in the "Scorecard" section on Oct. 17, 1983, and almost forty years later Will Leitch wrote an entertaining retrospective account of this joke for MLB.com, "The Harmless Practical Joke That Changed Baseball," Dec. 21, 2021. Howsam denied at the time that the satire had anything to do with Rapp's hiring.

227 He posted corny taglines: McCoy, interview with author, Jan. 6, 2022; "Will the Reds Rise Again?," *CP,* April 2, 1984.

227 fans could expect: "City, Stadium Stand Ready for the Reds," *CE,* April 2, 1984; Howsam, *My Life in Sports,* 168.

227 failed to earn the respect: McCoy, interview with author, Jan. 6, 2022.

228 "What if I brought Rose": Howsam, *My Life in Sports,* 174.

228 "do you think I can hit?": "Pete Says Team's Needs Come First," *CE,* Aug. 17, 1984.

228 Howsam had to decide: Details about Howsam's thinking come from two sources: Howsam, *My Life in Sports;* and Robert Howsam Jr., interview with author, Feb. 22, 2022.

228 married his girlfriend: Rose first mentioned that he planned to marry Carol in November 1983. They finally exchanged vows in Reuven Katz's home during an Expos road trip to Cincinnati in April 1984.

228 Carol was thrilled: Insight into Carol's thinking comes from multiple interviews she gave around this time, including "Coming Home," *DJH,* Aug. 18, 1984; "Romance and the Roses," *CP,* June 14, 1985; and "For Pete's Sake—Carol Rose Has Reason to Be Thankful," *DDN,* Aug. 11, 1985. In this last article, Carol said, "I felt I died and went to heaven. This is the most wonderful thing that's ever happened to me. Mainly just having the baby and a husband and a home—it's like finally it's all into shape. Before, I didn't know which way to turn."

229 "on the straight and narrow": Howsam, *My Life in Sports,* 175.

229 Dick Skinner: Details about Skinner and Rose come from interviews that the author conducted with two people: Wes Hills, formerly of the *Dayton Daily News,* a reporter who covered Skinner at the time, and a local gambler who ran in Skinner's circle in the 1980s, Keith Sexton. Hills, interviews with author, Nov. 4 and 14, 2022, and Sexton, interview with author, Nov. 11, 2022. Additonal details can also be found in Wes Hills's groundbreaking story about Skinner and Rose: "Tape Details Rose's Gambling Debt to Dayton Bookie," *DDN,* Dec. 22, 2002.

229 Joe Cambra: Details about Cambra's background come from multiple sources, including 1930 U.S. Census for his father, Jose Cambra; Cambra's World War II draft card, No. 11703; and records related to Operation Moby Dick.

229 In Pete's mind: In the 1980s, Rose denied betting placing bets with Cambra. But with the author, he admitted that Cambra was his bookie. Rose, interview with author, Oct. 20, 2021.

229 part of a spiderweb of bookies: In early 2021, the author tracked down and interviewed one of the lead investigators of Operation Moby Dick, the retired Massachusetts State Police trooper Jim Murray, as well as one of the men who served the warrant at Cambra's house that night, the former trooper Dick Rand. Details of the Cambra investigation come from interviews with both men, as well as a large box of Jim Murray's notes, records, and official State Police wiretap transcripts that Murray saved at his home in Massachusetts and shared with the author in 2022. Details about Cambra's bookmaking operation come from Murray, interview with author, Feb. 15, 2022; Rand, interview with author, Feb. 17, 2022; multiple stories from the New Bedford *Standard-Times,* including "Mob Sports Gaming Ring Raided," Nov. 14, 1984; multiple stories from *The Boston Globe,* including "Cambra: No Rose Game Bets," April 28, 1989; and hundreds of pages of documents gathered during Operation Moby Dick, including transcripts of wiretapped calls.

230 corked bats: Rose has denied ever using a corked bat, and two other members of the 1984 Montreal Expos, Doug Flynn and Terry Francona, told the author they never heard of Greenberg making bats for players. But three sources spoke to the author about Rose using corked bats—or about hearing about the existence of these bats at the time: Bryan Greenberg, the carpenter

who said he made the bat, interview with author, Oct. 14, 2022; Gioiosa, interview with author, Nov. 15, 2022; and Ron McClain (former Montreal Expos trainer), interview with author, Oct. 27, 2022. Reporter Joe Capozzi, who first broke the news about Bryan Greenberg's allegations, was also helpful in confirming details.

230 All Greenberg knew: "He Called Me 'Corky': Jupiter Man Says He Corked Baseball Bats for Pete Rose in 1984," *Palm Beach Post,* June 5, 2020; Greenberg, interview with author, Oct. 14, 2022.

46

231 Vern Rapp learned: Details about how Rapp was fired come from multiple sources, including McCoy, interview with author, Jan. 6, 2022; Howsam, *My Life in Sports,* 176; "Rapp's Swan Song Comes Just at Edge of Loss Streak End," *DDN,* Aug. 16, 1984; "Rapp Bows Out with His Dignity," *CP,* Aug. 16, 1984; and "Rapp Bows Out Gracefully," *CE,* Aug. 17, 1984.

231 "Pete Rose is Mister Cincinnati": "Schott Says Fans Will Go Bonkers," *CE,* Aug. 16, 1984.

231 $40,000 in tickets: "Return of Rose Means Bigger Stadium Crowds," *CE,* Aug. 17, 1984.

232 The press conference: "Press Conference Biggest in 25 Years," *CE,* Aug. 17, 1984; "Rose's Biggest Test Lies in the Long Run" and "Rose, Reds Ready for Fun," *DJH,* Aug. 17, 1984; "Rose Returns to Riverfront," *PI,* Aug. 17, 1984; "Rose's Work Cut Out on Two Fronts," *Chicago Tribune,* Aug. 17, 1984; "Rose Arrives on Wave of Good Feeling," *Detroit Free Press,* Aug. 17, 1984.

232 "better get ready to hustle": "Rose to Manage Reds," *DJH,* Aug. 16, 1984.

232 a relatively rare burst: The author asked the Elias Sports Bureau to track how many players, forty and older, had ever hit .365 or better over a twenty-six-game stretch. According to Elias, fifteen players did it between 1900 and 1962; two players did it during Rose's playing days between 1963 and 1984; Rose did it four times in the 1980s, including twice in 1984; and several players did it after him, including Tony Pérez and Craig Nettles in 1985, David Ortiz and Ichiro Suzuki in 2017, and Albert Pujols and Nelson Cruz in 2022.

233 the Reds were honoring him: "Here's the real story on 'Scoops' Lawson," *CP,* Oct. 1, 1984.

233 needed to work out that winter: "Rose Switches from a Lectern to Hitting Cage," Ibid., Jan. 29, 1985.

233 a healthy destination for beautiful people: Details about the Gold's Gym location in Forest Park come from advertisements that the gym placed at the time. Advertisement, *CE,* Feb. 20, 1986.

234 Fry ran the business side: Details of the business operation at Gold's Gym come from multiple sources, including *Dowd Report,* Exhibit 3, Mike Fry interview, April 11, 1989; Don Stenger's federal case file, CR-1-88-101, from his criminal charges in 1988; and the testimony of Stenger and others at Tommy Gioiosa's 1989 trial on drug and tax evasion charges, CR-1-89-038.

234 Mr. Ohio 1984: *CE,* Feb. 20, 1986.

234 Stenger was in the middle of that: In the sentencing memorandum prepared by his lawyer and submitted to a federal judge on Feb. 14, 1989, Stenger admitted to being involved with both steroids and cocaine over a period of time between 1984 and 1986. In his own words, penned to the judge on Dec. 8, 1988, Stenger admitted that he had struggled with addictions in the early and mid-1980s. Don Stenger, federal case file, CR-1-88-101.

234 Stenger injected Tommy: Stenger, testimony at Gioiosa's trial, CR-1-89-038, Transcript, 82–83.

235 Janowitz had tattoos: Details about Janowitz's life come from multiple sources, including Broward County court records for his 1981 marijuana arrest, case No. 81-466; U.S. Census records 1930; and "COPS, Business with a 'Sting,'" *Fort Lauderdale News,* Jan. 28, 1981.

235 per kilo: Stenger, testimony at Gioiosa's trial in federal court, CR-1-89-038, Aug. 1989.

47

235 "a danger to the community": This phrase appears in a federal judge's detention order, dated March 25, 1988, denying Janowitz bail in advance of his forthcoming trial. Norman Janowitz, criminal case No. 88-6402-CR, ordered by the author from the Federal Records Center in Atlanta and photocopied by the clerk of court at the federal courthouse in Miami.

235 a fully loaded handgun: Broward County, Fla., probable cause affidavit, signed by Det. Jerry Korte, Jan. 21, 1981.

235 Tommy didn't see the danger: Both in interviews with the author in 2021 and 2022 and at his trial in federal court in August 1989, Gioiosa said that his judgment was clouded by his own addiction to steroids.

235 wad of cash: Linda Kettle, testimony, Aug. 1989, CR-1-89-038.

235 convinced Mike Fry: *Dowd Report,* Exhibit 3, Mike Fry interview, April 11, 1989; Gioiosa testimony, Aug. 1989, CR-1-89-038.

235 never went to the gym: In an interview with the author on Oct. 1, 2021, Rose said, "I never went to Gold's Gym." But in 1985 and 1986, he told the press that he was working out there.

235 bragged to reporters: Several news items place Rose at Gold's Gym in the winter of 1984-85, including "Rose switches from a lectern to hitting cage," *CP,* January 29, 1985; "After Injuries of '84, Rose Trains His Way," *CE,* Feb. 2, 1985; and a half-page advertisement that ran in *The Cincinnati Enquirer* on Feb. 10, 1985, listing Rose as a member and displaying a photo of Rose holding two twenty-pound barbells in each hand inside the gym.

235 put his name on sweatshirts: Gioiosa testimony, Aug. 1989, CR-1-89-038.

236 "Pete Rose's Gold's Gym": Advertisement, *CE,* March 16, 1986.

236 "I have a key": "Reds' Player-Manager Not About to Give Up 1st Half of Title," *CP,* March 18, 1986.

236 Fry loved it: *Dowd Report,* Exhibit 3a, interview of Mike Fry, April 11, 1989, 7.

236 access to Pete's inner circle: Stenger, interview with author, Nov. 6, 2022.

236 "Just crazy": Ibid.
236 could hear Tommy at the front desk: *Penthouse,* Sept. 1989; *Dowd Report,* Exhibit 26, Janszen interview, Feb. 24, 1989, 6.
236 had to pull his car over: Stenger, interview with author, Nov. 6, 2022.
236 as much as $100,000: Stenger, testimony, Aug. 1989, CR-1-89-038.
236 Janszen helped distribute: Janszen testified about his activities at Gold's Gym during Gioiosa's trial in August 1989. CR-1-89-038, transcript of Janszen testimony, Aug. 30, 1989, 5.
236 one of Stenger's mules: Multiple people testified to this fact at Gioiosa's trial in August 1989, including both Gioiosa and Stenger, CR-1-89-038.
236 Why Tommy opted to do it: At his trial in 1989 for conspiracy to distribute cocaine and conspiracy to evade federal taxes, neither Gioiosa nor anyone else implicated Rose in being involved in cocaine, and federal agents found no connection. Gioiosa first mentioned Rose's interest in cocaine in an article for *Vanity Fair* more than a decade later: "A Darker Shade of Rose," *Vanity Fair,* Sept. 2001. He discussed it with the author in an interview on Oct. 25, 2021, and Janszen also discussed Rose's interest in cocaine in his first interview with John Dowd. *Dowd Report,* Exhibit 26, Janszen interview, Feb. 24, 1989, 67.
237 On two occasions in the summer of 1985: Stenger, Gioiosa, and Kettle testified to this fact at Gioiosa's trial in August 1989, CR-1-89-038.
237 One of the local papers: Advertisement, *CE,* March 27, 1985.
237 Budweiser made a series: MI-14-30 and MI-15-18, archival footage of Rose advertisements in advance of his record-breaking hit in 1985, Moving Image Index, Cincinnati History Library and Archives.
237 helped get General Mills: Robert Howsam Jr., interview with author, Feb. 22, 2022; "Pete Rose's Face to Be Championed," *DDN,* July 16, 1985.
237 "The potential for community embarrassment": "City Plans Daytime Ceremony for Pete," *CE,* Sept. 4, 1985.
237 "Hard work, hustle": "Pete Rose Has His Way—and Plaza—in City," *CP,* Sept. 6, 1985.
237 two million fans: "If Reds Top Two Million Fans, Banks Will Get an Assist," *CE,* July 7, 1985.
238 *The Today Show:* Bryant Gumbel interviewed Rose and Schott in Cincinnati on May 24, 1985.
238 Andy Warhol: In addition to the painting itself, the Cincinnati Art Museum created fifty silk-screen prints of Warhol's work and sold them to members for $2,500 and nonmembers for $3,000.
238 *Countdown to History:* "TV-Radio" column, *LAT,* Sept. 13, 1985.
238 book deals: Rose sold three books during his quest for Cobb's record or right after he claimed the record: *Pete Rose on Hitting; Countdown to Cobb;* and *Pete Rose: My Story.*
238 made an appearance: "Rose helps open Medford hall of fame," *The Oregonian,* Feb. 19, 1985.
238 "time-share condominiums": Ibid.
238 "in the Kingdom of Tonga": In 2022, the author filed a Freedom of Information Act request with the FBI, requesting any and all documents related to

this dealer, Dennis Lyle Walker—FOIPA request No. 1582925. This detail about "the Kingdom of Tonga" is contained within the records that the author received from the FBI in February 2023.

238 He first got Pete's attention: Bertolini, interview with author, Nov. 20, 2021.

239 "One wonders": Robert Howsam Jr., interview with author, Feb. 22, 2022; "A Few Memories of the Cincinnati Reds," a written account of Howsam's time there, shared with the author on Feb. 21, 2022.

239 cover story: "On Deck for the Big Knock," *SI,* Aug. 19, 1985. For the article, the writer Rick Reilly had unparalleled access to Rose in Cincinnati and produced a story that consumed thirteen pages inside the magazine. Yet in an effort to lionize Rose on the cusp of breaking Cobb's record, his piece for *Sports Illustrated* makes light of Rose's extramarital affairs and doesn't mention anything about gambling—at a moment when both of these things are about to derail Rose forever.

239 nearly did it on the road: Details of the day that Rose tied the record in Chicago can be found in multiple sources, including "Marge Warns Pete: Heart Won't Take It," *CE,* Sept. 10, 1985; "Cincinnati Fans Don't Mind Pete's Strikeout—This Time," "One More Hit and Bye-Bye, Ty," and "Witnessing a Bit of History Worth the Wait in Ticket Line," *CP,* Sept. 9, 1985; "Rose Is a Man-Boy Worthy of Becoming a Baseball Immortal," *DDN,* Sept. 9, 1985; and "Not Quite Like Any Other Day," *LAT,* Sept. 11, 1985; Gammons, interview with author, Oct. 14, 2022; and Rose, *Countdown to Cobb,* 199.

239 United Flight 352: "'Pete, Pete,' Fans Cheer as Rose Returns Home," *CE,* Sept. 9, 1985; "Patient Fans Steal Glimpse of Rose," *CP,* Sept. 9, 1985; *LAT,* Sept. 11, 1985.

240 went hitless: Details of his hitless night on Sept. 10, 1985, come from multiple sources, including "The Rose Watch," *BG,* Sept. 11, 1985; "Rose Hitless in 3–2 Loss to San Diego," "It's Rose Fever: A City Awaits the Ty-Breaker," "Reds Notebook," "Ticket Scalpers Do Better Than 0-for-4," and "Taking the View from the Top," *CE,* Sept. 11, 1985; "Pete's High Flies Deflate High-Flying Crowd" and "Pete's Empty Day, from Pals to Pop-Ups," *CP,* Sept. 11, 1985; "Pressurized Pitching" and "When Rose Talks, the Media Hang on Every Word," *DDN,* Sept. 11, 1985; "Rose, Reds Fall Short in 3–2 Loss" and "'All You Need Is a Base Hit, Huh?,'" *DJH,* Sept. 11, 1985; "Not Quite Like Any Other Day" and "Rose Doesn't Get Record Hit in 4 At-Bats," *LAT,* Sept. 11, 1985; and *Countdown to Cobb,* 201.

240 lifetime batting average of .370: Frank Labombarda, Elias Sports Bureau.

240 perfect late summer night: Details of Sept. 11, 1985, when Rose broke the record, come from multiple sources who were there that night, including Pete Rose, interview with author, Oct. 5, 2021; Karolyn Rose, interview with author, Dec. 2, 2021; Fawn Rose, interview with author, Feb. 2, 2022; Brennaman, interview with author, Aug. 1, 2021; Gioiosa, interview with author, Nov. 15, 2021; Gammons, interview with author, Oct. 14, 2022; Jeff Ruby (restaurateur), interview with author, Jan. 28, 2022; and Hal Bodley (reporter), interview with author, Jan. 4, 2022—along with television footage from NBC, voluminous newspaper coverage in *The Cincinnati Post, The*

Cincinnati Enquirer, the *Dayton Daily News,* and the Dayton *Journal Herald,* and Hal Bodley's blow-by-blow account of the quest to catch Cobb in Rose, *Countdown to Cobb,* 202.

241 Petey wasn't sure: Petey Rose has spoken about this moment a few times over the years, including in two key places utilized here: "Honor Thy Father," *SI,* July 11, 1997; and the 2010 documentary, *4192: The Crowning of the Hit King.*

48

242 Pete met Carol: The author spoke with three people who were with Rose after the record-breaking game that night: Gioiosa, interview with author, Nov. 15, 2021; Bodley, interview with author, Jan. 4, 2022; and Ruby, interview with author, Jan. 28, 2022.

242 beautiful young waitresses: Jeff Ruby, *Not Counting Tomorrow: The Unlikely Life of Jeff Ruby,* 154.

242 wasn't much time for sleep: Details about Rose's whirlwind night and schedule that week come from multiple sources, including Bodley, interview with author, Jan. 4, 2022; Gioiosa, interview with author, Nov. 15, 2021; Gammons, interview with author, Oct. 14, 2022; Ruby, interview with author, Jan. 28, 2022; "Rose Rests Before Chasing More Records," *CE,* Sept. 13, 1985; "They Came to See Pete," *CP,* Sept. 13, 1985; "The Music Won't Stop for Rose," *DDN,* Sept. 13, 1985; and television footage of the *Donahue* show, Sept. 12, 1985.

242 Bertolini had proof: Bertolini, interview with author, Nov. 20, 2021.

243 wrote columns: The first of these negative columns ran in *The Cincinnati Post* on Sept. 12, 1985, just hours after Rose broke the record. The young writer's name was Jay Mariotti. He was twenty-six years old at the time, new to the *Post,* and not long for Cincinnati. Mariotti would soon have a column for the *Chicago Sun-Times,* and by the early years of the twenty-first century he had become one of America's most famous—and controversial—sports columnists, with a platform at ESPN.

243 couldn't place bets anymore with Joe Cambra: Murray, interview with author, Feb. 15, 2022; Rand, interview with author, Feb. 17, 2022; Murray's personal records of Operation Moby Dick, shared with the author in 2021; "A Large Gray Area," *BG,* April 30, 1989; "Transcript Says Rose Made Bet with Mass. Bookie," *BG,* Aug. 16, 1989; *New Bedford Standard-Times,* Nov. 14, 1984; "Ex–City Cop Searched in Raid Was Charged in 1983 Video Probe," *New Bedford Standard-Times,* Nov. 15, 1984; "Area Gaming Raids Targeted 'Top Echelon' of Organized Crime," *New Bedford Standard-Times,* Nov. 18, 1984; Cambra's interview with Dowd's investigators in 1989, *Dowd Report,* Exhibit 66, Cambra interview, April 27, 1989.

243 his own knock at the door: Around 1987, Wes Hills, the reporter for the *Dayton Daily News,* learned of the existence of a tape recording that Dick Skinner had made of Rose discussing gambling debts. It took Hills about fifteen years to track down the tape, but he ultimately did. Details of Skinner's conversation with Rose published here come from Hills's story, *DDN,* Dec. 22, 2002;

Hills, interviews with author; and the tape itself. In late 2022, Hills played the Skinner-Rose tape for the author to hear.

49

245 Tommy found Ron Peters: The two men independently confirmed how they met—Gioiosa in interviews with the author and Peters in an interview with John Dowd. *Dowd Report,* Exhibit 50, Peters interview, March 23, 1989, 4–5.

245 Ron's father had escaped: According to 1940 U.S. Census records, Ron's father, John B. Peters, was born in eastern Kentucky and spent his childhood in the Lothair Black Gold Mining Camp in Perry County, where his father, Ron's grandfather, earned $1,000 a year, the equivalent of about $21,000 today.

245 wore out a path: Randy Bluhm (Ron's childhood friend), interview with author, Nov. 12, 2022; Jeff Woodward (Ron's childhood friend), interview with author, Nov. 13, 2022.

245 club member: According to the 2019 obituary for Ron's father, the family became members at the club in 1961.

245 leave richer: Woodward, interview with author, Nov. 13, 2022.

246 Ron told friends: Ibid.

246 a life of ease: Details of Ron's lifestyle come from multiple sources, including Keith Sexton, interview with author, Nov. 11, 2022; an interview that Dowd's investigators conducted with Ron's ex-wife, Lori Peters, on April 7, 1989, found in the *Dowd Report,* Exhibit 15; *Lori Peters v. Ronald Peters,* Complaint for Divorce, Case No. 3-11-87-208-11746, Warren County Common Pleas Court; and Ron Peters's criminal case file for his 1989 conviction on tax evasion and drug charges, CR-1-89-034, which the author reviewed in its entirety at the federal courthouse in Columbus, Ohio.

246 a two-story brick colonial: Butler County Auditor, property records for 7429 Cinnamon Woods Drive.

246 meet Ron for the first time: Details of this meeting, and how Tommy and Ron worked together afterward, are confirmed by the two principal sources, Gioiosa and Peters. Gioiosa, interview with author, Oct. 26, 2021; Peters, interview with John Dowd, March 23, 1989, *Dowd Report,* Exhibit 50, 4–5.

246 Once, in a snowstorm: Gioiosa, interview with author, Oct. 26, 2021.

247 Al Esselman told stories: Jackie Esselman Frey, interview with author, May 11, 2022; Jimmy Jones (a friend of Esselman's), interview with author, Oct. 22, 2021.

247 the Skin Man told his stories: Wes Hills, interview with author, Nov. 4, 2022.

247 Ron lied over a matter: Sexton, interview with author, Nov. 11, 2022.

247 didn't feel recreational anymore: Ibid.; Gioiosa, interview with author, Nov. 15, 2021; previously unreleased FBI records, obtained by the author under a Freedom of Information Act request, FBI FOIA Request No. 1517070-000, which reveals what the FBI knew about Peters's drug activities as early as 1987.

247 put Pete on speakerphone: Sexton, interview with author, Nov. 11, 2022.

Around this time, Ron told people, and later investigators, that he also made a tape recording of Pete Rose placing his bets—as insurance, just in case Rose stopped paying. After his marriage fell apart, however, Peters couldn't find the tape.

50

248 had a winning record: "All Want Pete to Play, but He Isn't Ready," *CE,* April 17, 1986.

248 three magazines predicted: *Baseball Illustrated, Bill Mazeroski's Baseball, The Sporting News,* and *The Cincinnati Enquirer* all picked the Reds to win the division in 1986. "Few Experts Like Reds' Chances for West Title," *CE,* March 19, 1986; "Color This a Red Season," *CE,* April 7, 1986; "N.L. Outlook: It's in the Cards, Rosy for Reds," *SN,* March 3, 1986.

248 series of maladies: "Reds Notes," *SN,* March 10, 1986; "Rose Buys Time on Disabled List," *CE,* April 8, 1986; "Manager Rose Sidelines Self as Player," *DJH,* April 7, 1986.

248 "Everybody was doing it": Details of Parker's testimony and the cocaine trial can be found in multiple sources including "The Resurrection of Dave Parker," *SN,* March 24, 1986; "Player Drug Involvement Far-Reaching," *SN,* Sept. 2, 1985; "Lonnie Smith: Bought Drugs for 2 Players," *Pittsburgh Press,* Sept. 5, 1985; "Hernandez Testifies He Used Drugs," *CP,* Sept. 6, 1985; "1980 Big Year for Cocaine, Player Says," *Pittsburgh Press,* Sept. 6, 1985; "Players Blame Cocaine Addiction on Lonely Road Trips and Money," *Pittsburgh Press,* Sept. 8, 1985; "Ex-Pirate Accuses Parker," *CP,* Sept. 10, 1985; "Berra: Got Pills from Stargell, Madlock," *Pittsburgh Press,* Sept. 10, 1985; "Parker: Used Cocaine Because It Was 'the In Thing,'" *Pittsburgh Press,* Sept. 12, 1985; "Focal Point on Players in Baseball Drug Trial," *SN,* Sept. 16, 1985; and "Convicted," *Pittsburgh Post-Gazette,* Sept. 21, 1985.

248 made his fortune: "Will Run Olympics with Firm Hand, Ueberroth Says," *LAT,* March 29, 1979; "Ueberroth: 'Way with People and a Buck,'" *LAT,* July 21, 1979; "Firm Buys 61.5% of First Travel; Tender Offer Set," *LAT,* Dec. 21, 1979.

248 "We'll be relentless": "Inside Baseball: Drugs, Money, and Expansion," *U.S. News & World Report,* Oct. 28, 1985.

249 two or three packs a day, maybe more: After his death, it was reported that Giamatti smoked three or four packs of cigarettes a day. "Myths Aside, Giamatti Not Typical of Heart-Attack Victims," *Miami Herald,* Sept. 12, 1989. In an interview with the author, his friend Fay Vincent said it was more like five packs a day.

249 Renaissance literature at Yale: Details of Giamatti's life come from multiple sources, including U.S. Census records, 1900–1940, for his grandfather Angelo Giamatti; Angelo Giamatti's World War I draft card, serial No. 807, Sept. 12, 1918; "Baseball's Renaissance Man: Bart Giamatti," *New York Times Magazine,* Sept. 4, 1988; "Professor Hardball," *Cincinnati Magazine,* Oct. 1989; Bill Mazeine (childhood friend), interview with author, April 7, 2023; and

the coverage of the *Yale Daily News,* including, most important, "A. Bartlett Giamatti: A Date-Line Biography," Oct. 14, 1978; "Real Life Adventures of Giamatti," April 10, 1979; and "A. Bartlett Giamatti, 1938–1989," "Giamatti Left His Mark on Baseball," and "Friends, Colleagues Remember Giamatti," Oct. 16, 1989.

249 "I don't want to": "Giamatti Elected," *Yale Daily News,* Dec. 21, 1977.

249 a book of vocabulary: "Inside Baseball," *CP,* July 31, 1986.

250 "to leave and to return home": "Green Fields of the Mind," *Yale Alumni Magazine,* Nov. 1977.

250 "The game begins in the spring": Ibid.

250 "frightfully distinguished": *Yale Daily News,* Dec. 21, 1977.

250 almost didn't take the job: Vincent, interview with author, Oct. 20, 2021.

250 "They're going to turn to you": Ibid.

250 "middle-class, middle-aged": "Giamatti Pans Book's Sentimentality," *Yale Daily News,* Nov. 4, 1983.

250 earned a pittance: U.S. Census records for Bart's grandfather Angelo Giamatti show that he immigrated to the United States from Italy around 1899 when he was sixteen years old, settled in New Haven, Connecticut, and initially lived as a boarder inside the home of another Italian who was employed as a woodchopper. Angelo later moved out and by 1920 owned his own home, paid for with his job as a watchmaker at a local clock factory. But by 1940, he still earned only $1,250 a year, the equivalent of about $26,000 today.

251 Pete liked Bart: Rose, interview with author, Oct. 6, 2021.

51

251 Pete can't remember: In his memoir *My Prison Without Bars,* Rose said he placed his first bet on baseball during the 1986 playoffs. *MP,* 123. Notes kept by his friend Mike Bertolini show that Rose was placing wagers on baseball at least months earlier.

251 the people around him: Gioiosa, interview with author, Oct. 28, 2021.

251 how many triples: Rose, interview with author, Sept. 22, 2021.

251 how many doubles: Rose, interview with author, Sept. 29, 2021.

251 Pete made a trip to Franklin: The trip happened sometime in late January 1986. "Renovated Building Turns into Relaxing Café," *Franklin Chronicle,* Feb. 5, 1986.

252 The café was located: The details of Peters's investment in the café come from three sources: *Franklin Chronicle,* Feb. 5, 1986; "Jonathan's Café One of the Fastest Growing Businesses in Area," *Franklin Chronicle,* July 29, 1987; and *Lori Peters v. Ronald Peters,* Complaint for Divorce, Case No. 3-11-87-208-11746.

252 Lori would work there: *Lori Peters v. Ronald Peters,* Complaint for Divorce, Case No. 3-11-87-208-11746, Closing argument memorandum, May 11, 1988.

252 "What I've done with Jonathan's": *Franklin Chronicle,* July 29, 1987.

252 ran a picture of Ron: *Franklin Chronicle,* Feb. 5, 1986.

252 The seats were free: *Dowd Report,* Exhibit 24, Rose ticket requests, May 30, 1986.

252 sat at the front window: Two of Dowd's investigators interviewed Lori Peters on April 7, 1989, and included a summary of her remarks in the *Dowd Report.* Exhibit 15, Lori Peters interview, 2.

253 Tommy began to worry: Gioiosa, interview with author, Nov. 15, 2021.

253 According to a notebook: ESPN first revealed the existence of this notebook in 2015, with reporting by William Weinbaum and T. J. Quinn. "Entries in long-hidden notebook show Pete Rose bet on baseball as a player," ESPN .com, June 22, 2015. Weinbaum had spent years trying to find it. The author obtained a copy of the notebook from John Dowd, former special counsel for Major League Baseball, in May 2023. This notebook, verified by multiple sources, shows that Rose was betting on baseball and Reds while he was still a player.

253 "Betting on the playoffs": *MP,* 123.

254 messier for Bertolini: According to the notebook, Bertolini bet against Rose and the Reds in at least five games in 1986. Bertolini confirmed at least one of these bets to the author. Bertolini, interview with author, Nov. 20, 2021.

254 "Pete owes me": These quotes come directly from the Bertolini notebook.

254 "Absolutely wrong": Rose, interview with author, Oct. 5, 2021.

255 "I'm rooting for somebody": Rose, interview with author, Sept. 24, 2021.

255 as Pete's losses mounted: Bertolini, interview with author, Nov. 20, 2021.

255 "The debt": Ibid.

255 Tommy couldn't sleep: Details of Tommy's state of mind in late 1986 come from multiple sources, including Gioiosa, interview with author, Oct. 28, 2021; Kim Hauck (former girlfriend of Gioiosa), interview with author, Nov. 16, 2022; and testimony given by others at Gioiosa's trial in August 1989, CR-1-89-038.

256 Twice, he borrowed cash: This is confirmed by Gioiosa, interview with author, Nov. 15, 2022, and Mike Fry's interview with John Dowd in 1989. *Dowd Report,* Exhibit 3, Fry interview, April 11, 1989, 17, 22.

256 turned to another friend: The details of how Janszen moved into Rose's inner circle come from the author's interviews with Gioiosa and Janszen, and from Janszen's testimony to Dowd back in 1989. *Dowd Report,* Exhibit 26, Janszen interview, Feb. 24-25, 1989.

256 "I don't know why": Rose, interview with author, Oct. 18, 2021.

256 stirred up a ruckus: Details of this night at the track come from interviews with three people who were there. Zimmerman, interview with author, Nov. 11, 2021; Gioiosa, interview with author, Nov. 15, 2021; Jerry Carroll, interview with author, Jan. 12, 2022. Rose also wrote about it in his memoir *My Prison Without Bars,* 131.

257 wrote a check: No one disputes that Katz's office wrote a check to Gioiosa in March 1987. It was confirmed by multiple sources, including *MP,* 131–32; Gioiosa, interview with author, Nov. 15, 2022; and *Dowd Report,* Exhibit 59, check from Rose to Janszen, March 18, 1989.

257 moving to California: Both Gioiosa and Hauck confirmed to the author that

they moved to California around this time. They also testified about their move at Gioiosa's trial in 1989.

52

258 "Does this mean": Associated Press, March 7, 1987.
258 piece in *Newsday:* "Fitting Athletics into Education," *Newsday,* March 29, 1987.
258 played catch with the commissioner Peter Ueberroth: "Red Sox Notebook," *BG,* March 15, 1987.
258 talking to Homer: "Sports Etc.," *Louisville Courier-Journal,* April 12, 1987.
258 "I'm kind of like a Martian": "Improving Atmosphere at Parks Top Priority of New NL President," *Palm Beach Post,* March 23, 1987.
258 "How can an ex–university president": "Personalities," *PI,* Sept. 7, 1986.
259 "You gotta get me out of here": Vincent, interview with author, Oct. 20, 2021.
259 couldn't believe the size: Janszen, interview with author, July 2, 2022; *Dowd Report,* Exhibit 26, Janszen interview, Feb. 24, 1989, 15.
259 taxi: *Dowd Report,* Exhibit 26, Janszen interview, Feb. 24, 1989, 15.
259 It had a racquetball court: The house was so opulent, and so famous, that the *Tampa Bay Times* wrote a story about it later that year. "Dubin Estate Goes on the Market to Pay Legal Defense and Tax Bills," *Tampa Bay Times,* Nov. 1, 1987.
259 He bragged about the house: "Basic as 1-2-3, a Book of Lists on the Reds," *CE,* March 6, 1987.
259 greeted Paul and Danita: *Dowd Report,* Exhibit 26, Janszen interview, Feb. 24, 1989, 15.
259 WELCOME TO HASSLEFREE: *Tampa Bay Times,* Nov. 1, 1987.
259 couldn't wait to go fishing: Janszen, interview with author, July 2, 2022.
259 busy falling in love with a blond dancer: Bertolini, interview with author, Nov. 20, 2021.
259 Pete's new sidekick: *Dowd Report,* Exhibit 26, Janszen interview, Feb. 24, 1989, 16.
260 Paul had heard: Ibid., 6.
260 He was a gofer: Ibid., 16.
260 cover losses: Both Janszen and Rose agreed that Rose was behind about $15,000 as he left spring training. *MP,* 133; *Dowd Report,* Exhibit 26, Janszen interview, Feb. 24, 1989, 22.
260 running with the wrong crowd: Janszen, interview with author, July 2, 2022.
260 believe that Pete was his friend: *Dowd Report,* Exhibit 26, Janszen interview, Feb. 24, 1989, 25.
260 Paul flew north: Ibid., 21.
260 People lined up that weekend: Details of the card show come from press accounts, including "Charlie Hustle," *Nashville Tennessean,* April 1, 1987; "Old Timers' Autographs May Be Costly," *Nashville Tennessean,* April 2, 1987; "DiMaggio: What's in a Name?," *Nashville Tennessean,* April 3, 1987; "Autograph Hounds Turn Out in Droves for Baseball Show," *Nashville Tennessean,*

April 4, 1987; advertisement, *Nashville Tennessean,* April 4, 1987; and "Baseball Dealers Complain," *Nashville Tennessean,* April 5, 1987.

53

261 started comparing the 1987 Reds: "Rose Claims Today's Reds Best He's Seen," *DDN,* April 21, 1987.

261 Lots of games: According to Rose's memories, he was betting as many as nine games a day that spring. *MP,* 135. Janszen also spoke about it at length in his interviews and deposition with Dowd, Feb. 24–25 and April 4, 1989. *Dowd Report,* Exhibits 26 and 38.

261 Paul wasn't even sure: *Dowd Report,* Exhibit 26, Janszen interview, Feb. 24, 1989, 28, 47.

261 down just $31,000: *MP,* 135.

261 more like $67,000: *Dowd Report,* Exhibit 26, Janszen interview, Feb. 24, 1989, 40. The figure $67,900 also appears in Janszen's handwritten notes. *Dowd Report,* Exhibit 12.

261 "Everybody worried about it": Metz, interview with author, Oct. 22, 2021.

262 dipped into his own personal savings: *Dowd Report,* Exhibit 26, Janszen interview, Feb. 24, 1989, 40.

262 $44,000: *Dowd Report,* Exhibit 38, Janszen deposition, April 4, 1989, 71.

262 on the road to Franklin, Ohio: According to Janszen's testimony, phone records gathered by Dowd's investigators, and the *Dowd Report,* Janszen was there in Franklin on May 25, 1987, at a minimum. *Dowd Report,* 80, 153. But likely on other occasions as well. *Dowd Report,* Exhibit 38, Janszen deposition, April 4, 1989, 70.

262 his wife, Lori, had left him: *Lori Peters v. Ronald Peters,* Complaint for Divorce, Case No. 3-11-87-208-11746.

262 fighting over money: This detail was confirmed in two places: *Dowd Report,* Exhibit 26, Janszen interview, Feb. 24, 1989, 56, and in a closing argument memorandum that Lori's lawyer filed on May 11, 1988, in her divorce case against Ron. *Lori Peters v. Ronald Peters,* Complaint for Divorce, Case No. 3-11-87-208-11746.

262 Tommy had never paid him: This was confirmed in two places: *Dowd Report,* Exhibit 38, Janszen deposition, April 4, 1989, 61; and *Dowd Report,* Exhibit 50, Peters interview, March 23, 1989, 21.

262 maybe $40,000: *Dowd Report,* Exhibit 50, Peters interview, March 23, 1989, 21.

262 Paul complained: According to Dowd's investigation and the author's interviews, at least three people heard complaints from Janszen: Charlotte Jacobs, a friend of Carol Rose; Jeff Ruby, Rose's friend and business partner; and Chuck Zimmerman, a Cincinnati police officer.

262 when he first heard: Zimmerman, interview with author, Nov. 11, 2021.

262 one of the worst gamblers he had ever met: Ibid.

263 He was on the run: Details about Dennis Lyle Walker's disappearance and death come from two souces: former FBI agent Jayme Gentile, interview with

author, Feb. 15, 2023, and previously unreleased FBI records, requested by the author, FOIPA request No. 1582925.

263 On a Monday in late June: Details of the search of Mike Fry's house come from multiple sources, including "Forest Park Businessman Pleads Guilty in Drug Case," *CE,* Oct. 14, 1987; "Body Builder–Cocaine Dealer Sentenced," *CE,* March 2, 1988; the case file for *United States of America v. Michael Fry,* CR-1-87-89, which the author reviewed in its entirety at the federal courthouse in Columbus, Ohio; the transcript of Fry's arraignment, Oct. 13, 1987; and the transcript of Fry's sentencing, Feb. 29, 1988.

264 "I will never be involved with drugs again": *United States of America v. Michael Fry,* CR-1-87-89, handwritten letter from Fry to his lawyer Warren Zevely, n.d.

264 Stenger, by then, had moved on: Stenger's dealings with cocaine and his cooperation with the government are documented by his own attorneys in his federal case file, *United States of America v. Donald Stenger,* CR-1-88-101, as they argued for him to receive a lighter sentence. The author reviewed the case file in its entirety at the federal courthouse in Columbus, Ohio.

264 Stenger's former girlfriend agreed to wear a wire: *United States of America v. Linda Kettle,* CR-1-88-100.

264 New Year's Eve 1987: Stenger detailed how he and his former girlfriend cooperated with federal authorities in the sentencing memorandum prepared by his lawyer and filed with the federal court on Feb. 14, 1989. *United States of America v. Donald Stenger,* CR-1-88-101

54

265 "The fourth time is a charm": "First Impression," *CP,* Jan. 19, 1988.

265 Cook turned his focus: Murray Cook, interview with author, Jan. 18, 2022.

265 a concern shared by baseball's newly hired director of security: Kevin Hallinan, interview with author, May 17, 2023.

265 Giamatti arranged to sit down: "Giamatti to Rose: Act Like a Manager," *CE,* Dec. 10, 1987.

266 significant enough: Hallinan, interview with author, May 17, 2023.

266 no big deal: "Rose's 'Honeymoon' with Players Ends with Tighter Clubhouse Control," *CP,* Jan. 19, 1988, and "Rose: Nice guy approach suits Reds just fine," *DDN,* Jan. 19, 1988.

266 "That was one of Dave Parker's problems": *DDN,* Jan. 19, 1988.

266 Parker didn't know: "Parker Questions Rose's Leadership," *CP,* Feb. 12, 1988.

266 "PETE ROSE!!!": Advertisement, Cleveland *Plain Dealer,* Feb. 12, 1988.

266 only staying close to Pete to collect: Janszen, interview with author, July 2, 2022.

266 Pete brought a woman with him: In an interview with the author, Rose said he could not recall this detail about the incident at the hotel near Cleveland. But he wrote about it in his memoir *MP,* 140. The author also confirmed these details with two eyewitnesses, Danita Marcum and Paul Janszen, and Rose's close friend Arnie Metz. Additionally, Janszen spoke at length about

this incident in his first interview with John Dowd. *Dowd Report,* Exhibit 26, Janszen interview, Feb. 24, 1989, 60.

266 for $8 apiece: The author confirmed this detail—and others about this autograph show—through multiple advertisements and stories in the Cleveland *Plain Dealer.* "Sign on Dotted Line," Cleveland *Plain Dealer,* Feb. 20, 1988.

267 Paul usually couldn't even get ahold of Pete: Janszen, interview with author, July 2, 2022.

267 On a Wednesday in early March: The most detailed account of Stenger's cooperation with federal agents comes from his sentencing memorandum, written by his own lawyers and filed with the federal court on Feb. 14, 1989. *United States of America v. Donald Stenger,* CR-1-88-101.

267 Paul heard a knock at the door: The details of the FBI's first visit to Janszen's house come from four sources: *United States of America v. Ronald Peters,* CR 1-89-034, affidavit of IRS investigator Lowell D. Wood, Aug. 17, 1989; Janszen testimony at Gioiosa's trial, Aug. 30, 1989, testimony transcript, 47; Janszen, interview with author, July 2, 2022; and Gentile, interview with author, Feb. 15, 2023.

267 Special Agent Jayme Gentile: Details about Jayme Gentile come from interviews with Gentile and her boss at the time, Assistant Special Agent in Charge Paul Mallett. Mallett, interview with author, May 19, 2023.

267 At the door of his condo: Details of Janszen's first meeting with the FBI agents come from interviews the author conducted with three people who were there that day: Paul Janszen, Danita Marcum, and Jayme Gentile.

268 "Did you tell Mr. Katz": *Dowd Report,* Exhibit 38, Janszen deposition, April 4, 1989, 75–76.

269 Reuven picked up the phone: Reuven Katz died in 2016. This recollection comes from three places: *MP,* 140; *Dowd Report,* Exhibit 2, Rose deposition, April 21, 1989, 288; and Rose, interview with author, Oct. 20, 2021.

269 He knew what he was doing: *MP,* 141.

269 a Friday in mid-March: The check was dated March 18, 1989. Details about what Rose was doing on this day come from press accounts including "Armstrong, Birtsas Among 10 to Farms," *CE,* March 19, 1988; "Reds Provide Answers to a Mound of Questions," *CP,* March 19, 1988; and "Reds Notes," *DDN,* March 19, 1988.

269 "Hit pretty good": *CE,* March 19, 1988.

270 "Set it up": Janszen, interview with author, July 2, 2022.

55

270 a regular-season record: Details about opening day in 1988 come from press accounts in *The Cincinnati Enquirer, The Cincinnati Post,* and the *Dayton Daily News* including "Schott Wants Bride," *CE,* April 5, 1988; and "Cincy Sunny, Bright, and Reds All Over," *DDN,* April 5, 1988.

271 Pete was angry: "Light-Hitting Reds Lose to Mets, 5–4," *CE,* April 30, 1988; "Big Bat Awakens—for Mets," *CP,* April 30, 1988; "Reds Sag, Finally Lose in 9th," *DDN,* April 30, 1988.

271 the second game of the Mets series: Details of the fights on this night between the Reds and the Mets, and Rose and Pallone, come from multiple sources, including Dave Pallone, interview with author, Jan. 27, 2022; Pete Rose, interview with author, Oct. 19, 2021; Tim Teufel, interview with author, Jan. 19, 2022; Keith Hernandez, interview with author, Jan. 13, 2022; John Franco, interview with author, Jan. 14, 2021; Dave Pallone, *Behind the Mask,* 273–76; "Mets Frustrate Reds" and "Stadium Uproar," *CE,* May 1, 1988; "Mets Beat Reds, 6-5, in Wild Finish," *DDN,* May 1, 1988; and "Red Menace at Riverfront," *NYDN,* May 1, 1988.

272 called him a scab: These complaints began way back in 1979 and were chronicled in many places, including "'New' Umpires Live Lonely Days," *TT,* July 3, 1979; "Scab Umps: Wounds Are Still Sore," *Fort Worth Star-Telegram,* Sept. 8, 1980; "Many at Fault for Dodgers' Loss to Expos," *LAT,* May 10, 1986; Pallone, interview with author, Jan. 27, 2022; and Pallone, *Behind the Mask.*

272 whispered about Pallone: Pallone, interview with author, Jan. 27, 2022; Rose, interview with author, Oct. 19, 2021; and *Behind the Mask,* 235.

272 an outburst: "NL Suspends Rose 30 Days," *NYDN,* May 3, 1988.

272 run interference for Pete: *CE* and *DDN,* May 1, 1988.

272 "Such disgraceful episodes": Giamatti statement, May 2, 1988.

273 "The National League," Giamatti said: Ibid.

273 "If I'm going to get thirty days": "Martin Goes Bump in the Night, Warns Umps," *NYDN,* May 3, 1988.

273 wondered if Pete had stabbed someone: "30 Days Leaves Rose's Players in a Daze," *CP,* May 3, 1988.

273 "Take him out to the Shakespeare festival": "Two Wrongs Don't Make Giamatti Right," *CP,* May 3, 1988.

273 Others took Giamatti's side: "Mets Feel Punishment Fits Pete," *NYDN,* May 3, 1988.

273 At a hearing in New York: Details of Rose's hearing before Giamatti on May 6, 1988, come from multiple sources, including "Katz Felt Appeal Was Longshot" and "Rose's Penalty Will Stick," *CE,* May 7, 1988; "Rose's Appeal Doomed from Start" and "Ruling Unchanged; Rose Out till June," *CP,* May 7, 1988; "Justice Grinds Slow, but Not Sure" and "Rose Strikes Out in Appeal of Suspension," *DDN,* May 7, 1988; "Rose's Suspension Is Upheld," *Newsday,* May 7, 1988; and "League Refuses to Cut Rose Suspension," *NYT,* May 7, 1988.

274 "I hate to say it": "Defiant Rose: Do It Again," *NYDN,* May 7, 1988.

56

274 Paul met with them twice: The best source of information on Janszen's undercover work with the FBI can be found in Ron Peters's federal case file, *United States of America v. Ronald Peters,* CR 1-89-034. In this file, there are two crucial documents that recount Janszen's cooperation in detail: a two-page report, filed to the federal judge by the FBI agents on the case as they sought

the original search warrant, and a twenty-seven-page affidavit, written by an IRS investigator the next day. The two key documents are: FBI Special Agent Jayme Gentile, "Affiant States the Following Facts Establishing the Foregoing Grounds for Issuance of a Search Warrant," Aug. 16, 1989; and IRS investigator Lowell D. Wood, affidavit, Aug. 17, 1989.

274 began recording conversations: *United States of America v. Ronald Peters,* CR 1-89-034.

275 Paul had begun to think: Janszen expressed this feeling in two places: Janszen, interview with author, July 2, 2022; and *Dowd Report,* Exhibit 38, Janszen deposition, April 4, 1989, 6.

275 "Wipe the slate clean": *Dowd Report,* Exhibit 38, Janszen deposition, April 4, 1989, 7.

275 Paul drove to Jonathan's Café: *United States of America v. Ronald Peters,* CR 1-89-034, FBI Special Agent Jayme Gentile, "Affiant States the Following Facts Establishing the Foregoing Grounds for Issuance of a Search Warrant," Aug. 16, 1989, and IRS investigator Lowell D. Wood, affidavit, Aug. 17, 1989.

275 The FBI had been watching: For his research, the author filed a request under the Freedom of Information Act asking for the previously unreleased FBI files for Rose's bookie Ron Peters. These records, given to the author in 2021, show that the FBI began to take an interest in Peters's activities at Jonathan's Café as early as 1986 and started to watch him there in 1987, months before knocking on Janszen's door. Details about what the FBI suspected or knew about Peters's operation can be found in these files, which are heavily redacted at times. FOIA Request No. 1517070-000.

275 couldn't be trusted: Ibid.

275 Paul's car ride with Ron: This meeting is chronicled in detail in the FBI and IRS filings in Ron Peters's criminal case file, *United States of America v. Ronald Peters,* CR 1-89-034.

275 obtained warrants: According to Peters's federal case file, CR 1-89-034, authorities executed their search warrants on Aug. 19, 1988.

275 "Do you understand that?": *United States of America v. Ronald Peters,* CR 1-89-034, transcript of Peters's formal guilty plea and sentencing, June 19, 1989.

276 Kevin Hallinan got a phone call: Hallinan, interview with author, May 17, 2023.

276 Giamatti informed Vincent: Vincent, interviews with author, Oct. 20, 2021, and Jan. 2, 2023.

276 unanimous: "Giamatti Picked as Next Commissioner of Baseball," *BG,* Sept. 9, 1988.

276 even after angry students: "Students Stage Protest," *Yale Daily News,* Jan. 15, 1985.

277 "we don't want what happened at Yale": "Giamatti Succeeds Ueberroth April 1," *Newsday,* Sept. 9, 1988.

277 Over dinner: Vincent, interviews with author, Oct. 20, 2021, and Jan. 2, 2023.

277 now valued at five times that figure: Several press accounts around this time chronicled the financial success of baseball owners under Ueberroth, such

as "Baseball Faces Pressing Problems with No Quick Fixes," *PI,* April 24, 1988; "Minor-League Health Report: Better Than Ever," *AC,* Dec. 1, 1988; "Corporate Ties Help Fill Tills in Major Leagues" and "Ueberroth Makes Souvenirs Major-League Money Maker," *Pittsburgh Press,* April 4, 1989.

277 "That's with a 'b'": "CBS Baseball Deal Worth $1.1 Billion," *AC,* Dec. 15, 1988.

277 the Madison Avenue hotel: "Baseball Wires in ESPN," *NYDN,* Jan. 6, 1989.

277 the gala that Ted Turner threw: "D.C. Contingent Just Wants Attention," *AC,* Dec. 1, 1988.

278 "I'm very sorry": The author retrieved the case file for Paul Janszen's criminal charge from a federal repository and copied it over two days at the federal courthouse in Columbus, Ohio. *United States of America v. Paul Janszen,* CR-1-88-99. This quotation comes directly from the transcript of his formal guilty plea on Jan. 13, 1989, 11.

278 "Last year, Danita and myself": *Dowd Report,* Exhibit 60, Janszen to Katz, Jan. 20, 1989.

279 nights were hardest for Paul: Janszen, interview with author, July 2, 2022.

279 Pete and Jerry hit it big: The story of the Pik-Six ticket was originally denied by Rose and Metz. But Jerry Carroll admitted it was true in the spring of 1989, and Rose ultimately followed suit, in his deposition with Dowd on April 20, 1989. Additionally, the author confirmed the details of this big win at the track in interviews with all three men involved: Rose, Carroll, and Metz.

279 "Pete will not pay": *Dowd Report,* Exhibit 61, Pitcairn to Janszen's lawyer, Merlyn Shiverdecker, Jan. 25, 1989.

279 Jerry Carroll wanted to wait: Carroll, interview with author, Jan. 12, 2022.

279 Pete had his friend the longtime groundskeeper Arnie Metz: Ibid.; Metz, interview with author, Oct. 22, 2021; *Dowd Report,* Exhibit 2, Rose deposition, April 20, 1989, 37.

280 to watch fantasy camp games: "Rose Takes Cuts with Campers," *TT,* Feb. 1, 1989.

280 Beat writers were hearing rumors: Multiple members of the local media confirmed this to the author in interviews, including Joe Cunningham, Wes Hills, Hal McCoy, and Ralph Morrow.

280 one last chance with her: "Is Schott's Rose-Colored View Fading?," *CE,* Feb. 10, 1989.

280 "another John DeLorean case": Three different sources independently confirmed this sentiment within the FBI: Gentile, interview with author, Feb. 15, 2023; Hallinan, interview with author, May 17, 2023; and Mallett, interview with author, Feb. 17, 2023.

280 He wanted to talk to someone: Details of Janszen's tip to *Sports Illustrated,* his demands for money, and what the magazine did after Janszen's phone call come from four former staffers at the magazine: Jerry Kirshenbaum (former assistant managing editor), interview with author, July 5, 2023; Craig Neff (former senior editor), interview with author, July 7, 2023; Sandy Padwe (former senior editor), interview with author, July 5, 2023; and Robert Sullivan (former staff writer), interview with author, July 5, 2023.

282 Ueberroth learned: Vincent, interview with author, Oct. 20, 2021.

282 Pete ran wind sprints: "Boys of Summer Were Ready Even Though Weather Wasn't," *CE*, Feb. 20, 1989; "Pee-Wee Herman Tekulve," *DDN*, Feb. 20, 1989.

282 all alone: McCoy, interview with author, Jan. 6, 2022.

57

282 casual to start: This account of the meeting comes from Vincent, interviews with author, Oct. 20, 2021, and Jan. 6, 2023; Rose, interview with author, Oct. 19, 2021; and *MP*, 146–47.

283 one sympathetic listener: The author conducted interviews with multiple people who worked in highest levels of the Major League Baseball office in 1989. Three different high-level sources agreed that Ueberroth wanted to find a quick solution, if possible.

284 "I'm not that stupid": Vincent, interview with author, Oct. 20, 2021.

284 they believed him: Ibid.

284 "There's nothing ominous": "Rose Is the Subject, Mum Is the Word," *NYT*, Feb. 22, 1989.

285 Dowd was overqualified: Details of Dowd's biography come from multiple sources, including World War II Draft Registration card for John's father, Paul L. Dowd, serial No. 1083; 1950 U.S. Census record for Paul L. Dowd and family; "Watch Out for Strike Force 18," *PDN*, July 21, 1977; "The Philadelphia Story," *New York Times Magazine*, Feb. 19, 1978; obituary for Paul L. Dowd, *BG*, Aug. 9, 1985; "Tracking the Man on Rose's Trail," *Washington Post*, May 21, 1989; and Dowd, interview with author, May 15, 2023.

286 Dowd had to remind himself: Dowd spoke about this in two places: Dowd, interview with author, May 15, 2023, and an hour-long talk that he gave at the Emory University School of Law in 2014. John Dowd, "Pete Rose's Ban from Baseball: 25 Years Later—an Inside Look into the Dark Side of America's Favorite Pastime," Oct. 2014.

286 the news of the secret meeting: Within a day of the meeting, the news that Rose had met privately with Ueberroth and Giamatti in New York started to appear in *The New York Times*, the *Dayton Daily News*, *The Cincinnati Enquirer*, and *The Cincinnati Post*.

286 Dowd had to be perfect: Dowd, "Pete Rose's Ban from Baseball."

286 "I was born in Cincinnati": *Dowd Report*, Exhibit 26, Janszen interview, Feb. 24, 1989, 3.

287 "A breeze": Ibid., 1.

287 "I said, 'Damn, Danita'": Ibid., 14.

287 Dowd didn't know if Paul: Dowd, interview with author, May 15, 2023; Dowd, "Pete Rose's Ban from Baseball."

288 "Don't you think he should?": This taped phone call took place on April 4, 1988. *Dowd Report*, Exhibit 27, 13.

288 play these tapes: Dowd, "Pete Rose's Ban from Baseball."

288 "Let me ask you this": *Dowd Report,* Exhibit 26, Janszen interview, Feb. 24, 16.
289 Paul would call Stevie: Ibid., 19.

58

289 With his girlfriend: Both Gioiosa and Hauck confirmed these details—in interviews with the author and at Gioiosa's trial in 1989. CR-1-89-038.
290 Twice in recent months: This detail was confirmed in Gioiosa, interview with author, Nov. 15, 2022; and Mike Fry's testimony to John Dowd, *Dowd Report,* Exhibit 3, interview of Mike Fry, in a federal prison in Terre Haute, Indiana, April 11, 1989, 22.
290 Yellow legal pads were on the bed: Gioiosa, interview with author, Nov. 15, 2021.
290 Kim didn't understand: Hauck, interview with author, Nov. 16, 2022.
290 when Dowd invited Tommy: *Dowd Report,* Exhibit 1, Dowd to Gioiosa, March 30, 1989.
291 "I'm with Pete": "Debt of Friendship to Rose," *BG,* March 26, 1989.
291 the easiest case he had ever prosecuted: Dowd, "Pete Rose's Ban from Baseball."
291 All Dowd had to do: Dowd, interview with author, May 15, 2023; Hallinan, interview with author, May 17, 2023.
291 It was a weeknight around closing time: The principals disagree on some of the details of the first meeting, but the gist is the same: baseball wanted to talk to Peters. Alan Statman (Peters's former lawyer), interview with author, Feb. 3, 2022; Hallinan, interview with author, May 17, 2023; and Dowd, interview with author, May 15, 2023.
291 he wanted to sell his story: Ibid.; "Rose Story Leads to Strange Places," *CE,* March 22, 1989; "The Rose Probe," *SI,* March 27, 1989.
291 By then, senior editor Sandy Padwe: Kirshenbaum, interview with author, July 5, 2023; Padwe, interview with author, July 5, 2023; Sullivan, interview with author, July 5, 2023; and Bruce Selcraig (former writer-reporter at *Sports Illustrated*), interview with author, May 18, 2023.
292 Instead of paying him: "The Rose Probe," *SI,* March 27, 1989.
292 forced to break their silence: "Ueberroth Confirms Inquiry on Rose," *NYT,* March 21, 1989.
292 behind closed doors: The author spoke to two people who attended this meeting: Kirshenbaum and Padwe. Details of the meeting, and the fallout, come from their recollections.
292 Padwe was told to shelve: Neff, interview with author, July 7, 2023; Padwe, interview with author, July 5, 2023.
293 Padwe was crushed: Padwe, interview with author, July 5, 2023.
293 "I did not bet": *SI,* March 27, 1989.
293 That morning: Details about the day the *Sports Illustrated* story broke were found in multiple places, including Brennaman, interview with author, Aug. 1, 2021; Dowd, interview with author, May 15, 2023; "Rose sells prize

memorabilia," *CE,* March 22, 1989; "Rose's Silence Not Such a Big Hit," *CP,* March 22, 1989; "Embattled Rose Digs in in Dugout" and "Rose Probe Focuses on Gambling," *DDN,* March 22, 1989; "Report: Rose probe eyes baseball bets," *Tampa Bay Times,* March 22, 1989; "Rose Cools Heat from Media," *CE,* March 23, 1989; and "Some Quips, but Little More from Rose," *NYT,* March 23, 1989.

293 tried to sell his story again: *CE,* March 22, 1989.

294 Pete picked up a pen in Florida: Dowd, interview with author, May 15, 2023; *Dowd Report,* Exhibit 71, handwriting analysis, written report by Richard E. Casey, April 11, 1989.

294 Dowd drove north: Dowd, interview with author, May 15, 2023.

294 killing the waitresses' tips: *CE,* March 23, 1989.

294 Statman wasn't worried: Statman, interview with author, Feb. 3, 2022.

294 Dowd agreed: Dowd, interview with author, May 15, 2023.

295 He sat before Dowd: Statman, interview with author, Feb. 3, 2022; Dowd, interview with author, May 15, 2023.

295 told him everything he knew: *Dowd Report,* Exhibit 50, interview of Peters in Statman's office, March 23, 1989.

295 "At a later time": Ibid., 63.

295 out a back window: Two of Peters's former lawyers confirmed this detail: Statman, interview with author, Feb. 3, 2022; and David Chicarelli, interview with author, Jan. 24, 2022.

295 what he wanted as a result: In his deposition of Ron Peters under oath on April 5, 1989, Dowd makes clear that in exchange for his "full and truthful cooperation" Giamatti would inform the sentencing judge that Peters had been helpful to Major League Baseball. *Dowd Report,* Peters deposition, 7.

295 "candid, forthright, and truthful": Giamatti to Judge Carl B Rubin, April 18, 1989, *Peter Edward Rose v. A. Bartlett Giamatti,* federal case file C2 89-577.

295 swooped in to arrest him: Details of Gioiosa's arrest come from multiple sources, including Gioiosa, interview with author, Oct. 27, 2021; Hauck, interview with author, Nov. 16, 2022; and "Gioiosa under indictment," *BG,* April 7, 1989.

296 In his expert opinion: *Dowd Report,* Exhibit 71, handwriting analysis, written report by Richard E. Casey, April 11, 1989.

59

296 Almost every day: Dowd, interview with author, May 15, 2023.

297 Dowd planned to show: Ibid.

297 give Dowd nothing: Pete described his frame of mind in Rose, interview with author, Oct. 18, 2021; and *MP,* 146.

297 "How the fuck am I going to eat?": Rose, interview with author, Oct. 18, 2021.

297 Dowd was surprised: Dowd, interview with author, May 15, 2023; John Dowd, "Pete Rose's Ban from Baseball."

297 "You understand": Dowd took Rose's deposition over two days in late April 1989. The entire transcript is included in the *Dowd Report* as Exhibit 2. It is 358 pages in total. This quote and others to follow come from the deposition, hereafter referred to as the Rose Deposition.
298 "Give me a thousand to win": Rose Deposition, 69.
298 He conceded that at times he lost money: Ibid., 72.
298 inviting Paul Janszen: Ibid., 57.
298 packed inside a satchel: Ibid., 43.
298 he'd met Ron Peters, once: Ibid., 136.
298 Ron wasn't his friend: Ibid., 137.
298 He blamed these calls: Ibid., 268, 272.
298 "Are we through with Paul Janszen?": Ibid., 300.
298 "If I was a betting man": Ibid., 303.
298 "I was a horse shit selector of friends": Ibid., 307.
298 Dowd thought he saw physical changes: Dowd, interview with author, May 15, 2023.
299 a good lawyer would have grabbed Pete: Dowd, "Pete Rose's Ban from Baseball."
299 Vincent discussed potential deals: This detail was confirmed by multiple sources including Vincent, interview with author, Oct. 20, 2021; Dowd, "Pete Rose's Ban from Baseball"; and Bart Giamatti, press conference, Aug. 24, 1989.
299 "Every day, people who are addicted": Dowd, "Pete Rose's Ban from Baseball."
299 unwavering on two points: Giamatti, press conference, Aug. 24, 1989.
300 They demanded that Giamatti: The author retrieved the case file for this court case from a federal repository and copied it over two days at the federal courthouse in Columbus, Ohio. *Peter Edward Rose v. A. Bartlett Giamatti,* C2 89-577.
300 Giamatti, Vincent, and Dowd: Vincent, interview with author, Oct. 20, 2021.
300 the local judge sided: Details of the judge's ruling come from multiple sources, including federal case file for *Peter Edward Rose v. A. Bartlett Giamatti,* C2 89-577; "Fans at Ballpark Bank on Rose," "Tension, Then Round of Sighs in Clubhouse," "Waiting, Watching, and Listening," and "Rose Wins Round One," *CE,* June 26, 1989; "Baseball Tries to Block Order" and "Excerpts of Nadel's Ruling in Favor of Rose," *CP,* June 26, 1989; "Pete Rose 1, Commissioner 0," "Reds Fans Issue Concurring Opinions," "Call Goes for Home Team, but Game Has Only Begun," and "Dibble Stands By His Manager," *DDN,* June 26, 1989.
300 a steadfast presence: Dowd, interview with author, May 15, 2023.
300 "It was the low point": Vincent, interview with author, Oct. 20, 2021.
301 Pete seemed to relax: Details of how Rose and others responded to the ruling can be found in multiple places, including *The Cincinnati Enquirer, The Cincinnati Post,* the *Dayton Daily News,* and WLW Radio, June 26, 1989.
302 "Who *are* these guys?": "Add O'Neill to Growing Disabled List," *CE,* July 22, 1989.

302 "Get those cameras": "For Beleaguered Rose, the Show Must Go On," *PI,* June 24, 1989.

302 Television crews followed him: *CE,* April 7, 1989.

303 Carol went into labor: "Rose Family Adds Baby Girl to Lineup," *CP,* Aug. 23, 1989.

303 informed the Reds' traveling secretary: Dan Lunetta (the former traveling secretary for the Reds), interview with author, Feb. 3, 2022.

303 secret documents that Pete: Neither Marge Schott, the owner of the Reds, nor Murray Cook, the general manager of the Reds, was aware of what was happening until the morning of the press conferences. Murray Cook, interview with author, Jan. 18, 2022.

303 Pete flew to Minneapolis: Details of his night in Minnesota come from multiple sources, including Metz, interview with author, Oct. 22, 2021; Associated Press reports, Aug. 24, 1989; "Pete Rose Suspension Expected Today," *Minneapolis Star Tribune,* Aug. 24, 1989; and "Even to the End, Rose Sold His Soul," *CP,* Aug. 24, 1989.

304 ABC's *Nightline:* "Rose Goes as Giamatti Strikes Deal," *PDN,* Aug. 24, 1989.

305 Pete had no comment: *Minneapolis Star Tribune,* Aug. 24, 1989.

305 The three men: Metz, interview with author, Oct. 22, 2021.

60

309 weight of the moment: Hallinan, interview with author, May 17, 2023.

309 accurately reported: "Rose, In Deal, Is Said to Accept Lifetime Ban for Betting on Reds," *NYT,* Aug. 24, 1989.

309 managed to slip past: Hallinan, interview with author, May 17, 2023.

310 "The banishment for life": Giamatti, press conference, Aug. 24, 1989.

310 life stopped: Details about the morning of the announcement come from multiple sources, including "No Joy in Mudville," "Pete's Mom Waits Alone for Nightmare to End," "At Spinney Field, Skepticism Greets Rose's Betting Denial," and "Polls, Gab Shows Tap Divided Views," *CP,* Aug. 25, 1989; "'Death Sentence' Casts Pall over City," *CE,* Aug. 25, 1989.

310 too theatrical: "Rose's Settlement a Crying Shame," *Chicago Tribune,* Aug. 25, 1989.

310 quivering and for once afraid: Pete Rose, press conference, Aug. 24, 1989.

310 not enough air-conditioning: "Rose," *DDN,* Aug. 25, 1989.

310 miscalculated yet again: Rose, interview with author, Oct. 5, 2021.

311 "just so beastly hot": *DDN,* Aug. 25, 1989.

311 "I will be told that I am an idealist": Giamatti, press conference, Aug. 24, 1989.

312 called Giamatti brilliant: "As Rose Steps Aside, Baseball Goes Forward," *SN,* Sept. 11, 1989.

312 handling the situation: "Charlie Hustle Wears a New Suit," *NYT,* Aug. 27, 1989.

312 praise his eloquence: "Bart Eloquent in Baseball's At-Bat," *CP,* Aug. 25, 1989.

312 He wasn't going to spend: "The Punishment Earns Giamatti a Spot in History," *PI,* Aug. 25, 1989.

312 "I'm looking forward": "Time to Close Book on Pete, Look to Playoffs, Giamatti Says," *CP,* Aug. 30, 1989.

312 Canseco was injecting himself: According to Canseco, he began taking steroids before the 1985 season, his last season in the minor leagues. Canseco, *Juiced,* 50.

312 McGwire had joined him: In his book *Juiced,* Canseco suggests that McGwire started using steroids in 1988. McGwire said in 2010 that he didn't start using until after the 1989 season. "Mark McGwire Finally Admits to Using Steroids," *LAT,* Jan. 12, 2010.

313 OWNERS & PLAYERS: "Opener an Adjustment for Fans, Reds," *CE,* April 27, 1995.

314 Strikeout rates soared: Elias Sports Bureau.

314 Television ratings: According to the Baseball Almanac, the ratings for the World Series reached historic lows between 2020 and 2022, but had been declining steadily for most of the past fifteen years.

314 new, fast-growing: "Commercial Gaming Revenue Tracker," American Gaming Association, May 16, 2023.

314 "a very high probability of more Pete Roses": Vincent, interview with author.

315 On the Friday before Labor Day: Details of Giamatti's death come from multiple sources, including Vincent, interview with author, Jan. 6, 2023; Peter Gammons (former *Boston Globe* reporter), interview with author, Oct. 14, 2022; interviews that the author conducted with two first responders on the scene the day of Giamatti's death—Richard Krauss (Edgartown Police) and Paul Condlin (Edgartown Police); and voluminous press accounts from *The New York Times,* the New York *Daily News,* and *The Boston Globe,* namely the *Globe* story written by Ron Borges in which he interviewed the paramedic who arrived on the scene that day. "EMT Just Tried to Save a Life," *BG,* Sept. 2, 1989.

61

316 careful not to blame: "Baseball's Giamatti Dies of Heart Attack," *NYDN,* Sept. 2, 1989.

316 constrictive coronary artery disease: "Giamatti Died from Heart Attack and Autopsy Shows Prior Attack," *NYT,* Sept. 3, 1989.

316 His old driver at Yale: "An Affair of the Heart," *NYDN,* Sept. 2, 1989.

316 "two-bit thug": Ibid.

317 "You have the authority": Giamatti, press conference, Aug. 24, 1989.

317 Tommy kept waiting: Gioiosa, interview with author, Nov. 15, 2021.

317 Tommy finally told ESPN: "Gioiosa on His Silence: I Didn't Want to Lie," *CE,* Feb. 2, 1990; "Gioiosa's Final Cry of Freedom: Rose Bet Reds," *CP,* Feb. 2, 1990; "Gioiosa: Rose Bet on Reds," *BG,* Feb. 2, 1990.

317 recast his story: "The Selling of Pete Rose," *Cincinnati Magazine,* Dec. 1989.

317 lied to Kahn: In 2004, when Pete finally admitted that he had bet on baseball—thirteen years after Kahn's book came out—Kahn wrote an editorial in the *Chicago Tribune* saying he felt "embarrassed" and could never vote him into the Hall of Fame. "Ghostwriter 'Embarrassed,'" *Chicago Tribune,* Jan. 6, 2004.

318 "It was strange": Rose, interview with author, Oct. 20, 2021.

318 "If Pete's elected": "Writers Will Get over Stress Left by Rose Mess," *Chicago Tribune,* Jan. 13, 1991.

319 "Give me the opportunity": "If Rose's Name Is Omitted from Hall of Fame Ballot . . . ," *Hartford Courant,* Jan. 6, 1991.

319 "It's crazy": *Chicago Tribune,* Jan. 13, 1991.

319 "The Committee to Make Sure": "Pete Rose Was the Real Issue," *PI,* Jan. 11, 1991.

62

319 "Pete should apologize": "Rose's Fate Should Be Left to Hall of Fame Voters," *Kansas City Star,* Jan. 11, 1991.

319 "It would've made him a better person": Gioiosa, interview with author, Nov. 15, 2021.

319 "I went to two or three meetings": Rose, interview with author, Oct. 18, 2021.

320 One national poll: "Poll: Bring Pete Back; Put Him in Hall," *CE,* Oct. 22, 1999.

320 "I'm human": WLW Radio, Jan. 9, 2004.

320 blindsided: Some of Rose's closest friends, including Arnie Metz and Jeff Ruby, had no idea that he was about to announce in his book that he had bet on baseball.

320 critics panned the book: "Rose: Yes or No?," *Chicago Tribune,* Jan. 6, 2004; "Our Review Says . . . ," *CE,* Jan. 9, 2004.

321 He lost his job: Rose, interview with author, Oct. 18, 2021.

321 "I'm fucking eighty": Rose, interview with author, Oct. 20, 2021.

322 "Every night because of Pete's unyielding": Janszen, interview with author, July 2, 2022.

322 "He didn't run": Dowd, interview with author, May 15, 2023.

322 Alan Statman took his old client: Statman, interview with author, Feb. 3, 2022.

322 Depressed and unsatisfied: "Bookies Regret: Rose as Client," *CE,* Aug. 22, 1999.

322 got arrested for stealing: "Cops Bust Pete Rose's Ex-bookie," *DDN,* Jan. 15, 1998.

322 "the Pete Rose incident": *CE,* Aug. 22, 1989.

323 failing to pay child support: "Rose Ex-bookie Owes Support, County Says," *CE,* Oct. 5, 2001.

323 He died there alone in 2016: "Pete Rose Bookie Found Dead in His Franklin Apartment," *Hamilton (Ohio) Journal-News,* Dec. 4, 2016.

323 "There's going to be illegal gambling": *CE,* Aug. 22, 1989.
323 Pete met twice: The former commissioner of baseball Bud Selig spoke to the author about the first of these two meetings. Selig, interview with author, Feb. 22, 2023.
323 Garber felt he couldn't support: Garber, interview with author, Jan. 20, 2022.
324 "You could probably commit": Lynn, interview with author, Sept. 23, 2022.
324 "If Rose had been a druggie": "Schmidt Makes Plea for Induction of Rose," *PI,* July 31, 1995.
324 the largest crowd: "Notes," *PI,* July 31, 1995.
324 "Pete stood for winning": Mike Schmidt, Hall of Fame induction speech, July 30, 1995.
324 But to his left and to his right: Details about the induction speech that day, and the Hall of Famers in attendance, come from multiple press accounts, including "Baseball Turns Its Eyes to Cooperstown," *Glens Falls (N.Y.) Post-Star,* July 29, 1995; "For Leon Day, Dream Is No Longer Deferred," *Baltimore Sun,* July 31, 1995; "Standing Tall on Way into Hall," (Camden, N.J.) *Courier-Post,* July 31, 1995.
324 "You can have him": "A Day for Phillies Fans," *NYDN,* July 31, 1995.

63

325 "Pete loves two things": Terry Rubio Fernandez, interview with author, Feb. 12, 2023.
325 some kind of compromise: Francona, interview with author, Nov. 18, 2022.
326 Karolyn Rose isn't sure: Karolyn Rose, interview with author, Dec. 2, 2021.
326 Tommy Gioiosa worries: Gioiosa granted ten hours of interviews to the author and repeatedly expressed his concerns for Pete.
326 He bounced around: *United States of America v. Thomas P. Gioiosa,* CR-1-89-038.
326 seven days a week: Ibid., memo from Gioiosa to Ms. Boutelle, regarding "Information to be presented to my Parole Board," Sept. 10, 1991.
326 an enduring belief: The views of the warden Dennis Luther were so notable that *The Atlantic* profiled him in the mid-1990s, a few years after Tommy got out of prison. "A Model Prison," *Atlantic,* Nov. 1995.
326 He thanked him: Dennis Luther (warden) to Gioiosa, July 12, 1990, *United States of America v. Thomas P. Gioiosa,* CR-1-89-038.
327 "I want you to know": Letter from a mother to Gioiosa, July 21, 1990, *United States of America v. Thomas P. Gioiosa,* CR-1-89-038.
327 Tommy felt the anger: Gioiosa, interview with author, Oct. 25, 2021.

64

328 He thought a lot about dying: Rose, interview with author, Oct. 20, 2021; Bertolini, interview with author, Nov. 20, 2021.

328 "I didn't hurt you": These quotations—and the following scene—come from time the author spent with Rose in Las Vegas in Oct. 2021.

328 "$100 million": Rose, interview with author, Oct. 1, 2021.

330 Pete took a seat in the back of the room: The author spent the evening with Rose while he was signing at the Sports Gallery in Cincinnati on Dec. 3, 2021. All the scenes rendered here come from that night and that reporting.

BIBLIOGRAPHY

Anderson, Sparky. *Sparky!* With Dan Ewald. New York: Prentice Hall Press, 1990.

Anderson, Sparky, and Si Burick. *The Main Spark.* New York: Doubleday, 1978.

Bass, Mike. *Marge Schott Unleashed.* Champaign, Ill.: Sagamore, 1993.

Bench, Johnny. *From Behind the Plate.* Englewood Cliffs, N.J.: Prentice-Hall, 1972.

Bouton, Jim. *Ball Four: My Life and Hard Times Throwing the Knuckleball in the Big Leagues.* Edited by Leonard Shecter. New York: World, 1970.

Canseco, Jose. *Juiced.* New York: HarperCollins, 2005.

Carbo, Bernie, and Dr. Peter Hantzis. *Saving Bernie Carbo.* Fort Pierce, Fla.: Diamond Club, 2013.

Corzine, Nathan Michael. *Team Chemistry: The History of Drugs and Alcohol in Major League Baseball.* Urbana: University of Illinois Press, 2016.

Hertzel, Bob. *The Big Red Machine: The Inside Story of Baseball's Best Team.* Englewood Cliffs, N.J.: Prentice-Hall, 1976.

Howsam, Robert Lee. *My Life in Sports.* With Bob Jones. N.p., 1999.

Kennedy, Kostya. *Pete Rose: An American Dilemma.* New York: Sports Illustrated Books, 2015.

Lawson, Earl. *Cincinnati Seasons: My 34 Years with the Reds.* South Bend, Ind.: Diamond Communications, 1987.

Lerch, Randy. *God in the Bullpen: The Randy Lerch Story.* Middleburg, Pa.: Word to the World Ministries, 2019.

Mantle, Mickey. *The Mick: An American Hero: The Legend and the Glory.* With Herb Gluck. New York: Doubleday, 1985.

McDowell, Sam. *The Saga of Sudden Sam: The Rise, Fall, and Redemption of Sam McDowell.* With Martin Gitlin. Lanham, Md.: Rowman & Littlefield, 2022.

Michaels, Al. *You Can't Make This Up: Miracles, Memories, and the Perfect Marriage of Sports and Television.* With L. Jon Wertheim. New York: William Morrow, 2014.

Morgan, Joe, and David Falkner. *Joe Morgan: A Life in Baseball.* New York: W. W. Norton, 1993.

Parr, Jeanne. *The Superwives.* New York: Coward, McCann & Geoghegan, 1976.

Posnanski, Joe. *The Machine: A Hot Team, a Legendary Season, and a Heart-stopping World Series: The Story of the 1975 Cincinnati Reds.* New York: William Morrow, 2009.

Proto, Neil Thomas. *Fearless: A. Bartlett Giamatti and the Battle for Fairness in America.* Albany: State University of New York Press, 2020.

Reston, James, Jr. *Collision at Home Plate: The Lives of Pete Rose and Bart Giamatti.* New York: Edward Burlingame Books, 1991.

Robinson, Frank. *My Life Is Baseball.* With Al Silverman. New York: Doubleday, 1968.

Rose, Pete. *Countdown to Cobb: My Diary of the Record-Breaking 1985 Season.* With Hal Bodley. St. Louis: Sporting News, 1985.

———. *My Prison Without Bars.* With Rick Hill. New York: Rodale, 2004.

———. *The Pete Rose Story: An Autobiography.* Cleveland: World, 1970.

Rose, Pete, and Peter Golenbock. *Pete Rose on Hitting: How to Hit Better Than Anybody.* New York: Perigree Books, 1985.

Rose, Pete, and Roger Kahn. *Pete Rose: My Story.* New York: Macmillan, 1989.

Ruby, Jeff. *Not Counting Tomorrow: The Unlikely Life of Jeff Ruby.* Cincinnati: Black Tie Productions, 2013.

Sokolove, Michael Y. *Hustle.* New York: Simon & Schuster, 1990.

Turbow, Jason. *Dynastic, Bombastic, Fantastic: Reggie, Rollie, Catfish, and Charlie Finley's Swingin' A's.* New York: Houghton Mifflin Harcourt, 2017.

Wilson, Dan. *Pudge.* New York: Thomas Dunne Books, 2015.

INDEX

A NOTE ABOUT THE AUTHOR

Keith O'Brien is the *New York Times* best-selling author of *Paradise Falls, Fly Girls,* and *Outside Shot,* a finalist for the PEN/ESPN Award for Literary Sports Writing, and an award-winning journalist. O'Brien has written for *The New York Times, The Washington Post,* and *Politico,* and his stories have also appeared on National Public Radio and *This American Life.* He lives in New Hampshire.

A NOTE ON THE TYPE

This book was set in a modern adaptation of a type designed by the first William Caslon (1692–1766). The Caslon face, an artistic, easily read type, has enjoyed more than two centuries of popularity in our own country. It is of interest to note that the first copies of the Declaration of Independence and the first paper currency distributed to the citizens of the newborn nation were printed in this typeface.

Composed by North Market Street Graphics
Lancaster, Pennsylvania

Printed and bound by Berryville Graphics
Berryville, Virginia

Designed by Michael Collica